A History of Intercollegiate Athletics at Florida Institute of Technology from 1958 to 2023

By William K. Jurgens and William C. Potter

With contributions from
Father Douglas Bailey
Dr. Anthony J. Catanese
Dr. Frank Webbe

Independently published

ISBNs
979-8-9889048-0-9 HC
979-8-9889048-1-6 SC
979-8-9889048-2-3 EPub

©2023 William C. Potter
Melbourne, Florida, U.S.A.

Table of Contents

INTRODUCTION

By William C. Potter

Intercollegiate athletics in the United States are on the brink of confronting some issues that will determine whether intercollegiate athletics will remain relevant to the objectives of many colleges and universities. This is not necessarily a new development since concerns about the proper role of intercollegiate athletics within institutions of higher learning have persisted for several decades. As the revenue from intercollegiate sports has exploded for many universities, the temptation to compromise academic standards and to distort the historical role of athletics has become compelling. For many fans of college sports, the distinction between collegiate athletics and professional teams has become almost irrelevant. The pressure to field winning teams has frequently caused schools to discard academic standards, to invest enormous sums in athletic facilities and coaching salaries, and to lose sight of the idea that college athletes should be real students. Although one thinks of these issues as affecting primarily large schools in NCAA Division I athletics, even smaller schools in Divisions II and III have not been immune to these concerns.

These problems are now being exacerbated greatly by two more recent factors. The first of these factors arises from the rights that have been accorded college athletes to profit from their name, image and likeness (NIL). Again, this issue is generally thought of as being an issue affecting large Division I colleges, but, again, other schools are also faced with this issue. The expectation by college athletes that they will be able to earn income, in some cases very substantial income, from their NIL, is having a dramatic impact on recruiting and retaining college athletes. *Florida Today* newspaper reported on September 13, 2022, that NCAA President Mark Emmert acknowledged the organization's inability to address this problem. Emmert admitted that, although the NCAA had adopted a broad rule that schools should not use NIL as a recruiting inducement, the rule was routinely ignored and the NCAA took no action to enforce it, recognizing that it was unlikely that it could prevail in litigation on the issue.

The Florida legislature addressed the NIL issue in 2020 when it followed several other states and enacted a statute codifying the rights of intercollegiate athletes to earn compensation in this manner. Section 1006.74, Florida Statutes, further requires any state university or college, or a private college or university that receives aid from the State of Florida, to provide at least two "financial literacy, life skills, and entrepreneurship workshops," each at least five hours in duration, prior to the graduation of an intercollegiate athlete.

Florida Tech has adopted an NIL Policy that permits a student-athlete to receive compensation from a third party, but not from Florida Tech, in exchange for services, activities, intellectual property, appearances, or other value provided by the athlete so long as the compensation is not being provided in exchange for athletic performance. The policy also permits student-athletes to retain agents to assist them with NIL activity.

Some have argued that the advent of NIL will have a positive effect on intercollegiate athletics by allowing student-athletes to remain in school rather than succumb to the lure of money in professional sports. An article in *The Athletic* by Stewart Mandel on June 7, 2023, urges college administrators to stop pretending that they are not engaged in professional sports.[1]

If anyone harbors any remaining doubt about the incompetency of the NCAA, they need only look to the failure of the NCAA to deal with the NIL issue. In June 2023, the NCAA issued a memo mandating that schools in states whose laws conflicted with NCAA NIL rules are required to follow NCAA rules. That, of course, is in direct conflict with prior NCAA directives to comply with state law in the event of a conflict.

Perhaps even more alarming is the fact that the National Labor Relations Board has filed an unfair labor practice claim against USC, the PAC-12 and the NCAA seeking to classify college athletes as employees rather than student-athletes. Additionally, two pending lawsuits against the NCAA, House v. NCAA and Johnson v. NCAA, seek relief that would abolish limits on athlete compensation and classify athletes as employees. A declaration classifying college athletes as employees rather than student-athletes would fundamentally alter the relationship between coaches and their teams and irrevocably change the very nature of college athletics.

The second recent factor impacting college sports is the NCAA transfer portal. The relative ease with which an athlete can leave one school and transfer to another is a game-changer for college sports. Athletes now can transfer between institutions for the most trivial of reasons or for no reasons whatsoever. This may be more equitable for **athletes,** but it dramatically changes the relationship between coaches and athletes and between institutions and their athletes. It makes the challenge of recruiting and retaining student-athletes an even more tenuous task.

The NCAA rules for Division II in all sports allow a one-time transfer without sitting out a year. The NCAA transfer portal is a database which facilitates the process for student-athletes seeking to transfer between member institutions. It allows student-athletes to place their names in the on-line database by notifying their current school of

---

[1] See: https://theathletic.com/4591232/2023/06/07/hunter-yurachek-sec-nil-laws-congress/.

their desire to transfer. The current school must then place the name of the student-athlete in the database within 2 days. Once the name has been entered, then coaches and staff members of other schools are free to make contact with the student-athlete.

A guest essay in the *New York Times* on March 23, 2023, by John I. Jenkins, president of the University of Notre Dame, and Jack Swarbrick, Notre Dame's director of athletics, noted about college athletics: "It faces threats on a number of fronts: the growing patchwork of contradictory and confusing state laws regulating it, the specter of crippling lawsuits, the profusion of dubious name, image and likeness deals through which to funnel money to recruits, the misguided attempts to classify student-athletes as employees. Underlying all that is the widespread belief that college athletics is simply a lucrative business disguised as a branch of educational institutions."

It is too early to know with certainty the long-term effects that these developments will have on intercollegiate athletics, but it does seem certain that the relationship between players and their universities has been changed forever. These developments account for part of the incentive that Bill Jurgens and I felt to write this book. We felt that the history of athletics at Florida Institute of Technology, a private university of modest size with limited financial resources and somewhat rigorous academic standards might provide some value in analyzing the future direction of intercollegiate athletics. Hopefully, the book will provide some useful lessons as we relate the challenges faced by Florida Tech as it instituted its athletic programs in the early 1960's and labored during the ensuing fifty-plus years to sustain and grow those programs in a manner consistent with the mission and goals of the university. The essential message of this history will be that the athletics program must be consistent with the overall mission of the institution. It may well be the greatest accomplishment of athletics at Florida Tech is that it has remained consistent with the academic objectives of the university and has fulfilled its role of supporting the mission of the institution by providing lessons to student-athletes that are consistent with and complimentary to the classroom lessons of these student-athletes.

The second incentive for writing this book is, of course, the retirement of Bill Jurgens. Bill served as Athletics Director at Florida Tech for nearly fifty years. It is fair to say that the athletics program at the school is the product of the vision of Bill Jurgens. In my view, Bill had a vision for intercollegiate athletics that is worthy of emulation. Bill understood that intercollegiate athletics should support, rather than supplant, the academic objectives of the university. Bill also understood that the athletics program should live within the available resources of the institution. Bill's influence and his philosophy of intercollegiate athletics reached beyond Florida Tech. As the chair of athletics directors in the Sunshine State Conference, Bill placed his indelible imprint upon the conference as he strived to assure that the conference maintained the proper view of its role within its member institutions. Similarly, Bill conveyed his ideas and philosophy upon the Dad Vail Regatta, the largest intercollegiate rowing event in the nation, where he served as a director for many years and continues to serve. Thus, Bill's retirement seemed to be a propitious time to record for posterity the lessons to be learned from his tenure at Florida Tech.

This book has a couple of objectives. One is to recognize those individuals who have had an impact on the athletics program at Florida Tech and, most importantly, an impact upon the lives of the thousands of student-athletes whose lives have been enriched because of their participation in athletics at the university. Florida Tech was founded only in 1958 with limited financial support, and the athletics program was founded just a few years later. The success that the program has experienced is quite remarkable when one considers its young age and limited resources. It has been able to achieve success and positively affect the lives of those student-athletes because a number of selfless individuals have devoted their time, energy, and skills to the program and the student-athletes. It is only fitting that those individuals should be recognized, and their efforts recorded for posterity.

The second objective is to illustrate an example of how an athletics program can be managed in a manner that fulfills the supportive and complementary role, consistent with the primary goals of the university, that an intercollegiate athletics program ought to provide. The fact that the program is relatively young and has succeeded with a limited financial foundation makes these lessons even more useful. It is my hope that the book may cause some readers, particularly those able to influence the direction of intercollegiate athletics, to consider the appropriate role of intercollegiate athletics within a post-secondary institution and to use their influence to ensure that athletics fulfill that appropriate role.

Author's Notes

- The university was founded in May 1958 as Brevard Engineering College. In March 1965, the name of the institution was changed to Florida Institute of Technology. Since changing its name in 1965, it has been commonly referred to as both "F.I.T." and "Florida Tech." Throughout this book, those names will be used interchangeably.
- Since chapters of this book have been contributed by various authors, the reader may discern some differing interpretations of events and even conflicting conclusions about the merits of some activities and occurrences. We have made no attempt to reconcile these differences or conflicts since it is to be expected that different individuals will interpret events differently. We will leave it to the reader to determine the relative weight of these views.

TIMELINE OF HISTORY OF ATHLETICS AT FLORIDA INSTITUTE OF TECHNOLOGY

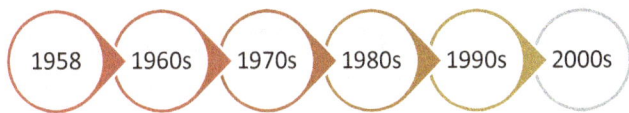

1958 | 1960s | 1970s | 1980s | 1990s | 2000s

This aerial photo shows several of the varsity athletic facilities. The white building in the lower right corner is the Clemente Center with the Panther Aquatic Center to its left. In the upper left corner is the Bottge softball field with the practice field to its right and the Catanese Varsity Training Center to the right of the practice field. The dirt field on the left side of the photo is the Stottler soccer/lacrosse field which was undergoing resurfacing at the time of this photo. The Hall-Seminick baseball field is to the right of the soccer/lacrosse complex. The Wakefield batting practice facility is between the softball field and the soccer/lacrosse complex.
Photo by William Potter.

May-58	**School founded as Brevard Engineering Institute**
Jun-58	Name of school changed to Brevard Engineering College (BEC)
Sep-58	First classes began at the college
Jun-61	First commencement conducted
Aug-61	BEC moves to its current main campus on a site donated by the former University of Melbourne
Jan-62	BEC granted new charter by Florida Secretary of State Tom Adams
Oct-62	Dr. Jerome Keuper retires from RCA to become full-time president of BEC
1964	BEC forms basketball team which practices and scrimmages against local teams
Dec-64	BEC receives accreditation from Southern Association of Colleges and Schools (SACS)
Dec-64	Groundbreaking for first dormitories
Jun-65	BEC fielded its first varsity baseball team coached by Andy Seminick
1965-66	Basketball season - Consists of games against junior colleges
Aug-66	BEC amends its Articles of Incorporation to become Florida Institute Technology, Inc.
1966-67	Basketball season - Team adopts "Engineers" as the name for its team
1966	Varsity tennis team instituted
Jan-68	Florida Tech undertakes intercollegiate rowing as a varsity sport
1968	Varsity golf team inaugurated
Feb-69	Newly constructed Florida Tech Gymnasium inaugurated with basketball win over Augusta College
1970	Men's soccer added as varsity sport
1969-70	Bill Jurgens becomes crew coach
1971	Men's rowing hosts first Governor's Cup Regatta

1971	Teams begin to use "Falcons" as mascot in lieu of Engineers
1972	Florida Tech men's crew wins Southern Intercollegiate Rowing Association Regatta
1972-73	Women's rowing added as varsity sport
Apr-76	Bill Jurgens appointed Athletic Director in addition to duties as crew coach
1977	Women's volleyball added as varsity sport
Oct-77	Les Hall hired as baseball coach
1979	Florida Tech joins National Collegiate Athletic Association (NCAA) Division II
1979	Women's softball (slow pitch) inaugurated
1981	Florida Tech becomes a member of the Sunshine State Conference
1981	Men's and women's cross country inaugurated as varsity sports with Bob Perry as coach
1982	Men's rowing varsity eight wins Dad Vail Regatta
1982	Men's and Women's rowing wins its first combined overall championship at Dad Vail Regatta
1983	Panther adopted as Florida Tech's mascot
May-84	Tom Folliard hired as basketball coach
1984	Men's cross country wins first SSC championship
1984	Florida Tech gymnasium expanded and improved as part of accommodating training by Pittsburgh Maulers
1985	Women's cross country wins first SSC championship
1985	Men's cross country wins second SSC championship
1986	Women's cross country wins second SSC championship
1986	Men's cross country wins third SSC championship
1986	Panther Athletic Association established
1986	Florida Tech Sports Hall of Fame established
1986	Women's basketball inaugurated as varsity sport
1986	Softball converts from slow to fast pitch

Jan-86	Florida Tech Gymnasium renamed in honor of Percy Hedgecock
May-86	Rick Stottler takes over as men's soccer coach
May-87	Men's and Women's Rowing wins its second combined overall championship at Dad Vail Regatta
1987	Women's cross country wins third SSC championship
1987	Men's cross country wins fourth SSC championship
1987	Baseball field is upgraded and renamed in honor of Andy Seminick
Aug-87	John Reynolds appointed as head coach of women's basketball
Aug-87	Dr. Lynn Weaver becomes third president of Florida Tech
May-88	Men's rowing wins third overall Dad Vail Regatta and its second varsity eight championship
1988	Men's soccer wins SSC championship and proceeds to win NCAA Division II championship
1990	Men's basketball for the first time finishes first as regular-season champion tied with University of Tampa; wins SSC Tournament championship for first time
1990	Men's cross country wins fifth SSC
1991	Men's cross country wins sixth SSC championship
1991	Men's soccer wins its second NCAA Championship
1992	Men's sports teams win their first ever SSC Mayor's Cup as the best male sports program in the conference
1992	Women's basketball wins its first SSC Championship Tournament and advances to the Elite Eight in NCAA Tournament
1992	Baseball advances to NCAA Division II World Series for first time in program history
1992	Women's crew wins Lightweight Eight at Dad Vail Regatta
1999	F.W. Olin Sports Complex completed
1999	New baseball field named "Andy Seminick-Les Hall Field"

Sep-01	Charles and Ruth Clemente Center for Sports and Recreation dedicated
Mar-02	Dr. Anthony J. Catanese selected as fourth president in history of Florida Tech
2003	Men's and women's golf, men's and women's tennis and women's soccer added as varsity sports
Fall 2004	Soccer field named "Rick Stottler Field"
Jan-05	Fitzgerald (Fidgi) Haig hired as women's soccer coach and Robin Chan hired as men's soccer coach
Oct-06	Softball field named renamed "Nancy Bottge Field"
May-07	Women's golfer Daniela Iacobelli wins NCAA Division II national championship
2010	Women's soccer wins its first SSC regular-season title and advances to the Final Four of the NCAA Division II Championship
2012	Men's sports teams win their second SSC Mayor's Cup (tied with Florida Southern College) as the best overall male sports program in the conference
Jun-11	Panther Aquatic Center completed
2011	Men's and women's swimming added as varsity sports
2011-12	Basketball season - Men win first-ever regular-season men's basketball championship
2012	Men's lacrosse added as varsity sport
Aug-12	Varsity Training Center (VTC) completed
Sep-13	Florida Tech football plays its first-ever game, defeating Stetson University
2013	Women's lacrosse added as varsity sport
May-15	Men's varsity eight captures Dad Vail title for third time in program history
May-16	Men's varsity eight captures Dad Vail title for fourth time in program history
2017	Men's sports teams win their third SSC Mayor's Cup as the best male sports program in the conference

Jul-16	Dr. T. Dwayne McCay becomes president of the university
Mar-17	Men's swimming 200 freestyle relay team wins NCAA Division II national championship
Nov-17	Women's soccer wins SSC Tournament Championship
May-19	Women's golf wins NCAA Division II national championship
Apr-19	Women's crew wins third consecutive SSC championship
Jun-19	Women's crew finishes runner-up at NCAA Division II National Championship
Nov-19	Men's soccer wins its first NCAA Tournament victory since 1993
Jan-20	Bill Jurgens promoted from Athletic Director to Vice-President for University Relations
Jan-20	Pete Mazzone becomes Interim Athletic Director
May-20	Football terminated as varsity sport at Florida Tech
Jun-21	Jamie Joss appointed as Director of Athletics at Florida Tech
Jun-22	Men's and women's crew, men's golf and men's and women's cross country/distance track programs eliminated as varsity sports
Oct-22	Men's rowers sue university under Title IX seeking to reinstate men's crew as a varsity sport
Feb-23	U.S. District Judge Carlos Mendoza issues preliminary injunction ordering Florida Tech to reinstate men's crew as a varsity sport
Mar-23	Dr. John Nicklow selected as president of Florida Tech

FOREWORD BY
DR. ANTHONY J. CATANESE, PH.D., FAICP

Photo from University Archives.

Athletics at the college and university level have been a major part of American culture for a long time. Most would agree that collegiate athletics was organized in the mid-19ᵗʰ Century when universities began to develop sports at the club level. Then in the 1880's, athletics took on a more formal organization. I would argue that it became significant on 6 November 1869 when Rutgers University played football against Princeton University. The game, sort of a combination of soccer and rugby at that time, was won by Rutgers with a score of 6 to 4. Other colleges took notice and started to issue challenges. Football grew rapidly and tremendous rivalries were started. The games became so intense, and injuries common, that President Theodore Roosevelt later called for restrictions on the game.

In 1906, the National Collegiate Athletics Association (NCAA) was created in part to deal with these issues but also to set up the rules and regulations for college athletics. Overall, the ideal was to create the so-called "level playing field." While the early football teams often had non-students, and some were even paid to perform, the NCAA would change that. Players must be students, hence the term "student-athlete" came into being. Players could receive scholarships to help pay for the education, but they were not to receive compensation or special treatment. They were there to get a college education first and play football or other sports as a secondary undertaking. The NCAA was a group of voluntary member colleges, but championships could only accrue to members.

Football became the bedrock of intercollegiate athletics by the 1920's, but slowly other sports came into being and popularity. To create an even more level playing field, divisions were created by the NCAA ranked primarily on size of the student body as well as funding. Funding became a major part of university budgets. Revenues from ticket sales, alumni gifts, student recruiting, and general fund-raising evolved. With the advent of mass media, college athletics became a major financial enterprise for universities. Events such as the National Championship for Football and the Final Four for Basketball became multimillion-dollar undertakings. With the recent additions of social media, streaming, and cable/ROKU/satellite, college athletics have become big business. At some colleges, expenditures and revenues of over a hundred-million dollars a year are frequent. The idealistic college president will soothe the faculty and students by passing along some of this money to academic uses, such as the library. Most of the surplus, however, would go to stadiums, field houses, locker rooms, and other athletic facilities. Athletics budgets have grown so large that it is common for top coaches in football and basketball to earn several times the annual salary of the president.

With all of this growth, and the wild devotion to your favorite college teams, and despite the best efforts of the NCAA, there has arisen great controversy of intercollegiate athletics. The major critique is that athletics takes away the attention and commitment for the academic mission. For many student-athletes, this is true. Many athletes leave college to pursue professional careers in the National Football League (NFL) and National Basketball Association (NBA). While there have been modest efforts by the NBA, and few if any by the NFL, the top players usually go for the money. That is, after all, the rational choice, despite the NCAA credo. How much then is the scholarship and even the degree worth to the best performers on the playing fields?

Some of the harshest critics say that college athletics in football and basketball is becoming the athletic trials for the NBA and NFL. Most other sports, such as baseball, have alternative ways to enter the professional ranks without going to college. A very small number of football and basketball players go directly to the professional ranks after age 18. NCAA rules for eligibility and continuing attendance are also changing, as will be discussed later. Degree completion rates for athletes are still held as a value, but they vary widely with colleges and majors, even by sport. As football coach Vince Dooley once said, "I see nothing wrong with a college athlete getting some education while they are here that can be useful when their playing days are over."

When I became President of Florida Tech, this was all familiar to me. As an athlete myself, as well as an NCAA President's Council Member, I knew I would have quite a challenge. It was a highly selective university with tough majors such as engineering, science, and information technology, but no easy fields or courses. Florida Tech had achieved success in soccer and rowing, but it had a long way to go for conference and national recognition in athletics. That was the kind of challenge I wanted.

When I became President of Florida Tech in 2002, there were seven college athletics teams. The Men's Soccer Team had won two Division 2 NCAA championships in 1988 and 1991. The Men's Basketball Team had shared a Sunshine State Conference championship. The Men's and Women's Rowing Teams, however, were the best known nationally and even internationally. This was a fine base to build upon. When I retired as President in 2016, we had grown to 23 intercollegiate sports teams, including Football.

Why did I do this? There were several reasons in addition to my basic philosophy that athletics were an important tradition in American universities. I believe that sports add to the college academic experience. They can provide loyalty to the college, an ease to difficult studies, and fun. College sports can unite the many constituencies of the university—faculty, students, staff, alumni, advisory and governing boards, and the wider community. Sports do not distract from the scholarly mission if properly managed and directed—indeed, they add to the learning experience through teamwork, practice, and goal setting. College athletics programs that are successful and have integrity can enhance the reputation of the university amongst its peers. As the great Football Coach Howard Schnellenberger once told me: "You can be compared academically by how you play athletically among your peer group." As I mentioned, some of my critics said that Florida Tech was too STEM-oriented to field good athletics teams. Having graduated Rutgers University, where it all started, and spending a good part of my career at Georgia, I did not agree with those pessimists. I resented the stereotype of the "dumb jock" in college athletics, and I wanted to counter it.

An important reason for my goals was to increase the number of women on campus and in the STEM fields of study. Florida Tech was a predominantly male institution when I started, and that was well reflected in the athletics programs. We took opinion surveys and found that the male students and athletes could not agree more on that idea. What better way to attract young women to Florida Tech than by adding several teams. We added women's teams in soccer, tennis, golf, lacrosse, swimming, diving, track and field, and cross country. By the time I left, we had more women athletes than men even counting football.

Several of my critics said that athletics were too expensive at a medium-sized school like Florida Tech. The most expensive sport, football, actually made money. The revenues from attendance at the games was among the Top Ten in NCAA Division II.

The other financial aspect, that too often is overlooked, is tuition income at a private school can increase with additional teams. The NCAA sets strict limits on the number of scholarships that can be awarded by sport. That means we had to distribute the scholarship money wisely and not everyone got one. Many players received partial scholarships. Many players did not have scholarships and paid tuition so they could play. We had to come up with academic scholarships to complement the athletic scholarships in many cases, so that meant we had to recruit good players who were also good students.

The number of students increased dramatically during my term, and much of it was related to intercollegiate athletics. While some of this was due to more athletes, we were happy to see that many came to Florida Tech because as one student told, "Now it is a real college." Also interesting, we found a significant increase in women who wanted to go to a school with a football team. The facts speak for themselves. In 2002 we had 3600 students seeking degrees. By 2016, there were 16,000 students seeking degrees. Was this cause and effect? Probably not. Much of it was due to the online and off-campus programs I added, but a lot of it was due to the athletics programs and the reputation it gave us.

The financial picture for athletics also proved my point. According to College Factual, a reputable group that measures expenses and revenues, college athletics at Florida Tech made money using their objective accounting, using all revenue sources and all expenses. They estimated average expenses of $12 million per year and average revenues of $13 million per year by 2016. Quite simply, the critics were wrong, and we were making at least $1 million per year.

Experience by leadership helps a lot. This was not my first rodeo. As President of Florida Atlantic University, I also expanded the athletics programs from 1989 through 2002. During that time, FAU grew from 10,000 students to 25,000 students, and two campuses were expanded to seven campuses over a five county South Florida Region. College athletics was a primary factor in giving these disparate campuses a common sense of loyalty and collegiality. A Division 1 Football Team was created, and Coach Schnellenberger became the Founding Coach. He established the record for the fastest rise to a bowl game in the NCAA. There is now a great Football Stadium on the Boca Raton main campus that attracts fans and is televised nationally. I upgraded Men's and Women's Basketball, and all FAU Teams, to Division 1. Again, being told that we could only be competitive in Division 1 Baseball, FAU Men's Basketball went to the Final Four in 2023.

My experience at FAU taught me a lot about people in this business. As a neophyte member of the NCAA President's Commission, I learned a lot from the great Notre Dame President Theodore Hesburgh. He taught me that the president's job is to hire the best coaches with the highest integrity and to make sure that they follow the NCAA Rules and serve as a role model for their players. I did that. I hired Schnellenberger, a national champion at Miami, for Football. I brought in the Orlando Magic's Sydney Green for Men's Basketball. I hired Chanceller Dugan for Women's Basketball. I brought in two Olympians, Bob Beemer for Track and Field and Marathoner Keith Brantly for all running sports. One of my proudest hires was the legendary Queen and her Court Pitcher, Joan Joyce for both Softball and Women's Golf. I learned definitively that coaches make the difference in intercollegiate athletics, just like Father Hesburgh told me.

I continued my lessons at Florida Tech, and the successes came flowing in. Daniela Iacobelli won the NCAA Singles Championship in golf in our first few years. She is now on the LPGA Tour. We had never expected that our players might become professionals, but we were pleasantly surprised. The Football Program had 18 All-Americans, three of whom went to play on Sunday with the NFL. We went to the Futures Bowl in West Virginia during our inaugural year and won. A highlight of my career and Florida Tech history was in 2014 when we played a top-ranked team at Dallas Cowboys Stadium and won.

We also won championships in Swimming and Diving as well as Track and Field. The Women's Golf Team later won the Division II National Championship. Even the teams that existed when I arrived excelled. The Men's Basketball Team won the Sunshine State Conference outright. The Women's Basketball Team went to the Division II Elite Eight. The iconic rowing teams won several Dad Vail Regatta rowing championships, placed well in the Intercollegiate Rowing Association National Championship, and won at the Head of the Charles regattas. They even were competitive at the Henley Royal Regatta in England.

This is all part of Florida Tech history, and Florida athletics lore, but most importantly, it is imbued in the memories of our student athletes. Nobody can ever take that away from them.

One outstanding piece of athletics should be mentioned. We needed a lot of money to start Football. We started a Founders Club for 10 people who we asked to give $100,000. We brought in some superstars to help. From the baseball world, we brought in our alumnus Tim Wakefield from the Boston Red Sox. Football greats like Heisman Trophy Winner Doug Flutie, Wisconsin Coach Barry Alvarez, Dallas Cowboy Tony Dorsett, and Coach Schnellenberger. And we were successful.

We learned that the community loved Football and wanted to be a part of the story. Our attendance at the games, amongst the highest in NCAA Division 2, was mostly community, students, and alumni. Even overall fund-raising for the university greatly increased due in some degree from our higher visibility from college athletics.

There have been some major changes in recent years that provide challenges to the state of intercollegiate athletics. They somewhat go against the traditional concept of the student-athlete as defined by the NCAA. The NCAA has always argued that college athletics were about higher education and not money. That viewpoint is now dubious with the advance of the Name, Image, Likeness (NIL) rules, regulations and laws which means that a student athlete can be compensated for the use of his/her name, pictures, and other forms of visual expression. Thus, the college athlete can now earn money because of their participation. On its face, this seems fair enough, but of course money changes everything. Agents, organizations, and businesses have come forth to help these individuals. Many universities have set up for-profit and/or non-profit entities to help or even exploit these opportunities. Football Coach Billy Napier of the University of Florida said that "this is the new arms race for the top students. Indeed, the quarterback of the University of Alabama is said to receive over a million dollars for his NIL. It clearly is now a major issue for the recruitment of top athletes and is a bidding war in many cases. Even sports like Gymnastics are finding huge payments for a student's NIL. Many critics of intercollegiate athletics say that this is the beginning of compensation for players. How far can that be since the principle has already been established. It sort of takes us back to 1869 when both Rutgers and Princeton were alleged to have paid non-students to play in the first intercollegiate football game. An even greater concern—how can the NCAA survive when its original premise has been rejected?

Another major change is the so-called Transfer-Portal. Staying true to its original student-athlete mission, the NCAA had rules that greatly controlled how a student could change colleges in order to play on another team with probably better prospects. Similarly, some students who had some eligibility for playing time left as a result of redshirt years or even graduation, had to follow the rules and either wait or sit out before they could play at another college, and even that with the coaches' permission. The Portal changed all that. Essentially, all a student-athlete now needs to do is declare for the Portal. Football Coach Deion Sanders of the University of Colorado has eliminated over half of the players he inherited in order to fill their slots with top players in the Portal. Many argue that this destroys the comraderies, team spirit, and loyalty of college athletes. Rather than take one for the team, in the old "Win one for the Gipper" norm, student-athletes now look out for number one. That is human nature, of course, but it does erase the nostalgia of the team spirit. Coupled with the loosening of turning pro rules and behavior, such as not playing in bowl games for fear of being injured before pro tryouts, as well as NIL, this is, if you will excuse the pun, a whole new game.

Some see this as an inevitable evolution of intercollegiate athletics with the advent of mass media, social media, streaming, pay-per-view, and cable/satellite television. There is simply too much money and fame to be ignored. Economists and Philosophers will state that this is rational behavior, and it is. The nostalgia and memories of the past are gone. It is sad, but it is reality. There is no doubt in my mind that professionalism will dominate intercollegiate athletics in the future.

This story does not have a happy ending for the Nation or Florida Tech. In my mind, much of the greatness in college sports has been diminished during the 2016 to 2022 administration that drastically cut the sports program in half. College athletics, coupled with pandemic cutbacks, drove leadership to seek other priorities. Now there is new leadership, and I am hoping that intercollegiate athletics will be a priority.

While I enjoy being told by alumni and community that I was President of Florida Tech "during the Golden Years," I would rather be regarded as the father of a great university with a great intercollegiate athletics program. What would I change if I could? What would I do differently. I refer those questions to the late, great Hawaiian singer, Likui Lee. His lyrics go something like this: "If I had to do it all over again, I would do it all over again."

Dr. Catanese was the President of Florida Tech from 2002 to 2016.

FOREWORD BY
FATHER DOUGLAS FRANCIS BAILEY, SDS

Photo from University Archives.

Author's Note

In any university, athletics have existed to encourage a strong mind in a strong body. At Florida Tech, we have included body, mind, and spirit. To that end, we have been very fortunate to have the services of our University Chaplain and Catholic Campus Minister, Fr. Douglas Bailey, SDS. He has been a part of the University and a part of athletics since 1983 until his retirement in 2020 and beyond. Fr. Bailey has been a mentor to and fan of Florida Tech athletes for the past 40 years. We have been blessed to have him lead our prayers at athletic banquets, award ceremonies and kick-off events. He has insisted that these prayers should be uplifting, inclusive, and earthy. The following is one example of his inspiring prayers.

Steve Goodier has written about life lessons learned from racquetball. Life lessons can come from unexpected places. Here are some important lessons that have come from that court.

People play better when they're encouraged. It's true in life, too. People do better when they're encouraged rather than criticized, condemned, and judged.

When two or more people occupy a small space, they should learn to share. It goes for planets and classrooms and houses, too.

Pay attention. Those who lose their focus lose or at least get knocked upside the head. And those who are too distracted by yesterday or tomorrow will never live today full and joyously. Focus on the present.

The only way to score is to serve. Individuals and institutions that make a difference find ways to serve others. Those people are happiest and most satisfied with their lives have learned to serve. Great lives are built on service.

This caused me to think about life lessons that can be learned from other sports. For instance, in baseball on the field and soccer on the pitch, you learn how to become a team, a cohesive family. All throughout history, armies, countries, peoples, teams that have been united are the ones who succeed. The same goes for crew, you have to learn to work as one and to be in perfect balance, just as you must keep your life in balance.

In soccer, you also learn how to anticipate and not merely react. You want to be where the ball or player is going to be and not where they are. In life too you don't want to be merely reactive.

In tennis, you learn never to give up, not on the play, not on the game, not on yourself.

In baseball, it's easy: sometimes you have to sacrifice to win and even if you play right field, you still get to bat.

In golf, you learn that all the important lessons of life are contained in the three rules for achieving a perfect golf swing: 1. Keep your head down just like when you're praying; 2. Follow through; 3. Be born with money.

The best athletes ask themselves: "What have I done today to make myself a better player?" Practice, practice and practice is an important element in becoming your best. The same is true for our spiritual life.

What have I done today to make myself a better person. Lord God, please help us to encourage one another, to not lose focus on what really matters and to be able to share and serve.

Amen.

CHAPTER ONE:
THE FOUNDING OF FLORIDA INSTITUTE OF TECHNOLOGY, NEE BREVARD ENGINEERING COLLEGE, 1958-1964

By William C. Potter

Ad Astra Per Scientiam
"To the stars through science"

Florida Institute of Technology is a rather remarkable story of higher education in the late Twentieth Century. It is remarkable in that it was founded in 1958 with virtually no assets other than the entrepreneurial spirit and unflagging energy of its founders. This occurred during a time when colleges and universities throughout the United States were suffering from declining enrollments and intensifying questions as to the value of the increasing costs of higher education.

Brevard County stretches approximately seventy-five miles along Florida's central east coast with Cape Canaveral at its northern feature. For much of its existence, it was a rather sleepy community marked by its citrus industry, excellent fishing and pervasive mosquitos. Its population in 1940 was 16,142 with citrus and fishing as the backbone of its economy. the county experienced a notable evolution during World War II when the U.S. Navy established three Naval Air Stations there to train pilots for the war. However, by 1950, the population had only increased to 23,653.

In the late 1940's and early 1950's, however, the county underwent a massive change with the advent of the U.S. space program. On June 1, 1948, the Navy transferred the former Banana River Naval Air Station to the United States Air Force. In May 1949, President Truman signed the legislation which established the Joint Long Range Proving Ground (JLRPG). The Air Force renamed the base the Joint Long Range Proving Ground, but shortly thereafter changed the name to Patrick Air Force Base. Work began in May 1950, to build an access road and launch facility at Cape Canaveral. The first rocket launched at the Cape was a V-2 rocket named Bumper 8 on July 24, 1950. In 1951, the Air Force established the Air Force Missile Test Center at Patrick AFB.

Cape Canaveral was chosen as the site for rocket launches in order to take advantage of the Earth's rotation. The linear velocity of the Earth's surface is greatest toward the equator and the relatively southern location of Cape Canaveral allowed the launching of missiles in the same direction as the rotation of the Earth. It was also helpful that the area was relatively sparsely settled and that missiles could be launched over the ocean rather than populated areas.

Between establishment of JLRPG in 1949 and 1957, launch activities at Cape Canaveral were intermittent and were given a relatively low priority by the U.S. Government. That changed immediately when the Soviets launched Sputnik in October 1957. That event was a wake-up call to the United States and caused grave alarm in the country as to not only the space and missile program but as to American technological education. Not only did the launch of Sputnik serve as an impetus to revamp and reinvigorate U.S. space programs but it caused a reexamination of the American education system. Experts noted with alarm the decline in the number of college enrollments in science and engineering. They also noted the lack of opportunities for continuing education among the scientists, engineers and technicians at Cape Canaveral.

These activities of the U.S. space program dramatically and almost instantly changed the essential nature of Brevard County as tens of thousands of technicians, scientists and engineers relocated to east central Florida to support the activities at Cape Canaveral. Among those who were drawn to the Cape and the U.S. space program was a young senior engineer in RCA's Systems Analysis section of the Missile Test Project by the name of Jerome Keuper. Keuper held a doctorate from the University of Virginia and a master's degree from Stanford University in addition to his undergraduate degree from Massachusetts Institute of Technology. Prior to joining RCA in 1958, Keuper had worked for Remington Arms Company in Bridgeport, Connecticut. While at Remington, Keuper had taught calculus at night at the Bridgeport Engineering Institute (BEI). BEI had been established to provide education to people working in technical jobs seeking to further their education. BEI instructors were people employed in the subject matter that they taught at night.

Even before arriving in Florida with his wife and daughter in early 1958, Dr. Keuper had given thought to the possibility of creating something akin to BEI that would allow engineers and scientists at Cape Canaveral to continue their education. He had even explored the idea of establishing a branch of BEI near the Cape but was urged to begin an independent institution of his own. Upon his arrival at RCA, Keuper immediately embarked upon this venture.

Keuper began discussing his idea of starting a college modeled after BEI with three of his team members at RCA, George Peters, Donya Dixon and Robert Kelly, all of whom enthusiastically embraced the idea. They were soon joined by Harold Dibble, an RCA inertial guidance engineer who had taught in UCLA's evening engineering program.

This group, led by Keuper, soon put together a plan to establish Brevard Engineering Institute. The plan contemplated that classes would be conducted three nights per week and would include classes in mechanical and electrical engineering leading to an associate degree. Graduate level courses, it was planned, would be added later. Faculty and administration of the college would consist of people employed in local industry who would teach in the subject area related to their employment. There would be no full-time professors or administrators. Keuper would serve as President, Dibble as Dean, Peters as head of the Mathematics Department, Kelly as Chief Financial Officer and Dixon as the school's corporate Secretary.

Founding President Jerome Keuper recognized the importance of athletics from the earliest days of Brevard Engineering College. *Photo from University Archives.*

In May 1958, Dr. Keuper publicly announced that classes would begin in the fall of that year. Brevard County Public Schools agreed to rent the new college three classrooms in what was then Eau Gallie Junior High School (present-day West Shore Junior/Senior High School). In response to the opinions of prospective students, the name of the institution was changed from Brevard Engineering Institute to Brevard Engineering College (BEC) in June 1958. In July, BEC announced that it would offer nine classes: Advanced Calculus, Transients in Linear Systems, Statistics and Probability Theory I, Modern Algebra, Advanced Circuitry Analysis, Servomechanisms, Electromagnetic Fields, Transistor Theory I, and Numerical Analysis.

An initial faculty meeting consisting of prospective faculty members was held in September 1958. At the meeting, it was disclosed that 114 undergraduates and 40 graduate students had enrolled. Notable were the facts that six of the students were women and that the average age of the students was thirty-three. Twenty-three faculty members were appointed, eight of whom held doctorates. Almost all students and faculty members were employed by contractors at Cape Canaveral, including seventy-five students employed at RCA.

In February 1959, Ray Work was appointed as Chair of the Electrical Engineering Department at BEC. Work was to have a profound effect upon the future of BEC and, in particular, upon its athletic programs.

BEC faced a crisis in March 1959, when the Brevard County School Board threatened not to renew BEC's lease on the classrooms in Eau Gallie Junior High School. Woodrow Darden, the Superintendent of Brevard Public Schools, voiced a number of reasons for this action, including parking congestion and speculation that BEC would duplicate a junior college which was contemplated but not yet established. However, it is probable that Darden's opposition to BEC arose from the fact that he had discovered that BEC's students included two African-American students. Only when those two students voluntarily dropped out was Darden's objection placated.

By the fall of 1959, the issue of classrooms had been resolved with the aid of Homer Denius and George Shaw, the founders of Radiation, Inc. (Radiation was acquired by Harris Intertype Corporation in 1967 which became Harris Corporation, which merged with L3 Technologies in 2019 and is now known as L3 Harris, the sixth largest aerospace company in the country which maintains its headquarters in Melbourne). Shaw and Denius were avid supporters of BEC from the outset and remained supporters until their deaths. They came to the rescue in 1959 by persuading the First National Bank of Melbourne, a bank of which they had been among the founders, to permit BEC to occupy a building owned by the bank. The building on Waverly Place in Melbourne had previously been occupied by the Methodist Church. Thus, in the fall of 1959, BEC began its second year of classes in the old Methodist Church building. African-American students returned to BEC. In September 1959, when BEC began its second year of classes, 247 students enrolled, including 149 graduate students and 98 undergraduates.

Following its year in the old church building, BEC relocated its classes to an old building at the Melbourne Airport. That building was a former Navy barracks used during World War II when the airport was a training base for Naval aviators. The building had been leased to Radiation which subleased a portion of the building to BEC.

Another problem which faced BEC at the outset related to finances. Although RCA and other contractors at the space center had policies reimbursing their employees for college courses, those policies required that the courses be taken from an accredited institution. Although BEC had undertaken the process of becoming accredited, that was a long process which would not be completed for several years. Keuper wrote a letter to Dr. Robert Sarnoff, CEO of RCA, explaining the dilemma. Sarnoff delegated Irving Wolff, a vice-president of RCA and Chair of its education committee, to visit BEC and make a recommendation on the issue of tuition reimbursement. Wolff visited Keuper and BEC in June

1959, and became fast friends with Keuper and a great advocate for BEC. Pursuant to Wolff's recommendation, RCA began to reimburse its employees for tuition paid to BEC and most of the other contractors at the Cape followed suit.

In 1961, BEC's prospects brightened considerably when it was the fortunate beneficiary of the demise of the University of Melbourne. In 1951, a group of local residents had a vision of establishing a liberal arts college in Melbourne, to be known as the University of Melbourne. The University of Melbourne succeeded in obtaining a gift of thirty-five acres of land on Country Club Road in Melbourne from a local funeral home owner, V.C. Brownlie. The University of Melbourne also went so far as to construct a small classroom and library building on the site. However, by 1961, the leaders of the University of Melbourne recognized that they lacked the resources to continue their dream of a liberal arts college. They closed the university and donated the assets of the defunct college to BEC. On August 21, 1961, *The Cocoa Tribune* reported that BEC had moved its operations to the site. On July 31, 1962, *The Cocoa Tribune* reported that BEC, with 457 students now enrolled, was undertaking the construction of two additional classroom buildings on the site. By March 1963, *The Evening Tribune* reported that work had commenced on the sixth building on the site. In January 1965 *The Evening Tribune* reported the dedication of a library building which had been built on the campus (that building is not the current library but was converted to the Keuper Administration Building when the Evans Library was constructed).

The Cocoa Tribune reported on June 14, 1961, that BEC would conduct its first commencement on the following day. The ceremony was held at Melbourne High School and Joseph Weil, Dean of the School of Engineering at the University of Florida, was the commencement speaker.

Keuper, Work and other officials of BEC continued to press for accreditation of the college. During 1960, the Florida Association of Colleges and Universities (FACU) had rejected BEC's application for membership. In 1962, FACU held its annual meeting in conjunction with a meeting of the Southern Association of Colleges and Schools (SACS), the regional accrediting body. BEC was permitted to attend that meeting as an observer but continued to encounter strong opposition from other Florida colleges. BEC continued its efforts for accreditation, and on December 3, 1964, *The Cocoa Tribune* reported that BEC had succeeded and was now "an accredited resident senior college of engineering and science."

In 1961, BEC applied to the Florida Secretary of State for a new charter. In January 1962, the request was approved by Florida Secretary of State Tom Adams. Included with the approval was the authority for exclusive use of the name "Florida Institute of Space Technology."

BEC demonstrated that it intended to become a more broadly-based university when it announced its intent to expand its curriculum beyond science and engineering. *The Cocoa Tribune* reported on March 14, 1962, that it was creating an Institute of Management Studies. The stated intent of the institute was to "provide the broad base of management studies upon which the company training function can build and develop the specific company's philosophies, methods and procedures."

As a newly founded institution with no endowment, BEC was in a constant state of financial instability. An effort to address the financial needs of the college led Keuper to enter into discussions with the Disciples of Christ church which had founded Texas Christian University. Robert Bruce, former Executive Director of the St. Petersburg Chamber of Commerce, had been instrumental in the founding of Florida Presbyterian College (now Eckerd College) in St. Petersburg. Bruce convinced Keuper that they could establish a similar institution in Brevard County by entering into an agreement with the Disciples of Christ. Bruce also represented to Keuper, either explicitly or implicitly, that the church would be able to invest several million dollars in the college. The proposal generated substantial enthusiasm from both BEC and the church. At the 71st annual meeting of the Disciples of Christ in May 1962, Keuper addressed the meeting and presented a preliminary agreement which had been negotiated by BEC and church representatives. The Disciples enthusiastically endorsed the plan, and it began to appear likely that Florida Christian University would be created. However, financial issues soon doomed the project. Apparently, Bruce, while assuring Keuper that the church would invest millions, had assured the church that no financial investment would be required. The negotiations quickly came to an end when it became clear that no funds would be forthcoming.

Another challenge that faced BEC during the early 1960's was the possibility of a state university being established at Cape Canaveral. In 1960, Florida Governor Farris Bryant had recognized the need for expanding the post-secondary education system in Florida. Bryant tasked the Education Committee of the Governor's Council of 100 to recommend a plan for Florida's post-secondary education needs. For BEC, the possibility of a state institution at the Cape was viewed as an existential threat. The creation of a new state institution in central Florida became a contentious political issue that attracted the attention of the most powerful political interests in the state, as well as business interests that could profit from such a venture. BEC, of course, used all of its influence to discourage establishment of a state institution, arguing that

BEC was willing and able to meet educational needs in the region. The political debate on both sides was vigorous. In May 1962, the Education Committee of the Council of 100 recommended to Governor Bryant that the state establish a space science university in central Florida. This, of course, resulted in the establishment in 1963 of Florida Technological University (FTU) east of Orlando, later renamed to University of Central Florida, which is now one of the largest undergraduate universities in the country. FTU opened in 1968 and, as Keuper predicted, has posed challenges to F.I.T., competing not only for students but for research money.

In June 1962, BEC conducted its second commencement, awarding degrees to thirty-eight graduates, including one woman. Honorary degrees were awarded to Secretary of State Tom Adams and astronaut Gus Grissom. The summer term of BEC in 1962 saw 448 students enrolled. Enrollment included 313 undergraduates and 135 graduate students.

In 1962, Keuper recognized that the college could not progress with part-time leadership. Dr. Keuper retired from RCA in October 1962 in order to devote all of his energies to BEC.

After BEC received full accreditation from SACS, the door was opened for BEC to receive research contracts. *The Evening Tribune* reported on December 4, 1964, that BEC had received its first industry-sponsored research contract. The contract with Dow Chemical obligated BEC to develop a mathematical model relating to the release of gases resulting from fuel releases.

The construction of dormitories signaled that BEC had evolved far beyond the idea of night classes for part-time students. On December 28, 1964, *The Cocoa Tribune* reported that a groundbreaking had been held for construction of Brownlie Hall, the first dormitory at the school.

In 1966, BEC amended its Articles of Incorporation changing its name to "Florida Institute of Technology, Inc." Since that time, the school has been informally referred to as "F.I.T." and, more recently, "Florida Tech."

With the construction of dormitories and the increasing number of full-time students at the university, it was predictable that there would be students who would advocate for the introduction of intercollegiate athletic teams. That request was soon forthcoming.

Notes

- Information regarding the establishment of the JLRPG and the first launches at Cape Canaveral is taken from "Evolution of the 45th Space Wing"(https://www.patrick.af.mil/library/factsheet)
- Information regarding Keuper's arrival at RCA, his desire to establish an education institution and the challenges during the first two years of the college is taken from Patterson, Gordon "Countdown to College: Launching Florida Institute of Technology," *Florida Historical Quarterly*, Volume 77, Number 2, Fall 1998.
- The description of the challenges faced by BEC during the early 1960's, including its efforts to gain accreditation, its negotiations with the Disciples of Christ and its efforts to forestall a state university in the area are discussed in the article by Patterson, Gordon "Space University: Lift-Off of Florida Institute of Technology," *Florida Historical Quarterly*, Volume 79, Number 1, Summer 2000.
- The information regarding the University of Melbourne and its gift to BEC is described in an article in *Florida Today* newspaper on May 25, 1969.

Other sources describing the founding of the college and its early challenges include:

- Cleveland, Weona. "Crossroad Towns Remembered: A Look Back at Brevard and Indian River Pioneer Communities." *Florida Today*, 1994. See page 87.
- Patterson, Gordon. "Florida Institute of Technology." Arcadia Publishing, 2000.
- Raley, Karen, and Ann Raley Flotte. "Melbourne and Eau Gallie (Images of America)." Arcadia Publishing, 2002.
- Stone, Elaine Murray. "Brevard County: From Cape of the Canes to Space Coast." Windsor Publications, 1988. Page 55.

CHAPTER TWO:
INTRODUCING INTERCOLLEGIATE
ATHLETICS AT FLORIDA INSTITUTE OF
TECHNOLOGY: 1965 TO 1976

By William C. Potter

Former Philadelphia Phillies Whiz Kid Andy Seminick was a vital part of early
development of the athletic program at Florida Tech.
Photo from University Archives.

According to Gordon Patterson's book, *Florida Institute of Technology*, a group of students approached Dean of Students Ray Work in 1964 with a request to organize a basketball team. In an interview with Bill Jurgens on September 21, 2022, John Courtney informed Jurgens that he and Melvin Fickett were the students who approached Dean Work. As Courtney related to Jurgens, Work returned to Courtney and Fickett a few days later and invited them to his office where he presented them with yellow basketball jerseys with red numerals. Work further informed them that he had arranged for them to practice at a local junior high school. Within a few weeks, Work introduced Tony Valenti as the newly employed basketball coach and practices began. For the remainder of the 1964-1965 school year, the newly formed basketball team practiced in the evenings at Hoover Junior High School under the tutelage of Valenti while also playing scrimmage games against local junior high school teams.

Photo from University Archives.

During the 1965-1966 season, Brevard Engineering College's fledgling basketball team began playing junior colleges. *The Cocoa Evening Tribune* reported on July 1, 1965, that Brevard Junior College would dedicate its new gym with a basketball game against Brevard Engineering College in late November 1965. The news article disclosed that Brevard Engineering College would be kicking off its first sports season that year. Unfortunately, Brevard Junior College was a state and national powerhouse in basketball that year. As reported by *The Evening Tribune* on November 29, 1965, the match-up with BEC resulted in a 117 to 33 rout in favor of the junior college. The box score indicates that BEC played only five players: Garcia, Lane, Guidner, Fickett and Courtney.

Not content with that ignominious experience, BEC took on Brevard Junior College again on January 28, 1966. This time, as reported by *The Cocoa Tribune* on January 31, 1966, BEC was able to make it a bit more competitive, losing 112 to 48. This time, BEC played six cagers, Garcia, Farrar, Guidner, Fickett, Courtney and Bergon.

During that 1965-1966 season, BEC played a total of eight games. In addition to the games against Brevard Junior College described above, BEC played St. Johns Junior College and Indian River Junior College.

An article in *The Crimson*, the student newspaper of Florida Tech, authored by Bill Tiso and published on June 4, 1968, purported to be a history of sports at the school. It indicated that baseball and basketball had existed at the school for the past three years. The article related that the basketball team did not win a game during the 1965-1966 season. The article stated that the team was coached by Tony Villani. That coach was actually Tony Valenti.

Valenti coached the team again in 1966-1967, playing a schedule of junior college teams and also a few four-year colleges. The team, with the school now renamed Florida Institute of Technology, was able to improve its record by winning three games. *Florida Today* reported on November 22, 1966, that Florida Tech had again lost to Brevard Junior College in a game played the previous night, this time by a score of 93 to 43. The Florida Tech line-up for that game included Courtney, Bostwick, Kandone, Atterton, Habbad, Thes, Stracker, Canter, Tarr and Goff.

Courtney related that at some point during that season, Dean Work asked the team what name should be on the uniforms. The consensus of the team was that they should be known as the "Engineers" and that would be the moniker for Florida Tech athletic teams until the Panther was adopted as the mascot in 1983.

Courtney also recalled that the 1966-1967 team played a total of twelve games, including games against Rollins College, Saint Leo, Barry and Embry Riddle Aeronautical University. Courtney recalled that the scores were generally lopsided against Florida Tech. However, the highlight of that season occurred at the last game of the season when Florida Tech defeated Embry Riddle with Courtney scoring 25 points. Courtney recalls that game as Florida Tech's first intercollegiate victory but Tiso's article reported that Florida Tech won a total of three games that season.

Prior to the 1967-1968 basketball season, Florida Tech hired Dick Bowman to serve in several capacities. Bowman would serve as residence director but also as head basketball coach and head baseball coach.

Bowman had been a high school coach in Ohio and West Virginia who migrated to the space program to work as a mathematician specializing in post-flight analysis at RCA. Bowman also coached RCA's company basketball team.

According to Tiso's history, the 1967-1968 team, now coached by Bowman, played games against "small colleges like F.I.T.," winning four games. During December 1967, The Engineers participated in a four-team Holiday Invitational Tournament in Augusta, Georgia, but lost both games. *Florida Today* reported on January 17, 1968, that F.I.T., was "enjoying its finest hour" and had won two basketball games in a row after overwhelming Drake College of Fort Lauderdale 115 to 84 in the Melbourne High School gymnasium. The starting line-up for that game included Rick Dodd, Jim Carter, Murray Lee, Jim Tharp and Dave Nankville. Dodd led the scoring with 27 points, while Carter added 25 points and 17 rebounds. Bob Hubbard, a 6-5 forward, added 11 rebounds.

Florida Tech faced a strong schedule during that 1967-1968 basketball season, starting with a road game against Troy State University in Alabama. The Engineers then went on to play a brutal schedule of six road games in seven days, including games against Southeastern Louisiana University, Mississippi Baptist, Nichols State, the University of Southern Mississippi, the University of South Alabama and the University of West Florida. The extended road trip was funded by a large guarantee paid by Southern Mississippi. Unfortunately, Jim Carter, F.I.T.'s leading scorer, suffered a season-ending knee injury during the Nichols State game.

In addition to that road tour, the 1967-1968 team played home and home games with Augusta College, Georgia State, the University of South Florida, Florida Memorial College, Saint Leo University and Embry Riddle Aeronautical University. They played single games against Bethune Cookman College, Armstrong State University and Biscayne College. Home games were played in the Melbourne High School gymnasium.

On February 14, 1968, *Florida Today* reported that F.I.T. had lost to Biscayne College the previous night in an overtime game at Melbourne High School. Rick Dodd led scoring with 22 points while Jim Carter added 21. The 86-84 loss left the Engineers with a record of 4 wins and 20 losses. In addition to the December win against Drake College, the Engineers defeated Florida Memorial and Saint Leo.

Tiso noted that a gym had been planned and construction was planned to begin in late June or early July 1968, and to be completed by the fall. Tiso was optimistic that with the gym and the improved 1967-1968 record, the future of Florida Tech basketball was bright.

On June 7, 1965, *The Evening Tribune* disclosed that BEC had fielded its first varsity baseball team. The team was coached by former Philadelphia Phillies catcher Andy Seminick. The report stated that the team was composed entirely of full-time students and played against local high school and college teams. The article further disclosed that BEC had hopes that a new small-college conference would be formed by the following year.

Tiso's article in *The Crimson* indicated that the baseball team had not won a game during the previous two seasons despite playing all junior college teams. It described baseball as having had "a half dozen" coaches during that time.

The Cocoa Tribune reported on April 18, 1966, that Brevard Junior College's baseball team had thrashed Brevard Engineering College by a score of eighteen to zero. Billy Stein pitched a one-hitter for the junior college.

The Cocoa Tribune reported on March 13, 1967, that Brevard Junior College had swept a baseball double-header from F.I.T. on March 11 by scores of seven to zero and six to four. *The Cocoa Tribune reported* on April 6, 1967, that F.I.T. had dropped another double-header to Brevard Junior College by scores of six to one and ten to zero. The F.I.T. line-up included Troy, Brakin, Secogges, Shaffer, Steinhauer, Whitney, Worthington, Reuther, Wendt and Kronish.

Despite Tiso's rather gloomy assessment of Florida Tech baseball, he did note that baseball had won its last two games of 1968 "in a blaze of glory."

Tiso's article reported that a tennis team was formed in 1966 with Dr. John Thomas as coach. The 1971 school yearbook, *Ad Astra*, describes the coach as Garland Thomas rather than John Thomas. The authors have not been able to verify Thomas's correct given name.

Tiso's article quoted Dick Bowman as advocating beginning "minor sports" because "we can excel in these sports without spending too much more money for scholarships, equipment, etc." Hence, golf, crew and wrestling teams have been formed with plans for intercollegiate competition next year (1968-1969). Bowman only coached at F.I.T. for one year but he demonstrated the same versatility shown by many of the school's coaches by serving as Director of Residence Halls as well as basketball coach, golf coach and baseball coach.

Tiso further reported that a group of "ambitious, hardy" students along with Robert Dunlap have formed a crew and purchased a shell. He reported that practice was underway and intercollegiate competition in the south would begin next year. Dunlap, an assistant to Dr. Keuper, had secured Keuper's enthusiastic endorsement prior to undertaking this venture.

This followed a plea that Dunlap had sent to the "Help" column of *Florida Today*. The January 13, 1968, edition of *Florida Today* included Dunlap's letter pleading: "Florida Institute of Technology will enter intercollegiate crew racing competition this fall. We've ordered two new racing shells but need the HELP! Of someone who knows all aspects of the sport to assist us in the planning and organization required. Can HELP! Locate the man we're looking for?" The newspaper referred Dunlap to Tom Dolan, a banker in Cocoa Beach who had rowed at Rollins College. It is unclear whether Dolan was able to assist.

Tiso reported that a golf team had recently been formed. Port Malabar Country Club was to be the home course for the team. Dick Bowman was apparently coaching the team in addition to his many other duties with the school. The 1969 *Ad Astra* pictured a golf team of nine members.

Tiso also reported that a wrestling team was formed in 1968. The team competed in an AAU tournament in Tampa in May 1968.

Tiso further reported that a "poor excuse" for intramurals was initiated in 1968. He said that intramural football was good. Basketball, however, failed to take off due to lack of a court. He noted that a football and baseball field was being laid out and would be in operation next year. Tiso concluded that, with the gym, new fields and the new student union, F.I.T. "will be a school of well-rounded stature, academically, socially and athletically."

During the remainder of the 1968-1969 basketball season, most of the games were home and home matchups with nearby colleges, including Augusta College, Embry Riddle, Saint Leo and Florida Memorial. The Engineers also had away games at the University of South Florida, Armstrong State University and Georgia State University. Perhaps the most significant win of the year for Florida Tech was its victory over nationally-ranked Bryant College in a game played at Melbourne High School. The 1968-1969 basketball season ended on a high note when Coach Bowman and the Engineers inaugurated the new gymnasium which would later be named in honor of Percy Hedgecock, an early supporter of F.I.T. athletics. The facility had been constructed at a cost of $135,000.00. The inaugural game against Augusta College on February 21, 1969, was won by the Engineers, setting the tone for future success at the new venue. The 1968-1969 team finished with a record of 5 wins with 21 losses.

The 1969 *Ad Astra* also disclosed that a judo team had been organized by Bill Harkins. The 1970 *Ad Astra* revealed that judo now had a full schedule, with fifteen team members, including three women. The 1970 team competed in the Florida Judo Association, the Southern Collegiate Judo Association and the East Coast Judo Association.

Don Rutledge took over as basketball coach for the 1969-1970 season. Rutledge was an interesting fellow. He came to F.I.T. after serving as an assistant coach at Florida Presbyterian (now Eckerd) College. Later in his career, he would become a renowned basketball official and would top his career as a referee by officiating a national championship game at the NCAA Division I Final Four. During his brief one-year stay at Florida Tech, he would coach not only basketball but also baseball and golf. Considering that the seasons for these sports overlap significantly, one can only imagine how adaptable Coach Rutledge must have been.

The 1969-1970 basketball team began its season by winning its first three games. Notably, it won its third game against Embry-Riddle by the lopsided score of 123 to 36. These victories inspired new hope for the team that quickly evaporated when it lost its next eleven games. The Engineers snapped that losing streak by beating Palm Beach Atlantic by a score of 91 to 74. When it beat Palm Beach Atlantic a second time, that was the team's fifth win, thereby tying the school record for wins in a season. It followed that win by beating Florida Presbyterian 96 to 84, thereby setting a new record for wins in a season. The Engineers closed their season by losing to Rollins, completing the season with 6 victories and 17 losses. According to the 1970 *Ad Astra*, Bill Zieher led the team in scoring with an average of 15.7 points per game.

Soccer was added in 1970. As disclosed in the 1970 *Ad Astra*, soccer was added as a varsity sport that year. Brian Hogg served as head coach of that initial team, assisted by Jim Irvin. Freshman Tom Bruno served as captain of that first team.

The 1970 yearbook also highlighted the cheerleading squad, which had twelve members that year. Although the number of cheerleaders would vary from year-to-year, their enthusiasm rarely waned.

Crew competed for its second season in 1970 and, as reported in the yearbook, had an excellent season, placing first in the Freshman Class State Championships. The crew had twenty-seven oarsmen and were captained by Ken Watts and Ray Walker. The crew also had a new coach that year, an enthusiastic young fellow named Bill Jurgens who would become the face of Florida Tech athletics for another fifty years.

1971 meant continued growth for the F.I.T. crew with thirty-two oarsmen competing for Coach Bill Jurgens and his assistant coach Augie Burrichter. Among the rowers was a young member of the junior varsity eight by the name of Casey Baker. Baker would go on to make his own mark on the Florida Tech crew as a rower, including rowing on the U.S. national team, and as a coach. *Florida Today* reported on January 28, 1971, that the crew of Princeton University was practicing in Melbourne as the guests of F.I.T. Bill Jurgens who noted that F.I.T. would have two pre-season races, freshmen and varsity, against Princeton later that week.

Florida Today reported on May 9, 1971, that the F.I.T. crew had placed sixth in the Dad Vail Regatta, which it described as "the small college national championships." It quoted Coach Bill Jourdan (sic) as saying: "I was a bit surprised. It's quite impressive though considering it's our first entry here."

The 1971 yearbook also disclosed that Leonard "Bing" Yandle had been hired as a coach and, in what was soon becoming a tradition at F.I.T., he would be a multi-tasker, coaching both basketball and baseball. *Florida Today* reported on January 31, 1971, that Yandle had promised a new look and a winning season in basketball. Unfortunately, he was unable to fulfill that promise. Bill Zieher, the team's leading scorer, took the losses well, however, noting that: "We have fine support from the fraternities, the cheerleaders and the school's crew team." The team would finish with a record of five wins and twenty-one losses.

The June 4, 1971, edition of *Florida Today* noted that Bing Yandle had signed five basketball players, including the school's first African-American athlete, Norm McMinns. McMinns had averaged thirty-one points per game at Lake Placid High and was described by Yandle as a "super leaper."

On November 21, 1971, *Florida Today* reported that Florida Tech defeated Palm Beach Atlantic in Melbourne 88 to 63, after having lost to them in West Palm Beach only four nights before. Yandle attributed the difference to the presence of Milton Walker, a freshman guard who scored eighteen points in the victory but who had not made the journey to West Palm Beach for the first game. As explained by Walker, he was behind in his classroom work and needed to study for a test. Yandle noted: "The studies come first."

On December 12, 1971, *Florida Today* described a loss by F.I.T. to Otterbein College of Westerville, Ohio. The article referred to F.I.T. as the "Falcons," the first reference we found that the Engineers name had been forsaken in favor of the newly designated Falcon mascot. That game was also noted by the actions of Milton Walker who placed his uniform at Yandle's feet as Walker left the court in his street clothes in the middle of the game, apparently terminating his basketball aspirations at Florida Tech. That loss placed the Falcons at one win and eight losses on the season.

On December 26, 1971, *Florida Today* reported that the basketball fortunes of F.I.T. may have hit their nadir. Not only did it lose its sixth straight game, 71 to 59 to Aquinas College, but the entire team lost their wallets and other personal items when someone broke into the team's locker room during the game.

The 1971 *Ad Astra* also disclosed that the golf team had a new coach, John Cooney. The team had five golfers representing the school that year. The yearbook further disclosed that Yandle had fielded a baseball team consisting of seventeen players.

Florida Today reported on January 11, 1972, that the Falcon cagers had narrowly lost an important game when they fell to Massachusetts Institute of Technology by a score of 79 to 76. With the loss, Florida Tech's record fell to 2 wins and 11 losses.

On January 23, 1972, *Florida Today* reported that Yandle had resigned as basketball coach in order to assume duties as athletic director, a role that he had been performing without the official title. Yandle left with a record of seven wins and thirty-six losses. Pete Navaretta immediately assumed the role as basketball coach. Navaretta had come to F.I.T. not as a basketball coach but as head of student affairs at Hydrospace Technical Institute, a division of F.I.T. Navaretta proclaimed himself a defensive specialist and brought a new-found sense of optimism to the program. Navaretta proved that his optimism was not totally unrealistic as the Falcons put up a fierce fight in his first game as coach, losing to Florida Technological University (now University of Central Florida) by a score of 68 to 60. Only two weeks before, FTU had beaten F.I.T. by fifty-nine points. A few days later, on February 12, 1972, *Florida Today* reported that the Falcon cagers "came of age" in a hard-fought 113 to 94 defeat at Rollins College. Navaretta described this game as their "best performance to date."

An article in *Florida Today* on March 4, 1972, disclosed the rapid development of the crew team. It reported that twenty-six returning crew members had been practicing, together with eighteen freshmen. Competition would open with a race against the University of Alabama and would include meets with three major powers in the sport, Brown, Columbia and Dartmouth. The schedule would also include appearances at the Dad Vail and the Miami Invitational Regatta. A letter to the newspaper published a few days later on March 9 admonished the publication that the crew included three women who were coxswains. That letter seemed to catch the attention of the newspaper since it published a story on April 9, 1972, describing the roles of the women coxswains, with particular emphasis upon Beth Hebert, a 112 pound oceanography major from Shrewsbury, Vermont, known affectionately to her teammates as "Buff." Buff charmed readers by observing: "I get wet in every race, but really wet when we win. Right – I get thrown in. It's some tradition to throw the coxswain in. But I don't mind – it's all part of being on the crew. It means you belong."

Another *Florida Today* article on April 9, 1972, disclosed that the Florida Tech varsity eight had narrowly lost the featured race at the

Miami Invitational to Oxford University. The English crew edged the Falcons by a narrow three-fourths of a boat length over the 1,500-meter course.

On April 23, 1972, *Florida Today* reported that the F.I.T. crew had captured the overall point trophy at the Southern Intercollegiate Regatta at Stone Mountain, Georgia. The Falcons had tied with the University of Virginia but were awarded the championship based upon the scoring system. The varsity eight crew finished third while the freshmen won.

On September 27, 1972, *Florida Today* reported on the continued expansion of the crew program at Florida Tech. The story reported that there were thirty returning oarsmen who had been joined by fifty freshmen August Burrichter would coach the freshmen while Todd Craun would coach the lightweight teams. The article further disclosed that Coach Bill Jurgens would take the team to the Head of the Charles race in October.

On December 7, 1972, *Florida Today* reported that twelve female students at Florida Tech had organized a crew team and begun practicing with two men's varsity crew members, Chuck Hildebrand and Doug Linden, serving as coaches. The article disclosed that on the previous Saturday, December 2, the women had rowed to victory in the first women's intercollegiate rowing event ever held in the South, beating Jacksonville University by three boat lengths. Ann Gauzens, it was reported, was the team captain.

The 1973 *Ad Astra* reflected that the 1972-1973 athletics program at F.I.T. was continuing to expand not only in terms of the number of teams but more importantly in terms of number of student-athletes. The soccer team had thirty members that year.

Soccer was developing a substantial following by 1972. Thirty players comprised the team that year. The team scored a big victory on October 17, 1972, by defeating Florida Technological University (now University of Central Florida) by a score of two to one. Goalie Fran Corlis turned away twenty-two shots. *Florida Today* reported on November 4, 1972, that F.I.T. had fallen three to two to Florida Southern in soccer, dropping its record to two wins and five losses. The goals for F.I.T. were scored by Milton Julien.

The 1972-1973 basketball team was coached by first-year coach Art Loche and included a fourteen-man roster. The season began somewhat ominously for Loche, as he was hospitalized the day of the opening game. It was discovered that Loche had been stricken with Hodgkin's Disease, a malady with which he would battle for several years. As reported by *Florida Today* on November 14, 1972, Assistant Coach Tom Howard took over the coaching duties for the opening game against Embry Riddle. The Falcons were looking forward to improving upon the previous year's mark of two wins and 26 losses. Their newfound hopes seemed to be justified when they routed Embry Riddle 113 to 68 in that opening game, led by freshman Eddie Vegas' twenty-eight points. The season continued on a positive note as *Florida Today* reported on January 17, 1973, that F.I.T. had won its eighth game of the season, setting a new record for wins in a season. On February 11, 1973, *Florida Today* reported that F.I.T. had lost a heartbreaker to Florida Technological University, 81 to 78, taking its season record to nine wins and twelve losses. The team would complete the season with a record of nine wins and eighteen losses.

Coach Eaton headed a tennis team of twelve netters, including one woman. Jim Wooten coached the golf team, which fielded a team of thirteen linksmen. Judo fielded a team of six.

Crew, however, continued to grow both in terms of the number of participants and the success of the program. Head coach Bill Jurgens was joined by lightweight coach Todd Craun and freshman coach August Burrichter. The team included fifty-nine members, including four women coxswains. *Florida Today* reported on March 17, 1973, that F.I.T. would host the Indian River Intercollegiate Regatta on a one-thousand-meter course off the Indialantic Causeway. The guests for that race were Rollins College, Jacksonville University, Marietta College and Florida Technological University. On April 1, 1973, *Florida Today* reported that F.I.T. had swept the Governor's Cup Regatta, defeating Jacksonville University, The Citadel and the University of Nebraska. On April 8, 1973, the newspaper reported that F.I.T. remained undefeated after rowing past the University of Tampa and was looking forward to the Miami Invitational Regatta in a few days. On April 29, 1973, the newspaper reported that the Engineers had "breezed past the 13-team field" in Atlanta to capture the Southeastern Intercollegiate Rowing Championship.

On May 23, 1973, *Florida Today* reported that five F.I.T. oarsmen had been named to the eight-man crew that would represent the U.S. against Europe's top crews in a four-week tour of Europe, culminating with participation in the Henley Regatta. The five selected included Coach Bill Jurgens and assistant coaches Augie Burrichter and Tod Craun, together with two undergraduate rowers, Casey Baker and Joe Eckelman.

The 1973 baseball team was coached by Otto Reyas that year. The team included twenty-one players.

Prospects for the 1973-1974 basketball season took an optimistic turn on May 10, 1973, when *Florida Today* reported that Don Gabbard, a six-five, two-hundred-and-thirty-pound star at Melbourne Central Catholic High School had signed to play for the Engineers. Gabbard, who had led Central Catholic to the state Class 2A basketball championship that year, turned down an offer to play football at Florida State University in order to play basketball at F.I.T. Gabbard would lead the team in scoring with an average of 13.3 points per game, including forty-five points in one game. The season began well for Loche and his team when F.I.T. defeated Clearwater Christian College on November 12, 1973, by a score of 88 to 64. These kinds of wins were rare, however, and the season took a turn for the worse as described in *Florida Today* on January 17, 1974, when three of Loche's top guards were declared academically ineligible for the remainder of the season. By January 25, 1974, when the Engineers lost to Eckerd College, its record had fallen to four wins and eleven losses. A couple of days later, however, playing its fourth game in six nights, F.I.T. got back on track by defeating St. Leo, 76 to 73.

The crew team continued to thrive during the 1974 season. In May 1974, the Falcons won three races at the Dad Vail Regatta in Philadelphia.

The 1974 soccer team had a strong season, winning nine and losing two. That was the best record in the school's history.

An article in *Florida Today* on November 7, 1974, set an optimistic tone for the 1974-1975 F.I.T. basketball season. Art Loche, beginning his third year at the helm, predicted that this would be his best team to date. The optimism was somewhat tempered, however, when the school announced that it would drop athletic scholarships for basketball. He pointed to six returning lettermen, including last year's leading scorer Don Gabbard. That optimism seemed justified when the team began the season by winning the opening game of the West Palm Beach Tip-Off tournament by beating Florida Memorial college 87 to 74, led by thirty-one points from Bernie Wigley, another local product from Melbourne High School. However, the Engineers proceeded to lose two games in a row before crushing Embry-Riddle 80 to 47, led by Chuck McShane with twenty points. By February 21, 1975, as described in *Florida Today*, the team had a record of eight wins and twelve losses following a recent loss to Rollins College by a score of 110 to 63. The team would complete the season with nine wins and thirteen losses. Bernie Wigley was the top scorer, averaging 17.9 points per game, followed by Pat Lang at 11.3, Don Gabbard at 10.6 and Tom Brown at 10.0.

Crew had another exceptional year in 1975. Coached by Bill Jurgens and assistant coach Norton Schlachter, the crew included 30 upper-classmen and 18 freshmen. F.I.T. won the freshman heavyweight, varsity lightweight and junior varsity lightweight at the Dad Vail Regatta, to finish second to the Coast Guard Academy in the team standings. An article by Art Brooks in *Florida Today* on May 30, 1975, recounted the extraordinary season of the crew that year, which included winning five races at the Southern Intercollegiate Championships which gave the Engineers the team title by a wide margin. That victory included a win in the varsity eight over Florida Technological University which was particularly sweet.

Women's crew that year was coached by Norton Schlachter. Seventeen women rowed with the crew.

Brooks' article also noted that F.I.T.'s 1975 baseball team, coached by the versatile Art Loche, completed its season with a record of four wins and nine losses. Among the mainstays of the team were pitcher Carl Reckstein, third baseman Bo Ramowitz, first baseman Rob Bleyman and pitcher Craig Pomeroy. Another notable member of the team that year was Randy Muns who would become a long-time supporter of the school and serve on its Board of Trustees.

The 1974-1975 school year was a strong one for the F.I.T. soccer program, consisting of sixteen players coached by Nick Pahiyiannakis. Brooks reported that the team had its best season ever with a record of nine wins and only two losses, outscoring its opponents for the season by forty-two to fourteen.

The tennis team struggled that year. Although the team included fourteen men and one woman, the team dropped all of its twelve matches.

The 1975 soccer team consisted of seventeen players. The team was coached by Gary Hogg and captained by Gary Rosenbloom. Among the teams on their schedule were the University of Florida, Stetson, Florida Southern and Florida International.

The 1975-1976 men's basketball team had the most successful year in its history. Coached once more by Art Loche in what would be his final year, and Assistant Coach Stone, the team had a record of nineteen wins and eight losses, including a nine-game win streak. Don Gabbard, Bernie Wigley and Captain Tom Brown once again led the team. Optimism about the team seemed justified when the Engineers blasted Embry-Riddle on November 22, 1975, by a score of 106 to 38. The team reached its record tenth win on December 20, 1975, when it defeated Miami Christian College, 91 to 75, with Bernie Wigley leading the way with thirty points. As reported by *Florida Today* on January 11, 1976, after a notable win against Western New England College, 89 to 72, Loche announced that he was stepping down as basketball coach at the end of the season. Loche cited the decision to eliminate basketball scholarships as the reason for his resignation and predicted that he believed that "the program will be operating on a club basis after next season." On February 20, 1976, Loche closed out his career at F.I.T. with a season-ending loss to Florida Bible College. Jerry Stone, the Dean of Men, who assisted Loche during his final season, presumably would take over as coach. It was notable that F.I.T., although not yet a member of the newly formed Sunshine State Conference, had defeated two members of the conference, St. Leo and Eckerd. The prediction that Stone would assume coaching duties proved inaccurate when *Florida Today* reported on April 21, 1976, that recently appointed Athletic Director Bill Jurgens announced that Norm Cockrell, an assistant coach at Melbourne Central Catholic High School, would take over.

The appointment of Jurgens as Athletic Director was reported by *Florida Today* on April 16, 1976. Jurgens replaced Art Loche who had decided to enter private business in Miami. The appointment of Jurgens seemed to be almost inevitable in view of the fact that Jurgens was easily F.I.T.'s most successful coach, both in terms of competitive success and student participation. What was less foreseeable was that, with the school having gone through several athletic directors during its short existence, Jurgens would remain in that position for the ensuing forty-four years. Ken Clarke noted in *Florida Today* on July 15, 1976, that since his appointment, Jurgens had been "consulting, listening, experimenting and planning." Jurgens set the tone for his forty-four-year tenure when he said: "We can't design our programs on going out and getting athletes. F.I.T. has a quality academic program that will attract certain athletes. That is something many schools don't have."

The appointment of Bill Jurgens as Athletic Director in addition to his duties as Head Crew Coach was a turning point for intercollegiate athletics at Florida Tech. Jurgens' leadership would provide a certain stability to the program which would transcend individual coaches and individual administrators. As we shall see in subsequent chapters, his administration would give athletics a new significance at Florida Tech.

- Gordon Patterson's book "Florida Institute of Technology" is part of the College History Series and was published by Arcadia Publishing in 2000.
- Bill Tiso's article in *The Crimson* on June 4, 1968 is titled "*A History of F.I.T. Sports.*"
- Bill Jurgens interviewed John Courtney on September 21, 2022, and Courtney's recollections set forth above are taken from Jurgens' notes of the interview.
- The name of the university was changed from "Brevard Engineering College" to "Florida Institute of Technology" on August 3, 1966. Since that time, the school has been informally referred to as "F.I.T." and "Florida Tech." Those names will be used interchangeably throughout this book.
- Bill Jurgens interviewed Dick Bowman twice during October 2022, and much of the information about the 1967-1968 and 1968-1969 basketball seasons is based upon Bowman's recollections during those interviews.
- An article in *Florida Today* by Lyle Graves on February 3, 1988, under the byline of "Panthers handle college sports growing pains" indicated that the first sport at what was then Brevard Engineering College was baseball, which was instituted in 1961 and remained the only sport for the next three years. The article noted that during the 1963-1964 school year, basketball was added, with Dean Ray Work serving as the first coach. A year later, under Coach Tony Valenti, the basketball team won its first game, defeating Stetson's freshman team. Crew was added in 1968.
- Coach Valenti's name continued to take a beating as Graves called him "Villanti" which was somewhat more accurate than *The Crimson* article by Tiso which had called him "Villani."
- On October 17, 2008, *Florida Today* published an extensive article describing the origins of intercollegiate athletics at Florida Tech. The article was published as part of the recognition of the fiftieth anniversary of the founding of Florida Tech. That article includes information about the sports which were introduced during the period covered by this chapter. There are some conflicts between that article, the earlier article by Graves and the records discovered during writing this book. For example, the article states that the 1966-1967 was the inaugural season for Florida Tech basketball while it is clear that games were played during the 1963-1964 season.
- Most of the information about Don Rutledge's season at F.I.T., including the results of the basketball team under his tutelage, are taken from two scrapbooks maintained by Rutledge which he shared with Jurgens and Potter at a meeting in October 2022.

CHAPTER THREE:
HIGHLIGHTS OF BILL JURGENS AS ATHLETICS DIRECTOR

By William K. Jurgens

When I arrived on the Florida Tech campus to be the head rowing coach in 1969, I did not have high expectations for having all the resources needed to run a successful rowing program, especially given that I received no salary. What I did find was a culture of support and encouragement that allowed me the autonomy to build a rowing program for which the student rowers and administration could be proud. At that time, 11 years after the founding of the university, all the administrators involved in the emerging years of the university were active in their roles. This included Dr. Jerome Keuper, president, Dr. John Miller, vice president for academic affairs, Dr. Ray Work, vice president for student affairs, Dr. Harry Weber, associate vice president for academic affairs, and Dr. Andy Revay who later became vice president for academic affairs. It was truly a pleasure to work with each of these administrators, knowing that they were there to assist me in any way they could. I recall walking across campus when I encountered Dr. John Miller. Miller stopped me to ask what a rowing ergometer was and why was it important to the rowing program. Miller said that my request for this piece of equipment had come up in the executive committee and he wanted to know more about it. I explained how it would benefit. the program and shortly thereafter it was ordered. I knew the university had limited funds and to approve such a request showed me that they trusted my judgment and really cared about what the rowing team was doing to become a successful program. During my 19 years as the head rowing coach, the crew members and I fundraised for every rowing shell that was purchased for the program. Another indication of limited funds was when many of the university's support staff took off during the summer months to help the university meet payroll.

Also, during these early years before I became athletics director, I was able to watch my predecessors in that position. What I gained from Don Rutledge in his first year at Florida Tech was that he was a positive person who was complimentary on what I was doing with the rowing program. Rutledge had the difficult task of being the head coach for men's basketball, baseball, and men's golf. Unfortunately, Rutledge only stayed at Florida Tech one year before he progressed to a career as a basketball official, which led him to become an NCCA Final Four official. Bing Yandle was the second athletics director who was a very capable basketball coach, but he put too much pressure on himself to succeed and resigned as coach midway through his second season after the team did not do as well as he had hoped. The third athletics director was Arthur Loche who had a twenty-game winning season with Jerry Stone, dean of students, as his assistant coach. Loche came to Florida Tech from the University of Vermont where he was the head basketball coach from 1965 to 1972. As the athletics director he felt that Florida

Tech was not providing enough funding for the athletic teams and he expressed his feelings in no uncertain terms to President Keuper, which led to his departure from the university. Coach Loche served as the athletics director at Florida Tech from 1972 to 1976.

To fill the athletics director position, Dr. Ray Work, vice president for student affairs, began a national search. I went to Dr. Work shortly after the search was announced and shared with him my desire to become the next athletics director. I expressed to Work that I wanted to take on this position because it would be a great challenge for me to transform Florida Tech athletics into a successful program using the many principles that I had learned while being the rowing coach. This included building the best program possible with the limited funds of the university, showing trust in the administration who oversaw athletics, and displaying the perseverance to stay with athletics until the goal of being a strong and successful program was achieved. I further said to Dr. Work that given what had happened in the past, if he hired an athletics director from outside, there is a great likelihood the new athletics director would only be at the university for a couple of years. In a few days Dr. Work called me back to his office to let me know I would be the next athletics director. I recall that I did not receive a pay raise, but it didn't matter to me because that was not the reason that I wanted to be Florida Tech's athletics director.

When I took over the position, I was the only full-time member of the athletics program. I hired Norm Cockrell as the new basketball coach, Mike Eldridge as the soccer coach, and Bill Bartlett as the baseball coach. One year later Les Hall was hired as baseball coach replacing Bill Bartlett who resigned. Eldridge and Hall had long tenures at Florida Tech (Eldridge eight years and Hall 25 years) After their years at Florida Tech, both Eldridge and Hall joked about their salaries and operating budgets. However, this did not keep them from doing an outstanding job with both their coaching and administrative duties.

One of my first objectives as athletics director was to identify a national athletics association in which Florida Tech could become a member. In my early years at Florida Tech, I heard the university had been a member of the National Association of Intercollegiate Athletics (NAIA), but from the time I arrived in the fall of 1969 there was never an indication of this association. However, in an interview with Dick Bowman, Florida Tech's head basketball coach from 1967-69, I found out that Bowman had attended NAIA conventions at the direction of Dr. Work for each of the two years he served as basketball coach. When Don Rutledge was appointed head basketball coach the following year (fall of 1969), he informed me that the program had not been associated with the NAIA during his one-year tenure at the university. This two-year association with the NAIA was confirmed by NAIA administrators. Though many of the intercollegiate competitions in the 1960s had been with NAIA institutions, in the '70s Florida Tech increased its competitions with NCAA division II institutions that included Florida Southern, Rollins College, Saint Leo University, Eckerd College, and Florida Technological University (FTU), which subsequently became known as the University of Central Florida (UCF). Consequently, Florida Tech began the process of applying for NCAA Division II membership. Florida Tech became a member of the NCCA DII in 1979.

Once NCAA membership was achieved, the next step was to become a member of a division II conference, and the only division II conference in the state of Florida was the Sunshine State Conference (SSC). This was a big step for Florida Tech Athletics, and it was important for the evolution of the program. I remember talking to baseball coach Les Hall in 1980 about joining the SSC and he said, "We will take our lumps, but it will also provide us with a challenge to grow the athletics program." The member institutions of the SSC currently were competing at the highest level of NCAA DII. Florida Southern College had already won three NCAA DII baseball titles before Florida Tech joined the conference. Other members of the conference at this time were Rollins College, Eckerd College, Saint Leo University, Biscayne College, and FTU. After I met with conference athletic directors regarding membership requirements and answering questions they had about Florida Tech Athletics, the conference approved Florida Tech as a member on July 1, 1981. Les Hall was right about the conference challenging Florida Tech athletics to become better, and this was evidenced years later when Florida Tech won the men's all-sports trophy (Mayor's Cup Trophy) in 1992, 2012, and 2017. When Jen Mercurio (associate athletics director) and I received the 2017 Men's Mayor's Cup Trophy, I remember telling everyone how proud Florida Tech was to receive this trophy as a member of the conference known as the "Conference of National Champions." Florida Tech also won a total of 14 SSC men's regular-season championships and 20 SSC women's regular-season championships.

The Athletic Advisory Council (AAC) was established in 1977 by President Jerome P. Keuper. As stated in the September 1979 university guide on *F.I.T. Intercollegiate Athletics*, "The purpose is to develop ideas which promote the Department of Athletics to the service of the university and the student body, and to advise (the president) on matters pertaining to athletics." In the first five years of the council the members included as chair the vice president for student affairs (initially Dr. Ray Work and later Dr. Barry Fullerton), the director of athletics, the faculty representative to the NCAA (Dr. Frank Webbe), the director of student activities, a member of the Student Government Association, and community representatives which included Andy Seminick, Joe Doller, and Percy Hedgecock. As the AAC expanded in the early 1980s community leaders took over as the chairpersons, which included Ned Wilford, president of Holmes Regional Hospital, Percy Hedgecock, former mayor of Satellite Beach and philanthropist, and Bill Potter, a local attorney and member of Florida Tech's board of trustees. As the council expanded there became an interest to take on fundraising activities to supplement the university's athletic scholarship budget, which totaled $430,000 in 1985. The first project to raise needed athletic scholarship dollars was the establishment of the Athletic Scholarship Fund. To get this fund started, Percy Hedgecock pledged $15,000 and said he would match that amount with his own fundraising. Further, he encouraged everyone to raise another $30,000 for this fund.

To expand its fundraising efforts, the Athletic Advisory Council recommended to the university the establishment of the Panther Athletics Association (PAA), which was established in 1986. This new association became the fundraising arm of Florida Tech athletics. Membership dues were established for this association that provided as one of its benefits is admission to all athletic events. There were also different levels of membership, which included reserved seating for basketball games. As athletic teams improved during the 80s, the need for concessions grew and the PAA took over this responsibility with Phil Gaarder heading up this effort. Phil Gaarder also proposed having a Spring Wine Festival on the northeast corner of Babcock St. and University Blvd. This event featured a tent for entertainment and carnival rides.

Another major fundraising project was the establishment of Sporting Affair in 1991. This fundraiser involved auctioning sports memorabilia and other items donated by local businesses and organizations associated with Florida Tech. Also auctioned were international destinations that included airfare and hotel lodging for two people. Darcia Francey was asked to oversee this major event. The first Sporting Affair was held in 1991 and this event was held in the Hartley Room on the campus of Florida Tech. It featured Pat Clarke, well-known sports anchor at WFTV in Orlando, as the emcee, guest speaker Sam Rutigliano, former head football coach of the Cleveland Browns, and an auction with hundreds of items. Throughout the event tables of auction items were shown on screens with the latest bids being displayed, so everyone kept bidding on the items and runners kept picking up their bid forms for immediate display. When Coach Rutigliano, featured speaker for the event, began to speak most of the crowd was focused on the screens and not him, which led him to say, "this was the toughest crowd

I have ever spoken to." Consequently, the long history of Sporting Affair continued without the need for a guest speaker. In the early 2000s the Sporting Affair evolved to a golf outing, a tented outdoor smorgasbord with over 1,000 guests, mostly those who had bought Chopper Dropper tickets. Chopper Dropper was added to Sporting Affair in 2002. Chopper Dropper was the brainchild of Joe Flammio, a member of the Sporting Affair committee and a member of the Florida Tech Board of Trustees. It started with the sale of 1,000 golf ball tickets at $50 each and grew to the sale of 2,000 tickets at $100 each. At the Sporting Affair event, the winners of the golf tournament received team and individual prizes and cash prizes were awarded for Chopper Dropper winners. Sporting Affair was a social event with beer, wine, and food from vendors throughout the community. An exciting part of the Sporting Affair was watching the helicopter drop up to 2,000 balls and the balls closest to the pin won cash prizes that totaled $72,000. This one-day event raised over $100,000 for the athletics department.

The fundraising efforts by the Athletic Advisory Council and the board members of the Panther Athletic Association proved to be a catalyst for the successes of the men's soccer and baseball teams, with both teams rising to prominence in the late 1980s and early 1900s. In 1988 both the men's soccer team and rowing team won national championships, and men's basketball defeated UMass and Boston College in the Holiday Classic. In 1989 men's basketball won their first regular-season Sunshine State Conference championship. In 1991 men's soccer won another NCAA championship; this time on the campus of Florida Tech in front of over 3,000 fans. In 1992 women's basketball won its first conference championship; baseball advanced to the NCAA World Series; and Florida Tech won the Sunshine State Conference's Mayor's Cup for being the top men's all-sports champion.

Establishing the "Panthers" as the university mascot took place in 1983. Prior to becoming the Panthers, Florida Tech was known as the Engineers. There had been an earlier effort in 1975 to change the mascot's name when a contest was held in which students were asked to submit their recommendations. The winning mascot name was the Falcons. This mascot name never really caught on in part because the Florida Air Academy, located a mile from campus, was known as the Falcons. In a meeting with Les Hall (associate athletics director and baseball coach), Marie Flanigan (administrative assistant), and myself (athletics director), I asked what they thought a good name would be for the Florida Tech mascot. After several names were brought up, Marie Flanigan suggested Panthers. Panthers was a good suggestion since a year earlier (1982), the state of Florida asked its public-school students to recommend a state animal for Florida and they chose Panthers. It made sense for Florida Tech to consider an animal that was indigenous to the state and recognized as the state animal. The recommendation of the Panthers as the new mascot was discussed with members of the Florida Tech Athletic Advisory Council (AAC) and upon their approval, Robbie Green, a member of the AAC, said she would present this recommendation to the president. President Keuper thought this would be a great mascot for the university, so he approved the Panthers as the Florida Tech mascot. To show his support for the new mascot, Dr. Keuper put on the Panther outfit and performed at the half-time of a basketball game and at the end of his performance, to everyone's surprise, he pulled off the Panther head so the fans could see it was he. A little-known fact is that Florida International University (FIU) wanted to adopt the Panthers as their mascot less than a year after Florida Tech chose Panthers as their mascot, which upset many at Florida Tech. After Tom Adams, vice president for development, discussed the university's dissatisfaction with Florida's commissioner of education, Charlie Reed, FIU agreed to become the Golden Panthers, which Florida Tech administrators thought was a satisfactory compromise.

In 1984 the Pittsburgh Maulers, a professional football team, trained at Florida Tech in preparation for the inaugural season of the United States Football League (USFL). Mike Rozier was a player with the Pittsburgh Maulers who had been selected as the Heisman Trophy winner the previous year (1983). The connection with the Pittsburgh Maulers was Edward DeBartolo, Sr. who owned the team and had purchased from Florida Tech the land on which the Melbourne Square Mall was built. Mr. DeBartolo needed a training site for his team, and he asked Florida Tech if it would be interested in hosting the Maulers. A condition for hosting the Maulers was that a facility be built that met all their needs, which included an athletic training room, laundry room, a locker room with 120 large-size lockers, a large strength training room, two offices, and an open area for team meetings. Tom Adams, vice president for development, worked with the Maulers to arrange an exhibition game at Satellite High School's football stadium to help cover the costs for constructing this building. Another funding source was the anticipated rental charges for use of this facility. The building was designed so when the Maulers were through using it, the facility could be occupied by Florida Tech's athletic teams. As it turned out, the USFL lasted just one year, and the facility was converted into full use by the Athletics Department. When the Maulers left, they took their strength training equipment, which the students sorely missed using. Hearing their desire for this equipment, university president Jerome Keeper, said the university would cover the cost of replacing this equipment for use by the students and varsity teams. This facility was designed so it could be converted into separate locker rooms, which became men's and women's locker rooms with each having restrooms and shower facilities. Having this new athletics complex was a big step forward for Florida Tech athletics, which previously had inadequate strength training equipment, only one locker room, and offices that had been converted from their original purpose. This new locker room complex was later used by major college football programs that came to Florida to play in one of the bowl games. Those programs that used this facility were The Ohio State University, University of Michigan, University of Virginia, and twice by Penn State University.

The Florida Tech Sports Hall of Fame was established in 1986. As stated in the constitution of the Florida Tech Sports Hall of Fame, the purpose "to honor those persons who have made outstanding contributions to Florida Tech Athletics and to perpetuate the memory of those persons who have brought distinction, honor, and excellence to Florida Tech in athletics." The first inductee into this special group was Jeanne Flanagan who two years earlier was part of the United States women's rowing eight who won an Olympic Gold medal in the 1984 Los Angeles Olympics. The Florida Tech Sports Hall of Fame has become a point of pride for Florida Tech, its athletics program, and most importantly those individuals who were inducted. This bi-annual event has grown through the years to become a highlight of the year for the athletics program.

As a tribute to Andy Seminick's two decades of service to Florida Tech athletics, the baseball field located to the west of the Percy Hedgecock Gymnasium was named the Andy Seminick Field in 1987. In preparation for this important event, a two-story press box was constructed behind home plate. The press box was constructed so it could be used for announcing both baseball and soccer games with a concession stand on the first floor. In preparation for the dedication of the field, Seminick and I traveled to Philadelphia to meet with the president of the Phillies, Bill Giles. The purpose of this meeting was to see if the Phillies would play Florida Tech in an exhibition game for the dedication of the field. Bill Giles, without hesitation, said he would send a "B" squad to Melbourne for the dedication, and among the team members would be Mike Schmidt (future Baseball Hall of Fame member) who had played for Andy Seminick when he managed in the minor league. The Phillies conducted their spring training in Clearwater, Florida, so the distance they would have to travel would not be that far away. The original date scheduled for this event was March 8, 1987. In preparation for the dedication, bleachers were brought in to go the entire length of the right and left field foul lines. Unfortunately, on the scheduled date there was a downpour that left puddles on the field. The

Phillies agreed to return the following weekend but got as far as St. Cloud when they encountered rain, and when they called, I told them that there was again standing water on the field. The dedication occurred two weeks later with a minor league team from the Minnesota Twins, which was arranged by the owner of the Twins, Calvin Griffith.

Another memorable event in the history of Florida Tech athletics was the men's basketball Holiday Classic on December 29-30, 1988. This tournament featured in Friday's first round games Florida Tech playing the University of Massachusetts and Boston College playing Coastal Carolina. The major sponsors for this game were *Florida Today* and McDonald Douglas. In a meeting with Frank Vega, publisher of *Florida Today*, he expressed an interest in bringing major college basketball to Brevard County. Also, George Faenza, vice president for McDonald Douglas, was a big fan of Florida Tech basketball and he also wanted to be supportive in attracting major college basketball to Florida Tech. This game was televised live over local television station WAYK. When Florida Southern College (FSC) heard that Boston College was going to play in Florida Tech's Holiday Classic, an assistant coach at FSC called Boston College's assistant basketball coach, Paul Ward, to ask him if he had seen Florida Tech's gymnasium, and the Boston College assistant coach responded by saying he was familiar with Florida Tech's basketball facility since he had been the men's assistant basketball coach and the women's head basketball coach at Florida Tech. Needless to say, Coach Paul Ward's background at Florida Tech and his long coaching history with Coach Folliard had a great influence in attracting Boston College to the Holiday Classic. In Florida Tech's first game of the tournament, Tech defeated John Calipari's UMass basketball team 106 to 87. Coach Calipari said he would return to the tournament if he did not have to face Florida Tech in the first round. In Saturday's championship game of the second round, Florida Tech was matched up against Boston College (BC) who had defeated Coastal Carolina on Friday. This was a very close game, which featured BC's All-America guard Dana Barros. After a hard-fought game, Florida Tech ended up on top 77-75. Florida Tech basketball was a ticket that everyone in Brevard County wanted to have. On many occasions there were 1,100 people packed in the stands, over 400 standing behind marked off areas around the court, and at least 200 people standing outside trying to get in the Percy Hedgecock Gymnasium.

The event that was the most emotional for me was the 1999 dedication of the Andy Seminick – Les Hall Baseball Field in the new F. W. Olin Sports Complex. The previous baseball field, the Andy Seminick Baseball Field, was cleared away to make room for three new academic buildings made possible by a grant from the F. W. Olin Foundation.

Unfortunately, there were no funds available from the university to replace the baseball field, which resulted in the baseball team playing their games off-campus at a baseball field that was part of the Palm Bay Recreation Department's facilities. The city of Palm Bay was very accommodating to modifying their baseball facility to meet the dimension requirements set forth by NCAA Baseball Rules. This left the university through its athletics department with the task of raising the necessary funds. A fundraising campaign began with soliciting corporate sponsors and acquiring donations for naming opportunities of different baseball related features within the new field, which included home plate, pitcher's mound, first base, etc. Donations were also requested for naming opportunities by purchasing square feet of the new field. Over 200 donors contributed to this fundraising project. The F. W. Olin Foundation had in its bylaws that it did not fund athletic facilities; however, they made an exception when they heard from a parent of a baseball player who mentioned in his letter to the foundation that Mr. Olin, for whom the foundation was created, would not have wanted a gift from the foundation to result in a baseball team not having a field, especially since Mr. Olin had been a professional baseball player. The awareness by the foundation of these circumstances resulted in the university receiving a $250,000 grant from the F. W. Olin Foundation to assist with the construction of a sports complex that included both baseball and softball. In appreciation for this generous grant, Florida Tech proposed to name the new complex the F. W. Olin Sports Complex, which also encompassed an area for a future soccer field and a future multipurpose field. Before the construction could begin there was still a shortfall needed to cover the construction costs. With time running out to begin construction of the baseball field for it to be ready in time for the start of the 1999 spring baseball season, President Weaver, Les Hall, and I met with Tim Wakefield to request support for this project. At this meeting Tim Wakefield graciously pledged a donation so construction of the new baseball field could begin.

The dedication of Andy Seminick – Les Hall Baseball Field took place on March 27, 1999. The Crimson (Severin, February 5, 1999) reported the following individuals who took part in the dedication: Dr. Lynn Weaver, president of Florida Tech, Jack Hartley, chair of the Florida Tech Board of Trustees, Lawrence W. Milas, chair of the F. W. Olin Foundation, Tim Wakefield, Boston Red Sox pitcher and Florida Tech baseball alum, Andy Seminick, Philadelphia Phillies catcher and Florida Tech volunteer, Les Hall, Florida Tech head baseball coach, and myself, Florida Tech Director of Athletics. Also present was the Florida Tech Pep Band. After President Lynn Weaver dedicated the field, the first game on the new field began with Tim Wakefield throwing out the first pitch to former Phillies All-Star catcher Andy Seminick (Severin, February 5, 1999). What made this dedication so special was seeing the joy and excitement of everyone in attendance and realizing that this would not have happened without the concerted effort of many people by showing their generosity and caring attitude for the baseball program and Florida Tech. For Tim Wakefield's generous donations to the construction of a new field, subsequent donations for lighting the baseball field, and numerous other gifts, the Tim Wakefield Batting Cage was built for the baseball and softball teams and named for Wakefield to show the university's appreciation for all he has done to improve the quality of the baseball facilities.

Les Hall speaks at the dedication of the new baseball field as Tim Wakefield, Andy Seminick look on. *Photo from University Archives.*

The dedication of the Charles and Ruth Clemente Center for Sports and Recreation on September 14, 2001, was a major step in moving the Florida Tech athletics program forward by providing year-long locker rooms for all sports, a spacious strength training room with a large assortment of equipment so students did not have to wait to use their favorite machines, and coaches and administrative offices outfitted with attractive furniture and the latest technology to meet their needs. Also available for students is a large recreation room outfitted with mirrors and a raised wooden floor in which a variety of recreational classes could be taught to students. Also, a recreational gymnasium and racquetball court students could reserve and have greater access to than previously possible. After the Clemente Center opened, every day for two years when I walked into the facility, I was in awe that this quality facility existed. In my previous 30 years at Florida Tech if I wanted office equipment I would have to go to the university's surplus furniture and equipment storage facility to see if they had what was needed. The Clemente Center with all its features and technological advancements began a new era in Florida Tech Athletics.

With this new facility, I thought it would benefit the Florida Tech athletics program to host the Sunshine State Conference's (SSC) men's and women's basketball tournament. I proposed to the SSC the idea of rotating the tournament among member institutions and Florida Tech would be the first in this rotation. For years prior to 2002, the SSC was using basketball arenas located in cities throughout the mid-state area, and I knew there would be some hesitation by conference members to change back to institutions. However, after a lengthy two-hour meeting of SSC athletic directors for the purpose of identifying the tournament site for the following year, one of the athletic directors said that Florida Tech wants to host the tournament and there are no other arenas that seem to want to host this event, so why not try rotating the tournament to member institutions who want to host the tournament. Another reason I wanted to host this event was to create greater university and community awareness and support for being a member of the SSC. This tournament would bring all private member institutions together in one spot to compete against one another, and I also thought it would benefit the Florida Tech athletics program by having our administration take part in the tournament banquet. In the past several years, there had been talk within Florida Tech of moving the athletics program to NCAA Division III (Helms, February 26, 1999). One of the reasons for considering Division III was that members in this division were not permitted to provide athletic scholarships, which the university felt would be a big cost-saving measure. However, there were no Division III institutions in the state of Florida and the only way this could be accomplished was to get other institutions, i.e., SSC members and NAIA programs, to change their affiliation to NCAA Division III. Several Florida Tech administrators visited several institutions within the state of Florida and found that though there were two who felt this was a good idea, there were other colleges/universities that felt this move would result in controversy that they did not want to be a part of.

The commissioner of the Sunshine State Conference, Don Landry, impressed on me that Florida Tech should serve as a model for other institutions hosting the basketball tournament, and he was right. When each of the institutions had their turn at hosting the basketball tournament, they showed a lot of pride in making sure they did a great job for the conference. Like Florida Tech, they had their coaches and staff working together to pull off an event which all the conference teams enjoyed attending. The 2002 SSC Basketball tournament held at Florida Tech went off without a hitch. Though the men's team did not make the final, the women's team made it to the championship game in which they defeated Rollins College. The attendance was very good for this tournament, which meant the guarantee was met and a surplus of $8,000 was left for Florida Tech.

The 2002 Florida Tech women's basketball team won the NCAA Division II South Regional Championship at Delta State University, which was a first for women's basketball and a memorable moment for the program. Prior to the NCAA regionals, the women's team tied with Rollins College as the SSC regular-season champion and won the SSC Basketball Tournament. The confident Florida Tech Lady Panthers were ready to take on the best teams in the NCAA DII South Regional Tournament hosted by Delta State University. The top six teams in the South Regional included Central Arkansas, Fort Valley State, Arkansas Tech, West Alabama, Florida Tech, and Delta State (Wikipedia, June 1, 2023). Delta State University is in Cleveland, Mississippi, a short drive to the Mississippi River. The Delta State women's basketball fans are as engaged in games as any place in the country, which adds to the ambiance in the arena. On entering the arena, you cannot help but feel excited about the storied tradition of the Delta State Lady Statesmen. In the '70s the Delta State Lady Statesmen won three consecutive national championships as a member of the Association for Intercollegiate Athletics for Women (AIAW), and in the '90s they won two consecutive NCAA Division II national championships.

As the second ranked team going into the NCAA DII Women's Basketball South Regional, Florida Tech received a bye in the first round, which resulted in them playing the winner of the Arkansas Tech – Fort Valley State game. In the second round Florida Tech defeated Arkansas Tech 61-57 to advance to the final. In the final, Florida Tech defeated Central Arkansas 71-64 to advance to the NCAA DII Elite Eight Championship for the first time in program history. Though the Florida Tech women lost in the first round of the Elite Eight to SE Oklahoma State 68-84, it does not take away from the outstanding season and performance of the Lady Panthers, which included future Florida Tech Sports Hall of Fame member Paulette King.

Receiving the Mayor's Cup trophies three times for being the top men's overall sports champion was a highlight for the Florida Tech athletics program. The first time the Panthers won this title was in 1992, the second time was in 2012 when the Panthers shared this honor with Florida Southern College, and the third presentation of the Mayor's Cup trophy to Florida Tech was in 2017. Another highlight was the women winning 20 regular-season conference championships and the men winning 14 regular-season conference championships. Florida Tech athletics has come a long way since 1981 when it entered the Sunshine State Conference.

There were many exciting times during the history of the Florida Tech football program. The program was discontinued in May of 2020 citing financial reasons just less than a decade after it began. However, this does not diminish what the team accomplished under Head Coach Steve Englehart during his tenure. There were many exciting moments and accomplishments by the team, and one that stands out for me is when the 2018 Panthers defeated the University of West Florida (UWF) to capture the Coastal Classic Trophy, which is awarded to the victor of this intrastate rivalry. Prior to this game, the Panthers had lost the two previous years to the Argonauts and last year's loss to UWF was a bitter one after Florida Tech made a miscue after leading and West Florida capitalized on it with under 10 seconds to go. With this come from behind victory the Argonauts went on to make the finals of the NCAA Division II national championship. In 2018 with Florida Tech facing the University of West Florida, ranked no.19th the country, the Panthers were not to be denied. Falling behind 21 to 3 in the first half, the Panthers went on a 27-point run and made a defensive stand that denied the Argonauts' comeback with little time left (*Florida Today*, October 22, 2018). After the game there was complete jubilation by the Panthers, which included an impromptu singing of the Florida Tech fight song while gathered on the field with the Coastal Classic Trophy on the ground in front of them. Whenever you defeat a ranked team at their home venue, you can expect the losing team to be disgruntled, and this game was no exception. The Panther football team made Florida Tech Athletics a stronger program in many ways, such as creating a fight song for the Panthers, adding a strength training room along with strength training coaches.

Watching the construction and subsequent opening of the Florida Tech Aquatic Center in the fall of 2011 was another highlight in my career as athletics director. This state of the art, beautiful facility was constructed so the varsity swim program could practice in the nine-lane pool, while the recreational pool, in which the pool temperature is set a few degrees warmer, could be used more for recreational purposes and lap swimming in the three available lanes. Additionally, there is a locker room on the south side of the pool for faculty, students, and staff use. To coincide with the opening of the pool, the men's and women's varsity swim teams were established.

Another highlight for me was being present when Florida Tech won the 200-freestyle relay at the 2017 NCAA Division II Swimming Championship in Birmingham, Alabama. The members of the winning relay team were Nir Barnea, Victor Rocha Furtado, Matthew Gallene, and Filip Dujmicand, with Justin Andrade as their coach. The joy of achieving this major goal will remain with these swimmers and their coach for a lifetime.

The successes of the Florida Tech's women golfers in 2007 and 2019 are nothing short of spectacular. It started with Daniela Iacobelli winning the individual NCAA Division II Women's Golf Championship in 2007 and continued with the 2019 Florida Tech women's golf team winning the NCAA Division II Women's Golf Championship.

Daniela Iacobelli reached the pinnacle of success for a collegian as a member of the Florida Tech women's golf team by winning the NCAA Division II individual Golf Championship. Just prior to the 2007 NCAA golf championships, Iacobelli captured the individual title of the Sunshine State Conference's women's golf championship in a playoff against Nova Southeastern's Maria Garia Austt, who was ranked #1 in the nation (Parsons, May 13, 2007). Janie Farina, Iacobelli's coach, had a long history with Iacobelli going back to when she coached Iacobelli at Satellite High School. Farina was confident that Iacobelli would win the NCAA Division II championship. According to Mike Parsons, *Florida Today* sportswriter, Farina said the following to Iacobelli about her chances of winning the NCAA title: "this is your week. I really never doubted it all week" (Parsons, May 13, 2007). On May 12, 2007, Iacobelli defeated second place Maria Garcia Austt of Nova Southeastern and third place Lindsey Bergeon of Florida Southern to become the first NCAA individual national champion for Florida Tech. To accomplish this NCAA championship title, she shot 72, 74, 73, and 74 to finish 5 over par. A reception honoring Daniela Iacobelli for her national championship was held in the lobby of the Clemente Center. President Catanese had earlier presented Iacobelli with a bouquet of flowers and after he expressed his pride in what Iacobelli had accomplished, he asked her to come forward to be recognized by the students, faculty, and staff. Later, when I met with Iacobelli, she said, "I would like a big ring because the championship that I just won was a big one." After her college career, Iacobelli went on to become an LPGA professional golfer. As a professional, Iacobelli in June of 2019 shot rounds of 69, 71, and 65 to finish 11 under par in the Island Resort Championship to capture first place (Grossman, June 25, 2019). This victory provided her with an exemption to the Evian Championship in France, which, according to Hillard Grossman (June 25, 2019) of *Florida Today*, is a major on the LPGA tour.

As an athletics director, one of the most difficult responsibilities is having to tell a team that their sport is being cut by the university. There is no easy way to accomplish this task other than to just tell them that you understand how they feel, and that you and the university are available to help them get through this painful situation. The team and Coach Saltmarsh were as respectful as they could be given the circumstances. What transpired after they were informed was truly amazing. The very best in sports was exhibited by these players and their coach. The players and coach, before the day was over, communicated with one another, and one of the players, Lucy Eaton, had these encouraging words for her teammates, "Let's go win nationals." The magnitude and resolve of the team members to achieve this goal, given that the team had never made the finals of the NCAA Division II Women's Golf Championships, was far beyond just having a hopeful desire to win. They were confident in their ability to achieve this goal. Their quiet determination and resiliency helped them keep focused, while they progressed through the season. Beth Ann Nichols (May 21, 2019), in her article *One last Stand* that appeared in *Florida Today* captured this quote from Coach Saltmarsh, "It was about trying to keep winning, keep making history." After winning three tournaments during the regular season, the team finished sixth at the Sunshine State Conference and fourth in the NCAA South Region to advance to the NCAA Championships. There are two parts to the NCAA golf championship: the first is a 54-hole playoff and the second part is match play based on how the teams were seeded from the 54-hole playoff. The Florida Tech women were seeded number one from the playoff round. The match play had each player competing against a player whose team had advanced from the playoff round. Lucy Eaton, Paolo Ortiz, Megan Dennis, and Lauren Watson won their matches to defeat Cal State San Marcos 4-1 for the national championship (Nichols, May 21, 2019). The team's success in winning the NCAA golf championship received extensive coverage throughout the US. Never in the history of Florida Tech athletics has more publicity been generated than by the women's golf team winning the women's golf NCAA championship. Coach Saltmarsh was destined to win a national championship, and there was no one better prepared to lead this women's golf team than him. A moment that I will never forget was the 2020 Florida Tech Athletic Awards Banquet when the women's golf team was called forward to be recognized for their accomplishment, and immediately 500 student-athletes and guests stood and cheered.

Another highlight of my career as athletics director was the privilege of working closely with Dr. Frank Webbe for 37 years in his capacity as Florida Tech's faculty athletics representative. I could not have asked for a more supportive and professional faculty athletics representative than Dr. Webbe. His strong ethical values and in-depth understanding of athletics guided him in his decision making. Dr. Webbe's knowledge of athletics included being a former soccer official, a distance runner, and father to a high school state champion soccer player. His background in athletics, along with his faculty status, gave him a good perspective on what it takes for a student-athlete to be successful in the classroom and in intercollegiate athletics.

Dr. Webbe is the ultimate professional who has always been there to serve the university on matters pertaining to athletics. He served on our Athletics Advisory Council for over 20 years, and recently helped develop the Athletics Mental Health Committee to better serve the needs of student-athletes. He also served as the chairperson for the athletics' grievance committee. This was not a requirement for the faculty athletic representative; however, there was no one outside of athletics more qualified to render a fair and unbiased decision for those student-athletes being affected.

He also oversaw our concussion management program. Through his dedicated service to this program, Florida Tech was able to provide student-athletes with a program that was one of the top programs among all NCAA institutions. His support of the physicians, neuropsychologists, and athletic trainers is a big reason our student-athletes knew they received the best care possible when they experienced a concussion.

Dr. Webbe's dedicated service to intercollegiate athletics at Florida Tech and the NCAA did not go unnoticed. Dr. Webbe was inducted into the 2022 Sunshine State Conference Sports (SSC) Hall of Fame for his dedicated service and leadership as part of the Faculty Athletics Committee of the SSC. In 2019 Dr. Webbe was inducted into the Florida Tech Sports Hall of Fame for his meritorious service to the university's varsity sports program. In 2018 Dr. Webbe received the highest award a faculty athletics representative can be given when he was selected as the recipient of the David Knight Award, which is presented by the NCAA and the Faculty Athletics Representative Association (FARA) to one individual from all NCAA divisions (I, II, and III) who has provided outstanding service to FARA and collegiate athletics.

The last highlight to mention is attending the graduation ceremonies for student-athletes. When there was available seating in the gymnasium, I would sit there, otherwise, I would sit in my office and watch over the live stream. When the graduation ceremony was winding down, I would go outside near the exit doors to acknowledge their accomplishments. When possible, I would personally meet with them and their parents. On several occasions, the rowing team participated in the finals of the Dad Vail Regatta on the day of graduation. On these occasions a graduation ceremony was held in a boathouse (Vesper Boat Club) on Boathouse Row immediately after the races concluded, which was approximately 5 p.m. Like the graduation ceremony on campus, the student-athletes, joined by their parents, were in their graduation robes and caps. The ceremony was conducted by university officials and each student-athlete was awarded their bachelor's degree diploma. There were tears of joy shown by many of the graduates and their parents. I appreciated the significance of graduation and how athletics was an important part of the educational process in preparing each student-athlete for the challenges and accomplishments they will face throughout their lives.

Bill Jurgens, inducted to F.I.T. Sports Hall of Fame, February 19, 1999.
Photo from University Archives.

References

- Clark, C. (February 17, 2017). *Trailblazer of their time.* Delta State Web Site. Retrieved from: https://gostatesmen.com/news/2017/2/16/womens-basketball-trailblazers-of-their-time.aspx.
- Commissioner Ed Pasque of the Sunshine State Conference assisted with research.
- Discussion with Chris Saltmarsh, head women's golf coach, circa 2019.
- Discussion with John Reynolds, head women's basketball coach, on June 1, 2023.
- Discussion with Les Hall, head baseball coach, circa 1980.
- *Florida Today* (October 22, 2018). *F.I.T.s big rally, clinches Coastal Classic.* Retrieved from Newspapers.com: https://www.newspapers.com/image/497891955/?terms= Coastal%20Classic%20Trophy&match=1.
- Gina Yates provided information on Sporting Affair and Chopper Dropper on May 18, 2023.
- Grossman, H. (June 25, 2019). *Iacobelli posts third pro golf victory. Florida Today.* Retrieved from: https://www.newspapers.com/article/florida-today-iacobelli-wins-in-2019/125358066/.
- Helms, K. (February 26, 1999). *Forum held, Division III move postponed. The Crimson*, Volume XXXII, No. 18. Retrieved from Evans Library Archives.
- Nichols, B. (May 21, 2019). *One last stand: Florida Tech wins women's golf title in program's final event. Florida Today.* Retrieved from: https://www.floridatoday.com/story/sports/2009/05/20/florida-tech-womens-golf-wins-ncaa-title-but-falls-victim-sports-cuts/3740590002/.
- Parsons, M. (May 13, 2007). *Iacobelli's eagles land NCAA title. Florida Today.* Retrieved from: https://www.newspapers.com/image/363020585/?fcfToken= eyJhbGciOiJIUzI1NiIsInR5cCI6IkpXVCJ9.eymcmVlLXZpZXctaWQiOjM2 MzAyMDU4NSwiaWF0IjoxNjg1MTM4MjI2LCJleHAiOjE2ODUyMjQ2 MjZ9._SfS10TSc-FYXCFoNV5QXVBgSrBGWGxYJBtD6k4M1Uo.
- Severin, M. (February 5, 1999). *President Lynn Weaver dedicated new baseball field to Seminick, Hall. Florida Tech Crimson*, Vol. XXXII, No. 15. Ed Pasque, (May 15, 1023).

- Wallace, E. (October 20, 2018). *PNJ Scoreboard FINAL: Florida Tech smothers No. 19 UWF. Pensacola News Journal.* Retrieved from: https://www.pnj.com/story/sports/college/university-west-florida/2018/10/20/pnj-scoreboard-live-florida-tech-no-19-uwf/1711059002/.
- Wikipedia (June 1, 2023). *2002 NCAA Division II women's basketball tournament.* Retrieved from: https://en.wikipedia.org/wiki/2002_NCAA_Division_II_women%27s_Basketball_tournament.

CHAPTER FOUR:
FOLLIARD TRANSFORMS BASKETBALL AT FLORIDA TECH AND MIMS BUILDS A LEGACY

By William C. Potter

A significant step forward for Florida Tech athletics was announced by *Florida Today* on November 23, 1983, when it was disclosed that the Pittsburgh Maulers of the United States Football League had selected the F.I.T. campus as its training site. The agreement between the Maulers and Florida Tech enabled the university to construct a two-story addition to its gymnasium for new locker rooms, training rooms and offices. These facilities would be shared by the Maulers and the university.

Roger Dufour resigned as men's basketball coach at the end of the 1983-1984 season. Florida Tech undertook a nationwide search which attracted more than seventy applicants. Among the applicants was forty-three-year-old Tom Folliard. F.I.T. Vice President for Student Affairs Barry Fullerton had worked with Folliard at Bryant College in Rhode Island and was a vocal advocate for him.

Folliard had an impressive resume, having played college basketball at Providence College when it won the National Invitational Tournament in the days when the N.I.T. attracted a field as strong as the NCAA Tournament. That Providence team included Lennie Wilkens who would go on to be a Hall of Fame coach and player, another NBA player Johnny Eagan, Hall of Fame coach John Thompson, and a future mayor of Boston, Ray Flynn. After graduation, Folliard became coach at Bryant College in Rhode Island, followed by service as basketball coach and Athletic Director at Stonehill College in Massachusetts. Folliard has since been inducted into the Halls of Fame at both Stonehill and Bryant.

In reporting Folliard's hiring as F.I.T. coach on May 24, 1984, Peter Kerasotis of *Florida Today* noted that the university had last won a game in the Sunshine State Conference three years before. Dufour had left with an overall record of 28 wins and 85 losses, including records of 4 and 20, 4 and 22 and 3 and 23 over the last three years of his tenure. The article quoted Folliard as saying: "My immediate goal would be to try to become competitive as quickly as possible and become front-runners in the conference."

Folliard's tenure at Florida Tech began inauspiciously with four straight defeats to begin the 1984-1985 season. But, as reported by *Florida Today* on December 5, 1984, Folliard had a plan, as he noted when saying: "Recruiting is ninety percent of the game in college basketball. I spent most of the summer on airplanes, flying around from Massachusetts to Newark trying to recruit players." He also noted that three transfer students would be eligible during the following year, including his son Tom, a transfer from Bryant who had averaged 26 points per game in high school, Henry Gibbs, a transfer from Tennessee State and George Leonard, who had been the leading scorer at Bryant the previous year.

Tom Folliard was a great motivator as well as a clever strategist.
Photo from University Archives.

On December 16, 1984, *Florida Today* reported that F.I.T. had won its first game under Folliard with a 65 to 64 come-from-behind victory over Coastal Carolina. Eli Lofton hit two free throws with two seconds remaining to win the game. The Panthers followed up that victory by beating Barry College a couple of days later.

By February 4, 1985, *Florida Today* noted that Florida Tech now had a record of 8 wins and 11 losses and that the school's rebuilding program was "a shot on the mark." Folliard noted wryly that he was "happy as hell" to get the eight wins, but quickly added: "my job is not to let them be happy about it." But it was difficult not to be enthusiastic when considering that the record in the previous five years had been 26 wins and 101 losses.

The 1985-86 season began with great optimism. As reported in *Florida Today* on November 22, 1985, the entire starting line-up from the previous year returned. They were joined by several transfers, including Folliard's son Tommy. Notably, Folliard's younger son Kevin, who had starred the previous year at Melbourne High School, also joined the team. In analyzing prospects in the Sunshine State Conference, Folliard noted: "We should be the most improved team." Former Panther standout Nino Lyons would serve as assistant coach that season.

The optimism quickly proved to be justified. On December 30, 1985, *Florida Today* noted that F.I.T. now boasted a record of 6 wins and 2 losses after beating Dartmouth 81 to 67. One of those losses was to Division I Florida State University.

Another season highlight was reported in *Florida Today* on January 6, 1986, when the Panthers downed Rollins College in Winter Park by a score of 86 to 75. Tommy Folliard paced the scorers with 24 points.

F.I.T would finish the 1985-1986 season with a record of 12 wins and 14 losses, including a 4 and 9 record in the conference. The Panthers lost narrowly 64 to 62 to Eckerd College in the first round of the conference post-season tournament.

Folliard immediately began scouring the country for recruits for the following year, noting in *Florida Today* on March 24, 1986, that: "now Division I schools are also interested in a lot of the same players."

On June 2, 1986, *Florida Today* reported that Paul Ward, who had worked with Folliard at Stonehill College, would become head women's basketball coach at F.I.T. In addition to coaching the women, Ward's duties included recruiting for the men's team.

On November 5, 1986, Roger Brown wrote in *Florida Today* that Folliard was hoping that his third time around would be a charm. The article noted that there were nine players returning from the previous year and three outstanding freshmen coming in. Leading scorer John Cooper was returning together with Tommy Folliard "who is considered the best outside shooter on the team." Davon Kelly was a freshman who showed great promise. Two freshmen from Queens, New York, Ron Ulmer and Ray Paprocky, also raised great anticipation.

Florida Tech opened the 1986-1987 season by defeating Nova by a score of 93 to 77 *Florida Today* reported on November 22, 1986, that the victory had brought the standing-room-only crowd of 1600 "to a feverish pitch at the Hedgecock Gymnasium." The fact that there was a standing-room-only crowd was a dramatic illustration of how far basketball had come under Folliard. Most promising was the fact that Kelly, Paprocky and Ulmer combined for 37 points while Kelley also pulled down 12 rebounds. Ron Harris added 16 points and Tommy Folliard chipped in 15 points. The Panthers followed up that victory with a 92 to 74 victory over Palm Beach Atlantic. *Florida Today* noted that the victory was the 300th of Folliard's coaching career.

However, by New Year's Eve F.I.T. stood at a record of 2 wins and 3 losses when it fell by one point to Nebraska Wesleyan. Over the New Year holiday F.I.T. hosted an invitational basketball tournament. It opened the tournament with a 76 to 64 triumph over Folliard's old school, Bryant College. By January 24, 1987, Florida Tech had amassed a record of 11 wins and 4 losses, including 2 wins and a loss in the conference. As they proceeded into the heart of their conference schedule, however, things came tougher. By February 14, their record had fallen to 12 and 11, with a 2 and 8 conference record. A promising sign, however, was a near upset of the University of Central Florida on February 21, 1987, when the Panthers led 42 to 33 at halftime before falling 79 to 72.

On July 15, 1987, *Florida Today* reported that Folliard had recruited three Canadians to play basketball for Florida Tech. These recruits would prove to be transformational for Florida Tech. Dwight Walton was a six-foot-five, 220 pounder who was "very tough." Astley Smith was a 6-foot-3 1/2, 230 pounder and Garfield Glasgow was a 6-foot-5-1/2, 235 pounder. Folliard was confident that these players could assist in pushing the Panthers into the upper part of the Sunshine State Conference standings. Walton was a transfer student from Siena College and, in accordance with NCAA transfer regulations, would have to sit out the 1987-1988 season.

The 1987-1988 season began on a positive note when the Panthers captured their own Tip-Off Classic by winning their first two games, defeating St. Joseph's of Maine and St. Leo. Davon Kelly was named Most Valuable Player of the tourney and joined Tommy Folliard and Garfield Glasgow on the all-tournament team. *Florida Today* reported on November 21, 1987, that Coach Folliard was pleased with his "new-found Canadian connection." That same edition reported that Nino Lyons had resigned as assistant coach to devote full-time to his business interests.

Florida Today reported on December 6, 1987, that the Panthers had improved their season record to 4 and 0 with a 116 to 98 win over Palm Beach Atlantic. The game was marred by a bench-clearing brawl in the first half. Astley Smith with 26 points and 15 rebounds led the team while Davon Kelly added 20 points and Tommy Folliard chipped-in 17 points.

With an 87 to 75 victory over Flagler College on December 15, 1987, the Panthers improved to 5 and 0 on the season. Tom Folliard led the way with 26 points, including 10 of 10 from the foul line, while Ron Harris and Garfield Glasgow added 15 and 14, respectively.

Florida Tech lost its first game on December 19, 1987, a heartbreaker at Division I Mercer by a score of 80 to 78. It followed that game by visiting Boston College on December 22, 1987. The Panthers lost their second consecutive game to a Division I school by a score of 116 to 93. Davon Kelly led the Panthers with 27 points.

Florida Tech followed-up the Boston College game by participating in the Bentley Classic in the Boston-area where they played Stonehill on December 28, 1987, and Tommy Folliard led the way by scoring 22 points against his former teammates. However, the Panthers lost in a heartbreaker 76 to 73. The following night, the Panthers lost another close game, falling to the University of Buffalo 82 to 79.

The Panthers completed their tour of New England by playing Bryant College, another place where Folliard had previously coached, on December 31, 1987. Fittingly, Tommy Folliard scored 27 points against his former team to lead F.I.T. to a 97 to 90 victory. Garfield Glasgow added 19 points.

On January 16, 1988, Florida Tech played what *Florida Today* described as "the most important three minutes in the history of the Florida Institute of Technology basketball program." The article was referring to the final three minutes of the first half of the Panthers' game against previously undefeated Florida Southern College, the top-ranked Division II team in the country, when Florida Tech rallied from 10 points down to take the lead at halftime and went on to win by a score of 72 to 70. In snapping a streak of twenty-six consecutive losses to Florida Southern, the Panthers achieved the biggest win in the history of the program and, in the words of *Florida Today*, halted "its image as a pushover."

On February 14, 1988, *Florida Today* reported that the Panthers had beaten number-one ranked Florida Southern for the second time that season the previous night. The game went down to the buzzer when Kevin Folliard, not known for his outside shooting, banked-in a shot from twenty-five feet as the clock expired to give them a 66 to 65 win. Kevin's father noted that: "He's never made a shot like that in his dreams." That win over the nationally top-ranked Moccasins brought Florida Tech's record to 15 wins and 7 losses overall and 5 wins and 2 losses in the Sunshine State Conference.

Florida Today published an extensive article on February 20, 1988, describing the Canadian recruiting pipeline that Folliard had created. Two years before, Folliard related, he had called a friend who had previously been an assistant coach at St. Bonaventure in the northeast looking for potential recruits. The friend gave him the names of Dwight Walton, Astley Smith and Garfield Glasgow. He also gave him the names of two Canadians who would be joining the team the following year, Robert Sewell and Astley's younger brother, Michael Smith. Folliard noted that all of the Canadian players were strong students, which he attributed to the Canadian educational system.

On February 27, 1988, the Panthers secured their second-ever victory against a Division I school when they defeated the University of Central Florida by a score of 98 to 83. As reported in *Florida Today,* one of the highlights of the game was that Tom Folliard, Jr. scored his 1,000th career point.

Although the Panthers' season would end with a defeat by Tampa in the conference tournament, Florida Tech would complete that 1987-1988 basketball campaign with 18 wins, including a winning record in the Sunshine State Conference for the first time in school history and a win over Tampa for the first time. Tom Folliard, Jr. and Davon Kelly led the team while Astley Smith made the conference All-Freshman team. With Walton slated to join the team for the 1988-1989 season, hopes were high and enthusiasm at the college and in the community ran rampant.

On April 14, 1988, *Florida Today* would report that Folliard had signed three new recruits for his team, including Astley Smith's younger brother Mike Smith and another Canadian, 6-5 Robert Sewell. He also signed 6-11, 240-pound Jamie Lathrop, the tallest player to ever don a Florida Tech uniform at that time.

On August 30, 1988, *Florida Today* announced the line-up for the annual holiday basketball tournament at Florida Tech, scheduled for December 29 and 30, 1988. It was a sign of the progress of Florida Tech basketball that the tournament was able to attract three Division I teams: Boston College, University of Massachusetts and Coastal Carolina. Folliard noted: "I hope the community gets excited about it because we certainly are." Later, on September 1, 1988, *Florida Today* reported that McDonnell Douglas had agreed to co-sponsor the tournament with *Florida Today*. Folliard explained that he had been able to attract Boston College to the tournament by guaranteeing them that it would not dip below 70 degrees while they were here. Folliard noted: "I just hope we don't have a cold front move through."

Florida Today reported on November 18, 1988, that the Panthers would open the 1988-1989 season by hosting its Tip-Off Classic with Nova, St. Leo and Georgia College. Although Dwight Walton had yet to play a game for Florida Tech, Coach Folliard pronounced him to be the best player in the Sunshine State Conference. Folliard announced that the starting lineup would include Walton, together with fellow Canadians

Astley Smith and Garfield Glasgow, sophomore forward David Love and guard Davon Kelly, a first-team all-conference selection the previous year. The following day, the newspaper reported that the Panthers had opened the season with a 75 to 69 victory over Nova, led by Kelly with 19 points. The Panthers proceeded to win their tournament with a victory over St. Leo.

By December 27, 1988, the Panthers had a record of four wins and one loss, the only loss being a double-overtime loss to Armstrong State. As reported by *Florida Today* on that date, their latest victory was a 75 to 60 win over College of Charleston.

On December 29, 1988, *Florida Today* reported on the upcoming *Florida Today*/McDonnell Douglas Classic Basketball Tournament under the byline, "Folliard takes F.I.T. into big times." Folliard noted: "Name recognition is critical in college basketball. And there's no better way for us to get our name out than this tournament." F.I.T. would host Boston College, University of Massachusetts and Coastal Carolina. UMass was coached by John Calipari who would go on to a legendary career at Memphis and Kentucky and would coach in the NBA for several years. Boston College was led by Dana Barros who had averaged 21.9 points per game the previous year and would go on to play more than ten years in the NBA.

F.I.T. topped UMass in its opening game of the tournament. Dwight Walton scored 30 points to lead the way. Folliard told *Florida Today* that: "This has got to be the best we've played in the five years that I've been here." Walton, however, noted: "We played well, but we can play a lot better." The win put the Panthers in the championship game against Boston College which had defeated Coastal Carolina.

The following night, December 30, 1988, the Panthers registered what may to this day be the greatest basketball victory in the history of the school when it defeated Boston College, 77 to 75. Barros showed his extraordinary shooting skills in registering 33 points but Kevin Folliard and Ray Paprocky took turns guarding him and had some success in denying him the ball in the second half. Florida Tech, on the other hand, had remarkably balanced scoring, led by Walton with 17, Astley Smith with 17, Kelly with 15, Sewell with 13 and Glasgow with 8. Dwight Walton pulled down 13 rebounds. Walton observed to *Florida Today*: "This is the biggest win ever for this program."

The Panthers had little time to enjoy the reflected glory of this victory, however. The following week, they hosted the F.I.T. Classic, with an opening game win against St. Anselm. In the championship game of the classic, F.I.T. defeated Sacred Heart, 76 to 64, behind 20 points each by Walton and Astley Smith. Smith was named Most Valuable

Player of the tournament while Walton joined him on the all-tournament team.

The Panthers followed-up the tournament by running their record to 10 wins and 1 loss with a 100 to 86 win over North Carolina-Greensboro. Davon Kelly led the way with 28 points. Kelly related to *Florida Today* that: "They really took it to us early, but then everybody dug down deep and pulled us back into it."

Coach Folliard missed two games in February due to a herniated disc. He was able to join the team for the Sunshine State Conference tournament in Tampa only due to travelling in a custom van with a bed in the back. Tampa also accommodated him by providing a sofa on the sidelines during the game which enabled him to lie down. Unfortunately, the Panthers lost to Florida Southern in the conference tournament by a 73 to 71 margin, to take their record to twenty-two wins and six losses.

Despite the tournament loss, the South Regional advisory committee selected F.I.T. for inclusion in the thirty-two team NCAA field. *Florida Today* reported on March 10, 1989, that the Panthers were ranked fourth in the South Region and would likely play their first-ever NCAA tournament game against South Regional host Jacksonville (Ala.) State. As the newspaper reported on March 20, 1989, F.I.T. lost that opening game to Jacksonville State 89 to 67, followed by a loss the following night to Florida Southern by a score of 85 to 75.

On March 21, 1989, Lyle Graves wrote an article in *Florida Today* pondering the future of F.I.T. basketball in light of their first NCAA Division II tournament appearance the previous weekend. Although the Panthers had lost both games of the weekend, Folliard noted: "But this was a tremendous learning experience for us. We're a team dominated by freshmen and sophomores, and it is very important for them to get a taste of what it's like to play in an NCAA Tournament this early in their careers." Folliard also noted that he had many contacts from schools in the northeast but that he had no intention of returning to that area, noting: "With my bad back, all the snow and ice of the North would be the worst thing in the world."

On June 7, 1989, *Florida Today* reported that Folliard had signed two players who would have a significant impact upon F.I.T. basketball. Igor Beros, a 6-foot-5 forward from Yugoslavia was not only a solid physical presence but also a skilled outside shooter. Chris Rose had led all Florida junior college players in scoring the previous year and was expected to contribute immediately as a point guard.

Kevin Folliard would earn recognition in *Florida Today* on July 4, 1989, not for his basketball prowess, but for his academic achievements. He was named one of the eight civil engineering students in the country to be selected for a National Science Foundation summer research appointment at Cornell University.

On July 15, 1989, *Florida Today* released the names of the teams which would compete in the second annual *Florida Today*/McDonnell Douglas Holiday Classic on January 5 and 6, 1990. Like the previous year, three Division I teams would join the host. George Washington, Alcorn State and Murray State would provide the competition.

On July 28, 1989, *Florida Today* reported that Coach Folliard was attempting to arrange a September trip to France for the team where they would play teams from the Soviet Union, France and Spain. Folliard also reported in the article that Garfield Glasgow had dropped out of school the previous spring and that all attempts to find him had gone for naught. Unfortunately, the tournament was cancelled when the French Basketball Federation failed to approve it. There is no evidence that efforts to locate Glasgow ever bore fruit and he never played for F.I.T. again.

Florida Tech basketball tipped-off the 1989-1990 season on November 18 with a 74 to 71 victory over St. Thomas University. Dwight Walton led the way with 28 points and 17 rebounds, while newcomer Igor Beros added 15 points. Folliard observed that Astley Smith, who had not practiced for nine days due to injuries, probably saved the win with his 11 points at crucial times.

On December 20, the Panthers ran their record to 4 and 0 by defeating Queens College by a score of 86 to 59. The victory was particularly significant since Queens had defeated the University of Central Florida a few nights before. Dwight Walton and Davon Kelly led F.I.T. with 18 points each while Chris Rose added 12 and Astley Smith scored 11.

The Panthers travelled to New England in late December to participate in the Bryant College Christmas Basketball Tournament. They opened the tournament with a 97 to 79 win over Stonehill. Florida Tech won the tournament with a dominant 97 to 74 win over New York Tech in the championship game. *Florida Today* reported that Astley Smith was voted Most Valuable Player of the tourney while Dwight Walton, Ray Paprocky and Davon Kelly joined him on the all-tournament team. Folliard observed: "I'm very pleased with our overall offensive and defensive performance."

That tournament crown, however, was sullied when the team fell victim to the infamous brutality of the Providence, R. I. police. After the tournament, a group of Panther players and their families were in a hotel lounge in Providence when a bouncer and a friend of the Folliard family were involved in a dispute. As the F.I.T. players and families attempted to leave and get to the elevators, the Providence police brutally attacked them with night-sticks. Tom Folliard, Jr., an assistant coach, attempted to shield his father from the attack but was bludgeoned by an officer and thrown against the wall, bleeding profusely. Tom, Sr., Tom, Jr. and Kevin Folliard were all arrested and jailed for the night. The Providence police were well-known at the time for their brutality and corruption. Florida Tech president Dr. Lynn Weaver appointed a committee to investigate the incident. After interviewing all available witnesses, the committee found that Folliard and his team had committed no wrongdoing and that the actions of the team were "exemplary under the circumstances." As later reported in *Florida Today* on April 27, 1990, a trial began in Providence on April 26, 1990, against all three Folliards. However, after hearing the first three witnesses, the presiding judge dismissed the charges against Tom, Sr. and urged the city and the other defendants to settle the matter. The settlement resulted in the dismissal of all charges against all Folliards. As part of the settlement, Tom Sr. agreed to waive his right to take civil action against the city and the police. Tom, Jr. and Kevin made no such agreement and retained their rights to sue.

On January 5, 1990, Florida Tech opened the Holiday Classic by defeating George Washington by a score of 71 to 53. Astley Smith with 20 points and Dwight Walton with 19 points led the Panthers' scoring. Walton added 11 rebounds while Ray Paprocky contributed 11 assists. In the championship game on January 6, Murray State proved to be too much, handing the Panthers their first loss of the season by a score of 72 to 62. Murray State was led by 27 points from Popeye Jones who would go on to a lengthy NBA career. Chris Rose led Florida Tech with 29 points. Astley Smith and Dwight Walton were named to the all-tourney team.

By January 25, 1990, when the Panthers defeated Florida Atlantic University, F.I.T.'s record stood at 14 wins and 2 losses.

On February 10, F.I.T. beat Tampa by a score of 75 to 68. That win lifted the Panthers to a tie with Tampa for first place in the Sunshine State Conference. Davon Kelly led the way with 25 points while Walton added 22 points and 11 rebounds.

On February 21, 1990, Florida Tech trounced St. Leo by a score of 94 to 74, marking its tenth consecutive victory and raising its record to 22 and 2. By then, the Panthers were rated eighth nationally among Division II teams. Davon Kelly scored 22 points to lead the way and also become the top-scorer in program history with 1,661 points during his career.

Florida Tech registered one of the most impressive wins in its history when it won at Barry University on February 24 by a score of 131 to 84. Seven Tech players scored in double figures, including Kelly with 17, Sewell with 16, Igor Beros with 14, Astley Smith with 13, Chris Rose with 12, Ray Paprocky with 12 and Doug Newbert with 12. That brought the season record to 23 and 2 with a 10 and 1 record in the conference.

On March 3, Florida Tech clinched a share of the conference championship when it defeated Florida Southern 75 to 69. That left the Panthers with a 25 and 2 record, 11 and 1 in the conference, tied with Tampa for first place. A coin-flip determined that Tampa would host the post-season tourney. David Jones of *Florida Today* commented about the coin flip: "It's the stuff that makes class leagues into sad jokes."

Unfortunately, the Panthers would fall to Florida Southern in the semi-finals of the conference tourney, losing 89 to 74 on March 9, 1990. Folliard noted: "We played awful. We couldn't score."

Fortunately, despite the loss in the conference tournament, Florida Tech was selected to play in the NCAA Division II tournament. The Panthers played Norfolk State in Norfolk in the opening game of the South Atlantic region on March 16. Florida Tech prevailed in that regional semi-final game by a score of 73 to 63, led by Dwight Walton's 24 points and 12 rebounds. The following night, the Panthers played Morehouse College in the championship game of the NCAA South Atlantic Regional, falling behind early but rallying to fall just short, losing 81 to 77. Folliard noted: "After the Norfolk State game, we just didn't have anything left." Walton led the way with 26 points and 17 rebounds, while Kelly added 20 points and Robert Sewell contributed 14 points. Walton and Kelly were named to the all-tournament team.

Florida Tech would finish that 1989-1990 season with a record of 26 wins and 4 losses. They would be co-champions of the Sunshine State Conference and make their second consecutive appearance in the NCAA Tournament. Folliard would be named one of eight NCAA Division II coaches of the year. Dwight Walton was named to the NCAA Division II All-America third team. Folliard was quoted in *Florida Today* on March 21 as describing Walton as "the guts of our team."

The 1990-1991 season began with great optimism. Dwight Walton, Astley Smith and Robert Sewell all returned to the front line. Although guards Davon Kelly and Ray Paprocky had graduated, Chris Rose returned and was joined by Brian Keenan, a transfer from Hartford. Folliard also had high hopes for James Odeh, a 6-foot-7 Nigerian. The optimism seemed justified when the Panthers opened with a 109 to 56 rout of Nova University on November 17, 1990, led by Odeh's 20 points.

On December 12, the Panthers defeated Armstrong State College by a score of 71 to 64, taking their record to 5 and 1 for the season. Astley Smith led the way with 23 points.

A few nights later, on December 15, the Panthers defeated Florida Atlantic by a score of 90 to 77. The depth of the team was demonstrated by the balanced scoring with Walton with 25 points, Astley Smith with 16, Mike Smith with 14, Rose with 12 and Sewell with 11.

On December 29, 1990, the Panthers crushed Milwaukee School of Engineering by a score of 118 to 63. F.I.T. had six players score in double figures, led by Chris Rose's 19 points and Mike Smith's 13 rebounds. That improved the team's record to 8 and 1.

The line-up for the McDonnell Douglas Classic for 1991 included Brown University, University of Detroit and University of District of Columbia. The Panthers entered the tournament with a record of 9 and 1. They opened with an easy 72 to 37 win over University of District of Columbia, with balanced scoring led by Doug Newbert's 12 points. The championship game against the University of Detroit proved to be a tougher battle but the Panthers prevailed by a score of 56 to 53. Chris Rose led the scoring with 18 points and was named Most Valuable Player of the tournament.

F.I.T. completed its non-conference schedule on January 9, 1991, with a 96 to 74 victory over St. Thomas University. That brought the Panthers' record to 12 wins and 1 loss. Rose had 21 points, while Astley Smith added 18 and Robert Sewell added 15. Mike Smith contributed 11 rebounds.

Florida Tech lost its first game in the conference, losing to Rollins on January 19 by a 78 to 68 score. A few nights later, however, they returned to form by beating St. Leo, 91 to 70, behind Dwight Walton's 25 points.

On January 30, 1991, the Panthers picked up a big win by defeating Tampa, 90 to 84. Rose had 19 points, Astley Smith 19, Walton 18 and Beros 16. Sewell, Walton and Mike Smith fouled out of the game. Unfortunately, they followed that game with a 56 to 53 loss to Florida Southern a few nights later, dropping the Panthers to 4 and 2 in the league.

F.I.T. quickly turned things around, however, on February 9 when they defeated league-leading Rollins by a score of 74 to 71. Astley Smith led the scoring with 19 points while Walton snared 7 rebounds and Rose dealt 7 assists. By February 16, Florida Tech was 5 and 2 in the league and tied for second with Florida Southern behind league-leading Rollins.

A crushing loss at Tampa on February 20 dropped the 20th ranked Panthers to 19 and 4 overall and 7 and 3 in the league. Folliard commented about the 90 to 56 loss by saying: "They just totally took us out of the game."

On February 27, 1991, Florida Tech's 23-game winning streak in Percy Hedgecock Gymnasium came to a halt when Florida Southern defeated the Panthers by a score of 68 to 59. That ended the Panthers' regular season with a record of 20 and 5 overall and 8 and 4 in the league.

Dwight Walton led the way for the Panthers with 19 points while Astley Smith added 16.

Florida Tech reached a big milestone on March 5, 1991, when it defeated Eckerd College by a score of 65 to 52, marking the first victory ever in the Sunshine State Conference tournament. Folliard noted: "The jinx is gone, if there is such a thing." Chris Rose led the scoring with 19 points and Walton added 13.

The victory over Eckerd put F.I.T. in the semifinal game against Rollins, a team with whom they had split during the regular season. F.I.T. upset Rollins at Winter Park with an impressive 90 to 76 victory. A determined second half comeback brought the Panthers' record to 22 and 5. The Panthers outrebounded the Tars 51 to 29, led by Odeh's 13 rebounds, Walton with 24, Beros with 22 and Rose with 18 led the scoring.

Florida Southern dashed the Panthers' hopes for the tournament crown by defeating them 77 to 66 on March 9, 1991, in the championship game. Florida Tech was led by Walton and Rose, with 16 and 14 points, respectively. They both were named to the all-tourney team. That victory took Florida Southern to its sixth consecutive conference tournament championship. Folliard told *Florida Today*: "We are a team of streaks – good streaks and bad streaks. Tonight, the bad streaks outnumbered the good streaks,"

The Panthers failed to receive an NCAA Tournament bid that year. Dwight Walton was named to the NCAA Division II All-America second team by the National Association of Basketball Coaches. F.I.T. Assistant Coach Kevin Dunne told *Florida Today* on March 19: "I'm very happy for him. This makes up for last week a little bit."

On August 23, 1991, *Florida Today* reported that Tom Folliard had announced his resignation the previous day. The coach was 51 years of age and had accumulated 123 wins and 73 losses in seven years at a school where wins were rare prior to his arrival. Folliard was quoted as saying: "I just don't feel like I could generate the enthusiasm necessary to do this for another year." A later article by David Jones in *Florida Today* on September 19, 1991, quoted Folliard as saying: "College athletics is changing. It is changing right before our eyes and I don't like where it is going." Jones also discussed with Folliard how the incident with the Providence police had affected him and continued to haunt him. It seemed clear that the event in Providence continued to affect Folliard and his family. A few days before the interview with Jones, Folliard had filed a civil lawsuit in U.S. District Court against the City of Providence and 10 police officers.

Folliard's record at Florida Tech was as follows:

SEASON	WINS	LOSSES	SSC WINS	SSC LOSSES
1984-85	10	17	3	9
1985-86	12	14	4	9
1986-87	12	15	2	11
1987-88	19	9	6	5
1988-89	22	8	9	5
1989-90	26	4	11	2
1990-91	22	6	10	5
TOTAL	123	73	45	46

Tom Folliard had changed forever the expectations for basketball at Florida Tech. The coaches that followed him would struggle to emulate his success. Tragically, Coach Folliard would die of cancer at age 61. However, he left behind indelible marks. Not only did he have remarkable coaching success at three different universities, but he conveyed to his family the formula for success. His oldest son Tom, Jr. became Chief Executive Officer of CarMax, a publicly traded used vehicle retailer with annual revenues in excess of $18 billion. His younger son, Kevin, graduated from F.I.T. with a degree in Civil Engineering, earned his PhD in Civil Engineering from California-Berkley and is now a tenured professor of Civil Engineering at Texas-Austin. Coach Folliard obviously taught his children what it takes to be a winner as well as a responsible citizen.

Folliard was succeeded as coach by Andy Russo who had experienced success as a coach at Louisiana Tech and the University of Washington. In an article in *Florida Today* on October 1, 1991, David Jones praised the hiring of Russo but noted that, unlike Folliard, Russo had no "Canadian connection," noting that under Folliard the Panthers had "found a very unusual market and took advantage of it." This, of course referred to the pipeline of Canadian players who had been the heart of Folliard's most successful teams. Jones noted that F.I.T.'s academic standards posed an additional challenge for Russo but noted that: "It's nice to see a coach who, like Folliard, appreciates brains."

Russo remained at Florida Tech for 8 years, from the 1991-92 season through the 1998-1999 season. During his tenure at Florida Tech his teams won 125 games while losing 94 games. In the conference, his record was 56 and 50. Russo was selected as the Sunshine State Conference Coach of the Year for the 1993-94 season. His most successful season was in 1996-1997 when the Panthers won 21 games and lost 8. The conference record that year was 11 and 3, good for second place in the conference. Russo coached several remarkable players during his time at Florida Tech. Canadian Robert Sewell was a 1st team all-conference selection in 1992. Peter Wolcott, another Canadian import, was 1st team all-conference in 1993, 1994 and 1995. Sherman Hamilton was a 2nd team pick in 1993. Rob Terry was an honorable mention pick in 1994, a 2nd team pick in 1995 and a 1st team pick in 1997. Terry left Florida Tech holding most of the school's records in those categories. He was elected to the Florida Tech Sports Hall of Fame in 2003. In 1996, Nebojsa Damjanovich and Junior Allen were honorable mention picks while Allen made the 1st team in both 1997 and 1998. Brandon Palmer was an honorable mention selection in 1998 before being selected as a 1st team pick and Co-Player of the Year in the conference for the 1998-1999 season.

Percy Hedgecock Gymnasium was a tough place for visiting teams.
Photo from University Archives.

An important step in the history of Florida Tech sports was announced in *Florida Today* on December 31, 1999, when it was disclosed that Hedgecock Gymnasium would be razed, and The Charles and Ruth Clemente Center for Sports and Recreation constructed on the site. Hedgecock Gymnasium was a 27,800 square foot facility which had been built in 1967 at a cost of $203,000.00 and seated 950 spectators. The Clemente Center would be a 57,250 square foot facility constructed at a cost of $6.8 million and would seat 1,800 to 3,200 people. The structure was funded by a gift from Florida Tech trustee Charles Clemente and his wife, Ruth, which was matched by the F.W. Olin Foundation. While the new facility was being constructed, Florida Tech men's and women's basketball and women's volleyball would play their home games at nearby Brevard Community College. *Florida Today* would reveal on September 8, 2001, that the first athletic event played in the Clemente Center was a volleyball game between Florida Tech and St. Thomas. The women's basketball team would play their first game in the facility on November 16, 2001, against Florida Memorial while the men's basketball team would play their initial game in the facility on November 18 against Puerto Rico-Rio Piedras.

Kris Olson coached the Panthers for 6 seasons from 1999-2000 until 2004-05. Olson's teams compiled a record of 48 wins and 116 losses. Eric Jackson was selected to the 1st team all-conference team for the 1999-2000 season under Olson's tutelage. Billy Mims was hired as coach on June 27, 2005, and remains coach as of the writing of this book. In his 18 seasons at Florida Tech, he has amassed the most wins of any men's basketball coach at Florida Tech with 251 wins. A highlight of Mims' career at Florida Tech occurred during the 2011-12 season when the Panthers compiled a record of 23 wins and 7 losses with a 12 and 4 record in the conference. This won Florida Tech its first outright Sunshine State Conference regular season championship, although they fell in the semi-finals of the conference tournament. That team won its opening game in the NCAA tournament by beating St. Leo by a score of 61-56 before falling to Alabama-Huntsville by a score of 82 to 71. That team was led by senior center Edgars Eglitis, forward Anthony Jackson from Viera High School and veteran forward Derek Helleman.

Mims has coached some of the most notable basketball players in Florida Tech history. E.J. Murray was an honorable mention all-conference selection in 2006 and a 2nd team selection in 2007. In 2008, Carl McNally was selected to the 1st team and Justin Sedlak to the 2nd team. Sedlak would be selected to the 2nd team in 2010 and the 1st team in 2011. In 2009, Derek Helleman was selected to the 2nd team while Ryan Ballard gained honorable mention. In 2012, Simon Cummings was selected 1st team all-conference while Helleman and Julius Reid received 2nd team recognition. The 2013 all-conference 2nd team included Panthers Chris Carter, Jermaine Jackson and Julius Reid. Jermaine Jackson would gain 1st team honors in 2014. Corbin Jackson may have been the finest defensive player in the history of Florida Tech basketball, gaining recognition as conference Defensive Player of the Year in 2014, 2015 and 2016. This gained him 2nd team all-conference recognition in 2015 and 2016 as well as honorable mention-All-American recognition in 2016. The Spring 2016 edition of *Florida Tech Today* recognized senior forward Corbin Jackson, a former Melbourne High School star. Jackson had averaged 15 points, 9.4 rebounds and 2.1 blocks during the 2015-2016 season. Even more significantly, Jackson earned his 3rd-consecutive Defensive Player of the Year recognition from the Sunshine State Conference.

Billy Mims enjoyed coaching one of the school's all-time best, Justin Sedlak.
Photo from University Archives.

The spring 2018 edition of *Florida Tech Today* related that senior guard Jordan Majors had become the all-team leading scorer in the men's basketball program when he ended his career with 1,898 points, surpassing the previous mark set by Justin Sedlak. That same edition of *Florida Tech Today* reported that senior forward Sam Daniel had broken the program's season record for 3-pointers with 96 and also broke the career record for treys with 247. Jordan Majors was a 2nd team all-conference selection in 2017 after having been an honorable mention All-American selection in 2015. Sam Daniel was a remarkable player under Mims, receiving honorable mention All-American honors in 2018 and all-conference recognition in 2017 and 2018. Derek Murphy received 2nd team all-conference recognition in 2019 and 2020.

The winter of 2023 edition of *Florida Tech Today* had a poignant article by Christina Hardman which described the accomplishments of Chris Carter, a 2015 graduate who had starred for the Panthers before playing professional basketball in the German Pro A League. Not content with merely winning a championship in basketball, Carter also wrote a children's book, published in German and English, titled *Joy,* a novel about a young girl who overcame adversity to become a professional basketball player. Carter said: "I have to credit much of my success to Florida Tech. The leadership skills he (Mims) taught me have stayed with me during my pro career."

At the time of the writing of this book, the Panthers completed a successful 2022-2023 season with 19 wins and 11 losses. Their conference record was 11 and 9. The season ended with a 95 to 89 overtime loss to Nova Southeastern, the top-ranked team in the country and the eventual national champion, in the semi-finals of the conference tournament. It was a heartbreakingly close loss after a valiant effort. Nova went on to win not only the conference tournament but the NCAA Division II national championship with a perfect 36 and 0 record. During their run to the championship, no team challenged Nova like the Panthers had done. The Panthers played with notable energy and determination over the last half of the season. They were led by guards Sean Houpt, who averaged 21 points per game, and Sesan Russell, who averaged 18.9 points per game. Russell and Haupt were each named to the All-Sunshine State Conference second team. Haupt was named to the All-South Region second team.

The Maple Leaf Five consisted of Dwight Walton, Astley Smith, Garfield Glasgow, Michael Smith and Robert Sewell, Canadians who led the school to unprecedented basketball success. *Photo from University Archives.*

Another notable player of the 2022-2023 team was Niall Harris, a 6'4" guard from Leicester, England. Harris had an outstanding year on the court, starting 26 games while averaging 11.1 points per game, a team-high 7.4 rebounds per game with 3.25 assists per game and 1.9 steals per game. However, Harris' performance in the classroom was even more important as he maintained a 3.9 grade point average while majoring in aeronautical engineering.

Mims was inducted into the Space Coast Sports Hall of Fame in 2018. In reporting his induction, Space Coast Daily noted on May 7, 2018, that Mims had achieved his 600th win as a basketball coach during that year. Mims told the magazine: "I just want to be remembered as someone that used basketball and a little southern hospitality to bring smiles to a lot of faces."

Davon Kelly helps to cut down the net after leading Florida Tech to victory.
Photo from University Archives.

Notes

- Jerry Durney and Daniel Supraner wrote an article for *Florida Tech Magazine,* Spring 2021, Volume 30, Issue 1, titled "The Maple Leaf Five: A Canadian Quintet Leaves an Impact on Florida Tech Basketball." The five players referred to are Robert Sewell, Astley Smith, Mike Smith, Peter Walcott and Dwight Walton. As the article describes, these five Canadians were essential participants in creating the most successful era in program history. A sixth Canadian, Garfield Glasgow, was a significant contributor in the 1987-88 and 1988-89 seasons but did not return after that. The article describes the impact that these five Canadians had on Florida Tech basketball and follows the players after graduation.

- All basketball scores and statistics are taken from the archives of *Florida Today.*

- Information regarding the assault by the Providence police and the disposition of the case are taken from the archives of *Florida Today* of January 2, January 9, January 27, April 25, April 26 and April 27, 1990.

- Information regarding Folliard's resignation and his comments about it are taken from *Florida Today* archives of August 23 and September 19, 1991.

- The account of Andy Russo's time at Florida Tech was retrieved on January 14, 2023 from Wikipedia: https://en.wikipedia.org/wiki/andy_Russo.

- The information about Billy Mims and his hiring and record at Florida Tech are taken from the archives of Florida Tech at news F I T.edu.archive>florida-tech and the official website of Florida Tech athletics at http://www.floridatechsports.com/, retrieved on January 14, 2023.

- The information about all-conference and All-American recognition of individual players was compiled from the archives available at the website of the Sunshine State Conference at sunshinestateconference.com

CHAPTER FIVE:
STOTTLER BRINGS SOCCER NATIONAL CHAMPIONSHIPS TO FLORIDA TECH

By William C. Potter

*F*lorida Today reported on May 11, 1969, that Don Rutledge had been hired as head basketball coach at F.I.T. but had also been tasked with additional duties. In announcing the hiring of Rutledge, assistant athletic director Joe Doller noted that Rutledge would also be responsible for developing the new soccer program, noting that "if there is enough interest at the school, soccer will be played for the first time next year." By November 1969, F.I.T. was indeed playing intercollegiate soccer. As described in the 1970 *Ad Astra*, Brian Hogg served as coach of that first team, assisted by Jim Irvin. Hogg was a native of England and an engineer at Harris Corporation. The team consisted of 15 players and, notably, freshman Tom Bruno served as captain.

Soccer was developing a substantial following by 1972. Thirty players comprised the team that year. The team scored a big victory on October 17, 1972, by defeating Florida Technological University (now University of Central Florida) by a score of 2 to 1. Goalie Fran Corlis turned away 22 shots. *Florida Today* reported on November 4, 1972, that F.I.T. had fallen 3 to 2 to Florida Southern in soccer, their 10th straight loss to the Moccasins, dropping its record to 2 wins and 5 losses. Both goals for F.I.T. were scored by Milton Julien.

By 1974, Florida Tech soccer, led by Coach Nick Pahiyiannakis, achieved its first winning record in school history. As reported by Florida Today on November 19, 1974, Florida Tech concluded that season with a record of 9 wins and only 2 losses. Its final win of the season was a 4 to 2 victory over Flagler College which had come into that game undefeated. The Engineers outscored their opponents that season by 42 to 14. Two brothers, Kamran Kaviani and Manouchehr Kaviani led the team in scoring. Goalie Dave Rollins registered 3 shutouts.

In 1976, Mike Eldridge assumed the role of coaching men's soccer at F.I.T. Although the team had a record of 2 wins, 6 losses and a tie, the team fielded 26 players, 20 of whom were freshmen. The highlight of the season was a hard-fought tie with Stetson.

The 1977 team concluded its season with a resounding 4 to 0 victory over Embry-Riddle, wrapping up its season with a record of 8 wins, 5 losses and 3 ties. The team consisted of only 1 senior, 2 juniors, 14 sophomores and 16 freshmen. The future of F.I.T. soccer appeared bright. It was, however, marred when several Iranian players, dissatisfied with their playing time, quit the team and formed their own soccer club.

During the 1970's Florida Tech soccer played both a fall and a spring season. *Florida Today* reported on April 26, 1978, that the Pepsi-F.I.T. Invitational soccer tournament would be held in Melbourne on April 28 and 29. Florida Technological University would play F.I.T.-Jensen Beach in the first game and Flagler would play F.I.T. in the second. This was the first mention that F.I.T.-Jensen Beach was playing intercollegiate sports.

At the outset of the 1978 season, Eldridge noted in a *Florida Today* article on September 10, 1978, that the team was limited by its lack of affiliation with a conference as well as its lack of athletic scholarships. The fall season in 1978 was highlighted by a road trip to North Carolina. After first playing Jacksonville University, F.I.T. then played to a 2 to 2 tie with Davidson College. *Florida Today* reported on September 15, 1978, that Davidson was "a team using modern defensive techniques developed in Europe."

The following day, F.I.T. continued its road trip with a loss to Belmont Abbey in a game beset by controversy. According to the *Florida Today* article on September 16, the game was preceded by a dispute over whether to use a 16-pound English ball or a 32-pound American ball. Not surprisingly, Belmont Abbey prevailed and the English ball was used. The folly continued with numerous controversies and questionable officiating during which 3 Engineers were ejected from the game. In sum, Coach Eldridge, with typical English understatement, concluded that it was "a very inhospitable situation."

That 1978 team would conclude the season with a record of 8 wins, 9 losses and 2 ties. Seven of those games were played against nationally ranked teams.

According to the 1979 *Ad Astra*, during spring break of 1979, the team travelled to Bogota to play Colombian teams in "friendlies." Eldridge described that trip as, "a trip of friendship and soccer." No record of the outcomes of those games was found.

Mike Eldridge continued to coach the soccer team during the 1979 fall season with 12 returning lettermen and the team improved to a record of 6 wins, 6 losses and a tie. The 1980 *Ad Astra* noted that there were only 4 seniors among the 27 players on the team. The 1979 squad opened the season with a game against Flagler College.

Eldridge continued to coach the team for the ensuing 1980, 1981 and 1982 seasons. The 1980 season began with participation in the Methodist College Invitational Tournament in Fayetteville, N.C. An article in *Florida Today* on September 10, 1980, noted that the Engineers would also play a "friendly" with the University of Dublin, Ireland, at F.I.T.'s new soccer field in Melbourne.

On October 21, 1982, *Florida Today* reported that Florida Tech, having joined the Sunshine State Conference in 1981, had won its first conference game by defeating St. Leo 2 to 0. Mohsin Zakeri led that victory with his eighth goal of the season.

Following the 1982 season, Mike Eldridge resigned as coach in order to pursue business interests. Eldridge left with a record of 55 wins and 39 losses in his 6 years as coach. Eldridge had constructed a solid men's soccer program at F.I.T., a team which was consistently competitive not only in the Sunshine State Conference but throughout the southeast.

Athletic Director Bill Jurgens conducted a nationwide search for a successor to Eldridge. Over 60 applicants sought the job. On June 8, 1983, *Florida Today* reported that 29-year-old Gianni Grimaldi had been selected as the next soccer coach at F.I.T. Grimaldi had played collegiately at Rutgers University and had been an assistant coach at Princeton. Jurgens noted: "He seems like the type of person who would fill in where Mike left off." Grimaldi added in an article on June 23, 1983: "My objective is winning, but more than that, my objective is performing."

On November 5, 1983, goals by Moshen Zaderi and Nick Lane led F.I.T. to a 2 to 1 victory over Palm Beach Atlantic. That brought the Panthers' record to 5 wins, 7 losses and a tie for the season, with 5 of those losses coming by a single goal.

Grimaldi apparently worked diligently to spread the sport in central Florida. *Florida Today* announced on May 26, 1985, that day was the final time for tryouts for an under-19 U.S. Soccer Federation select team to travel to Colombia and Italy and directed interested players to contact Grimaldi at F.I.T.

Florida Today reported on September 14, 1985, that F.I.T. soccer had defeated Barry University a few days earlier by a score of 2 to 1. On September 18, 1985, the Panthers fell to the University of Tampa, ranked third nationally in Division II, by a score of 3 to 0. By September 27, 1985, their record had dropped to 3 wins and 5 losses by virtue of a 2 to 1 loss to Florida Atlantic University. The Panthers moved their record to 3 wins, 5 losses and a tie on October 2, 1985, with a 1-1 tie with Stetson. They followed that game with a 2 to 0 victory over St. Leo a few days later. *Florida Today* reported that the Panthers fell to Florida International University, the top-ranked Division II team in the country, on October 27, 1985, in a game that Grimaldi described as "playing on a lake." By November 6, 1985, when *Florida Today* reported that F.I.T. had tied Flagler College, the top-ranked NAIA team in the country, the Panthers had run their record to 4 wins, 7 losses and 2 ties. By November 9, F.I.T. had achieved a record of 5 wins, 8 losses and 2 ties as it approached its last game of the season, a meeting with Brooklyn College. On November 10, 1985, *Florida Today* reported that the Panthers' season had ended with a 2 to nil loss to Brooklyn, leaving F.I.T. with a season record of 5 wins, 9 losses and 2 ties. Nick Lane of Palm Bay and Rachid Sefrioui of Morocco were named most valuable players of the team and both were invited to participate in the Florida All-Star Soccer Classic.

Gianni Grimaldi resigned as coach at F.I.T. in early 1986 to pursue coaching opportunities in the Washington, D.C. area. *Florida Today* reported on May 16, 1986, that Rick Stottler would take over as coach of the Panthers. Stottler was president of a local engineering firm and also the soccer coach at Cocoa Beach High School, where he had notable success. Stottler had played soccer at the University of Maryland and, because college and high school soccer seasons did not overlap, would continue to coach at Cocoa Beach. On June 12, 1986 *Florida Today* reported that Stottler had appointed 23-year old Giles Malone as assistant coach, noting that Malone would be responsible for most of the recruiting and scheduling duties. Later, Stottler added Homer Bozorg as another assistant coach. Although the appointments of Stottler, Bozorg and Malone were met with enthusiasm, few would have predicted the heights to which Florida Tech soccer would rise under their leadership. Stottler, however, had big dreams and was quoted in *Florida Today* on August 30, 1986 as saying: "We expect in three or four years to be a team of national stature. We want to be able to compete at the highest level." His vision proved to be prophetic. Both Malone and Bozorg would prove to be brilliant picks. Bozorg was a skilled strategist and a source of great stability for the team. Malone, a native of the U.K. with ties to youth soccer in the U.K. and elsewhere internationally, would prove to be an invaluable recruiter of talent.

By October 30, 1986, the Panthers had improved their record to 9 wins and 4 losses, with a 5 win and 1 loss record in the conference, good for second place. Their latest victory was a 5 to 1 romp over Florida Atlantic University, led by 3 goals and 2 assists from freshman Bino Campanini. Stottler told *Florida Today* that their goal was a bid to the NCAA tournament, a goal which they would not achieve that year but soon would realize.

The 1987 team was met with great optimism. Of the 17 players on the roster, only 6 were from the United States. As reported in *Florida Today* on September 17, 1987, two of the team's top players, sophomore forward Bino Campanini and goalkeeper Jason Carpenter, were from Jersey in the Channel Islands. Campanini had led the Sunshine State Conference in scoring the previous season. The season began with a flourish when F.I.T. routed Flagler on September 8 by a score of 4 to nil and then drubbed Auburn University-Montgomery on September 17, 1987, by a score of 6 to nil. Campanini scored the first goal against both Flagler and Auburn and was supported by goals from freshman forward Fitzgerald (Fidgi) Haig, sophomore forward Steve Freeman and freshman defender Joe Francono. Carpenter made several acrobatic saves.

By September 29, 1987, the Panthers had dropped to 3 wins, 2 losses and 2 ties, with a 0-1 record in the conference. When they lost to Tampa by a 2 to nil score, Stottler was greatly disappointed and insisted that "we dominated the game."

On October 19, 1987, in what Stottler described as the "biggest comeback in Florida Institute of Technology soccer history," the Panthers defeated Rollins College in double overtime by a score of 5 to 4. It was F.I.T.'s first victory at Rollins in history and took the Panthers to a record of 6 wins, 3 losses and 2 ties. Down 3 to 0 with 22 minutes left in regulation, goals by Jarrad Isherwood, Fitzgerald Haig and Robin Chan tied the game. Steve Freeman scored the winning goal in the second overtime.

By October 28, 1987, *Florida Today* reported that the Panthers had recently beaten both Central Florida and Rollins, two schools whom they had never before defeated, and their record now stood at 7 wins, 3 losses and 2 ties. The team was now ranked 19th in the NCAA Division II soccer poll.

On November 5, 1987, *Florida Today* reported that the Panthers were now 9, 3 and 2 on the season, ranked twelfth nationally and "fighting for the school's first NCAA tournament bid." With 2 regular season games remaining, the team was given an even chance to be selected for the tournament. On November 19, 1987, *Florida Today* reported that, for the first time in 18 years of NCAA competition, a Florida Tech athletic team had landed a postseason tournament bid. The Panthers' record now stood at 11 wins, 3 losses and 2 ties. Having received a first-round bye, they were slated to play Tampa in the second round of the tournament.

Tampa defeated F.I.T. in the second round of the NCAA tournament on November 21, 1987, by a 2 to 1 score on a very controversial call when the referee disallowed what the Panthers thought was clearly a goal with 18 seconds remaining in the game. Stottler told *Florida Today*: "I thought it was a very bad call. I just don't see how they could have missed it." Robin Chan scored the lone goal for F.I.T. Bino Campanini, who received a yellow card for arguing with the officials, added: "I thought there were some bad calls and that we should have won."

F.I.T. kicked off the 1988 soccer season with an exhibition game against defending NAIA champion, College of Boca Raton (now Lynn University). *Florida Today* noted that the team would be led by Bino Campanini, Steve Freeman and Robin Chan. The season started in a disappointing manner for the Panthers, losing 2 games on a 5-game road trip to North Carolina, Virginia and Georgia. When they defeated Alabama-Huntsville on September 17, the win brought their season record to only 4 wins and 3 losses. Stottler noted that: "We have a better team than last year, but there have been some problems. We've got some things to work out." However, the Panthers' record fell to 4 and 4 when they lost to the University of Central Florida on September 21.

The Panthers seemed to pick up dramatically when Bino Campanini, who had been sitting out with a knee injury, returned to the lineup. After a victory over Barry on October 1 brought their record to 6 wins and 4 losses, Stottler explained: "Bino is our catalyst. He makes us go and he's missed 9 games."

They followed-up that victory with a 6 to nil victory over Florida Atlantic on October 4, led by 3 goals from Campanini and a third consecutive shutout by goalkeeper Alex Skodnik. On October 8, the Panthers won an overtime battle with Rollins when Eddie Grosso headed in a pass from Steve Freeman. William Twaite had recently been declared eligible and replaced Skodnik in goal.

Next, on October 14, F.I.T. faced conference rival Tampa, ranked second in the country. The Panthers, playing without injured Fidgi Haig, prevailed by a score of 2 to nil. Stottler described the significance of that victory by saying: "We're now the team to beat in this conference and I think we will be in the future." Robin Chan and Bino Campanini scored goals against Tampa.

They followed that victory with a 7 to nil blowout of St. Leo on October 18, raising their record to 10 wins and 4 losses. Steve Freeman collected 4 goals against St. Leo while Fidgi Haig, who had sat out several games due to an injury, returned to provide 2 assists. Midfielder Robin Chan, called by Stottler "one of the best college players in America," scored as well.

Unfortunately, the Panthers then proceeded to lose 2 consecutive games. First, they lost to College of Boca Raton, then ranked the top NAIA Division I team in the country. They followed that game with a loss to NCAA Division I power University of South Florida. As Freeman told *Florida Today* on November 2: "We just have to put those behind us."

With a 4 to nil victory over Eckerd College on November 2, F.I.T. had raised its record to 11 wins and 6 losses. As reported in *Florida Today*, that win assured the Panthers of at least a share of the Sunshine State Conference championship and a berth in the NCAA Division II tournament. By that point, the team was ranked fourth in the Division II national poll.

On November 5, 1988, F.I.T. routed Florida Southern by a score of 7 to 0. That victory closed the regular season for the Panthers with a record of 12 wins and 6 defeats and a perfect record of 6 and 0 in the conference. That gave Florida Tech its first conference championship in any sport other than cross-country. In 6 league games, the Panthers surrendered only a single goal. In this final regular-season game, everyone on the team saw time on the field, including 4 goalkeepers. Campanini scored 3 goals and, not surprisingly, was also the most verbose player when he noted: "I remember what we had three years ago, and when I look back at that, I am a little surprised at how quickly we have turned things around. But at the same time, I look at the players we have and I'm not surprised at our success. It would have been a disaster if we hadn't won it."

On November 20, 1988, F.I.T. hosted the NCAA tourney quarter-final game against Gannon University of Pennsylvania. Gannon, having lost only 1 game all season, had gained the quarterfinals with a 3 to 1 victory over Tampa. The Panthers won a thriller when Fidgi Haig fired a shot past the Gannon goalkeeper with 1:14 left in the game. Haig was an unlikely hero because he had missed 8 minutes in the second half after being kicked in the ribs and down on the field for 5 minutes. Goalie Bill Twaite had 8 saves to give F.I.T. its 11th shutout of the season.

The semi-final and final games of the NCAA Division II soccer championship were scheduled in Northridge, California, on the first weekend of December 1988. F.I.T. faced defending national champion Southern Connecticut in its semi-final game. As Campanini noted: "This is not a holiday. We've come out here with one purpose, and that is to win a national championship." The Panthers' stay in Northridge was made even more memorable when they experienced an early-morning earthquake that shook the Los Angeles area on December 3. Despite having their sleep interrupted by the earthquake, F.I.T. prevailed over the defending national champions by a score of 1 to nil when Tylan Hannan, a sophomore from South Africa, headed in a corner kick from Steve Freeman.

In the championship game, the Panthers faced the hosts from California State University-Northridge. Goalkeeper Bill Twaite proved to be the key in the championship game as his 4 saves preserved the 3 to 2 victory for F.I.T. Stottler noted: "If there's a better goalkeeper, I haven't seen him." Fidgi Haig scored the first goal, while Robin Chan added the second and Eddie Grosso headed-in the third off another corner-kick by Steve Freeman. Haig noted, "I knew it, I knew in here that we were going to win it," pointing to his heart. With that victory, the Panthers concluded their 1988 season with a record of 15 wins and 6 losses and having established a new standard of achievement at Florida Tech.

After winning a national championship the previous year, hopes for the 1989 season were sky high. On August 29, 1989, Stottler told *Florida Today*: "I think we'll be much stronger than we were last year." Not only was the team returning every starter from its championship team, but it added several talented newcomers. F.I.T.'s goal was clearly another national championship.

The season began with a 3 to 2 win over Alderson-Broaddus which had been the NAIA runner-up the previous season. Tylan Hannan, who had been the most valuable defensive player in the 1988 NCAA tourney, headed-in the first goal on an assist from Steve Freeman. They followed that win with a 1 to nil victory over Florida International.

The Panthers won their third game of the season on September 10, 1989, with a 2 to 1 victory over Flagler College. Chris Payne had an assist and a goal but lamented: "we couldn't really get it together tonight."

By September 13, the Panthers were the top-ranked Division II team in the country. That night, they defeated Florida Atlantic University by a score of 2 to nil.

On September 17, 1989, they faced the number two team in the country among NAIA schools, College of Boca Raton. Boca Raton brought a 40-game win streak into the contest. F.I.T. took its record to 5 and 0 with a 2 to nil victory. Steve Freeman scored 2 first-half goals to lead the way. Stottler commented: "It was a war." Bill Twaite made several outstanding stops.

The Panthers suffered their first defeat on September 23 when they lost to Division I Alabama A&M by a score of 1 to nil. Unfortunately, they played without three injured starters. It was a frustrating loss because the Panthers outshot their opponents 23 to 3.

By the opening game of the F.I.T. Tournament of October 14, 1989, the Panthers had dropped a notch in the national polls and bore a record of 10 wins and 2 losses. They opened the tourney with a 1 to nil victory over Oakland (Michigan) University, the sixth-ranked team in the country. Tylan Hannan scored the lone goal off an assist by Steve Freeman. Its next game in the tournament was a 4 to 1 victory over University of North Carolina-Wilmington. Ed Grosso scored 2 goals and was named the tournament's Most Valuable Player.

F.I.T. continued its winning streak with a 4 to nil victory over Nova University. Notably, 2 local players, Merritt Island's Keith Ames and Melbourne High's Greg Kemp, scored for the Panthers. Chris Payne had 3 assists.

The Panthers faced a monumental challenge on October 25, 1989, when they took on the University of Tampa. Tampa was undefeated in the Sunshine State Conference and ranked seventh in the country. An article in *Florida Today* on the day of the game focused on Fidgi Haig, who had led the conference in scoring the previous year as a freshman. Stottler said of Haig: "He's so quick and so skilled that he scares people to death." That night, Fidgi came through with a goal at the beginning of the second half on an assist from Steve Freeman to give the Panthers a 1 to nil win and a share of the lead in the league.

F.I.T. next faced Virginia Commonwealth University and prevailed easily by a score of 5 to nil. Steve Freeman scored the hat-trick with 3 goals and an assist. Freeman now had 11 goals and 15 assists on the season but commented: "It doesn't really matter. If the team is going well, that's what's important."

On November 4, 1989, *Florida Today* wrote about F.I.T.'s 3 seniors, Ed Grosso, Steve Freeman and Bino Campanini, who would be playing their final regular season home match that evening. Stottler explained: "Ed, Steve and Bino stand for everything we've strived for." That evening, the Panthers clinched the Sunshine State Conference championship with a 6 to nil blowout of Eckerd College. They were paced by 4 goals from the conference's leading scorer, Steve Freeman. Unfortunately, Bino Campanini received a red card which mandated a suspension for the next game.

Florida Today reported on November 7 that the Panthers' opening match in the NCAA tourney would be at home against conference rival Tampa. The team was the second seed in the Southeast Region.

Rick Stottler was selected as Coach of the Year in the conference, while Bill Twaite, Robin Chan and Steve Freeman were selected for the all-conference first team. Chris Payne, Gary Eyles, Fitzgerald Haig and Dylan Lewis were chosen for the second team.

On November 11, 1989, Florida Tech was bounced from the NCAA tournament by Tampa. Although the Panthers outshot Tampa 21 to 4, the Spartans prevailed by a score of 2 to nil. F.I.T. finished the season with a record of 17 wins and 3 losses.

On August 16, 1990, *Florida Today* reported that the Panthers had opened practice for the 1990 season. The article highlighted Melbourne High School graduate Greg Kemp who was expected to play an important role that season. The article also noted that Tylan Hannan and Dylan Lewis had been named team captains.

The 1990 season did not begin well for F.I.T., at least by recent standards. A 2-nil loss to Flagler on September 26 took their record to 5 wins and 3 losses. Bino Campanini, now an assistant coach, noted that injuries to Fidgi Haig and talented freshman Richard Sharpe had hurt the team.

The Panthers bounced back quickly with an 8 to 1 blowout of Northeast Missouri on September 30. Eddie Enders, a walk-on from Merritt Island scored the first goal.

Florida Today published an article on October 6 that praised Robin Chan's value to the team. The paper wrote of his quiet demeanor and said: "And yet, he speaks quietly and carries a mean kick."

On October 10, Melbourne High graduate Greg Kemp scored 2 goals to lead the Panthers to a 3 to 1 victory over Florida Atlantic University. That brought the team's season record to 9 wins and 3 losses. Stottler, however, was not pleased and said: "We should have scored 6 or 7 goals in the first half, no problem. I don't know, maybe one of these days we'll put it all together."

By October 17, the Panthers were rolling. They ran their record to 12 and 3 overall and 3 and 0 in the conference with a 10-nil crushing of Florida Southern. Chris Payne scored 5 goals and added 2 assists. To top things off, Eddie Enders was named the Sunshine State Conference player of the week after having scored 4 goals against the University of Central Florida the previous week.

The streak came to an end on October 27 when the Panthers fell to Tampa, 1 to nil. They came back on October 31 with a 3-nil shutout of Barry which kept alive its hopes for an NCAA bid. Stottler praised F.I.T.'s walk-on goalkeeper, John Loftis.

The Panthers closed out the regular season with a 5 to 1 victory over St. Leo on November 3. That brought the season record to 16 wins and 4 losses. Stottler noted that the team had scored 99 goals while giving up only 17 for the season.

On November 8, the all-conference team for the Sunshine State Conference was announced. Chris Payne, the leading Division II scorer in the nation, joined teammates Robin Chan, Tylan Hannan, Gary Eyles and Dylan Lewis on the first team. The second team included Eddie Enders and Richard Sharpe, while Kip Ortiz received honorable mention.

On November 10, F.I.T. defeated Tampa in the NCAA Division II South Region semifinals. A header by Tylan Hannan off an assist by Robin Chan gave them the 1-nil victory and sent them on their way to the regional championship game against the University of North Carolina-Greensboro.

Fidgi Haig and Keith Ames each scored to lead F.I.T. to victory in the regional championship game by a 2 to 1 score. As a bonus, the NCAA announced that the Division II Final Four would be held on the Florida Tech campus. That would be the first NCAA sanctioned national championship event in the county's history.

Florida Tech faced Seattle Pacific in the Division II semifinal game on November 30. A crowd of 2,200 watched a hard-fought game in which the Panthers outshot their opponents 15 to 2. Unfortunately, both Seattle Pacific shots went in the goal to give them a 2 to 1 victory. Stottler observed: "We had plenty of chances. This game shouldn't have been close but that's the way it goes." Thus ended the 1990 season with a record of 18 wins and 5 losses.

Florida Tech did not wait until the following fall to have its first game of 1991. On February 23, the Panthers played a friendly with the Tampa Bay Rowdies of the American Soccer League. Two of the players for Tampa Bay were familiar faces as both Steve Freeman and Robin Chan, having exhausted their college eligibility, were trying out for the Rowdies.

The Panthers opened the 1991 fall preseason training camp beginning August 23. *Florida Today* wrote on August 27 that preseason training included 3 sessions per day over a 4-week period. The article highlighted the important role expected from Dylan Lewis that season.

Florida Tech began the season ranked sixth in the country in Division II and opened the season on September 8 against seventh-ranked Sonoma (California) State University. After regulation and 2 overtimes, the game ended in a 2 to 2 tie. Both Stottler and Lewis received red cards and were ejected.

The Panthers followed quickly with a 2 to nil victory over Auburn University-Montgomery on September 11, despite the absence of Lewis and a couple of other injured starters. In a sign of things to come for the season, *Florida Today* noted that Richard Sharpe had scored 3 of the 4 Panther goals for the year.

Three days later, however, Florida Tech dropped a 2 to 1 match to College of Boca Raton. Local product Eddie Enders had the Panthers' lone goal. They followed that loss with a 1-nil victory over tenth-ranked Florida Atlantic a few days later.

By September 28, F.I.T.'s record stood at 5 wins, 1 loss and a tie, which resulted in the team being ranked fifth nationally in Division II. That day, they were matched against twentieth-ranked Rollins College in a match for which the game proceeds would be donated for a young local girl in need of a lung transplant. As was typical of Stottler, the idea to use the proceeds in that manner was his idea. F.I.T. blasted Rollins by a 6-nil score, marking its fourth consecutive defeat of a nationally ranked team. Richard Sharp scored 4 goals, giving him 16 on the season. Stottler, however, was less than effusive in his praise as he said of Sharpe: "He could be a very good player. He just needs to get a little tougher."

Stottler also spoke of Janet Jeffreys, the young girl for whom the game proceeds had been pledged. Stottler told *Florida Today* on September 29 that: "I think it was good for the players to be around her. She's fighting a battle and doing a good job. She's a winner, a good example for us to follow."

On October 5 and 6, F.I.T. hosted the F.I.T. Classic which opened with Florida Tech playing Oakland (Michigan) University and the University of Central Florida playing Virginia Tech, while the final games would pit Oakland against UCF and F.I.T. against Virginia Tech. Florida

Tech eked by Oakland 1 to nil but then exploded to defeat Virginia Tech 6 to 1. Defender Dylan Lewis was named Most Valuable Player of the tournament. Richard Sharpe brought his scoring up to 20 goals in the 10 games played thus far in the season.

Richard Sharpe with young fans. Photo from University Archives.

Florida Tech required double-overtime to defeat Nova University on October 11, taking F.I.T.'s record to 11 wins and 1 loss and a tie. Star defender Dylan Lewis had to sit out that game due to having received his fifth card of the season in the previous game against Florida Southern. Richard Sharpe, the leading scorer in NCAA Division II soccer, scored 2 penalty-kicks to lead the Panthers to a 3 to 2 victory.

That victory set up the game of the year on October 19 against Tampa. As reported in *Florida Today* on that date, both teams were ranked in the top-ten nationally and both were undefeated in league play. At stake were the conference championship and a likely first-round bye in the NCAA tournament. In a surprisingly one-sided game, F.I.T. scored 3 second-half goals to defeat Tampa by a score of 4 to 1. Richard Sharpe scored his 27th goal of the season, breaking Chris Payne's school record. Keith Ames played great defense, inspiring Stottler to observe: "Keith Ames is an All-American if there ever was one." Colin Semwayo, a junior midfielder from Zimbabwe, led scoring with 2 goals and an assist.

The Panthers rounded out the conference season with a 6 to nil rout of Eckerd College on October 23. Richard Sharpe led the way with 3 goals and 2 assists. Three days later, Florida Tech downed Flagler by a 2 to nil score, taking their record to 14 wins and only 1 loss and 1 tie.

On October 30, 1991, *Florida Today* reported that Florida Tech had moved into the top-ranked spot in NCAA Division II. Stottler noted: "This team just has an uncanny ability to win." The newspaper noted that three key players originate from Brevard County, including Eddie Enders and Keith Ames from Merritt Island and Greg Kemp from Melbourne.

A few days later, F.I.T. hosted the Panther Invitational. The opening opponent for the Panthers was Franklin Pierce College of New Hampshire, ranked fourth in the country in Division II. The Panthers demolished the visitors by a score of 9 to nil. Richard Sharpe scored 4 goals, giving him a nation-leading 36 goals for the season. Keith Ames noted: "They weren't used to playing in the heat and humidity like we are." Unfortunately, the Panthers were upset the following night by Alabama A&M, a Division I team, in double-overtime by a score of 2 to 1.

On November 12, *Florida Today* reported that Florida Tech had received a first-round bye and would host the South Region championship of the NCAA Division II tournament. The Panthers would be shooting for their third Final Four bid in the last 4 seasons. On November 19, David Jones quoted Stottler as saying: "This year, I think we're gonna be lucky and I think we're gonna win it."

On November 23, *Florida Today* reported that Florida Tech had defeated Tampa on November 22 by a score of 2 to 1 to win the NCAA Division II South Region championship. Dylan Lewis headed in the winning goal. The victory was particularly sweet because it gave the winners the right to host the Division II Final Four the following month. The win brought the season record for F.I.T. to 16 wins, 2 losses and a tie.

Stottler received a victory ride after winning the 1991 NCAA Division II championship. *Photo from University Archives.*

On December 6, F.I.T. narrowly defeated Franklin Pierce by a score of 2 to 1 in the national semi-finals. Eddie Enders scored both Panther goals. The victory meant that the Panthers would face Sonoma State (California) for the NCAA Division II championship. The following night, before a crowd in excess of 3,000 fans, the Panthers destroyed Sonoma by a score of 5 to 1 to win their second NCAA championship in 4 years. Sharpe scored 3 goals. Florida Tech completed the season with a record of 19 wins, 2 losses and a tie. Richard Sharpe was the outstanding offensive player of the tournament while Dylan Lewis was selected as outstanding defensive player for the championship.

Lewis was the only player who participated in both national championship wins for the Panthers. He was recognized as a first team All-American. Stottler was honored as the Division II national coach of the year. With typical grace, Stottler told *Florida Today* on January 21, 1992: "But when you get right down to it, I couldn't have won it without Giles and Homer." Sharpe was named player of the year for the Sunshine State Conference after leading the nation in scoring with 42 goals.

In an interesting development, Division I national champion University of Virginia agreed to come to Melbourne to play an exhibition game against Division II champion Florida Tech on March 21, 1992. Both teams played that friendly without some of their key players. Not surprisingly, Richard Sharpe led the Panthers in scoring with 2 goals. Virginia finally prevailed when it broke the 2 to 2 tie with a goal in the first of 2 overtime periods.

Florida Tech held its soccer awards banquet on June 13, 1992. As reported in *Florida Today* on June 16, the national champions named Dylan Lewis as Most Valuable Player while also announcing that his jersey would be retired. Stottler described Lewis as "the best player I've ever seen play at Florida Tech." Rhard Sharpe was recognized as the Most Valuable Offensive Player while goalkeeper Mark Cartwright was named Rookie of the Year and Eddie Enders received the Coaches' Award. Sharpe set an NCAA Division II record with 42 goals on the year.

Rick Stottler won his second NCAA title in 1991. *Photo from University Archives.*

As defending national champions with a solid group of returning players, expectations were high for the 1992 soccer season. Those expectations seemed well-based when the Panthers defeated defending NAIA champion Lynn University by a score of 4 to 1 on September 5. Eddie Enders led the way with a goal and 2 assists.

The explosiveness of the Panther offense quickly became apparent. On September 16, they demolished St. Leo by a score of 13 to nil. Enders had 4 goals while Greg Kemp and Richard Sharpe each had 3 goals. By September 23, Florida Tech was ranked first in the country in the Division II coaches' poll and Enders and Sharpe were tied for first in the nation in scoring with 22 points each.

A loss to Tampa a few days later dropped the Panthers' record to 5 wins and 2 losses and a fifth-place ranking in the polls. A 10 to 1 win over the University of North Florida on October 7 brought their record to 8 and 2. They followed that victory with an 11 to nil rout of Embry-Riddle on October 18, raising the Panthers' record to 12 and 2 on the season.

In keeping with his record of community service, Stottler organized a benefit for a young lady in need of a heart transplant. As reported on

October 20, a portion of the gate from Florida Tech's game with Florida Southern would be donated to the "Helping Hands for Cindy Fund."

On October 24, Florida Tech won its opening round game of the Florida Tech Invitational Soccer Classic by smashing Barry by a score of 7 to 1. They followed that with a 4 to nil victory over Wisconsin-Whitewater the following day. Sharpe scored 5 goals in the tournament, giving him 37 for the season.

The following week, Sharpe scored his 43rd goal of the season, breaking his national record that he had set the year before. That feat earned him an appearance in the November 9 issue of *Sports Illustrated*. Sharpe was the third Florida Tech athlete to be recognized in *Sports Illustrated* that year, following women's basketball players Paulette King and Christine Keenan who had appeared in the April 6 edition of the magazine.

Sharpe followed that recognition by scoring 5 goals on November 6 in a 5 to nil victory over Florida Southern. That brought Sharpe's scoring to 48 goals for the season and brought the team to a 17 and 2 record, 5 and 1 in the conference.

On November 10, 1992, *Florida Today* disclosed that Florida Tech would host the University of South Carolina-Spartanburg in the opening round of the NCAA Division II South Region Tournament. Surprisingly, Tampa received the top seed in the region and, hence, the first-round bye. After defeating USC-Spartanburg by a 4 to nil score on November 14, the Panthers travelled to Tampa to meet the hosts for the region title and a spot in the Final Four. That game ended Florida Tech's season when they lost to the Spartans by a 2 to 1 score in double overtime. Thus ended the Panthers' hopes of repeating as national champions.

Richard Sharpe was named to the Division II All-American team, as was teammate Eddie Enders. Sharpe had 49 goals and 112 points for the season, both national records. Enders had 22 assists and 27 goals to finish with 76 points. The team closed the season with a record of 18 wins and 3 losses.

Once again, expectations were high as the 1993 season got underway. *Florida Today* reported on August 19, 1993, that the Panthers had opened their preseason camp. Stottler observed: "About half our team is back and about half is new."

On September 11, 1993, Richard Sharpe scored the 100th goal of his Florida Tech career as the Panthers defeated Davis & Elkins College by a score of 4 to 2. Stottler proclaimed: "He's the greatest striker in college soccer." By September 24, Florida Tech boasted a record of 5 and 0 and were ranked number 1 in NCAA Division II. The only sour note for the Panthers was a lingering concern about an Achilles' heel injury plaguing Richard Sharpe.

On October 16, Florida Tech edged Tampa by a 2 to 1 score, behind Richard Sharpe's 2 goals. The victory brought the Panthers' record to 12 wins and no losses and put them in the driver's seat for the conference championship and a bid to the NCAA tournament.

The Panthers extended their record to 15 and 0 on October 24 with a 2 to nil victory over Lindsey Wilson College. Their home winning streak now stood at 23 games.

On November 20, 1993, the Panthers needed 2 overtimes to give them a 3 to 2 NCAA Division II South Regional victory over South Carolina-Spartanburg. The victory sent the undefeated and top-ranked Panthers to the Final Four for the fourth time.

Florida Tech was chosen as the host for the Final Four and would welcome Seattle Pacific, Gannon and Southern Connecticut to Melbourne for the championship. What followed for Florida Tech was an almost surreal experience when it faced Seattle Pacific in the semi-final match. The game lasted more than 4 hours and ended after midnight. The teams played 2 halves of 45 minutes each, followed by 2 overtime periods of 15 minutes each, followed by 2 sudden-death overtime periods. At one point in overtime, the Panthers had a 2-goal lead, only to see Seattle Pacific tie it with 2 goals within a couple of minutes. The game was finally decided on penalty kicks which gave Seattle Pacific a 10 to 9 victory.

Paul Robertson was a rarity among contemporary collegiate athletes in that he was a star at 2 sports. As a freshman, he made an immediate impact in both soccer and tennis. As his career at Florida Tech progressed, he would gather numerous honors in both sports. *Florida Today* reported on November 12, 1993, that Robertson had been selected to the Sunshine State All-Conference 1st team.

As if he did not have enough to fill his time, Stottler realized a long time ambition in 1994 when he became the co-owner of a professional soccer team, the Cocoa Expos. The Expos were members of the United States Interregional Soccer League. Now, in addition to his duties as soccer coach at Florida Tech and his role as CEO of his engineering firm, Stottler, Stagg and Associates, Stottler had a venture to keep him occupied during the spring season. It also was a place for Florida Tech players whose college eligibility had expired, such as Eddie Enders, Richard Sharpe and Dylan Lewis.

The 1994 season began with high hopes. By September 25, the Panthers had extended their record to 7 wins with no losses when they captured the title at the Gannon Invitational Tournament. James Phillips was selected as the most valuable offensive player of the tournament, despite having been ejected with a red card. They followed up that victory with a 4 to 1 victory over St. Leo which vaulted them to the top-ranking in the national polls.

By October 28, the Panthers were sporting a record of 12 wins, 1 loss and a tie. They found themselves in a familiar position of facing Tampa in a match that would likely determine the Sunshine State Conference championship and a guaranteed berth in the NCAA playoffs. Tampa prevailed by a 3 to 1 score when the Panthers were forced to play a man down due to Colin Prest's ejection early in the second half. That loss to Tampa was costly as it relegated Florida Tech to the last seed in the NCAA South Region. That meant that the Panthers would have to travel to Tampa again to face the Spartans in the first round. Unfortunately, the result was similar as Tampa ousted Florida Tech from the tournament with a 3 to 1 overtime victory. Stottler promised: "We'll be back again. We've been here eight straight years and eight of our starters are either sophomores or freshmen."

Florida Tech completed the season with a record of 14 wins, 3 losses and a tie. Goalkeeper Martin Peat and defender James Sharp were named first team all-conference selections while Colin Prest and Marco Genee were named to the second team and James Phillips was an honorable mention choice. Peat received second-team All-America honors.

The 1995 season began with a sense of optimism but that optimism soon proved to be illusionary. *Florida Today* reported on August 31, 1995, that no less than 5 players who had been expected to be in the starting lineup were either injured or had dropped off the team. One cause for optimism, however, was the arrival of Jesse Goldfarb, a heralded recruit from Melbourne High who had rejected Division I offers in order to play at Florida Tech and who was the all-time leading scorer in the Cape Coast Conference.

By September 21, the Panthers had lost 4 of its first 6 games and were facing the nation's top-ranked team, their old nemesis Tampa. The Panthers went up 2 to nil on Tampa but then gave-up a flurry of goals to fall 5 to 3.

A bright spot in an otherwise dismal season occurred when the university announced that its soccer field would be renamed Rick Stottler Field. In typical Stottler fashion, Stottler told *Florida Today* on October 26 that: "I'd enjoy it more if we were playing better." The newspaper noted that his record at the time was 145-38-5.

The team had a bit of satisfaction when it upset Gannon University on October 28 by a score of 5 to 1. Gannon had come into the contest ranked fourth nationally in Division II. Stottler noted: "This gives us a little bit of our self-respect and confidence back."

The Panthers ended the season on a positive note with a 6 to nil blowout of Eckerd College, led by a hat-trick from Jesse Goldfarb. That ended the season with a record of 5 wins, 10 losses and 2 ties, the worst record for Florida Tech in 10 years. Stottler commented to *Florida Today* on November 5: "We learned a lot about ourselves. And next year, we intend to be right where we were before. We're going to be back in the NCAA playoffs."

Stottler was determined that 1996 would see great improvement. As reported in *Florida Today* on August 31, one major step that he took was to entice Homer Bozorg to return as assistant coach. The 1996 season began well. When Florida Tech defeated Presbyterian College and Wingate College on a trip through the Carolinas, the team had run its record to 5 and 0 and earned a number 6 ranking nationally.

However, by October 11, when Florida Tech faced Tampa, its record had fallen to 6-3-1 and its playoff hopes were uncertain. Its loss to Tampa virtually eliminated it from tournament contention.

On October 16, 1996, a ceremony was held dedicating the soccer field to Stottler. Feeding from the emotion of that event, Florida Tech dominated the University of North Florida, which had been ranked in the top 20 nationally, by a score of 4 to nil.

On October 23, the Panthers fell to St. Leo by a score of 2 to nil, taking their record to 9-5-1 overall and 2-2 in conference play. Stottler told *Florida Today*: "We had lots of chances to make it to nationals and we just didn't get it done."

A 2 to 1 victory over Florida Southern on November 3 brought Florida Tech's 1996 record to 11-5-1 and 4-2 in the conference. That victory and a series of upsets among other conference teams left the Panthers with a slim chance to win the conference championship. On November 15, the Panthers completed their season with a 3 to nil victory over Rollins, bringing Florida Tech's record to 12-5-1 on the season and a second-place finish in the Sunshine State Conference.

On August 31, 1997, *Florida Today* reported that the Panthers would open their 1997 season against Nova Southeastern in a "drive toward resurrection." Unfortunately, they were shutout by Nova, an NAIA school at the time. On September 10, 1997, the Panthers took their record to 2 wins and a loss after defeating North Carolina-Pembroke by a 2 to nil score. A 3 to nil loss to Tampa on September 21 marked the Panthers' fifth straight loss to the Spartans. A 5 to 2 victory over Rollins on October 1 gave the Panthers a record of 8-2 overall and 2-1 in the conference. They won that game despite playing a man down for more than 30 minutes when Greg Knight received his second yellow card and was ejected from the game.

The Panthers ran their record to 9-4-0 when they rallied past Mars Hill College on October 18 by a 7 to 3 score. They completed their 1997 home schedule on October 29 with a 3 to 2 overtime victory over Webber College, bringing their season record to 10 wins, 5 losses and a tie. A 2 to 1 victory at Barry University on November 8 brought the season record to 12-5-1 overall and 4-1-1 in the conference.

On November 13, 1997, *Florida Today* reported that senior forward James Phillips and freshman midfielder John Hudson had been named first team all-conference selections. Steven Barnes and Greg Knight were selected for the second team.

The 1998 season began with a lot of questions. August 14, 1998, *Florida Today* noted that the Panthers would have 8 English players on the squad for that season. It also noted that the team had suffered some key losses due to graduation. Jamie Byers made his goals clear when he said: "There's only one goal for our team. To win a national championship."

The Panthers opened the 1998 season with a 3 to 2 victory over St. Thomas University. Two penalty kicks by Melbourne High School alumnus Jesse Goldfarb led the way. However, the Panthers proceeded to lose 4 straight games before tying Tusculum College on September 19. Florida Tech's 1-4-1 start constituted the worst start for the team in many years. The dismal start may have been due, at least in part, to the fact that Stottler was not coaching because he was caring for his ill mother.

The Panthers did win their first conference game with a 2 to nil victory over Rollins College. On October 7, the team welcomed back Rick Stottler and celebrated his return with a 3 to nil victory over Florida Southern. The Panthers then went on to defeat Gardner-Webb on October 9 by a score of 6 to 1 behind 3 goals by Jesse Goldfarb. On October 10, however, they fell to NAIA powerhouse Life University by a score of 4 to nil. This dropped Florida Tech's season record to 3 wins, 7 losses and a tie on the season.

On November 2, Florida Tech rallied from a 2 to nil halftime deficit to win 3 to 2. Goldfarb again led the way with 3 assists. This brought the season record to 7-9-1 overall and 3-2 in the conference. They followed up that victory with a 5 to nil thrashing of Eckerd College on November 4. Once again, Goldfarb led the way with 3 goals and an assist.

The Panthers closed the 1998 season with a match against St. Leo on November 7. That victory brought the season record to 9-9-1 overall and 5-2 in the conference.

On November 18, *Florida Today* reported that Jesse Goldfarb had led the Sunshine State Conference in goals for the 1998 season and had been selected to the first team on the all-conference squad. That same edition also reported that Richard Sharpe, the most prolific scorer in

NCAA soccer history and a three-time All-American, would be inducted into the Sunshine State Conference Hall of Fame.

Florida Tech began its 1999 season at a substantial disadvantage. As reported in *Florida Today* on August 25, the Panthers were relying upon 10 freshmen to bolster the team and recover from the disappointment of the previous season. However, as the team travelled to St. Thomas University in Miami for its opening game, those 10 freshmen remained in Melbourne for freshmen orientation. The Panthers managed a 2-2 tie with St. Thomas despite the missing players.

Another early-season challenge for Florida Tech was the absence of an experienced goalkeeper. As reported in *Florida Today* on September 28, the anticipated keeper, Paul Badaracco, a transfer from Italy, had his eligibility delayed due to NCAA bureaucratic issues, while Stein Norman, the previous year's keeper, had issues with the Norwegian government regarding a student loan. Forced to improvise, Stottler drafted Justin Schanck, a little-used midfielder from Maine, to play goal. Schanck surpassed all expectations when the team won its first 6 games with Schanck in goal, including 3 shutouts. Schanck had allowed 4 goals in those 6 games while making 25 saves.

By that point in the season, the Panthers had a 7-game undefeated streak and a record of 6-0-1 after defeating Alabama-Huntsville 1 to nil in overtime in the Florida Panther Invitational Soccer Tournament. By October 19, Florida Tech had extended its record to 9-2-1 overall and 1-2 in the conference. However, a 4-1 loss to Eckerd that day dashed any hopes of winning a conference championship.

On October 29, the Panthers played their final home game of 1999 with a 1-1 tie against Tampa. That game was not concluded due to the fact that several banks of lights went out with 11 minutes, 40 seconds remaining in the first overtime. Although the players were eager to continue without all of the lights, the referee would not allow play to continue.

When Florida Tech fell to Lynn on November 3 by a 1 to nil score, its record dropped to 9 wins, 5 losses and 2 ties. The Panthers dropped their final 2 games to complete the season with a record of 9-7-2 and a 1-5-1 conference record.

Stottler retired as Florida Tech coach following the 1999 season. Throughout his tenure at Florida Tech, Stottler served without monetary compensation and raised a substantial amount of the funds in support of the program. Nor were any of his assistant coaches paid by the school. His teams compiled 190 wins during his 14-year tenure, with only 66 losses and 12 ties. It is not debatable that he transformed soccer at F.I.T. More than that, however, he transformed soccer in central Florida. Stottler and the players and coaches who he brought to the area have spread the popularity of soccer throughout the region and have caught the imagination of youth in a way that has caused the sport to boom.

Many of the people that Stottler brought to the area have remained and have become unusually productive citizens in the area, not only through soccer but through many other community activities. Several became coaches of local clubs and schools and conducted camps that inspired hundreds of young players. Fidgi Haig became coach of the Satellite Beach girls' soccer team and led them to 2 state championships before becoming women's coach at Florida Tech. Fidgi was adored by the players he coached and had an enormous impact on girls' soccer in Central Florida. His premature death evoked an outpouring of affection throughout the community. Robin Chan became coach of the Melbourne Central Catholic boys' team and steered them to 2 state championships before becoming head coach at his alma mater. He has experienced good success at Florida Tech and, like Fidgi, has had a substantial impact upon youth soccer in the area. Giles Malone has remained in the area and has become a notable leader in the business community, particularly in promoting tourism in the area. Giles has supported numerous charitable activities and remains an avid booster of Florida Tech. Bino Campanini has become something of a local icon. He first advanced to become CEO of Stottler Stagg. He then was elected as a trustee of Florida Tech before accepting a position at the school as Director of Alumni Affairs. He later advanced to Senior Vice President for Student Affairs. James Phillips remained in the area, became coach of the boys' team at Holy Trinity Episcopal Academy and, later, advanced to become Athletic Director. Steve Freeman also remained in the area and became a successful financial planner. He, too, was elected to the Board of Trustees of the university. Scott Armstrong has had an enormous impact on local soccer as Executive Director of Space Coast United Soccer Club, while also coaching West Shore Junior – Senior High School to a state championship.

A lengthy article in *Florida Today* by David Jones on February 20, 2004, paid tribute to Stottler's accomplishments. The article noted that Stottler retired after a 14-year SSC Hall of Fame career with a career winning percentage which ranked third all-time among Division II coaches. It was particularly moving in its description of the high character of the players that Stottler and Malone recruited to the area. Of particular note was a section of the article titled "Where are They Now" which described the current lives of former stars Keith Ames, Kieran Breslin, Bino Campanini, Robin Chan, Eddie Enders, Steve Freeman, Fidgi Haig, Greg Kemp, Dylan Lewis, Chris Payne, Paul Robertson and Richard Sharpe.

Florida Tech men's soccer experienced some tough times following Stottler's retirement. *Florida Today* reported on October 9, 2001, that the Panthers had beaten Thomas University the previous weekend, ending a 25-game winless streak. Coach Kevin Johnson told the newspaper: "I think we're very close to being a good team right now."

On January 20, 2005, *Florida Today* reported that Fidgi Haig had been appointed as women's soccer coach at Florida Tech while Robin Chan had been appointed men's coach. Both teams had been winless in the Sunshine State Conference the previous season. Chan had been at Melbourne Central Catholic High School for 8 years, compiling a record of 170 wins, 29 losses and 18 ties. His teams captured 2 state championships. Haig had coached the Satellite High School girls' team for 9 seasons, compiling a record of 231 wins, 18 losses and 8 ties. Haig, too, had 2 state championships to his credit.

At the time of this writing, Chan has remained as coach at Florida Tech for 17 seasons, guiding his teams to 134 victories, 111 defeats and 31 ties. His 2022 team had a particularly outstanding season with 10 wins, 1 loss and 7 ties, including an appearance in the NCAA Division II tournament.

An article by Jerry Durney and Christina Hardman in the winter 2023 edition of *Florida Tech Today* chronicled Chan's 21 years as a player and coach at Florida Tech. The article recited that the Panthers have finished in the top-4 in the conference 6 times since 2010, receiving 3 NCAA tournament bids during that time. The Panthers had been ranked in the top 25 nationally at some point during 6 of the past 7 seasons, reaching the top 10 on 3 occasions. Chan had been named conference Coach of the Year twice while coaching 30 all-conference players. In 2016, Tiey Collins, a mainstay on the soccer team, became the school's first-ever male Academic All-American after receiving first team honors from the College of Sports Information Directors of America. Sam Sawyer was named the Sunshine State Conference Defensive Player of the Year during the 2016 season, becoming the first Panther in program history to receive that award. Women's coach Ryan Moon, who had played for Chan and later served as an assistant to Chan, claimed that Chan's "biggest strengths are his man-management skills and his genuine care for his players that goes well beyond the pitch."

The winter 2018 edition of *Florida Tech Today* noted that two seniors on the soccer team, Evan Enders and Jan Hlavica, had been named to the second team Academic All-American team. They became the 7th and 8th Panthers in school history to receive that honor. Enders held a 3.93 GPA in Electrical Engineering while Hlavica maintained a perfect 4.0 GPA in business and management.

Tragically, Stottler became afflicted with Parkinson's Disease. He passed away on December 2, 2010, at the age of 75. He left an indelible mark on his community, not only due to his soccer achievements but also due to his professional accomplishments as well as the many charitable activities which he instituted and supported.

Notes

- The information in this chapter regarding the results for individual games and season records is taken from the archives of *Florida Today*, as are the quotes from individual players and coaches.
- In most cases the edition of *Florida Today* on the day following each game was the source of the information described.

CHAPTER SIX:
REYNOLDS BECOMES AN INSTITUTION

By William C. Potter

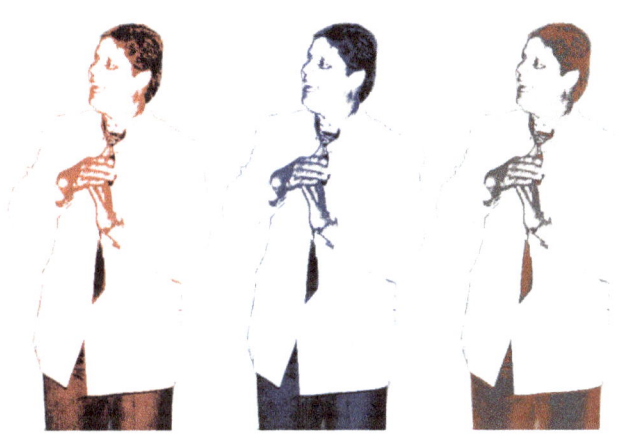

omen's sports in the Sunshine State Conference had begun in earnest in 1986 when the athletic directors had determined that basketball, volleyball and slow-pitch softball should be the "flagship" sports for women in conference play. On June 2, 1986, *Florida Today* reported that Paul Ward, who had worked with Folliard at Stonehill College, would become head women's basketball coach at F.I.T. In addition to coaching the women, Ward's duties included recruiting for the men's team.

Ward was not naïve about the challenges he faced. On June 2, 1986, he told *Florida Today*: "I think you're talking about a five-year program to get things the way they should be." Ward's assistant coach that year was a fiery young part-time coach by the name of John Reynolds. The Lady Panthers recorded their first victory in school history on December 3, 1986, with a 77 to 75 overtime victory over Edward Waters College. Melbourne Central Catholic graduate Barbara Barlow led the way with 24 points. They followed that win with a win over Webber College on December 6. Unsurprisingly, Florida Tech's first womens' basketball team in the 1986-87 season struggled to an overall record of 5 wins and 19 losses and a 2 and 10 record in the conference.

On August 20, 1987, *Florida Today* reported that Paul Ward had resigned to accept a position as assistant coach at Boston College and that John Reynolds had been appointed as his successor at Florida Tech. In promoting Reynolds, Athletic Director Bill Jurgens noted: "John is a very dedicated coach with a great rapport with the team. He's shown a strong commitment to the women's program." Jurgens' words proved to be prescient although few could have predicted the intensity and duration of Reynolds' dedication and commitment over the ensuing 37 years.

The 1987-1988 season began on a strong note as Florida Tech defeated Edward Waters on November 24, 1987, behind Miriam Shields' 25 points and 16 from Lisa Sims. Reynolds said of the game: "That tells me that the program is coming around a little bit."

As the 1987-1988 season progressed, the Lady Panthers made remarkable progress. By February 28, 1988, they had extended their record to 12 wins and 14 losses and eliminated St. Leo from the conference tournament with an 81 to 64 win. Barbara Barlow, the sophomore from Melbourne Village, led the team with 23 points and 6 rebounds. On March 3, Rollins eliminated the Panthers from the tournament with an 80 to 64 victory. Reynolds noted however: "We improved from 6-19 to 12-15, so if we improve by 100 percent again next year, we ought to be in the championship game." Point guard Miriam Shields made the first team All-Conference team.

The Lady Panthers received a big boost, compliments of men's coach Tom Folliard. Folliard had been transforming men's basketball partially through a surge of Canadian players. On one of his recruiting trips to Quebec, he discovered Christine Ferron, a 5'8" point guard. Reynolds told *Florida Today* on November 21, 1988, that: "A lot of our success this season will depend on how quickly she matures." She joined 7 returning players who started at various times during the previous season, Amy Farnhow, Mary Kispert, Kelly Leary, Barbara Barlow, Karen Horne and Lisa Sims.

The season opened with a 94 to 74 romp over Edward Waters. Ferron made her debut for Florida Tech with 30 points, tying the school record while adding 9 assists. On November 30, 1988, the Lady Panthers extended their record to 2 and 1 behind Ferron's 30 points in an 84 to 71 victory at Flagler College. Lisa Sims added 23 points and 19 rebounds.

A pre-conference tournament took place on December 2nd and 3rd with the Panthers taking home the title. A 3-pointer by Amy Fahrnow at the buzzer took Florida Tech to an 80 to 77 victory over Eckerd in the championship game. Lisa Sims was named Most Valuable Player, finishing the tournament with 32 points, 32 rebounds, 7 blocks and 3 steals. Ferron and Fahrnow joined her on the all-tournament team.

On January 18, 1989, Ferron broke the school single-game scoring record with 38 points in a 90 to 52 romp over Barry. That put the Lady Panthers' record at 8 and 5 on the season and 1 and 1 in the conference. When they lost to Florida Southern in an 80 to 78 heartbreaker on February 11, their record fell to 13 and 8 and 5 and 4. The season ended with an 86 to 75 loss to Florida Southern in the semi-finals of the Sunshine State Conference tournament on March 2, 1989. This Panthers team set team records with a 17-11 overall record and 8-4 record in the conference. Reynolds noted: "Our next step is to learn how to win the big games."

Ferron was named the conference's Freshman of the Year and was a unanimous pick for the all-conference team. Lisa Sims also was named to the all-conference team with her average of 15.3 points and 12.5 rebounds per game.

On July 1, 1989, *Florida Today* reported that Florida Tech had signed 2 promising recruits to join its returning corps of players. Rhanda Hinote had been a conference player of the year at Melbourne High School while Candee Zepka had averaged more than 21 points per game in high school in Virginia.

Christine Ferron, conference co-player of the year in 1988-1989, missed the first 5 games of the 1989-1990 season following a bout with chicken pox. They began the season with Mary Kispert and Kelly Leary at forwards, Karen Horne at center, and Rhanda Hinote and Amy Fahrnow at guards. When Ferron rejoined the team on December 12, the Lady Panthers stood at 4 and 2. The Lady Panthers won 11 of their first 13 games. When they fell to Rollins on February 12 by a 72-61 score, the Panthers' record was 17 and 5 overall and 7 and 2 in the conference. On February 21, they took their record to 19-5 overall and 9-2 in the conference with a 76 to 53 rout of St. Leo. Mary Kispert led the scorers with 27 points.

When the Lady Panthers defeated Tampa on March 1 in the opening round of the Sunshine State Conference tournament, they raised their record to 20 and 6, thereby posting the first 20-win season in school history. Ferron led scoring with 21 points in the 72-63 victory. The following night, Rollins defeated the Lady Panthers by a score of 74 to 58 in the championship game of the tournament. That closed the season with a record of 20 and 7 overall and 9 and 3 in the conference. Ferron and Kispert both were named to the all-tournament team.

The 1990-1991 season was, to say the least, a disappointment. It began ominously when Christine Ferron, now Christine Ferron Keenan as a result of her marriage to F.I.T. men's basketball player Brian Keenan, announced that she was expecting a child and would sit out the season. Ironically, Mary Kispert, now Mary Folliard by virtue of having married men's basketball player Tom Folliard, Jr., would also be sitting out the season to have a child.

An interesting footnote to the marriage of Christine Ferron and Brian Keenan appeared in a story by Jerry Durney in the Spring 2023 issue of *Florida Tech Magazine* (formerly known as *Florida Tech Today*). Durney's story related that Josie Keenan, Brian and Christine's daughter, was now playing volleyball for the Lady Panthers.

Florida Today reported on November 21, 1991, that Ferron-Keenan and Folliard were, however, back for the 1991-1992 season and anticipation was high. In a tragic turn of events, the team lost two prize recruits, 6-3 Candice Kleibrink and 6-7 Laurie Hockridge, when they were injured in an auto accident. Candee Zepka returned and was joined by transfer guard Margaret Farley. Also returning was 6-5 Jenny Andersson from Sweden. Paulette King was touted as a promising newcomer. One can only imagine what the team could have been had Kleibrink and Hockridge not been injured.

The potential of the 1991-1992 team quickly became apparent when they blew out Flagler College on December 3 by a score of 109 to 57. Keenan led with 28 points while Paulette King added 26 and Farley 17. Candee Zepka set a record with 14 assists.

By December 30 when the Lady Panthers defeated visiting Pfeiffer College, the Lady Panthers were 7 and 1. Paulette King was leading the conference in scoring and chipped in 37 points and 16 rebounds that night. Keenan added 26 points and 10 rebounds.

On January 3, 1992, the Lady Panthers won their own Holiday Classic with a 106 to 101 overtime victory over Northern Michigan University. Paulette King was selected Most Valuable Player of the tournament while Christine Keenan was an all-tourney selection. Mary Folliard made clutch shots at critical times.

By February 3, 1992, the Lady Panthers had extended their record to 18-2 overall and 6-0 in the conference. In their victory over Flagler College that day, Christine Keenan broke the school record with 46 points, including 11 three-pointers. Paulette King garnered 12 rebounds.

The Panthers closed out their regular season on March 1 by crushing Rollins by a score of 98 to 62. Candee Zepka tossed in 24 points while Mary Folliard, the lone senior on the team, added 23.

Florida Tech faced Rollins in the semi-final game of the Sunshine State Conference tournament on March 3. The Panthers prevailed by a score of 68 to 56 behind 21 points from Paulette King. They followed-up with a victory in the championship game, defeating Florida Southern by a score of 71 to 66. Keenan had 19 points, Farley 18 points and King 17 points. Farley had 14 rebounds and 6 assists while King added 12 rebounds. Altogether, it was a very impressive showing of a balanced team. Farley was selected as MVP of the tournament.

The conference championship earned the Lady Panthers a trip to the NCAA South Region Tournament where they faced Delta State. Unfortunately, the season ended there with a 97 to 70 loss on March 13.

John Reynolds was named the SSC Coach of the Year. Paulette King was named conference Player of the Year. Christine Keenan joined King as a member of the all-conference first team. King led all NCAA Division II in scoring with a 29.5 average while Keenan finished in the top 10 nationally with a 22.7 average. King was an honorable mention selection on the All-America team. April 6, 1992, edition of *Sports Illustrated* included King and Keenan in the "Faces in the Crowd" section.

The outlook for the 1992-1993 season was rosy. With all starters returning except Folliard, the team was deep and talented. David Jones wrote about the Lady Panthers in the October 28, 1992, edition of *Florida Today*. As Jones described it, Reynolds' biggest problem this season might be how to keep his stars happy with all of the returning performers, including 3 starting guards in Christine Keenan, Margaret Farley and Candee Zepka, together with forward Paulette King who had led the nation in scoring the previous year. Jones noted: "It could also end up being the most successful basketball team Florida Tech has ever had – in men's or women's play."

Florida Tech picked a tough opponent for its opening game of the season. They faced Delta State, which had trounced the Panthers in the NCAA tournament the previous season and was defending national champion, as their opening game. Unfortunately, the results were largely the same as Delta State romped to a 95 to 61 victory. Paulette King scored 22 points and Christine Keenan chipped in 16 for the Lady Panthers. The Panthers also lost their second game to Bellarmine on November 22 before finally getting a win with a 93 to 71 win over Edward Waters College on November 25 behind Paulette King's 38 points. They followed that game with a win over Florida Memorial on December 1 by a score of 80 to 54. A highlight of that game was the return of Laurie Hockridge after more than a year in rehabilitation from her injuries suffered after being hit by a car. On December 6, the Lady Panthers blasted St. Augustine College by a score of 102 to 82 behind King's 36 points and 17 from Hockridge. On December 14, an 89 to 61 victory over Seattle Pacific brought their record to 4 and 2. Christine Keenan led the way with 29 points.

On December 17, the Lady Panthers took on Virginia State in the first round of the Florida Atlantic Tournament in Boca Raton. They won that game 84 to 68 behind Paulette King's 21 points. The following night, they lost the championship game to Florida Atlantic by a score of 76 to 63, despite 30 points from King and 17 points from Keenan.

Florida Tech hosted the Florida Tech Holiday Tournament on January 2 and 3, 1993. The Panthers opened the tournament with a one-sided 102 to 60 defeat of the Air Force Academy. King scored 29, Keenan added 25 and 3 others were in double figures. The following night, the Panthers edged Michigan Tech by a 68 to 66 score to win the tournament. Margaret Farley was named Most Valuable Player of the tournament while Paulette King joined her on the all-tournament team.

The Lady Panthers stretched their record to 11 and 3 on January 13, 1993, when they cruised to a 106 to 50 win over St. Leo. Paulette King led the way with 35 points, followed by 23 from Christine Keenan, 15 from Laurie Hockridge and 11 from Margaret Farley. Candy Zepka contributed 9 assists. At that time, the Panthers boasted a ranking of 16th in the national polls.

A 77 to 63 victory over Tampa on January 20 boosted their record to 13 and 3 overall and 3 and 0 in the conference. King again led the way with 26 points while Hockridge snared 10 rebounds. A big victory over Florida Southern on January 27 was keyed by King's 32 points followed by Farley's 22 points. That game marked the first conference game between 2 women's basketball teams ranked in the top 20 nationally. A victory over North Florida on January 30 took their record to 16 and 3. The 80 to 50 win was sparked by Keenan's 22 points. That win set the school record of 11 straight victories.

Laurie Hockridge, the 6-foot-7 center, was the star when the Panthers ran their record to 17 and 3 (6 and 0 in the conference) with an

83 to 69 victory over Rollins on February 3. Hockridge contributed 19 points and 15 rebounds.

By February 17, 1993, the Panthers had run their record to 20 and 3 overall and 9 and 0 in the conference and were ranked 20th nationally. King led the nation in scoring with a 28.6 points average while pulling down an average of 8.7 rebounds. The team had won 15 consecutive games. They extended that record that night when they defeated Florida Southern by a score of 64 to 56 behind King's 22 points.

They wrapped up the regular season with a perfect 12 and 0 conference record when they routed St. Leo by a 105 to 52 score on February 27. Paulette King put on a show with 41 points and 15 rebounds. On March 2, King was named conference player of the year while Keenan joined her on the first team of the all-conference team. Farley was named to the second team. Reynolds was honored as Coach of the Year.

The Lady Panthers followed up their regular season championship by sweeping the post-season tournament. They opened the tournament on March 5 with an 87 to 63 romp over Rollins. They then defeated Florida Southern in the title game on March 6 by a score of 87 to 75. That ran their record to 25 and 3 on the season and their winning streak to 20. Farley and King were named to the all-tourney team while King was named Most Valuable Player.

The Lady Panthers travelled to Cleveland, Mississippi for the NCAA Division II South Regional tournament commencing March 12. They opened the tournament with an 86 to 74 win over Florida Atlantic. Christine Keenan, whose grandfather had died only a few hours before the game, led the team with a remarkable 22 points, 5 assists and 17 rebounds. King added 21 points.

Unfortunately, their extraordinary season and 20 game unbeaten streak came to an end in the South Regional championship game when they lost to defending national champions Delta State by a score of 75 to 51. Paulette King led Panther scoring with 16 points and was named to the all-tournament team. That marked the final game for 6 seniors who had made an indelible mark on Florida Tech women's basketball. Paulette King, Christine Keenan, Margaret Farley, Candee Zepka, Laurie Hockridge and Jenny Andersson had all played their final game for F.I.T. *Florida Today* reported on March 27 that King had been recognized as an honorable mention on the Kodak All-American team.

Both King and Keenan would be selected to the Florida Tech Sports Hall of Fame in 1998 and, fittingly, inducted at the same event. Keenan would leave as the career leader in 8 categories, including career 3-pointers and career steals. King, a first team All-America selection in 1991-1992 and 1992-1993, would depart having averaged 28.3 points per game during her career, the highest average in the history of NCAA Division II women's basketball. She would leave with 8 Florida Tech records, including points in a season, career field goal percentage, free throws made in a season and points in a game (49). Both King and Keenan would also be inducted into the Sunshine State Conference Hall of Fame.

Paulette King would eventually marry, become Paulette King-Morin and have children, a daughter Mikayla, and a son, Alex. As reported in *Florida Today* on May 11, 2014, Paulette and her daughter became known by creating a book and a video that teaches music in a kid-friendly way. *Florida Today* disclosed on February 23, 2007, that Paulette had been named as the top women's basketball player in the Sunshine State Conference during its first 25 years of women's competition.

Not surprisingly, the Florida Tech women's basketball team experienced a few seasons of mediocrity following the loss of this historic group of seniors. The 1993-1994 season was particularly frustrating. The Lady Panthers were rolling along doing pretty well, led by Sherri France, a product of Melbourne High School who had previously played at Valdosta State. By February 1994, the Lady Panthers had posted 14 wins and 7 losses and France was leading the nation in scoring with a 28.6 points average while also being among the nation's top 10 in rebounding and assists. However, as reported in *Florida Today* on February 11 and 12, 1994, it was discovered that France had previously exhausted her eligibility by playing not 3 seasons in Valdosta as she had claimed, but she had actually played several games in a 4th season. As a result, France was immediately declared ineligible and the Lady Panthers were obligated to forfeit several games which they had won with France.

By the 1995-1996 season, Reynolds had assembled another powerhouse. That team was led by Sonja Radenkovic, a 6-foot-4 post-player from Belgrade, Serbia, who had dominated the conference as a freshman the previous year, averaging 22 points and 10.3 rebounds per game. As noted in *Florida Today* on November 27, 1995, Radenkovic was joined by another import from the Balkans, Dunja Pacirski, a point guard from Zagreb, Croatia.

The 1995-1996 Panthers began the season inauspiciously. When they lost to Fort Valley State on November 28, that dropped their record to 1 and 2. However, by the time of the Florida Tech Holiday Classic in late December, the Lady Panthers had hit their stride. In the tournament opener, Florida Tech routed the Air Force Academy, 75 to 51, behind 20 points from Radenkovic. However, they dropped the tournament championship game with a narrow 68 to 63 loss to Pitt-Johnstown. Radenkovic scored 17 points while forward Gwen Clayton added 16.

By January 16, 1996, when the Lady Panthers defeated Barry by a 73 to 59 score, their record had progressed to 9 and 7 overall and 3 and 1 in the conference. Varel Clarke, a point guard from the Bahamas, had come forward as a force for Florida Tech and scored 20 to lead the team to victory.

Gwen Clayton and the Lady Panthers experienced many success stories on the basketball court. *Photo from University Archives.*

By the time of the conference tournament on March 1, the Panthers had advanced to 19 and 8 overall and 12 and 2 in the conference. Florida Tech moved to 20 and 8 with a victory over Rollins in the semi-finals of the tourney but dropped the championship game to Florida Southern by a 76 to 64 score. Radenkovic ran into foul trouble early in the game and played only 23 minutes. That ended the season for the women with a record of 20 wins and 9 losses and an optimistic outlook for the next season.

The 1996-1997 season began with high hopes and achieved many of those aspirations. When they defeated Valdosta State on November 26 by a 76 to 65 score, they ran their record to 4 and 0 on the season. A 63 to 50 road win over Savannah State on December 5 ran their record to 6 and 0 for the year. However, they suffered their first loss of the season on December 7 when they fell on the road at Valdosta State by a score of 91 to 84 in overtime. Three Panthers had fouled out by the time overtime was reached. The Lady Panthers defeated Husson College on December 27 by a score of 79 to 51, extending their record to 8 and 1 on the season. Gwen Clayton, a forward from Frostproof, Florida, led the team with 5 steals.

On December 30, 1996, the Lady Panthers hosted undefeated Harding University. The visiting Bisons extended their record to 13 and 0 with a 77 to 68 victory over Florida Tech. Radenkovic had 16 points and 11 rebounds in the losing cause.

When the Lady Panthers won a road squeaker over Florida Southern on January 25, 1997, by a score of 75 to 73, that ran their record to 16 and 2 overall and 6 and 0 in the conference. Varel Clarke had 12 points and 8 rebounds.

By the time of the Sunshine State Conference tourney on February 27, the Lady Panthers were 24 and 2 on the season and remained undefeated at 14 and 0 in the conference. They crushed Eckerd in the opening game of the tournament before facing Florida Southern in the semi-finals. They took care of business with an 88 to 72 victory over Florida Southern on February 28 behind Radenkovic's 30 points. Clarke added 20 points. The Lady Panthers went on to defeat Barry in the championship game by a score of 70 to 59. Radenkovic was named Most Valuable Player of the tournament while Clarke joined her on the all-tournament team.

Florida Today reported on March 3, 1997, that the Panthers were not only the top seed in the NCAA South Regional tourney but they were also hosting it. Florida Tech, then 27 and 2, would face the winner of the Valdosta State-Fort Valley State game in their opening game. Unfortunately, when they faced Fort Valley on March 7, they struggled against the Fort Valley press and fell 67 to 59, ending their season with 27 wins and only 3 losses.

Peter Kerasotis noted in *Florida Today* on March 8, 1997, that it had been a historic season for Florida Tech women's basketball. Their 27 wins were a school record as was their 19-game winning streak. Radenkovic was the Sunshine State Conference player of the year while Reynolds was coach of the year.

The 1997-1998 season was another successful, if not record-breaking, season. Although Radenkovic returned, she was surrounded with a primarily freshmen supporting cast. With an overall record of 18 wins and 8 losses, the conference regular season record was a modest 7 and 5. Radenkovic picked up where she left off with another remarkable season. On November 19, Radenkovic had 36 points to down North Florida by a score of 85 to 73. On December 16, 1997, she scored 30 points with 13 rebounds and 7 assists to lead the Lady Panthers to a 79 to 64 victory over Savannah State.

The Lady Panthers hosted the State Farm Insurance Holiday Classic on January 2 and 3, 1998. At that point, the Panthers were 9 and 1 on the season. A *Florida Today* story by Anna Maria Della Costa on January 2, 1998, discussed the relationship between John Reynolds and his players. Reynolds said: "I think coach-player relationships are very important. To be successful as a coach, they have to respect you." Della Costa went on to say: "Reynolds always has carried the policy of communication, trust and having fun with his players. The coaching strategy has worked: his team is 190-96 in the past 10 seasons, and Tech has won its own tournament 8 times in the tournament's 10-year existence."

The Panthers opened the holiday tournament with a 56 to 48 win over the University of British Columbia. The Panthers won the tournament the following night with a 75 to 58 win over Florida Memorial. Florida Tech's Natara Loose was Most Valuable Player of the tournament while Radenkovic and freshman LeiAnne Lindenberger were selected to the all-tournament team.

When conference play began on January 7, 1998, the Lady Panthers were 11 and 1 on the season. By January 17, when Florida Tech defeated Tampa by a score of 70 to 57, their season record was 14 and 2 with a 3 and 1 conference record. They followed that game with a 78 to 76 win over Florida Southern on January 24. When they beat St. Leo on January 31, they took their record to 18 and 2 and 6 and 1 in the conference.

The fortunes of the Lady Panthers took an abrupt turn when Sonja Radenkovic tore her ACL while working out. She had recently been honored for becoming the first player in Sunshine State Conference history to score 2,000 points. She was averaging 21.4 points per game. The injury would end her career at Florida Tech and send the Panthers' season in another direction. They entered the conference tournament on a 4-game losing streak and seeded third with a 19 and 7 overall record and 7 and 5 in the conference. The Panthers were bounced from the tournament by Barry by a score of 70 to 56. Thus ended a promising season sabotaged by fate. In addition to the loss of Radenkovic, Tech point guard Ursula Thomas, who was leading the conference in assists, was injured during the game and taken to a Lakeland hospital with a separated shoulder while guard Dunja Pacirski did not play due to an ankle injury suffered a few days earlier. Despite the unfortunate end of the season, Reynolds was named the NCAA Division II South Region Coach of the Year. Radenkovic completed her career as the all-time leading scorer at Florida Tech and in the Sunshine State Conference.

After a few modestly successful seasons, Reynolds was back with a powerhouse squad for the 2001-02 season. The season began on a high note when the Lady Panthers played their first game in their new home, the Clemente Center, with an 87 to 51 victory over Florida Memorial on November 16, 2001. After a year and a half of playing games at Brevard Junior College while the Clemente Center was under construction, it was an emotional homecoming. Senior guard Felicia Bell scored the first basket at the Clemente Center. Junior center Delicia Phillips had 13 points and 14 rebounds. The following night, the Panthers faced the University of North Dakota, the number two ranked Division II team in the country. The Panthers fell in a 67 to 65 heartbreaker despite 25 points from Shawntel "Peaches" Williams.

On November 28 and 29, 2001, the Lady Panthers participated in the Sunshine State Disney Challenge at the Wide World of Sports Complex. The tournament matched 4 Sunshine State Conference teams against 4 top Division II teams from around the country. Florida Tech won both of its games in the tourney, first defeating Winona State and then defeating Augusta State in the final game by a score of 74 to 63. That extended Florida Tech's record to 6 and 1.

On December 28, the Lady Panthers took their record to 8 and 2 on the season with an 82 to 59 victory over Nova Southeastern. Senior guard Felicia Bell led the way 22 points and junior center Delicia Phillips added 19 points and 14 rebounds.

By January 15, 2002, the Panthers were 12 and 2 overall and 2 and 0 in the conference. When they defeated Tampa on January 23 by a 73 to 64 score, their record went to 14 and 3 overall and 4 and 1 in the conference.

When the Lady Panthers celebrated Senior Day on February 23 against St. Leo, they were 20 and 5 overall and 10 and 3 in the conference.

The 77 to 55 win would give them a share of the conference title with Rollins. Phillips had 19 points and 12 rebounds while Bell had 14 points in the victory.

The Panthers picked up where they left off when they routed St. Leo in the opening round of the Sunshine State Conference tournament on March 1 by a 94 to 68 score. Phillips led the scoring with 15 points while adding 9 rebounds. In the semi-final game, Florida Tech knocked off Eckerd by a 67 to 55 score. Bell led the scoring with 16 points.

On March 3, the Lady Panthers knocked off Rollins College in a 59 to 56 nailbiter to win the conference tourney and an automatic bid to the NCAA Division II tournament. Natasha Griffin, Delicia Phillips and Felicia Bell all were named to the All-Tournament squad.

Felicia Bell was named to the first team All-Sunshine State Conference team while Peaches Williams was named to the second team. John Reynolds garnered his third Coach of the Year recognition.

The South Region tournament took place at Sillers Coliseum in Cleveland, Mississippi, beginning on March 8, 2002. The Lady Panthers won the opener in an overtime thriller over Arkansas Tech by a 61 to 57 score. They were paced by 15 points from Phillips. They then faced Central Arkansas in the battle for a trip to the Elite Eight. They rose to the challenge by defeating Central Arkansas by a 74 to 71 margin led by 20 points from Bell and 15 points and 14 rebounds from Phillips. Delicia Phillips and Felicia Bell were named to the All-Tournament team.

The regional win raised the Panthers' season record to 26 and 5 and sent them to the Elite Eight in Rochester, Minnesota for a shot at the national championship. Their remarkable season came to an end on March 21 with an 84 to 68 loss to Southeastern Oklahoma. The game took an abrupt turn when Southeastern Oklahoma went to a 1-2-2 zone defense after falling behind by 10 points. Florida Tech seemed confused by that move and never seemed able to adjust. The team completed that remarkable season with a record of 26 wins and 6 losses and a number 7 ranking in the national poll.

On March 22 Carl Kotala of *Florida Today* wrote a piece on Florida Tech discussing the void that would be left by the graduation of 5 seniors from this memorable team. Reynolds quipped:" It's not replacing the hole in my lineup. It's replacing the hole in my chest that they've just left." Felicia Bell spoke for the team in saying of Reynolds: "He's been like a father to all of us. You're not going to have too many coaches like that. There's no coach in the world like our coach." The 2001-2002 team would be inducted into the Florida Tech Sports Hall of Fame in 2014.

Bell left school as the number 2 scorer in school history and received honorable mention on the All-American team. Bell's 1,955 career points were second only to Radenkovic's 2,136.

After a couple of years of relative mediocrity, Reynolds would field another powerful squad for the 2004-05 season. The Panthers kicked off that season facing Flagler College on November 15, 2004. They started the season with a 68 to 54 victory, led by 13 points from freshman point guard Jennifer Tamilio. Danielle Quinn, a product of Cocoa Beach High School, would prove to be a valuable addition for the Lady Panthers. Reynolds' daughter Laurissa was another contributor to that squad as was freshman guard Amanda Muns. The team finished the regular season with a record of 19 and 8 with a 11 and 5 conference record.

The Panthers entered the conference tournament that season as the second seed. They knocked off Lynn in their opening and then won their semi-final game on March 5 with a 50 to 44 victory over Nova Southeastern. Tamilio led the team with 15 points and 4 assists. In the championship game, they faced Rollins and fell to the Tars by a score of 65 to 56. Jennifer Tamilio and Ty-anna Caravano of Tech made the all-tournament team.

Somewhat surprisingly, the Lady Panthers received an at-large bid to the NCAA South Region Tournament at the University of Central Arkansas in Conway, Arkansas. There, they faced Valdosta State on March 11. Unfortunately, their season ended with a disappointing 67 to 49 loss. That resulted in a record for the season of 21 wins and 10 losses.

The 2006-2007 squad would prove to be another strong Lady Panther team. When the Lady Panthers opened the conference schedule on December 2, 2006, with a 62 to 53 victory over Eckerd, their record stood at 7 and 1 for the season. Senior guards Danielle Vaughn and Jennifer Tamilio were pacing the team.

The 2006 Florida Tech Holiday Classic matched the Panthers with Albany State on December 29, followed the next day by a game against Fort Valley State. Florida Tech crushed Albany State in the opener by a score of 79 to 40, led by 25 points from Merritt Island High graduate Kristin Heminger. They followed that with a 62 to 56 victory over Fort Valley. Danise Fequire, a 6-1 senior center, led scorers with 14 points. The win extended the Panthers' record to 9 and 2 for the season.

When the Panthers faced Tampa on January 10, 2007, they had won 4 games in a row and 10 of their last 11 games. However, a disappointing performance against Tampa ended in a 55 to 46 home defeat.

However, they soon recovered and their 55 to 52 victory over Rollins on January 24 put them in first place in the conference with a 7 and 1 conference record and 15 and 3 overall record. Jennifer Tamilio's 27 points led the way against the Tars. By February 17, when they defeated Nova Southeastern by a score of 44 to 33, the Lady Panthers had run their record to 21 and 4 (13 and 2 in conference) and were ranked

20th in NCAA Division II. Danielle Vaughn came off the bench with 13 points and 6 rebounds to key the victory.

Florida Today reported on February 28, 2007, that John Reynolds had been named Coach of the Year in the Sunshine State Conference for the 5th time in his career. Jennifer Tamilio, who had averaged 14.1 points per game, was named as the conference's Woman's Basketball Player of the Year.

The Lady Panthers entered the conference post-season tourney seeded second. They began the tournament on March 1 with an 89 to 64 rout of Florida Southern, led by 20 points each from Tamilio and McKena Richardson. However, they were eliminated in the tourney semi-finals with a 66 to 58 loss to Tampa.

Despite the loss to Tampa, the Lady Panthers received an at-large bid to the NCAA South Region Division II Tournament where they would face Delta State which was ranked 5th nationally. That March 9 game was decided quickly when Delta State jumped out to a 17 to 2 lead in the first 7 minutes of the game on their way to a 66 to 50 win. Tamilio noted: "I think we played scared early." Reynolds added: "They just played great defense on everybody." This ended the 2006-2007season for the Panthers with a record of 23 and 7.

An article in the winter 2007 edition of *Florida Tech Today* magazine by Christa Parulis-Kaye celebrated Reynolds' 20 years of coaching at the school. The most moving passage in the article related the fact that Reynolds had coached his daughter Laurissa for 3-years at Florida Tech. Reynolds recalled witnessing Laurissa score a 3-pointer that tied the game in the semifinals of the 2024 Conference Tournament, sending the game to overtime where the Panthers would prevail and advance to the championship game.

Florida Today reported on October 26, 2010, that the Lady Panthers had high hopes for the 2020-2011 season. Tamara Dowdell, a 6-3 center, was returning from an injury suffered during the previous season. Lynisha Nelson, a local product and a two-time all-conference selection, returned at point guard.

As *Florida Today* reported on November 10, the opening game of the 2010-2011 season would mark Reynold's 662nd game as Florida Tech head coach and the commencement of his 24th season directing the program. At that point, Reynolds had a record of 421 wins and 240 losses.

The Panthers started the season strong with 4 wins before falling to Georgia Southwestern on November 26 by a 65 to 56 score in the Rollins Thanksgiving Classic. The following night, however, they bounced back with a 77 to 60 win over Missouri-St. Louis, behind Nelson's 15 points, 9 assists and 5 rebounds.

The Lady Panthers began the conference schedule on December 4 with a 59 to 53 victory over St. Leo. That took their record to 7 and 1 on the season.

On December 18, Florida Tech won its opening game in its Christmas Tournament by defeating Palm Beach Atlantic by a score of 67 to 56. The following night, they won the tournament with a 73 to 57 win over West Florida. Junior guard Ashton McClairen led the scoring with 17 points and was named the Most Valuable Player of the tourney. The win extended the Panthers' record to 10 and 1 for the season.

The Panthers lost 2 straight conference games in January 2011 before breaking the streak with a 72 to 48 win over Lynn on January 12 behind 23 points from Ashton McClairen. That brought them to a record of 13 and 3 for the season and 2 and 2 in the conference. A 59 to 58 squeaker over Barry followed on January 15. McClairen again led the scoring with 20 points. A 62 to 58 victory at Rollins on January 19 was highlighted by a perfect 16 for 16 free throw shooting. When they beat Tampa on January 26 by a 91 to 82 overtime score, their record improved to 17 and 3 overall and 6 and 3 in the conference.

The Panthers suffered their first home loss of the season on February 10 when they dropped an overtime thriller to Nova Southeastern by a 73 to 69 margin. February 23 was senior night for the Lady Panthers. Lynisha Nelson, Kristen Dixon and Tamara Dowdell were honored. Unfortunately, Rollins tainted the celebration by defeating the Panthers by a 66 to 60 score, dropping Florida Tech to 21 and 6 overall and 10 and 5 in the conference.

The Lady Panthers opened the Sunshine State Conference on their home floor with a 64 to 52 victory over Nova Southeastern. Lynisha Nelson led the way with 22 points, 5 rebounds and 4 steals. The Panthers faced Tampa in the semifinal game on March 5 and came away with a 75 to 62 victory behind Nelson's 16 points, 10 assists and 4 steals. That vaulted Florida Tech into the championship game against Florida Southern on March 6. However, Florida Southern proved to be too much for the Panthers as they cruised to a 79 to 66 victory, despite 26 points and 6 steals from Nelson.

Despite the loss in the conference championship, Florida Tech was selected for a berth in the NCAA South Regional in Russellville, Arkansas, where they would face their old foe Tampa on March 11. The game developed as a barn-burner won by Florida Tech by a score of 56 to 54 when Nelson hit 2 free throws with .7 seconds on the clock.

In the second round of the regional tournament on March 12, 2011, Florida Tech faced the tall task of playing the nation's number 1 ranked Division II team, Arkansas Tech. The Panthers gave Arkansas Tech all that it could handle before falling by an 83 to 74 score. McClairen led the team with 20 points while Nelson added 17 points. The Panthers ended the season with a record of 24 wins and 9 losses.

Lynisha Nelson ended her career as a three-time All Sunshine State Conference first team selection and two-time conference Defensive Player of the Year. Reynolds commented: "The saddest part about losing tonight's game is that's the last time I'm going to coach our three seniors on the floor."

Lynisha Nelson was a native of Melbourne who had played high school basketball at Melbourne Central Catholic. She played at Florida Tech from 2007 to 2011. She earned All-South Region honors in 3 of those seasons. She was twice selected Sunshine State Conference Defensive Player of the Year and 3 times selected to the first team All-Conference team. In her senior season, the women won 24 games and advanced to the second round of the NCAA tournament before losing to Arkansas Tech. John Reynolds stated that Nelson had the highest basketball IQ of anyone he coached. After graduation, she played basketball with the Brevard Flame, a women's semi-pro team before enlisting and serving in the U.S. Army. She was inducted into the Florida Tech Sports Hall of Fame in 2018.

On November 24, 2014, *Florida Today* reported that Reynolds was closing in on the milestone of 500 victories. The previous day, the Panthers had won their second straight game of the season by beating Fort Valley State 83 to 71 behind 36 points from Kayk Wilson, a senior from Viera High School. Reynolds achieved his 500th win with a 76-60 victory over Eckerd College on December 6. The following day, *Florida Today* wrote that Reynolds had grown to learn that there was more to basketball than winning. He said: "But I think what happens over the years is you realize it is the relationship with your players and alumni that is so much more important than that."

The winter 2015 edition of *Florida Tech Today* noted that the Panthers had run their unbeaten streak to 12 games when they defeated Eckerd on December 6. Even more notably, that win was Reynolds' 500th victory as coach of Florida Tech, making him only the 11th active Division II coach to attain that mark. Senior forward Jasmine Brown described Reynolds by saying: "He makes me a better person on and off the court. It's not just about basketball with him. He teaches life skills that will carry on after college."

John Reynolds and his team celebrated when he won his 500th coaching victory in 2014. *Photo from University Archives.*

By December 20, Florida Tech had run its record to 15 wins without a loss with a 95 to 75 win over Shaw in the final game of the CarMax Holiday Tournament at the Clemente Center. Kayk Wilson led the way with 31 points and was named Most Valuable Player of the tournament. Wilson was averaging 22.1 points per game at that time.

The Lady Panthers took their winning streak to a school record 15 games before losing to Rollins by a 72 to 65 score on January 21, 2015. Jasmine Brown had 20 points for Florida Tech but 18 turnovers doomed the Panthers. When the Panthers edged Florida Southern on February 14 by a 59-58 margin, their record stood at 19 and 3 overall and 9 and 3 in the conference. However, three straight losses in the conference dropped the Panthers to fourth place in the conference with a 9 and 6 record. A loss to Tampa in the opening game of the conference tournament on March 5 ended their season with an overall record of 20 and 7 and a conference record of 10 and 6. Kayk Wilson led the conference in scoring for the second consecutive year with 19.3 points per game. She also was named to the all-conference first team for the second consecutive year.

The 2015-2016 season was the 30th season for Florida Tech women's basketball. The Panthers anticipated that they would be young but talented. Tiesha Flagler would be team captain while Shequana Harris and DeLise Williams would share point guard duties. Tereza Sedlakova, sister of all-time leading scorer of men's basketball Justin Sedlak, was a highly anticipated newcomer.

The season started off slowly for Florida Tech. When the Lady Panthers fell to unbeaten Sioux Falls on November 27, their record fell to 3 and 2 on the season. Shequana Harris led the Panthers with 16 points, 7 rebounds, 4 assists and 4 steals.

On December 5, 2015, the Panthers knocked off previously undefeated and defending national champions Florida Southern, snapping their 12-game home winning streak. DeLise Williams scored 24 points to lead the 73 to 61 victory.

Florida Tech hosted the CarMax Holiday Classic at the Clemente Center on December 19 and 20, 2015. The Panthers romped in the opening game, beating Fort Valley State by the lopsided margin of 72 to 45. Tiesha Flagler had 19 points and 10 rebounds to pace the victory. The Lady Panthers suffered an 81 to 73 defeat at the hands of Drury on the final day of the conference. DeLise Williams led the Panthers with 18 points while Tiesha Flagler added 17 points. The loss brought the Panthers' season record to 8 wins and 3 losses.

The Lady Panthers gained possession of second place in the Sunshine State Conference on January 27, 2016, with a 49 to 46 victory over Tampa, improving the Panthers' record to 13 and 5. They entered the post-season tournament as the second seed. In the quarterfinal game of the tourney on March 2, Florida Tech defeated Eckerd by a score of 70 to 62, led by Harris' 26 points. Flagler added 12 points and 9 rebounds. The Panthers followed that up with a 71 to 62 win over Florida Southern in the semifinals. Shequana Harris led the Panthers with 21 points.

Florida Tech lost to Tampa in the final of the conference tournament on March 6. That brought the Panthers' record to 20 and 9 on the season, good enough to gain them an at-large bid to the South Region of the NCAA Division II Women's Basketball Tournament.

The Lady Panthers fell 51 to 30 to Benedict in the first round of the tournament on March 11, 2016 at Union, Tennessee. That completed Florida Tech's season with a record of 20 wins and 10 losses.

That 2015-2016 season was the last 20-win season for Reynolds. However, Reynolds' success cannot be counted by mere wins and losses. As Coach Reynolds told *Florida Today* on March 11, 2011: "At Florida Tech, I get to coach kids the rest of their lives because I'm always in touch with them and they're always in touch with me." The real impact of John Reynolds is measured by the lives he has changed. A poignant article in *Florida Today* on December 25, 2010, described the impact that he had on one of his players, Tamara Dowdell. Dowdell grew up in impoverished Pahokee, one of four children of a single mother. Dowdell herself had a child at age 15. Dowdell graduated from Florida Tech with an accounting degree, cum laude, playing her final year while pursuing a master's degree. Dowdell explained: "This program and Coach Reynolds. I just feel very blessed to be here." The bond between Reynolds and Dowdell is only one example of the hundreds of lives that Reynolds has positively impacted during his 37-year career as coach of the Lady Panthers.

Prior to the start of the 2022-2023 season Reynolds' overall record was 586 wins and 390 losses, with a conference record of 290 wins and 233 losses. That ranks him among the 20 winningest Division II coaches of all-time and among the 10 winningest active coaches. His record of lives changed is incalculable.

Notes

- The results of specific basketball games are, unless stated otherwise, derived from the edition of *Florida Today* on the day following the day of the game.
- Information regarding Reynolds has been gleaned from his biography posted on the Florida Tech Athletics website in addition to the newspaper articles cited.
- Information regarding King, Keenan, Radenkovic and the 2001-2002 team was also derived from the biographies of these players and the description of the team on the Hall of Fame section of the official website for Florida Tech athletics.
- Lanisha Nelson's play with the Brevard Flame was reported in the May 13, 2011, edition of *Florida Today*.
- I originally drafted this chapter to be titled "Reynolds Becomes a Legend." In his typically modest fashion, John strongly objected to being labelled a legend. He firmly explained that he envisioned his role as a coach as one of molding lives and developing relationships rather than seeking fame. He almost surely will object to being labelled an institution as well. I probably have not yet identified the correct descriptor of John but I can say with certainty that he is a great teacher of basketball and an even better teacher of life who has had a positive effect on dozens of young women and changed numerous lives for the better.

CHAPTER SEVEN:
MEN'S ROWING BECOMES A NATIONAL POWER

By William K. Jurgens

The two individuals who were significant in the establishment and development of Florida Tech rowing were Jerome P. Keuper, founding president of Florida Tech, and Robert H. Dunlap, assistant to the president and later director of boat acquisitions at Florida Tech. Dr. Keuper first acquired an interest in rowing as an undergraduate at the Massachusetts Institute of Technology (MIT) where he watched their rowing team practice on the Charles River. He envisioned that the prominence of rowing at MIT could also be realized at F.I.T. Robert Dunlap had a profound effect on the rowing program at Florida Tech. He not only shared in Dr. Keuper's vision of having a successful rowing program, he also oversaw the operations of the rowing program through its formative years. Dunlap's enthusiasm and commitment to the program resulted in him being presented on May 24, 1978, with a plaque recognizing him as "The Father of F.I.T. Crew."

Competitive Highlights

1960s

Florida Tech began its rowing program in the 1968-1969 academic year. There were just over two eights of rowers and coxswains who joined the first-year program. This provided good competition for making the first boat. The regular season competition consisted of dual matches between Rollins College, Florida Southern College, and University of Tampa. Though Florida Tech lost to these more experienced rowing programs, the varsity eight did finish within a boat length of the University of Tampa. The last race of the season was the Florida Intercollegiate Rowing Association (FIRA) Championship held in Jacksonville, Florida. The coaches from Rollins, Florida Southern, Tampa, and Jacksonville agreed to allow Florida Tech to row in the Freshman category since this was their first year of intercollegiate rowing. Jacksonville University, the host program, provided Florida Tech with one of its rowing shells to race in, which was an upgrade from the refurbished boat they were using, "Hugh F. McKeen."

The varsity eight that represented Florida Tech in the 1969 state rowing championship was comprised of rowers who were highly motivated, physically F.I.T., and rowed well together. Rowing against the other well-coached teams, Florida Tech managed an early lead and held on to win the race. Bill Jurgens, who officiated the race, had this response to Bob Dunlap when asked what he thought of their winning performance, "they did everything wrong, but they did it together." Jurgens then proceeded to congratulate Dunlap on the crew's victory at its first state rowing championship. The student coach of the Florida Tech rowing team was Alex Popow, who was a former Brown University rower now studying at Florida Tech. Also providing coaching assistance was student coach Charlie Griffiths. Additional coaching assistance for the Florida Tech rowing team were coaches and rowers from Princeton University, who had their winter training session based at the Florida Tech Anchorage, which had been arranged by Bob Dunlap working with Princeton's head rowing coach, Pete Sparhawk. Members of this first state championship crew were coxswain George Bangs, stroke John Westerman, 7-Mike Guile (captain), 6-Ray Walker, 5-Dave Marcus, 4-Dick York, 3-Ira Baskin, 2-John Roller, and bow Ken Watts.

1970s

The second year (1969-1970) of the program welcomed the addition of Bill Jurgens as the head rowing coach. Jurgens relocated to Melbourne, Florida after graduating from Jacksonville University where he rowed for four years. Returning to his hometown made the transition much easier, especially given that Jurgens needed to teach science at Eau Gallie Junior High School since Florida Tech was unable to provide a salary his first year.

The first race of the season was against the University of Tampa. This 2,000-meter (approximately one mile and a quarter) race started on the southeast side of the Melbourne causeway and proceeded across the open channel to the finish line on the west side of the Indian River. This first race for Coach Jurgens as Florida Tech's head rowing coach was far from what he expected. It turned out that on this day, March 7, 1970, there was a total eclipse of the sun (known as "the eclipse of the century") which may have influenced the windy and deteriorating water conditions at race time. There were three eight person shells lined up for the race: Florida Tech's varsity eight, University of Tampa's varsity eight, and Florida Tech's junior varsity eight. The crews handled the conditions well for the first 1,000 meters with Florida Tech's varsity rowing to one boat length of open water lead on Tampa, and Tampa with a boat length lead on Florida Tech's JV eight. However, as Florida Tech's varsity rowed through the bridge opening in the causeway they began taking on water until they swamped. This same scenario happened to Tampa's eight as it entered the open water of the channel. However, the Florida Tech junior varsity eight was able to row through the rough water while only losing an oar that was knocked out of its oarlock by the rough water. The submerged Florida Tech varsity eight was able to turn its hull before the wind blew the boat through the opening in the bridge, thus sustaining no damage. Unfortunately, Tampa's eight was unable to turn its boat in time and it became locked on the bridge pilings. A spectator's yacht was nearby and one of its members, Tom Adams (Florida's Secretary of State at the time) dove into the water fully clothed and tied a rope to one of the shell's riggers. The yacht pulled the shell off the pilings and returned it to the nearby boathouse. Fortunately, no one was injured in this race and the damaged shell was easily repaired; however, the lesson learned was that rowing across the Indian River channel was too much of a risk, which resulted in limiting future races across the channel.

The 1970-1971 season expanded from the previous year of having a varsity and junior varsity eight to having three eights with August Burrichter as the freshman crew coach. Jurgens and the crew set their sights on Rollins College, which became a rivalry throughout the decade. During the early '70s it was common for Florida Tech rowers and coaches to greet one another by saying, "beat Rollins." In a dual race with Rollins in the spring of 1971, Florida Tech beat Rollins in the varsity and JV eights and tying them in the freshman eight. Several weeks later, at the FIRA Championship, Rollins beat Florida Tech's varsity by two-thirds of a length. Also 1971 was the first year in which Florida Tech participated in the Dad Vail Regatta. The team finished a respectable fifth place overall, which included third place in the freshman eight event, sixth place in the JV eight, and seventh place in the varsity eight (*The Washington Post*, May 9, 1971).

In the 1971-1972 season the men's varsity continued to grow and become more successful. In a race with perennial Dad Vail power Marietta College, Florida Tech was victorious over Marietta's lightweight eight by almost a boat length on its home course. Jurgens remembers telling his lightweight eight before the race not to show any emotion when they beat the defending lightweight eight Dad Vail champion. However, their excitement over this accomplishment could not be contained as they yelled and splashed water on one another. The Florida Tech lightweight eight went on to finish third in the lightweight eight event at the Dad Vail Regatta behind the Coast Guard Academy and Marietta College (Lindamood, 1994). The Dad Vail Regatta, a National Open Intercollegiate Rowing Championship was established as a championship for rowing programs that were not major rowing programs in the United States. As such, it is annually the largest intercollegiate rowing championship in the country. Also, in 1972 the Florida Tech Rowing Team won the first FIRA Overall Florida Rowing Championship title, which was given for the first time, but again finished second to Rollins in the men's varsity eight.

The Florida Tech men's rowing program finally captured the men's varsity eight championship at the 1974 FIRA Championship. This event was held on Lake Buena Vista in Disney World. On hand for the event was Dr. Jerome Keuper, president of Florida Tech. He would not be disappointed, given that Florida Tech finally reached its goal of winning the men's varsity eight at the state championship, and again won the overall state championship title. The margin of victory for the varsity eight was one half length over Florida Technological University (FTU), and a length over Rollins College. The Lake Buena Vista course was 1,750 meters (250 meters short of the Olympic distance of 2,000 meters). Florida Tech got off to a strong start and led after 500 meters, but FTU edged ahead of F.I.T. at 1,000 meters. Florida Tech had waited too long for this opportunity and were not to be denied as they summoned the strength to row through FTU to win by two seconds (Crimson, April 28, 1974). The Florida Tech varsity eight was comprised of coxswain Gene Jeffords, stroke Matt Stoudt, 7-Casey Baker, 6-Joe Eckelman, 5-Howard Rivenburg, 4-Tom Breeden (captain), 3-Don Bee, 2-Bill Hoppe, and bow Bill McGovern. Dr. Keuper and Bob Dunlap had miniature gold trophies made for each member of the team. The inscription on the trophy was "F.I.T. Crew, State Champs, 1974."

Another significant year of improvement for the men's varsity rowing team was the 1974-1975 season. In the Dad Vail Regatta, the team finished tied with the Coast Guard Academy with 18 points apiece for the combined overall title that included 46 participating schools. The tie breaker was determined by the highest placed finish in the varsity heavyweight eight event, which resulted in the Coast Guard Academy being awarded the Dad Vail Regatta title. Florida Tech was first in the men's varsity lightweight eight, first in the JV lightweight eight, first in the men's frosh/novice heavyweight eight, and first in the men's frosh/novice heavyweight four-with. Bill Jurgens coached the winning men's varsity lightweight eight and men's JV lightweight eight crews; Norton Schlachter coached the winning frosh/novice eight crew; and John Hennon coached the winning men's frosh/novice four-with, which was from Florida Tech's Jensen Beach campus.[2]

The 1974-1975 season also marked the first time Florida Tech Jensen Beach competed in the Dad Vail Regatta. Coach Jurgens supported the Florida Tech Jensen Beach campus by providing them with an eight-person rowing shell and assisting the Jensen Beach rowing program during its start-up. Coincidentally, the shell provided to them was the same boat, the Hugh F. McKeen, that Florida Tech used when it started its rowing program.

---

[2] See Appendix 3: Dad Vail Regatta Men's Champions – names and coaches.

After a two-year lapse (1975 loss to Rollins and 1976 loss to FTU) in winning the varsity eight at the FIRA Championship, the 1977 men's varsity eight began an unprecedented win streak that continued through the '70s and '80s. This string of successes in the men's varsity eight and as overall FIRA champion established Florida Tech as the team to beat. The Florida Tech rowing successes also garnered attention from high school rowers as a university in which they would receive an outstanding education and be a part of a rowing program with a winning tradition. Consequently, the size of the men's rowing programs grew to between 55 and 85 student-athletes in the '80s.

The men's varsity eight began its focus on winning the varsity eight at the Dad Vail Regatta. In 1977 Florida Tech's varsity eight, coming off victories in the FIRA Champion and SIRA Championship, proved that it was a strong contender to challenge the U.S. Coast Guard Academy for the varsity eight title at the Dad Vail Regatta. In the 1977 final of the varsity eight, Florida Tech finished three seconds (three-quarters of a boat length) behind the Coast Guard Academy, who were the defending Dad Vail champion in this event.

The 1978 men's varsity eight race at the Dad Vail Regatta proved to be another close race in that Florida Tech again finished second (three-quarters of a boat length) to a strong Coast Guard Academy rowing program. There was a total of fifty schools participating in this year's regatta. Members of the 1978 men's varsity eight were coxswain Walt Faulconer, stroke Jim Vega, 7-Brad Peale, 6-Dan Copeland, 5-Mike Leblanc, 4-Biff Schied, 3-Eric Smith, 2-Pat Langley, and bow Steve Johnson.

The consistency of being one of the top rowing programs at the Dad Vail Regatta led Dr. Jerome Keuper, president of Florida Tech, to send the varsity eight to the Henley Royal Regatta as part of the university's 20th anniversary. The Henley Royal Regatta is the most prestigious rowing regatta in the world and participating in this rowing championship is a reward for many United States rowing teams who performed well in their regular season. Dr. Keuper asked his good friend, and member of the university's board of trustees, Ralph Evinrude, CEO of Evinrude Outboard Marine Corporation, to fund the varsity eight to the Henley Royal Regatta, which he agreed to do. In a board of trustees meeting following the event, Evinrude provided a summary of his rowing days at Wisconsin by saying he enjoyed his rowing days at Wisconsin under Emerson "Dad" Vail (for whom the Dad Vail Regatta is named) and he jokingly said, "I no longer want to be in a boat unless it has a motor." A framed Florida Institute of Technology pennant was presented to Florida Tech by Dr. O. A. Holzer. Holzer waved this pennant from the Henley Regatta Enclosure while cheering for Florida

Tech's varsity eight in its dual race against Harvard University. The plaque accompanying the framed pennant read, "Pennant waved by Dr. and Mrs. O. A. Holzer when F.I.T. defeated Harvard University at the Henley Regatta on June 29, 1978."[3]

1980s

The 1982 men's crew, coached by a young Bill Jurgens, brought home all kinds of hardware, including a national championship
Photo from University Archives.

The 1982 Dad Vail Regatta was seen by the Florida Tech rowing program as the culmination of over a decade of work. Florida Tech became the first team from the south to capture the men's varsity eight title and become the overall champion at the Dad Vail Regatta. Prior to the Dad Vail Regatta, the Panther season was going as planned until the men's varsity crew began its defense of the men's varsity and junior varsity eights at the SIRA Championship. Earlier in the year the Florida Tech men's varsity eight defeated Yale University in an exhibition race on the Tampa Bypass Canal. Yale went on to have an undefeated season. The last preparation before going to the Dad Vail Regatta was fine-

---

[3] See Appendix 3: Dad Vail Regatta Men's Champions – names and coaches

tuning the crews on one of the finest 2,000-meter courses in the country, the Melton Hill Lake in Oakridge, Tennessee. A strong Purdue University rowing program coached by Kevin Sauer defeated the Florida Tech men's varsity and junior varsity eights by one-half length in both races. Florida Tech had trained hard and was mentally prepared to do what was required of them to win, but it was not to be. As each of these Florida Tech crews placed their boats on the racks, rowers collapsed to the ground underneath their boats. It was obvious that it was not for a lack of effort that Florida Tech finished second in these two races. The Florida Tech coaches got together and developed a plan that would help the team reach its peak performance in two weeks for the Dad Vail Regatta, because it was going to take a peak performance to win this race. There was no complaining or questioning one another by coaches or rowers, it was about using the next two weeks to achieve a goal that everyone had hoped and worked hard for the past nine months. The intense seat racing and the three back-to-back 2,000-meter races on Sunday before the regatta were a testament that the team would not be outworked by any of the other 60 participating schools. The workload was reduced the four days before Friday's heats, so the glycogen stores could be replenished to full capacity by race day. The Florida Tech men's rowing program was up to the task, which showed in their first-place finishes in the men's varsity eight, men's junior varsity eight, and men's lightweight four. The Florida Tech men's frosh/novice program coached by John Stillings finished second in three races: men's frosh/novice lightweight eight, men's frosh/novice heavyweight eight, and men's frosh/novice four. The preparation for this successful day extended far beyond the previous nine months; it involved Coach Steve Wagner's 1979 Dad Vail victories in the men's frosh/novice four and the men's frosh/novice eight, and Glenn Bunting's winning 1980 men's frosh/novice eight. All these crews paved the way for the 1982 men's varsity eight victory. Norman Hildes-Heim's heading for his article in *The New York Times* read "Florida Tech Excels in Dad Vail Regatta," and he summarized the varsity eight race by saying, "Florida Tech and Temple battled for the lead over the entire 2,000-meter distance of the course. After an initial one-seat lead in the first 500 meters, Florida Tech was overtaken by higher-stroking Temple, who pulled ahead by 20 feet at the 1,500-meter mark. Florida Tech, seemingly biding its time until this point, drove its racing cadence to 38 strokes to the minute, and edged ahead, winning by 3 seconds in a time of 6 minutes 8.6 seconds." Also in 1982, with help from the winning women's varsity four-with, Florida Tech captured its first-ever Dad Vail Regatta Combined All-Points Trophy.

The overall success of the men's and women's rowing program is evidenced by the point trophies given to Florida Tech for its dominance in rowing in the southeast. The Cypress Gardens Combined All-Points Trophy for the FIRA Championship lists Florida Institute of Technology as the winner in this combined overall champion category every year from 1972 to 1992. The Stone Mountain Park Points Trophy lists Florida Institute of Technology as the winner from 1972 to 1987 except in 1984 when Marietta College captured it. After the 1984 SIRA Championship, Ralph Lindamood, head coach of Marietta College, sent the overall championship plaque to Bill Jurgens, head coach of the Florida Tech Rowing program and wrote in an accompanying letter that Florida Tech deserved the overall championship title more than Marietta since Tech had won all the major events. Jurgens wrote back to Lindamood that he appreciated his magnanimous gesture, but Marietta College would be inscribed on the plaque since they won it according to the rules.

After the 1982 season, Florida Tech continued its winning ways by capturing Dad Vail Regatta gold in men's frosh/novice events, men's junior varsity eight events, and lightweight events. Florida Tech won the frosh/novice event in 1984 and 1987. The men's junior varsity eight event was won in 1983, 1985, and 1986. The men's lightweight eight event was won in 1983 and 1987. In addition, Florida Tech won the 1983 men's lightweight four event. From '83 to '89 the men's varsity eight consistently boated outstanding crews: they were second in 1983, seventh in 1984, second in 1985, second in 1986, third in 1987, first in 1988, and second in 1989. In addition to the combined overall champion title, the Dad Vail Regatta in 1986 instituted a men's overall champion trophy as well as a women's overall champion trophy. The successes of the above-mentioned crews helped Florida Tech win the 1986, 1987, and 1988-men's overall champion trophies. Additionally, Florida Tech again won the combined (men and women) overall championship trophy in 1987.

The 1988 Florida Tech men's varsity eight knew it was going to be a challenge to wrestle away the men's varsity eight title from Temple University, especially since it was on their home course, and they had won this event the previous five years. But the Florida Tech varsity eight had prepared well for this race and their performances up to this race garnered them the number one seed. Their race strategy was either win or finish back in the pack; it called for them not to take the rating down until they had a half-boat length lead on Temple. They got the half-boat length lead by 750 meters then made the shift down to a more sustainable rating and maintained that lead to the finish. A photograph on the sports page of the *Philadelphia Enquirer* shows Temple in the foreground with Florida Tech in the background with raised arms, and the caption underneath reads, "Crew from Florida topples Temple in Dad Vail varsity eight contest." Norman Hildes-Heim's article in *The New York Times* stated: "Florida Institute of Technology ended Temple University's five-year reign as the men's varsity heavyweight rowing champion of the Dad Vail Regatta, defeating the Owls today in the eight-oared final to win the Tom Conville Cup. This was the 50th anniversary of the Dad Vail Regatta, the small-college season ending championship. It attracted more than 3,500 competitors from 89 schools."[4]

1988 Dad Vail Varsity Heavyweight Champions. *Photo from University Archives.*

1990s

In 1994 the men's varsity four, coached by Casey Baker, finished first at the Dad Vail Regatta. As a result of their outstanding performance, the Dad Vail Regatta Race Committee provided this crew with financial assistance to go to the Henley Royal Regatta in Henley-on-Thames, England.

In 1995 the Florida Tech's men's varsity four-with, coached by Casey Baker, finished first. As in 1994, the Dad Vail Regatta Race Committee provided financial support to defray the cost of sending the heavyweight four-with to the Henley Royal Regatta. Additionally, the men's lightweight four-with won in their event. Casey Baker had the following to say about the successes of the two fours in 1995, "What an

---

[4] See Appendix 3: Dad Vail Regatta Men's Champions – names and coaches.

accomplishment for both the lightweight varsity four-with and the heavyweight varsity four-with to not only win their events but set course records. The thrill for the entire team, and the coach, was exceptional." Baker added, "We could not leave the lightweights home after their win, so the team voted to raise the money needed to also send the lightweights to Henley," Baker also said, "When I was asked why I didn't combine the two fours to make a heavyweight varsity 8, I replied, they just rowed better in the fours and they proved it."

In 1996 the Florida Tech men's lightweight eight won their event at the Dad Vail Regatta. The success of this crew at the Dad Vail Regatta led the Race Committee to fund this boat (roundtrip transportation costs) to the Henley Royal Regatta. Florida Tech's men's lightweight eight was accepted by the Henley Royal Regatta to participate in the Temple Challenge Cup.

The 1998 Dad Vail Regatta saw Florida Tech men's crews capture medals in two events. The men's varsity lightweight eight captured gold by defeating second place Villanova University by seven seconds. The other crew to capture a medal was the men's varsity four-with-coxswain, which won a silver medal. Members of this boat were coxswain Alex Samaras, stroke Andreja Vasiljevic, 3 – Dan Dubiel, 2 – Adam Schoell, and bow Josh Green with Casey Baker as coach. The finals of the 1998 Dad Vail Regatta had to be postponed from Saturday to Sunday because of the damage done to the course by a powerful weather front that wiped out the lane buoys and left debris on the course. Without buoys, the course for Sunday's finals was shortened to approximately 1,200 meters beginning at the bridge, so the course was now straight to minimize problems.[5]

2000s

During the first five years in the new century, the rowing program was again without athletic scholarships. Though it was not common, there were, on occasion budget reductions by Florida Tech which impacted athletic scholarships. However, this lack of athletic scholarships did not affect the 2004 frosh/novice four-with who captured Florida Tech's first Dad Vail Regatta championship of the 2000s under Coach Marc Mandel. In 2005 Coach Mandel took the winning experience of the previous year's frosh/novice four-with to build a formidable varsity eight. It was remarkable how well Florida Tech's varsity eight did, given that they were in lane six.

---

[5] See Appendix 3: Dad Vail Regatta Men's Champions – names and coaches.

This historically is considered a slower lane to race in on the dog-leg course in which they start behind other boats and the current is typically slower. Coach Mandel said their strategy made a difference. He told his crew, "Go after it like we are racing a thousand meters and let the adrenaline carry you through the second thousand meters." They went through the bridge at the turn in the course (750 meters into the race) ahead of the field and went on to finish second to the University of Michigan by three-quarters of a boat length. Members of the 2005 men's varsity eight were coxswain Ken Gottschalk, stroke Andrew Merlino, 7-Ryan Burton, 6-Ryan Strauss, 5-Nick Nistal, 4-Steve Plunket, 3-Tim Watson, 2-Gabe Candelaria, bow Logan Soya and Coach Mark Mandel.

Similarly, in 2007, the men's varsity eight found themselves in lane six again at the Dad Vail Regatta. Like the '05 varsity eight, they powered through the first 750 meters and through the turn at the bridge to position themselves slightly ahead of the field. By the finish, the varsity eight rowed to a third-place finish, winning a Dad Vail Regatta bronze medal. This crew's positive attitude and belief in one another were reasons they were successful in confronting challenging circumstances. Members of the 2007 men's varsity eight were coxswain Aliyah Snyder, stroke Taylor Brown, 7-Kevin Moore, 6-Jimmy Woodard, 5-Gabe Candelaria, 4-Tyler Jandreau, 3-Paul Bunkers, 2-Chris Lambert, and bow Jeff Tessier. Also in 2007, the Men's Frosh/Novice Lightweight eight etched their names in history by winning the Dad Vail Regatta.[6]

2010s

The men's varsity rowing program achieved greatness during this decade, reaching the pinnacle of success in 2015 and 2016 by winning the varsity eight in the Dad Vail Regatta. Coach Jim Granger's rowing teams performed at record breaking levels during this time. One such accomplishment was that from 2010-2016 they were the only rowing program to medal every year at the Dad Vail Regatta. Additionally, they had two first place finishes in the varsity 8, and they were second in the varsity 8 three times. Another great accomplishment was winning the Dad Vail Regatta in the men's varsity four-with in 2013 and 2022.

The 2015 victory of the men's varsity eight at the Dad Vail Regatta was a special race that will go down in the annals of the Dad Vail Regatta as one of the best races ever rowed. Twenty-seven years had elapsed since Florida Tech last won (1988) the varsity eight race at the Dad Vail Regatta. In the previous four years, Florida Tech was literally inches away from victory. In 2012 they lost to the University of Michigan by .342 of

---

[6] See Appendix 3: Dad Vail Regatta Men's Champions – names and coaches.

a second. So, there was hope and anticipation that this was going to be the year. As the race proceeded it was clear that defending champion Michigan and Florida Tech were going to battle it out to see who would be the winner of the varsity eight, the premier event of the regatta. As the two crews passed under the bridge (1,200 meters to go) Michigan had a third of a boat length lead over Florida Tech. This led the Channel 6 (ABC in Philadelphia) announcer to say, "Florida Tech has always performed well at the Dad Vail but was always a bridesmaid." As the race progressed Michigan increased their lead to one full boat length at 700 meters to go, which led the Florida Tech varsity eight to increase their rowing cadence to 40 strokes a minute, an unheard-of rating for this far from the finish line.

Ernestas Zaeskis, who rowed in the seven seat, said, "We knew that to win we had to begin the charge at this point or not accomplish our goal." The television announcers were amazed by how Florida Tech kept increasing its rating from 40 to 42, to 44, to 46, all the way to 48 strokes per minute as the team began to move through Michigan. It was not just the high stroke rating but watching the crew continue to get positive run in that the two man's puddle was past the eight man's puddle by over a foot. It was clear that no other crew could withstand Florida Tech's magical performance by all eight rowers and the coxswain. At the finish line Florida Tech's varsity eight won in a photo finish by .75 of a second over Michigan. This led the announcer to say that Florida Tech was no longer a bridesmaid.

Other major accomplishments were the men's varsity eight gold medal finishes in the SIRA Championship in the following years: 2009, 2010, 2011, 2013, 2015, 2016, 2017, 2018, and 2019. Florida Tech also qualified for the Intercollegiate Rowing Association (IRA) Championship from 2013 to 2019, finishing as high as 14th in this major national rowing championship. In 2011 the men's varsity eight competed in the Henley Royal Regatta. In 2010 the varsity eight won the Head of the Charles Regatta in the men's collegiate eight, and in 2016 the men's collegiate four-with finished first at the Head of the Charles Regatta with a boat of freshmen. [7]

2020s (2020-present)

Continuing its winning ways, the men's varsity program competed in the men's varsity heavyweight four-with at the 2022 Dad Vail Regatta. LaSalle University was a favorite to win this event by those programs who had competed against them during the regular season. In the final

---

[7] See Appendix 3: Dad Vail Regatta Men's Champions – names and coaches.

---

of the four-with, Florida Tech and LaSalle were bow to bow with each exchanging the lead during the first 1,000 meters. As the race progressed, Florida Tech moved to a half boat length lead which they held to the finish. The other crews in this race were Lafayette in third, U.S. Military Academy in fourth, Marietta in fifth, and Grand Valley in sixth.

After the 2021-2022 season the men's varsity rowing program was cut as a varsity sport and designated a club sport by the university. After this announcement Coach Granger left the university to become the head rowing coach at Georgetown University. Coach Granger had this to say about his time at Florida Tech, "F.I.T. Rowing will always hold a special place in my heart and influenced me in many ways to be a better coach and leader."[8]

Florida Tech Men's Rowing Reinstated

In an article written by Arianna Schuck (Editor-in-Chief) and James Pillow (Managing Editor) in the February 22, 2023, publication of *The Florida Tech Crimson* it stated that on February 17, 2023, U.S. District Judge Carlos Mendoza ruled that Florida Tech must reinstate the men's rowing team back to varsity status (Schuck & Pillow, February 22, 2023). The Title IX lawsuit was initiated by six members of the men's rowing team: Mason Yaskovic, Thomas Francis, Jaden Krekow, Ben Komita, Joshua Navarro, and Kyle Stewart (Schuck & Pillow, February 22, 2023). *The Crimson* reported that rower Ben Komita said, "I am so excited that the legacy of F.I.T. rowing will be here in the past, present, and future" (Schuck & Pillow, February 22, 2023). Financially supporting the rowers in their legal effort to return to varsity status were the Friends of Florida Tech Rowing. The lead counsel for the plaintiffs was attorney Art Schofield who said, "the rowing program gave me so much and it was an honor and pleasure to serve the university's rowing program." Schofield was a member of Florida Tech's Dad Vail Regatta's winning varsity eight in 1988 and winning frosh/novice eight in 1987. The court stated that the university must return the program to full operating status by March 12, 2023, which coincides with the beginning of spring break so the team can begin preparations for the spring rowing season. Coach Adam Thorstad and assistant coach Catherine Davie have served as the club men's rowing team coaches as well as the club women's rowing team coaches. To assist with the transition of the men's rowing team back to varsity status, the university appointed long-time Florida Tech rowing coach Casey Baker as the interim men's varsity rowing coach. Florida

---

[8] See Appendix 3: Dad Vail Regatta Men's Champions – names and coaches.

Tech is undertaking a national search for a full-time men's varsity head coach.[9]

The 2023 spring season was an exciting time for the men's rowing team. With Casey Baker serving as the interim men's varsity rowing coach and Adam Thorstad assisting Baker in the team's transition back to a varsity program; they wasted no time in getting the varsity eight in top racing form. The first race of the spring was on March 18th at Rollins, in which the men raced in a four-with and other small boats. Florida Tech won the four-with event. Their second race was on March 25th at the Hatter Invitational (Stetson University). In the first round, Florida Tech finished first with Embry Riddle Aeronautical University placing second, and UCF in third. In the second round, Florida Tech defeated Stetson University. The men's varsity eight had another strong performance in the FIRA Championship by finishing first ahead of second place Jacksonville University (JU) and third place Stetson University. The next progression for the Panther men's varsity eight was the SIRA Championship. In this race Florida Tech just missed finishing second to JU by less than a bow length with Colgate University capturing first. In the Dad Vail Regatta, the varsity men's eight finished second to Rutgers University in the Petite Final, which placed the Panthers eighth in this premier event. On their way home, the men's varsity raced in the inaugural Atlantic Association of Rowing Colleges Invitational Regatta held on the Occoquan Reservoir in Virginia. The Florida Tech's men's varsity eight finished third in this race to first place Colgate University and second place Saint Joseph's University. In the final race of the season, the IRA National Championship, the men rowed in the varsity four-with event. In this 32-boat field, the Panthers finished fourth to first place University of California, second place Temple University, and third place Dartmouth College.

Florida Tech Men Who Competed Internationally

During the 55-year history of the men's rowing program, there have been 23 Florida Tech rowers who have competed for their country in international competition. Four of the 23 are Tom Bohrer, Fran Reininger, Wayne Macfarlane, and Casey Baker. Tom Bohrer '86 was a member of the U.S. Olympic Team in 1988 winning a silver medal; and he was also a member of the U.S. Olympic Team in 1992, winning another silver medal and serving as the captain of the team. Additionally, Bohrer participated in the World Rowing Championships in 1989, 1991, and 1993. Bohrer's success as a rower gained him recognition as the 1989

---

[9] See Appendix 3: Dad Vail Regatta Men's Champions – names and coaches.

Male Rower of the Year in the United States. Bohrer also became World Indoor Rowing Champion in 1992. Fran Reininger '81 stroked the 1983 U.S. Pan American Team's coxed four, which won a gold medal. In 1987 Reininger was a member of the national team in the double sculls that competed in the World Rowing Championships in Copenhagen. In the 90s, as a single sculler competing in the World Cup, Reininger achieved a rating of 6th in the world. Additionally, Reininger stroked Oxford University to a victory over Cambridge University in England's The Boat Race, and he went on to earn a doctorate from Oxford University. Wayne Macfarlane '90 was the stroke of the undefeated Ridley College (Canadian high school) crew that won the Thames' Challenge Cup at the Henley Royal Regatta. He was also stroke of the Florida Tech men's varsity eight that won the Dad Vail Regatta and advanced to the semi-final race in the Ladies' Challenge Plate at the Henley Royal Regatta. In 1987 Macfarlane competed in the Pan American Games in which he won a silver medal in the lightweight weight pair and a bronze medal in the lightweight four without coxswain. He also participated in the 1991 World Rowing Championship where he won the petite final (seventh place) in the lightweight four without coxswain. Casey Baker '74 was a member of the 1977 U.S. National Rowing Team that participated in the World Rowing Championship in the quad that finished ninth, and he was a member of the 1983 U.S. Pan American Rowing Team in the quad that finished fourth.

On July 28, 2023, Florida Tech's athletics director, Jamie Joss, announced in a release that Adam Thorstad would be the new head men's rowing coach. Adam Thorstad had been the successful women's varsity rowing coach from 2007 to 2022, after which the women's rowing program was changed from a varsity to a club sport. During the 2022-2023 season, Coach Thorstad oversaw the men's and women's club rowing programs and also assisted Coach Casey Baker when he was appointed interim men's varsity rowing coach in March of 2023. Jamie Joss had this to say about Thorstad, "As an alum and former Florida Tech men's rower, Adam brings a wealth of knowledge, passion for coaching with proven success, and unwavering dedication as we embark on this new chapter of Florida Tech men's rowing."

References

Background Information

- Anna Norris (Florida Tech archives librarian)
- Ken Watts interview (team member and student during the formative years).
- Ray Walker interview (team participant during this time)
- Rob Dunlap interview (son of Robert H. Dunlap)

60s

- Anna Norris (Florida Tech archives librarian)
- Ken Watts (team participant during this time)
- Ray Walker (team participant during this time)

70s

- *Crimson* (April 28, 1974). *F.I.T. Crew wins at state*. Volume VII, No. 7
- Glenn Bunting interview (team member and coach during this time)
- Lindamood, R. (1994). *Marietta crew: A history of rowing at Marietta College*
- Marietta College of College Advancement. Marietta, Ohio
- Steve Wagner (men's frosh/novice coach during this time)
- *The Washington Post* (May 9, 1971). *Georgetown wins Dad Vail as St. Joseph's crew fades.* Provided by Ken Watts.

80s (1980-1989)

- Anna Norris is Florida Tech archives librarian
- Glenn Bunting interview (men's frosh/novice coach during this time)
- Hildes-Heim, N. (1982, May 9). *Florida Tech excels in Dad Vail Regatta. The New York Times*
- Hildes-Heim, N. (1988, May 15). *Temple is upset in regatta final. The New York Times*
- Steve Fluhr interview (a team member and men's coach during this time)
- Wayne Macfarlane interview on July 20, 2022 (team member during this time)

90s (1990-1999)

- Anna Norris (Florida Tech archives librarian)
- Casey Baker interview (men's coach during this time)
- Steve Fluhr interview (men's head coach during this time)

2000s (2000-2009)
- Anna Norris (Florida Tech archives librarian)
- Jimmy Woodard interview (team member)
- Marc Mandel interview (men's head coach during this time)
- Tim Watson interview (coach of the men's frosh/novice lightweight eight)

2010 (2010-2019)
- Anna Norris (Florida Tech archives librarian)
- Jim Granger interview (men's head coach during this time)

2020 (2020-present)
- Jim Granger interview (men's head coach during this time)
- Schuck, A. & Pillow, J. (February 22, 2023). *Florida Tech men's rowing reinstated*
- *The Florida Tech Crimson*, Issue 2, Spring

CHAPTER EIGHT:
LES HALL BUILDS A BASEBALL PROGRAM

By William C. Potter

revard Engineering College had fielded its first varsity baseball team in 1965. *The Evening Tribune* reported on June 7, 1965, that the team was coached by former Philadelphia Phillies catcher Andy Seminick. The team was composed entirely of full-time students and played against local high school and college teams. The article further disclosed that BEC had hopes that a new small-college conference would be formed by the following year.

The *Cocoa Tribune* reported on April 18, 1966, that Brevard Junior College's baseball team had thrashed Brevard Engineering College by a score of 18 to 0. Billy Stein pitched a one-hitter for the junior college.

The *Cocoa Tribune* reported on March 13, 1967, that Brevard Junior College had swept a baseball double-header from F.I.T. on March 11 by scores of 7 to 0 and 6 to 4. *Cocoa Tribune* reported on April 6, 1967, that F.I.T. had dropped another double-header to Brevard Junior College by scores of 6 to 1 and 10 to 0. The F.I.T. line-up included Troy, Brakin, Secogges, Shaffer, Steinhauer, Whitney, Worthington, Reuther, Wendt and Kronish. Lincoln Jarrett coached the team that year. Butch Galante was the ace of the pitching staff.

Bill Tiso's article in *The Crimson* on June 4, 1968, indicated that the baseball team had not won a game during the previous two seasons despite playing all junior college teams. Tiso described baseball as having had "a half dozen" coaches during that time. Despite Tiso's rather gloomy assessment of Florida Tech baseball, he did note that baseball had won its last two games of 1968 "in a blaze of glory."

The 1973 baseball team was coached by Otto Reyas that year. The team included twenty-one players.

Art Brooks' article in *Florida Today* on May 30, 1975, reported that F.I.T.'s 1975 baseball team, coached by Art Loche, completed its season with a record of 4 wins and 12 losses. Among the mainstays of the team were pitcher Carl Reckstein and third baseman Bo Ramowitz, first baseman Rob Bleyman and pitcher Craig Pomeroy. The highlight of the season was a doubleheader sweep of Florida Bible College.

On April 11, 1976, *Florida Today* reported that the Engineers had once again defeated Florida Bible College, thereby running their record for the season to 5 and 14. Craig Pomeroy was the winning pitcher. Another significant accomplishment for F.I.T. baseball was reported in *Florida Today* on March 12, 1976, when it was disclosed that Randy Muns, the Engineers' catcher, had won a bid to a national forensic competition as part of the speech and debate team. It is unclear whether Muns' forensic talents enhanced his baseball skills or perhaps it was the other way around.

On February 19, 1977, the Engineers took a double header from Embry-Riddle by scores of 23 to 5 and 6 to 4. Randy Muns demonstrated that his skills were not limited to the debate team by contributing 4 hits in the first game and 2 in the second game. On March 6, 1977, *Florida Today* reported that the Engineers had swept a doubleheader the previous day by defeating Flagler by scores of 13 to 3 and 6 to 3. That improved their record to 5 wins and 6 losses on the season.

Three icons of Florida Tech baseball:
Andy Seminick, Les Hall and Tim Wakefield

The fate of Florida Tech baseball would take a notable leap forward when Les Hall was hired as head coach in the fall of 1977. As reported in *Florida Today* on October 1, 1977, Hall had compiled a record of 204 wins and 79 losses in 11 years as coach at Satellite High School. Even though F.I.T. baseball had no athletic scholarships to award and not even a field for its exclusive use, Hall was optimistic when he told the newspaper: "I hope I can get a good program going and we can be respectable. And in two or three years, I hope to be respectable."

Hall was able to make Florida Tech respectable much quicker than anticipated. When they swept a double header from Clearwater Christian on April 15, 1978, they extended their record to 17 and 10, more than doubling their wins from the previous season. *Florida Today* reported on April 19, 1978, that: "Hall's Engineers (were) on the winning track." The team went 20 and 11 that first year and then, 23 and 20 the following year against steadily improving competition.

The remarkable progress of Florida Tech baseball under Hall was chronicled in *Florida Today* by Shelby Strother on May 12, 1980. Strother noted that the Engineers had, for the first time, competed in NCAA Division II and constructed a record of 28 wins and 14 losses. Florida Tech, still without athletic scholarships, relied largely on recruits from local high schools. Strother noted that the teams bore Hall's trademark: "Fundamentally sound, aggressive and opportunistic players who enjoy playing the game." One of the players mentioned in the article was "ex-Melbourne High speedster" Jim McGinnis who led the team that year with a .394 batting average. McGinnis would go on to be an assistant coach for Hall at Florida Tech, a successful long-time coach at Melbourne High and an iconic and charismatic teacher at Melbourne High.

Joe Narciso was an outstanding pitcher for Hall in 1980, 1981 and 1982. Narciso compiled a career record of 22 wins and only 11 losses. In 1981, he set the single season record for wins with 9 wins and 5 losses. An outstanding student and winner of the Faculty Scholarship Award, Narciso was inducted into the Florida Tech Sports Hall of Fame in 1991.

President Lynn Weaver inducted Tim Wakefield into the F.I.T. Sports Hall of Fame in 1993. *Photo from University Archives.*

Indisputably, the most well-known player in Florida Tech baseball history played for the Panthers from 1986 to 1988. A graduate of Eau Gallie High School, Tim Wakefield set school records with 22 home runs in a season and 40 round-trippers in his career. He was selected as Most Valuable Player as a first baseman but pitched only once in a fall game at Florida Tech. He was drafted as a first baseman by the Pittsburgh Pirates in 1988. After a stint playing Single-A ball, he was advised that he would never rise above Double-A as a first baseman. In response, Wakefield began working on a knuckleball and in 1990 converted to a pitcher. He led the Carolina League in starts and innings-pitched and advanced to Double -A in 1991 where he led the Pirates' organization in innings pitched and complete games. In 1992, he began the season in Triple-A before being called to the major leagues where he won 10 games with a 3.06 earned run average. In 1993 and 1994, Wakefield struggled at times with his control and bounced between Pittsburgh and their Triple-A team. The Pirates released Wakefield on April 20, 1995. Six days later, he was signed by the Boston Red Sox where he would become one of the most iconic pitchers in the rich history of the team. When he retired in February 2012, he would rank third in wins in Red Sox history (behind Roger Clemens and Cy Young) with 186. He would also rank first in Red Sox history in games started as a pitcher and in innings pitched. Wakefield would also make a place in Sox history when he was awarded the Roberto Clemente Award in 2010 as a major leaguer who combines a dedication of giving back to the community with outstanding skills on the baseball field. His charitable work in both Melbourne and Boston was cited in the award. With typical modesty, Wakefield responded: "I feel very lucky to be living out my dream I had as a kid and I feel a responsibility to give back."

The 1987 version of Florida Tech began the season on a strong note. One of the season highlights was an 8 to 7 victory over Navy on February 25 when Brian Crane scored the winning run in extra innings. When the Panthers routed Ithaca College on March 9 by a score of 26 to 7 behind 25 Panther hits, it extended their record to 15 and 3. Catcher Chip Greek had 4 hits while Tim Wakefield had 5 hits, including his seventh homerun. They cooled a bit as the season progressed and by May 1, when they fell to Eckerd 10 to 9, their record had slipped to 26 and 17 overall and 7 and 13 in the conference and they were no longer in contention for an NCAA playoff berth.

Chip Greek would play at Florida Tech as the starting catcher from 1987 until 1990 and leave the program with numerous batting records. As reported in *Florida Today* on June 4, 1990, Greek graduated holding school records for career hits (246), doubles (51), runs batted in (168) and runs (165). He was named to the first team all-conference team and to the second team of the all-region team. He was inducted into the Florida Tech Sports Hall of Fame in 1995.

The 1991 team broke the ceiling by earning a berth in the NCAA Division II Tournament. *Florida Today* reported on May 5, 1991, that the Panthers' 5 to 1 win over Barry clinched a South Region top-3 finish that gained them a spot in the tournament. Tom Finney of Merritt Island, who had become the school's all-time wins leader, clinched the victory with a 3-hit complete game. The win brought Florida Tech's record to 27 and 15 (12 and 9 in conference). Finney noted: "This was one of the goals we talked about before the season started. That's one of them out of the way."

Florida Tech lost the first game of the regional tournament to Tampa on May 16 by a score of 6 to 5 and then lost its second game to Florida Southern by a 6 to 3 score, thus eliminating the Panthers from the tournament. Although the Panthers lost their first 2 games in the NCAA South Region Tournament, it remained a notable season with historic accomplishments. The *Orlando Sentinel* reported on May 24 that pitcher Tom Finney, first baseman Paul Ouellette, third baseman Dave Campbell and catcher Dave Schwefler all made the All-South first team. Schwefler set a school record with 74 hits and batted .385. Ouellette won the conference batting title with a .387 average and set Florida Tech career records for triples and total bases. Finney posted an 11 and 5 record while leading the conference in strikeouts, complete games and innings pitched. Finney, Schwefler and Ouellette were all selected to the All-Sunshine State Conference first team while Campbell was a second team pick.

Tom Finney was named to the third team Division II All-American squad. He became the first player in school history to earn a postseason All-America baseball selection. He completed his career as the school's all-time leader in wins, innings pitched and strikeouts. *Florida Today* reported on June 14, 1991, that Finney had signed a free-agent contract with the New York Mets. He would play 1 year in the Gulf Coast League. He was inducted into the Florida Tech Sports Hall of Fame in 2005.

Paul Ouellette was named to the All-Sunshine State Conference team in both 1989 and 2001. He was also named to the All-South Region team both of those years. He left Florida Tech as the career leader in triples and total bases and second in home runs, runs batted in and hits. He was inducted into the Florida Tech Sports Hall of Fame in 2020.

Hall's 1992 team was one of the strongest teams in Florida Tech history, winning the NCAA South Atlantic Region championship and advancing to the Division II College World Series. The regular season was not particularly notable as the Panthers ended conference play with an overall record of 25 wins and 21 losses and an 11 and 13 record in the conference. A 13 to 2 victory over St. Leo on May 3 enabled them to finish in third place in the conference and a chance for a bid to the NCAA Division II tournament. As reported in *Florida Today* on May 4, Jeff Faino pitched his eighth complete game of the season to defeat St. Leo.

Florida Today revealed on May 12 that the Panthers had received a bid to the South Atlantic Regional in Savannah. The tournament was a double-elimination format. Their first game in the regional was against the University of South Carolina-Aiken on May 14, a game they won 6 to 4 behind another complete game by Faino. The Panthers won it by scoring 2 runs in the ninth inning behind a walk to Mark Venditti, a sacrifice by Chad Shoultz, a walk to Jeff Driskell and a double by Pete Labbe that drove-in 2 runs.

Florida Tech faced Armstrong State in their second game on May 15. They won that game by a score of 7 to 5, coming from behind to score 4 runs in the fourth and 2 in the sixth behind the hitting of Venditti, Scott Brown and Phil Campbell.

In their third tournament game, the Panthers faced a rematch with South Carolina-Aiken. They were trailing the fifth-ranked Pacers in the fourth inning when Merritt Island High School grad Joel Stephens broke a 0 and 10 batting streak with a grand-slam homerun, leading to a 7 to 2 victory and the regional title. Venditti and Brown were all-tournament choices while Campbell was Most Valuable Player of the tournament.

That sent the Panthers to the 8-team Division II College World Series in Montgomery, Alabama. The Panthers were tossed from the double elimination World Series with an 8 to 4 loss to Missouri Southern, followed by a 2 to 0 loss to Lewis University. The loss to Lewis was particularly heartbreaking causing Hall to tell *Florida Today*: "That game right there is why I hate baseball sometimes." That completed the season for the Panthers with a record of 28 and 23 but a post-season run that exceeded all expectations.

After the post-season run in 1992, with much of the lineup returning, expectations were high for the 1993 season. Alas, as David Jones described it in *Florida Today* on May 14, 1993, the season was "a terrible start, a miserable mid-season slump and a hot finish that was probably too little, too late for a return ticket to the postseason." When the Panthers completed the regular season with a sweep of Florida Atlantic University, that made it 4 victories against Top 20 teams in the past 3 weeks and gave them some hope of a post-season bid. Merritt Island graduate Joel Stephens earned the final victory over Florida Atlantic with his eighth complete game of the season. Despite the sweep of the sixth-ranked Owls, Florida Tech was denied a post-season slot.

Hall picked up his 400th win at Florida Tech with a 6 to 2 win over Palm Beach Atlantic on February 7, 1994. A victory over St. Leo on April 16 took the Panthers record to 24 and 16 overall and 7 and 7 in the conference. The Panthers' post-season hopes for 1994 ended with lop-sided losses to Florida Southern at the end of April.

1996 was a frustrating season for Hall and Florida Tech. As Hall told *Florida Today* on April 29, 1996, after a loss to North Florida: "That game right there summed up our season. That's the way all 44 games have gone at the end. We had a chance to win and we just couldn't get them in." The Panthers at that time had a record of 26 and 24 (10 and 8 in conference) and had lost 7 games by less than 2 runs. Nate Falk, a senior pitcher with 12 complete games for the season was named to the

NCAA Division II All-South Region team. Falk was an electrical engineering major with a 3.3 grade point average who was also named Florida Tech's male scholar-athlete of the year. First-baseman Chris Santoro, who finished his career as the school's all-time career batting leader with a .367 average, was also named to the All-South team. Hall spoke about Santoro to *Florida Today* on May 22, 1996, and said: "I would have to rate him as probably the best hitter we've had here - as far as consistency, putting the ball in play from both sides of the plate."

In November 1996, after 14 consecutive years of winning more than 20 games per season, Hall was inducted into the Florida Tech Sports Hall of Fame. His 472 victories at Florida Tech at the time of his induction ranked him among the 30 winningest baseball coaches in NCAA Division II history. He had taken the Panthers to 2 NCAA tournaments and a trip to the College World Series. On November 20, 1996, David Jones wrote in *Florida Today* about Hall's graduation from Marshall University and his decision to come to Florida to teach and coach rather than pursuing professional baseball. Hall recounted: "I came here, I didn't have plans to stay in this area." But here he was, 36 years later, having shaped the lives of hundreds of young men.

The 1997 season was a productive one for the Panthers who completed the season with 31 wins and 16 losses. They were in contention for a post-season berth until a late season loss to 2nd-ranked Florida Southern. Perhaps the highlight of the season occurred on April 19 when the Panthers defeated North Florida 10 to 6 thereby giving Hall his 500th career victory at Florida Tech. Grady Ollis' home run provided the winning margin. Ryan Jackson pitched the complete-game win. Ryan Jackson and third baseman Ray Santos were named to the first team All-Conference team. Designated hitter Ramsey Halabi was named to the second team. *Florida Today* reported on May 29 that Jackson had been named to the third team All-America team by the American Baseball Coaches Association.

1997 brought new challenges for Florida Tech baseball when the university decided to construct a new academic building on the site of the baseball field. The F.W. Olin Foundation had made a $50-million grant to the school to construct new engineering and science buildings. The site of the baseball field was the logical site for those buildings but the grant did not include funds to replace the field. David Jones' byline on July 30, 1997, described the situation as "Stealing Home." That sent Panther baseball to West Oaks Park in Palm Bay where home games would be played for the 1998 season.

The good news was announced in *Florida Today* on November 23, 1997, when President Lynn Weaver announced that the Olin Foundation had awarded the school a grant of $250,000 to build a new baseball field on the southwest part of the campus. Larry Milas, president of the foundation, noted that Olin had played major league baseball for the Washington Senators. Tim Wakefield also agreed to donate to complete the new field.

The final game on Andy Seminick Field was a game between the 1998 squad and a group of alumni on January 10, 1998. The starting pitcher for the alumni was Tom Finney and Andy Seminick threw out the first pitch with Tim Wakefield catching Seminick's throw. Wakefield won the home run derby that took place before the game. Ryan Jackson was the starting pitcher for the varsity.

The 1998 Panthers experienced a frustrating season, due not only to playing on a strange field away from campus but also due to injuries to key players. The result was a record of 24 and 22 overall and 6 and 12 in the conference. *Florida Today* reported on May 20 that first baseman Kevin Milford was named to the All-South Region team after hitting .389 with 14 home runs and setting school records of 82 hits and 75 runs-batted-in.

The 1999 season began on an upbeat note when Florida Tech dedicated the new field Andy Seminick/ Les Hall Field on January 30, 1999. The *Florida Today* noted in an article that day that the project had expanded and was now named the Franklin W. Olin Sports Complex and that the Panthers also hoped to open play in March on a new softball field under construction adjacent to the baseball field. Wakefield threw out the ceremonial first pitch which was caught by Seminick. A game with Nova Southeastern followed the opening ceremony.

The Panthers' record for the 1999 season was 16 wins, 26 losses and a tie (6 and 15 in the Sunshine State Conference). The season ended on a positive note on May 3 with a 5 to 4 win over Rollins College behind a complete game pitched by freshman Ronaldo Richardson. Four Panther players who had played high school ball in Brevard County, John Kunkle, Matt Slate, Bryan Naylor and Dan Nungesser, contributed hits to the victory.

The 2000 Florida Tech baseball team was described by *Florida Today* on April 16 as having "overachieved this year considering the level of competition in the SSC – there are four teams ranked in the nation's top 30." At that point, the Panthers were 22 and 19 overall and 6 and 11 in the conference, including victories over the nation's top 2 teams, North Florida and Tampa.

The 2001 season was a disappointment for the Panthers, who suffered an inordinate number of injuries. By April 10, *Florida Today* reported that they were down to 12 players after losing Derek Wolske, one of their leading hitters. By that time, the Panthers' record had fallen to 12 and 28 overall and 2 and 1 in the conference. They finished the season with an overall record of 13 wins and 34 losses.

On January 23, 2002, *Florida Today* reported that Hall had announced that he would retire at the end of the 2002 season after 25 seasons at Florida Tech. Among those commenting on the announcement was Hall's most famous product, Boston Red Sox pitcher Tim Wakefield, who said: "I am very happy for him. He's done a great service to that school as far as bringing competitive teams to the field as long as he has. He's had to do a lot of the maintenance, the laundry and driving and all that stuff himself. It's sad that he's leaving." Hall would leave with a career record of 596 wins and 545 losses and a tie. That would rank him among the top 30 all-time winningest coaches in NCAA Division II baseball.

The Panthers struggled during the 2002 season. On March 26, 2002, *Florida Today* reported that Florida Tech stood at 14 and 19 overall and only 2 and 7 in the conference.

Hall's final celebration with Florida Tech took place on April 19 and 20, 2002, with a 3-game series with Eckerd College. The Panthers took 2 of 3 from Eckerd amid the celebrations. Hall was presented with a framed number 1 jersey. Florida Tech's pitcher in the first game of the Saturday doubleheader was Jeff Withers. In attendance was Jeff's father Alan Withers who had played for Hall at Satellite High School. In typical Hall understatement, he simply told *Florida Today*: "It was a heck of a nice day for me." Thus ended the career of a man who touched thousands of lives with his quiet, sincere and caring demeanor that ingratiated him to his players and colleagues. On October 23, 2002, *Florida Today* revealed that Hall would be inducted into the Sunshine State Conference Hall of Fame.

On May 7, 2002, athletic director Bill Jurgens announced that Paul Knight had been hired as baseball coach of Florida Tech. Jurgens told *Florida Today*: "Paul Knight is a perfect fit for our institution and athletic program." Over 100 applicants had sought the position.

Knight would coach at Florida Tech from the 2003 season through the 2007 season. He would compile a record of 139 wins and 128 losses before leaving to become the coach at Lenoir-Rhyne College. He coached several notable players while at Florida Tech, including All-Americans outfielder Jonathan Baksh and shortstop Steve Condotta.

Baksh was the Player of the Year in the Sunshine State Conference in 2005. In 2006, he was a first team All-America selection. He gained first team All-Conference recognition in both 2005 and 2006. He led the conference in batting in 2006 with a.489 average. When he was selected by the Toronto Blue Jays in 2006 in the 7th round, he became the 2nd highest draft pick in the history of Florida Tech baseball. *Florida Today* reported on June 10 that Baksh, from Mississauga, Ontario, had signed with the Blue Jays. He was inducted into the Florida Tech Sports Hall of Fame in 2015.

Condotta was also a native of Mississauga and was drafted by the Blue Jays in the 12th round in 2007. Condotta left Florida Tech with a .355 batting average after batting .431 in 2007. He left as the career leader at Florida Tech in at bats, runs, hits, sacrifice flies and stolen bases attempted. He was named first team All-Sunshine State Conference, first team All-South Region and third team All-American. Coach Paul Knight told *Florida Today* on June 6, 2007, that in addition to his hitting skills, Condotta had "a great glove, great range and a great arm. He could play any position on the field." Condotta was inducted into the Florida Tech Sports Hall of Fame in 2016.

The 2007 Panther team would set the standard for the Knight era. On April 6, 2007, *Florida Today* reported that the Panthers, with a record of 24 and 11 overall and 8 and 4 in the conference, had attained a ranking of 20th in the latest national poll. By May 4, the newspaper reported that the Panthers were now in 4th place in the conference with a record of 29 and 19 overall and 11 and 10 in the conference.

On August 4, 2007, *Florida Today* reported that Lenoir-Rhyne College in Hickory, North Carolina, had hired Knight as head baseball coach. On September 21, the newspaper disclosed that Greg Berkemeier had been hired as Panther head baseball coach, succeeding Knight. Berkemeier had been an assistant to Knight for the preceding 5 seasons.

Berkemeier would remain head baseball coach at Florida Tech for 14 years. He would compile a record as head coach of 389 wins, 271 losses and a tie. In his first season as head coach in 2008, the team finished the year with 35 wins, 20 losses and a tie. That team compiled a 13 and 11 record in the Sunshine State Conference and advanced to the NCAA South Region tournament.

His best seasons were 2010, when the team had a record of 39 and 16, and 2015, when they achieved a record of 38 and 13. The 2010 team, led by first baseman Michael Demma and pitcher Jonathan Cornelius, advanced to the NCAA regional tournament.

In 2011, the Panthers reached the 30-win level for the 5th consecutive year, finishing with a record of 30 wins and 20 losses, including an 11 and 13 record in the conference. Shortstop K.C. Clabough was named a 2nd team All-American. A significant event occurred on May 7, 2011, when the Panthers celebrated its 1st game under the new lights which had been installed on their home field with a 5 to 4 win over Florida Southern.

The 2012 team concluded their season with a 26-win, 23-loss record and an 11 and 12 record in the conference. Shortstop K.C. Clabough, 1st baseman Ryan McChesney and pitcher James Mannara were named to the All-Conference 1st team while pitcher Jason Boyer was selected for the 2nd team.

The Panthers had another solid season in 2013, posting a school record 14 wins in the Sunshine State Conference. Their overall record was 32 wins and 19 losses and, for the 3rd time in the last 6 years, they made the post-season regional tournament. Freshman catcher Austin Allen was conference Freshman of the Year, as well as 1st team All-Conference and 2nd team All-Region.

The 2014 team finished the season with an overall record of 25 and 22 and a record of 9 and 14 in the conference. Pitcher Scotty Ward was named to the All-Conference 2nd team.

The 2015 team also advanced to the regional tournament where they lost a 5 to 4 heartbreaker to Tampa in the tournament finals in extra innings to send Tampa to the NCAA Division II World Series. That closed the season for the Panthers with a record of 38 wins and only 13 losses. Among the outstanding players on that team were Scotty Ward and Austin Allen. Allen, named to a 2nd team All-American, hit .421 with a school-record 25 doubles. Scotty Ward was named 2015 Sunshine State Conference Pitcher of the Year. As reported by *Florida Today* on June 18, 2015, Austin Allen became the highest draft selection in school history when he was taken in the 4th round of the 2015 draft by the San Diego Padres. Ward went 9 and 4 on the season with a 2.48 earned run average. Ward was undrafted but signed an independent contract to play professional ball.

Florida Tech completed the 2016 season with a record of 29 and 21 overall and 11 and 13 in the conference. Pitcher Ty Cohen was selected to the All-Conference 1st team. Designated hitter Kevin Capella, reliever Drew Beyer, outfielder Daniel Szpik and 1st baseman/shortstop John Sternagel were all named to the 2nd team.

In 2017, the Panthers were back with another 30-win season, finishing with 30 wins and 20 losses, including a 14-win, 10-loss conference record. Pitcher Andrew Marzheuser was selected to the All-Conference 1st team while pitcher Tyler Deel, outfielder Daniel Szpik, infielder Nick Capra, and pitcher Ty Cohen all received 2nd team recognition.

The 2018 season was marked by the selection of pitcher Ty Cohen by the St. Louis Cardinals in the 2018 draft. As noted in the Fall 2018 issue of *Florida Tech Today*, Cohen compiled a record of 28 wins and 15 losses during his career at Florida Tech, good for the 2nd most wins in a career by any Panther pitcher. The 2018 season was a relatively unsuccessful year for the Panthers, as they finished with a record of 20 wins and 30 losses and a 12 and 18 record in the league. Cohen completed his career with a 3-hit complete game in a 6 to 1 victory over Rollins on May 12.

The 2019 team came back strong and completed the season with a 29 and 18 record, including a 17 and 11 record in the conference. First baseman Jacob Buser and pitcher Andrew Marzheuser won 1st team All-Conference recognition while infielder Rodnie Bernard received 2nd team honors.

The 2020 team struggled during a Covid shortened season, winning only 7 games while losing 17.

The 2021 Panther baseball season was another Covid limited season and concluded with an overall record of 17 and 10 (15 and 9 in league play). Shortstop Raul Quintero and pitcher Boris Villa were named to the 2nd team of the All-Sunshine State Conference team. Pitcher Justin Lorenz gained honorable mention honors while center fielder Sam Schner was named to the All-Defensive team. Villa also was named to the All-Region second team.

Jeff Tam was promoted to head baseball coach at Florida Tech on December 17, 2021, following the resignation of Berkemeier. Tam had experienced a 6-year career in the Major Leagues as a relief pitcher with 4 different teams.

Florida Tech concluded an outstanding 2022 season with a record of 30 wins and 19 losses. A notable game that season was a 17 to 5 victory over Lynn on March 22 when the Panthers put up 21 hits and 17 unanswered runs. Pitcher Alex Carpenter received Academic All-District honors and 2nd team Academic All-American recognition with a 4.0 GPA in psychology. Dylan Owens and Sam Schner earned All-Conference selections.

As this book is written, Florida Tech baseball has completed a rather unremarkable 2023 season. When they completed their season by splitting a doubleheader with Nova Southeastern on May 13, their record reached 23 wins and 26 losses and a 12 and 18 conference record. Going into the last game of the season Josh Ford, a catcher from Melbourne High School, was batting .336 while Jason Blackstone, another Melbourne High product, was hitting .335. Tyler Vermillion, a junior pitcher, led the hurlers with a 4 and 0 record.

Notes

- Information about individual games is, unless otherwise cited, taken from *Florida Today*, usually the edition published the day following each game.
- The description of Tim Wakefield's career relied upon *Knuckler: My Life with Baseball's Most Confounding Pitch*, by Tim Wakefield, published by Mariner Books; Reprint Edition March 6, 2012.
- The description of Tim Wakefield's receipt of the Roberto Clemente Award is taken from an article by Gordon Edes published in ESPN Magazine on October 28, 2010.
- Information about the 1992 baseball team is also taken from the official website of Florida Tech Athletics and the description of the team appearing in the Hall of Fame. The entire 1992 team was inducted into the Hall of Fame in 2013.
- Information about John Narciso, Paul Ouellette, Tom Finney, Jonathan Baksh and Steve Condotta also includes information taken from their biographies on the official website of Florida Tech Athletics in the section describing members of the Hall of Fame. The results of specific seasons, coaching changes and post-season honors are, unless otherwise cited, taken from news articles from https://floridatechsports.com/news. The news articles on baseball which were relied upon were those published on May 7, 2011, May 16, 2011, May 17, 2013, May 4, 2014, May 17, 2015, May 14, 2016, May 18, 2016, May 13, 2017, May 17, 2017, May 12, 2018, May 11, 2019, May 15, 2019, May 6, 2021, May 13, 2021, June 2, 2021, December 17, 2021, March 22, 2022, May 12, 2022, May 16, 2022, June 8, 2022, and April 1, 2023.
- Austin Allen was the subject of a story by Jameson Carter published in the Fall 2015 issue of *Florida Tech Today*.

CHAPTER NINE:
HOW TITLE IX SHAPED WOMEN'S
COLLEGIATE SPORTS AND SOCIETY

By William C. Potter

In 1970, Congresswomen Edith Green of Oregon and Patsy Mink of Hawaii drafted legislation that would prohibit sex discrimination in education. Indiana Senator Birch Bayh sponsored the legislation in the Senate. The legislation passed as Title IX of the Education Amendments Act of 1972. On June 23, 1972, President Nixon signed the act. Title IX of that act for the first-time recognized gender equity in education as a civil right. The amendment succinctly stated: "No person in the United States shall, on the basis of sex, be excluded from participation, be denied the benefits of, or be subjected to discrimination under any education program or activity receiving Federal financial assistance." Although we often tend to think of Title IX as primarily affecting gender equity in athletics, in fact, it has changed the face of all aspects of education. In 1972, college student bodies and faculties were overwhelmingly male. In 1970, only 59% of women in the U.S. graduated from high school and only 8% earned college degrees. Now, 50 years after the enactment of Title IX, that picture has dramatically changed. By 2021, women comprised virtually half of all faculty members at U.S. colleges. The percentage of female students at U.S. higher education institutions was nearing 60% by then and the percentage of female students was continuing to grow. Tellingly, female students were substantially more likely than male students to complete their degree.

Title IX's impact on those seeking advanced degrees is even more dramatic. In 1972, women earned a mere 9% of all medical degrees and only 7% of law degrees. Presently, nearly half of law and medical degrees are conferred upon women.

It is difficult to conclude with precision how much of that change has resulted from Title IX rather than other societal evolutions, but it is clear that Title IX has had an enormous impact on education which, in turn, has revolutionized society as women have increasingly assumed leadership roles in the professions, in business, in government and throughout society.

Participation in athletics rates among high school students has increased tenfold since the enactment of Title IX. In 1972, only 1 in 27 girls played sports compared to 1 in 5 in 2022. More than 200,000 women play collegiate sports in 2022 compared to less than 30,000 in 1972.

In 1972, at the time of enactment, most educators viewed Title IX in terms of its impact on classrooms, admissions policies, academic programs and facilities but did not generally consider the impact of the new legislation on athletic programs. When college administrators began to realize that Title IX applied to athletics, there was an initial outcry of opposition. Many athletic directors and men's coaches rose in alarm and argued that the need for equity in sports would spell doom for men's sports. Many schools simply ignored the law between its enactment in

1972 and the issuance of regulations implementing the law in 1988. At the NCAA convention in January 1979, the organization overwhelmingly adopted a resolution opposing Title IX compliance regulations as written, arguing that major revenue sports, basketball and football, should be exempt from equal per-capita spending requirements. But when the regulations were issued and the U.S. Department of Education began enforcing the regulations throughout colleges and universities, including their athletic departments, the requirements of Title IX could no longer be ignored.

Women's sports in the Sunshine State Conference had begun in earnest on April 15, 1982, when the athletic directors had determined that basketball, volleyball, and slow-pitch softball should be the "flagship" sports for women in conference play with cross country and tennis as additional conference sports. In 1987, slow-pitch softball was replaced with fast-pitch softball. Women's rowing was added in 1996 and women's soccer and women's golf followed in 1998. Swimming was added as the conference's ninth sport in 2010 while lacrosse became the tenth women's sport for the conference in 2014. Since the inauguration of women's teams in the conference in 1982, 47 women's teams from the Sunshine State Conference have won national championships. The conference now sponsors 10 sports for women compared to only 8 for men.

An article in *Florida Today* by David Jones published on October 28, 1994, described the budgeting challenges posed to Florida Tech by Title IX. The article disclosed that while women's programs were experiencing budget increases, men's budgets were being trimmed. The article related that the female population was about 28% of the student body but 35% of the athletes were women. During that fiscal year, women received 30% of the athletic budget and Athletic Director Bill Jurgens stated that he intended to increase the women's share to 35% for the following year.

Ironically, the only significant difficulties that Florida Tech has faced regarding Title IX have resulted from challenges in providing sufficient opportunities for male student athletes. In June 2022, Florida Tech terminated 5 varsity sports programs-men's and women's rowing, men's and women's cross country/distance track and men's golf. These sports were transitioned to club sports. Six men's rowers, backed by a group of former rowers at Florida Tech organized as The Friends of F.I.T. Rowing Association, filed a lawsuit in the U.S. District Court of the Middle District of Florida, seeking to enjoin the university from eliminating men's rowing as a varsity sport. A hearing in February 2023 on the plaintiffs' request for a preliminary injunction educed testimony claiming that Florida Tech violated Title IX requirements by failing to provide sufficient varsity sport opportunities for male students. The testimony claimed that the university had been out of compliance with Title IX for 16 of the previous 18 years. Testimony revealed that during the 2020-2021 school term, the school population was 69.4% male and 30.6% female while athletic participation was 58.7% male and 41.3% female. The university made a couple of arguments in support of its contention that it was in compliance with Title IX. First, it argued that e-sports should be recognized as a sport in calculating the participation rates. Secondly, it argued that on-line students should be included in the school population for purposes of calculating the composition of the student population. On February 17, 2023, District Judge Carlos Mendoza rejected the argument that e-sports should be included in the calculation and entered a preliminary injunction, ordering Florida Tech to reinstate the men's rowing team to varsity status and to provide it with "full funding, staffing and other benefits commensurate with its status as a varsity-level intercollegiate team." Additionally, the order enjoined the school from "taking any action in furtherance of eliminating the men's rowing team or any men's intercollegiate athletic team at the institution pending a full trial on the merits or until the Court orders otherwise."

The university has taken steps to reinstate men's rowing in accordance with the order. Shortly thereafter, the university, on its own initiative, reinstated men's cross country and men's track. The lawsuit remains pending as of this writing.

Title IX has also had similar unintended consequences for academic programs in universities and, alarmingly, has adversely impacted some efforts to provide opportunities for women. As demonstrated by the disparities in the gender mix at Florida Tech, women are often underrepresented in fields such as engineering and computer science. In order to correct that imbalance, colleges, including Florida Tech, have offered special scholarships or programs to attract women to these academic programs. However, Title IX prohibits such gender discrimination and prohibits awards or programs solely for women. The Department of Education has cracked down on scholarships and programs which it determines discriminate against men. As of 2019, the Department of Education had opened more than 2 dozen investigations into universities that offered female-only scholarships and professional development workshops. Even science and engineering camps for middle and high school girls have been under scrutiny.

It is important to note that increased athletic opportunities for women under Title IX have impacted society in ways that transcend the athletic fields. Research cited in the *Harvard Business Review* indicates that more than half of female senior business executives played a sport at the college or university level. The study surveyed more than 400 female executives in 5 countries and found that only 3% had never participated in sports at any level. Moreover, the study indicated that female senior business leaders who had played a sport had a strong preference for hiring other women who had played sports. Those surveyed cited "bringing projects to completion" and "discipline" as qualities instilled by sports that made athletes desirable employees. Even more important were the qualities of "competitiveness" and "teamwork" which were fostered by athletic experiences.

The success of former women collegiate athletes is not limited to the business world. In politics, too, former women athletes have applied their experiences as athletes to their positions in government. Former Illinois Congresswoman Cheri Bustos, a 2-sport college athlete at the University of Maryland, noted that: "You learn to win with dignity and always have a competitive spirit. And when you have a teammate who doesn't have a good game, you help them up. They're all lessons that parallel politics." One of Bustos' close friends in Congress was Senator Kirsten Gillibrand, who learned leadership as the captain of Dartmouth's women's squash team. Lori Trahan, a Congresswoman from Massachusetts who played volleyball at Georgetown added: "Women athletes have far more power and influence than I ever could have dreamed of when I was playing. They have a pivotal role in our country's public discourse especially right now and the coming years as we continue working to create a more equal playing field, whether it's in business, government or the economy."

- For the evolution of Title IX and its effect upon higher education, see "How Title IX Transformed Women's Sports" at https://www.hutirt.com/news/title-nine-women-sports retrieved on December 7, 2022.
- See also: Mertens, Maggie "50 Years of Title IX: How One Law Changed Women's Sports Forever." *Sports Illustrated*, May 19, 2022.
- As to the data on the numbers of female faculty members and students, see Carey, Kevin, "Men Fall Behind in College Enrollment: Women Still Play Catch-Up at Work." *New York Times*, September 10, 2021.
- The data regarding the participation rates in women's athletics were excerpted from an article by Lauren Camera titled "Title IX Marks 50 Years of Gains and Goals for Gender Equity in Education" published in *U.S. News and World Report* on June 22, 2022.
- Information regarding the institution of women's sports in the Sunshine State Conference is derived from "Celebrating 50 Years of Title IX" on the conference website at sunshinestateconference.com.
- Information regarding the Title IX lawsuit regarding rowing is derived from the filings in Navarro, et. al. v. Florida Institute of Technology, Inc., case number 6:22-cv-1950-CEM-EJK in the United States District Court, Middle District of Florida, Orlando Division. Rick Neale also wrote about the lawsuit in *Florida Today* on February 7, 2023, and February 19, 2023.
- As to the prohibition of programs designed to attract women to STEM programs, see "The Unintended Downside of Title IX for Women" by Kim Elsesser published in *Forbes Magazine* on June 23, 2022.
- See also "Women-only STEM College Programs under Attack for Male Discrimination" by Teresa Watanabe published in the *Los Angeles Times* on August 20, 2019.
- The study regarding the prevalence of college athletes among female business leaders was cited in "Research: More Than Half of Top Female Execs Were College Athletes" by Nanette Fondas, published in *Harvard Business Review* on October 9, 2014.
- The story about women athletes in politics was written by Shia Kapos and published in *Politico* on July 16, 2021.

As this book was nearing publication, it was announced by Florida Tech on September 26, 2023, that it had reached a tentative settlement of the lawsuit regarding men's rowing. The agreement had been executed by the university and the plaintiffs but was subject to the approval of the court. Under the agreement, men's rowing and men's cross country would remain varsity sports at least through 2028. Through 2026, Florida Tech would have an independent expert verify its compliance with Title IX. Additionally, Esports would not be counted as a varsity sport until it was recognized by the NCAA or by another court. In announcing the settlement, newly appointed Florida Tech President John Nicklow commended General Counsel Ryan Petersen and Athletics Director Jamie Joss for facilitating the settlement and added: "We are pleased that we have come to an agreement within Title IX law that balances the needs of our student-athletes and fits within our overall athletics program in a fiscally prudent approach."

- See Florida Today September 26, 2023.
- See also https://news.fit.edu/campus/florida-tech-reaches-equitable-settlement-in-rowing-lawsuit/

CHAPTER TEN:
THE EVOLUTION OF WOMEN'S SPORTS AT FLORIDA TECH

By William C. Potter

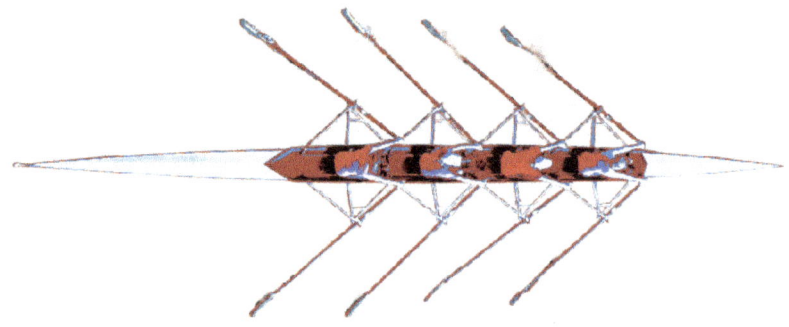

Title IX of the Education Amendments Act of 1972 was signed into law by President Nixon on June 23, 1972, Title IX of that act for the first-time recognized gender equity in education as a civil right. The amendment succinctly stated: "No person in the United States shall, on the basis of sex, be excluded from participation, be denied the benefits of, or be subjected to discrimination under any education program or activity receiving Federal financial assistance." When Florida Tech fostered its women's crew program in 1972, it was ahead of many schools in encouraging athletic opportunities for coeds.

A letter to *Florida Today* published on March 9, 1972, pointed out that the men's crew included 3 women who were coxswains. That letter seemed to catch the attention of the newspaper since it published a story on April 9, 1972, describing the roles of the women coxswains, with particular emphasis upon Beth Hebert, a 112-pound oceanography major from Shrewsbury, Vermont, known affectionately to her teammates as "Buff." Buff charmed readers by observing: "I get wet in every race, but really wet when we win. Right – I get thrown in. It's some tradition to throw the coxswain in. But I don't mind – it's all part of being on the crew. It means you belong." These 3 coxswains were probably the first coeds in school history to compete in intercollegiate athletics.

On December 7, 1972, *Florida Today* reported that 12 female students at Florida Tech had organized a crew team and begun practicing with 2 men's varsity crew members, Chuck Hildebrand and Doug Linden, serving as coaches. The article disclosed that on the previous Saturday, December 2, the women had rowed to victory in the first women's intercollegiate rowing event ever held in the South, beating Jacksonville University by three boat lengths. Ann Gauzens, it was reported, was the team captain.

The Florida Tech women proceeded to take the team title at the state championship 5 years in a row. In 1976, *Florida Today* reported on April 18 that they had won the varsity eight race by 7 seconds (2 boat lengths) over FTU (now U.C.F.).

In 1976, F.I.T.'s women's crew won the Southeastern Intercollegiate Championship at Stone Mountain, Georgia, thereby qualifying for the small college national championship at the Dad Vail Regatta in Philadelphia. *Florida Today* reported on April 30, 1976, that the women were raising money to finance the trip by holding a car wash.

One of the members of that team was Jeanne Ann Flanagan. Flanagan would graduate in 1979 after majoring in biology. She won a bronze medal at the 1979 world rowing championship in the women's 8. She then qualified for the 1980 Olympics, only to be denied a chance to compete due to the U.S. boycott of the Moscow Olympics. However, she would win a silver medal at the 1981 world championship as a member of the women's 8. She culminated her career with a gold medal at the 1984 Olympics, rowing in the women's 8. She earned a master's degree in exercise science from the University of Massachusetts. She was inducted into the Florida Tech Sports Hall of Fame as part of the first class of inductees in 1986.

Another member of that F.I.T. team was Valerie Barber, who was a 4-year rower for the Panthers. She had never rowed when she arrived at Florida Tech but led the team to 3 state championships and 2 South Region championships. After her graduation in 1978, she was selected for the U.S. Rowing Team. She represented the U.S. in the 1978 World Championship, finishing 4th. She earned a seat on the 4-woman shell for the 1980 Olympics. She was denied an opportunity to compete when the U.S. elected to boycott those Olympics. *Florida Today* reported on February 1, 2013, that she had been inducted into the Florida Tech Sports Hall of Fame. At the time of her induction, she had earned an MS and PhD from the University of Alaska-Fairbanks and was a research professor specializing in climate change at that university. The 2022-2023 Academic Catalog of the University of Alaska Southeast lists Dr. Barber as a member of the adjunct faculty of chemistry.

The 1982 women's varsity 4 shell was coached by Mike Davenport and became the first women's boat to win gold at the Dad Vail Regatta after winning the Southern Intercollegiate Rowing Association and Florida Intercollegiate Rowing Association championships. They also helped the team win the combined overall championship at the Dad Vail Regatta. This varsity 4 shell, through its members, was inducted into the Florida Tech Sports Hall of Fame in 2014. Members recognized included JoAnn (Alden) Michalsky, Christine Bredenkamp, Laurie Kuestner, Sharon Trepiccione, Sue (Brown) Wasik and Sharon Gallagher.

One of the most ardent promoters of women's sports at Florida Tech was Martha Work, wife of Dean Ray Work. Martha was a founding member and board member of the Panther Athletic Association when it was founded in 1986, as well as a founding member of the Women's Locker Room. She rarely missed a Florida Tech athletic event and was known as the "Cookie Lady" as she frequently brought cookies to distribute at games. Dozens of Florida Tech female athletes considered her as a mentor. She was inducted into the Florida Tech Sports Hall of Fame in 2003.

According to an article in *Florida Today* on February 12, 1986, women's sports in the Sunshine State Conference had begun in earnest on April 15, 1982, when the athletic directors had determined that basketball, volleyball and slow-pitch softball should be the "flagship" sports for women in conference play. In addition, Cross-country and tennis were instituted as conference sports for women. Fast-pitch softball would replace slow-pitch softball in 1986. Women's crew would be added as a conference sport in 1996, followed by soccer and golf in 1998. Women's swimming would be added to the conference slate in 2010 and women's lacrosse, added in 2014, would be the latest women's sport in the conference. At present, the Sunshine State Conference sponsors 8 men's sports and 10 women's sports.

Florida Today reported that F.I.T. was searching for a women's basketball coach and that the coach must be hired within three weeks in order to compete in the conference next season. Athletic Director Bill Jurgens was quoted as worrying that time was running out for recruiting prospective players. On June 2, 1986, *Florida Today* reported the hiring of Paul Ward as women's basketball coach. It noted that Ward would also recruit for the men's team. He, of course, would remain the women's coach for only a single season and would be succeeded by his assistant, John Reynolds, whose remarkable accomplishments are described in another chapter.

There are 15 individual women among the members of the Florida Tech Sports Hall of Fame. In addition, there are 2 women's teams, the 2001-2002 women's basketball team and the 1982 Dad Vail champions women's 4 rowing shell. This book will chronicle the athletic accomplishments of these women at Florida Tech and, in many cases, also demonstrate their impressive contributions to society following their athletic careers. It is safe to say that without Title IX, many of these accomplishments on and off the playing fields would not have occurred.

Ironically, Florida Tech's most significant Title IX challenge in athletics has been providing sufficient opportunities for male student-athletes. Title IX is commonly viewed as a requirement to provide opportunities for female students. However, at Florida Tech, a STEM institution with a predominantly male student body, the challenge has proven to be to maintain an appropriate balance that provides adequate opportunities for male students. The abolition of the football program in May 2020 recreated a substantial imbalance which had existed prior to inauguration of the football program in 2011. The Title IX lawsuit resulting from the termination of men's crew as a varsity sport is described in Chapter 9 of this book which discusses the effect of Title IX and the challenges that can arise from its application.

The NCAA Woman of the Year award was established in 1991 and honors senior female student-athletes who have distinguished themselves throughout their college career by their achievements in academics, athletics, service and leadership. In 2022, Florida Tech swimmer Savannah Brennan was nominated and was among the top-30 finalists for the award. There were 577 nominees for the award and the top-30 included 10 from each NCAA division. Brennan, from Oviedo,

Florida, was the first 3-time winner of the Sunshine State Conference's Female Scholar-Athlete of the Year award. She was also a First Team CoSIDA Academic All-America honoree. She completed her undergraduate studies after achieving a 3.97-grade point average with a double major in Genomic and Molecular Genetics and Biomedical Science. After graduation, she then began pursuit of a master's in biotechnology. Head swimming coach Dave Dent noted: "During her illustrious career, Savannah was the first female to score any points at NCAA's, the first female All-American, the first female swimmer to win the SSC Scholar-Athlete of the Year award, the first athlete to win the SSC Scholar-Athlete award 3 times in a row, the first Florida Tech scholar-athlete to win the SSC Woman of the Year, and now she is the first Florida Tech scholar-athlete to be named in the Top 30 for the NCAA Woman of the Year. Savannah has garnered an impressive number of accomplishments during her career, no one is more deserving than Sav, she worked harder than anyone day in and day out to accomplish everything she did." Brennan was a 4-year member of the TriBeta biological honors society, where she served as chapter president. During the pandemic, she volunteered in the emergency department of Holmes Regional Medical Center. She also volunteered with Team IMPACT which matches collegiate teams with children dealing with chronic diseases. There could be no more compelling example of the results of Title IX than Savannah Brennan.

Notes

- For the evolution of Title IX and its effect upon higher education, see "How Title IX Transformed Women's Sports" at https://www.hutirt.com/news/title-nine-women-sports retrieved on December 7, 2022.
- See also: Mertens, Maggie "50 Years of Title IX: How One Law Changed Women's Sports Forever," *Sports Illustrated*, May 19, 2022.
- The information regarding Flanagan, Barber and Work is derived primarily from the biography of each athlete posted on the Hall of Fame section of the Florida Tech athletics website.
- The Complaint and resulting Order regarding men's rowing are found in the case of Navarro, et. al. v. Florida Institute of Technology, Inc., Case Number 6:22-ev-1950-CEM-EJK, in the U.S. District Court for the Middle District of Florida (Orlando Division).
- Savannah Brennan's achievements were chronicled in an article by Christina Hardman published on October 13, 2022, on the website of Florida Tech Athletics at floridatechsports.com.

CHAPTER ELEVEN:
A BRIEF EXPERIMENT WITH FOOTBALL

By William C. Potter

I am acutely aware that some of the conclusions about football at Florida Tech set forth in this chapter contradict the conclusions set forth in the Foreword written by my friend Dr. Catanese. I have great respect for Dr. Catanese and his contributions to Florida Tech. I don't believe that the reader needs to make a decision that one of us has made the correct assessment while the other is mistaken. Rather, I believe that our differing viewpoints about the football program at Florida Tech may be attributed to our differing educational backgrounds and work experiences. While Dr. Catanese is respected for his visionary thinking, creativity and optimism, I must confess that I am often constrained by the cynicism that arises from more than 40 years of practicing law. While my legal training tends to cause me to view issues in terms of their short-term challenges, President Catanese more often tends to look at the long-term impacts of his decisions. While I tend to look at the direct and immediate tangible risks and results of decisions, I must acknowledge that Dr. Catanese may be better at assessing the overall, long-term impact of initiatives undertaken such as the general enhancement of the school's "branding" brought about by football. In any event, the reader will have the benefit from a couple of viewpoints about the issue.

The inauguration of varsity football was an exciting time for Florida Tech.
Photo by William Potter.

Football is undoubtedly the most expensive intercollegiate sport and, for most colleges which have football teams, the most high-profile sport. It is also in sharp decline in terms of participation rates prior to college as well as in terms of attendance at college games. Participation in youth football declined by more than 30% between its peak in 2008 and 2020. Participation in high school football declined by almost 10% during the time between its peak in 2009 and 2020. College football attendance hit its peak in 2013 and declined about 7% between the peak and 2020.

Despite these trends, colleges have continued to launch new football programs. The number of NCAA schools fielding football teams has increased from less than 500 in 1978 to more than 650 in 2018. Between 2008 and 2022, 16 teams instituted football at the Division II level while 15 began Division III play. The NAIA added 34 new football programs during that timeframe while Division I FCS and FBS added 14 teams.

One of the schools that began playing intercollegiate football during this period was Florida Atlantic University, a college of about 20,000 students with its main campus in Boca Raton, which began playing intercollegiate football in 2001. The president of FAU who spearheaded the advent of football was Anthony J. Catanese. In 2002, Dr. Catanese left FAU to become president of Florida Tech.

Catanese was an energetic advocate of intercollegiate sports who would dramatically expand the scope of intercollegiate athletics at Florida Tech during his tenure. Under his leadership, men's and women's lacrosse, men's and women's tennis, men's and women's golf, men's and women's swimming and men's and women's track and field would all be instituted at Florida Tech.

In early 2010, Catanese appointed a group of administrators and faculty members to explore the possibility of establishing an intercollegiate football program at Florida Tech. The committee presented a couple of preliminary reports which Catanese rejected, instructing the committee to continue its work. Finally, on April 26, 2010, the committee presented its final report. The report made the following conclusions:

1. The most cost-effective football program would be non-athletic scholarship NAIA football;
2. Football could begin in the fall of 2011 with competition beginning in the fall of 2013;
3. It would be necessary to raise donations of $821,000 in fiscal year 2011 and $1,880,000 in fiscal year 2012;

4. If the fund raising described above was attained, cash flow for football would be continually positive;
5. The ultimate goal should be scholarship, Division II, football but it would take at least 6 years to attain that goal;
6. The goals of increased enrollment, campus spirit and community involvement could be achieved by establishing football;
7. Football could be established without damaging the academic culture at the school;
8. Visibility of the school would be enhanced by adding football.

In concluding that Division II football was impractical at that time, the committee noted that there were currently no Division II football teams in Florida and that Division II teams typically had 6 or more full-time coaches. It also pointed out that football is an athletic scholarship sport in Division II.

When the report was presented to the Board of Trustees, it engendered a vigorous discussion. Some trustees were irrevocably opposed to the establishment of a football team while others gave only lukewarm support. After a lively discussion, on April 30, 2010, the board approved the findings of the report and authorized the administration to proceed to institute a football program.

Shortly after the Board of Trustees gave the go-ahead for football, Florida Tech announced that it had named John Thomas, former football coach at Holy Trinity Episcopal Academy, to be Director of Football Operations at the university. Thomas's duties, as reported in *Florida Today* on May 12, 2010, would include fundraising, hiring of the coaching staff and managing football facilities.

The idea of playing non-athletic scholarship NAIA football disappeared shortly after the Board of Trustees approved the concept. *Florida Today* reported on May 14, 2011, that Florida Tech was in discussions with the Gulf South Conference regarding the school joining the conference as a football-only member. Thomas told the newspaper: "The NAIA is not out but we are aggressively exploring the GSC." The Gulf South Conference was a NCAA Division II conference which required its members to provide 36 athletic scholarships for its football teams.

On June 16, 2011, *Florida Today* reported that Steve Englehart, the offensive coordinator/quarterbacks and running backs coach at Indiana State University, had been named as Florida Tech's first head football coach. Thomas was quoted as saying of Englehart: "He's young, he's progressive, he's enthusiastic. The one thing that really impresses us, he's a coach who will be a player's coach." On June 18, *Florida Today* reported on the press conference held by Englehart the previous day. The newspaper reported that Englehart, 34 years old, was "tall, square-shouldered, corn-fed and confident." Englehart had also served as head coach at Rose-Hulman Institute of Technology, a small, private engineering school in Terre Haute, Indiana, after having been a 3-year letterman at quarterback at Indiana State, as well as an "academic standout."

Englehart's hiring would prove to be a positive step for Florida Tech football. Englehart proved to be an effective coach who brought instant success to the program on the field. More importantly, he proved to be an ethical, caring and engaging leader who not only reflected great credit upon Florida Tech but transmitted laudable lessons to his players. He worked hard to recruit players whose character reflected the values of Florida Tech as well as players who would be consistent with the academic standards of the University.

Florida Tech quickly developed a football rivalry with the University of West Florida. *Photo by William Potter.*

On August 20, 2011, *Florida Today* announced that Florida Tech had accepted a bid to play as the first football-only member in the "powerhouse Gulf South Conference," an NCAA Division II conference which required its members to provide 36 athletic scholarships for its football teams. This decision, of course, negated many of the assumptions and conclusions that had been made in the report of the exploratory committee. The financial projections set forth in the report had been rendered meaningless now that the decision to play NCAA Division II football was made, a possibility which the report had said would not be feasible for at least 6 years. Thus, the financial projections were no longer valid, even if the fundraising goals could have been attained, which, in the end, they could not.

The members of the GSC at that time were Delta State, North Alabama, West Alabama, West Florida, Valdosta State and West Georgia. Shorter would join the conference in 2012 and Mississippi College would join in 2014. North Greenville would join the conference for football-only in 2018. North Alabama would leave the conference in 2018 in order to transition to Division I.

From the time of John Thomas' appointment in May, 2010, until the first game to be played in the fall of 2013, Thomas and the university faced the daunting task of hiring a coaching staff, recruiting players, finding facilities for training, practicing and playing games and raising the $2.7 million contemplated by the plan approved by the board.

Englehart's hiring was a good start to building a coaching staff. He immediately set about building his staff using the numerous contacts that he had made at Indiana State and Rose-Hulman.

The need for training and practice facilities was addressed by the construction of a new Varsity Training Center and an artificial turf field on the southwest side of the Florida Tech campus. As reported in *Florida Today* on August 12, 2012, the Varsity Training Center would house football offices, football locker rooms and weight and training facilities for use by all varsity sports.

The need for a playing field for games would be realized when Florida Tech negotiated with Brevard Public Schools for the use of Palm Bay High School stadium. The agreement required Florida Tech to make more than $100,000 worth of improvements to the stadium, including upgrading the press box and building a press box on the visitors' side which would provide television broadcast capabilities and restroom facilities for announcers. These improvements were mandated by the GSC in order to make the facility comply with its requirements. Between the varsity training center, the practice field and the upgrades to the Palm Bay stadium, $3.82 million was spent in construction for football according to the *Florida Today* article of September 13, 2014, by Michael Parsons.

Englehart and his staff immediately undertook an energetic recruiting campaign. Ray Herring, a Holy Trinity graduate and an outstanding defensive back at Notre Dame, was appointed as Recruiting Coordinator. Much of their initial effort was placed on finding junior college players. An article in *Florida Today* on May 21, 2012, disclosed that Herring had visited every junior college in Mississippi while Englehart saw all of the junior college teams in Arizona. Offensive line coach Mike Nahl, offensive coordinator Jayson Martin and defensive coordinator Willie Tillman covered the 70 junior colleges in California. Notably, Englehart acknowledged that junior college players often are perceived as having academic deficiencies so that he established a rule that both junior college transfers and four-year transfers were required to have at least a 3.0 grade point average.

Fundraising would prove to be another challenge and those efforts would be met with limited success. The report of the exploratory committee had posited that more than $2.7 million should be raised in order to implement football. That projection was readily reduced and by September 26, 2011, when *Florida Today* ran an article headlined "Football Makes Perfect Sense at Florida Tech," the university was proclaiming that only $1 million needed to be raised. By the following year, the Fall 2012 edition of *Florida Tech Today* would announce that $1.2 million had been contributed for football funding. Unfortunately, that figure included pledges, several of which were never paid so that the actual amount donated was substantially less than $1 million.

Fund raising difficulties aside, Englehart and his staff continued to recruit vigorously. The Spring 2012 issue of *Florida Tech Today* reported that 22 recruits signed National Letters of Intent on February 1, 2012, for Florida Tech's first recruiting class. By then, Englehart and his staff had visited more than 250 Florida high schools. Defensive back Aneus Sangster from Lauderhill, Florida, faxed his NIL at 7:01 A.M., thereby becoming the school's first ever official commitment for football. The first commit from Brevard County, Mike Ferguson from Cocoa High, faxed his NIL at 8:55 A.M.

On August 12, 2012, John A. Torres would report in *Florida Today* that Florida Tech would begin its first-ever football practice that day with 120 players. Torres reported that, although the team would not begin formal play until 2013, Coach Englehart would run practices this year as though they were already playing official games. Torres related: "There will be daily practices, weekend scrimmages and all the expectations that come with being a member of a college football team." Englehart added: "We want to try and do everything we would do during regular seasons. That's the main goal-to give them the experience."

Florida Tech played a couple of intra-squad games that fall. The first was closed to the public. The second scrimmage was held at Palm Bay stadium on October 27, 2012, and, as reported by Chris Bonanno in *Florida Today*, the fans were treated to a triple-overtime contest. Englehart expressed disappointment that the team had "too many penalties, we lined up wrong a ton, just wasn't quite what I was hoping from our guys-a lot sloppier than what I would have hoped we'd have been." On the other hand, Englehart noted: "These guys just need experience."

National Signing Day in 2013 was another big day for Florida Tech football. As reported by John A. Torres in *Florida Today* on February 7, the Panthers signed 22 players to letters of intent. Among the most notable signees was Jarvis Giles, a highly sought-after running back who had played extensively at the University of South Carolina. Joe Batch, a skilled defensive back from Merritt Island High School, was another big catch for the Panthers. Another recruit Skylar Sheffield, a 305 pound offensive lineman from Tennessee, had been recruited by Tennessee and Ole Miss.

The highly anticipated first intercollegiate football game for Florida Tech took place on September 7, 2013, when the Panthers took on Stetson at Palm Bay High School stadium. As related in the Fall 2013 issue of *Florida Tech Today*, 5,400 fans saw The Panthers defeat Stetson University by a score of 20 to 13. The article related that 50% of the team were freshmen and 35% were sophomores. The historic first points were scored when Brion Ashley kicked a 49-yard field goal. The first touchdown was a 26-yard pass from Sean Ashley to Xavier Milton. The first rushing touchdown was a 5-yard run by Ashley. The first tackle for the Panthers was a 9-yard sack by defensive lineman Tevin Kirkland.

As that first season progressed, the injury bug began to take its toll on the Panthers. By September 27, as they faced the prospect of travelling to Delta State for their first Gulf Coast Conference road game, *Florida Today* reported that 4 key starters were unable to play. Quarterback Sean Ashley would be replaced by Bobby Vega. Defensive standouts Tevin Kirkland, Trai Cadore and Nate McDowell would also miss the game. The return of running back Jarvis Giles was a cause for optimism for the Panthers whose record stood at 1 win and 2 losses. Unfortunately, Giles was injured again early in the game.

After Delta State, the Panthers faced a daunting task when they travelled to play Valdosta State, then ranked as the number 1 Division II team in the country. Although Valdosta State prevailed by a 52 to 14 score, the score was deceiving in that the Panthers actually held the opponent's offense to only 3 points in the first half. A *Florida Today* article by John A. Torres on October 10, 2013, focused on the outstanding play of Florida Tech cornerbacks Manny Abad and Aneus Sangster. Unfortunately, running back Trevor Sand was injured in that game.

The Panthers got back on the winning track with a 28 to 24 victory over Shorter University on October 19, when it stormed back from a 17-point deficit. Florida Tech stayed on the winning track on October 26 when it defeated Warner University on homecoming weekend by a score of 37 to 3. That brought their record to 3 and 5 overall and 3 and 1 at home.

The Panthers were pleasantly surprised when they were invited to play Alderson-Broaddus College, another first year program, in the ECAC Division II Futures Bowl in Philippi, West Virginia, on November 23, 2013. Florida Tech ended the season on a winning note, defeating Alderson-Broaddus by a score of 32 to 20. Quarterback Bobby Vega finished his career by completing 27 of 40 throws for 295 yards and 4 touchdowns. Xavier Milton had 14 catches for 177 yards and 2 touchdowns. Trevor Sand led the team in rushing with 872 yards. On defense, Nathan McDowell led the team in tackling.

Florida Today featured Florida Tech football in the highlights of its year in review on December 31, 2013. It noted that the Panthers had finished the season with 5 wins and 7 losses and had faced 3 nationally ranked conference foes. It also pointed out that the team had appeared on CBS Sports Network and ESPN3.

As Englehart led the Panthers into spring practice in 2014, there was an air of optimism about the team. Englehart told *Florida Today* on February 17, 2014: "I think we have a lot better idea of who we are, both offensively and defensively, and we have an idea of what we are going against." He reported that he and his staff had brought in a good recruiting class which would result in some interesting position battles. The team would have 14 practices leading up to a March 22 spring game.

An article in *Florida Today* on August 3, 2014, illustrated the kind of values that Englehart and his staff promoted among their team. Defensive coordinator Willie Tillman disclosed that all players were required to give a minimum of 12 hours of community service each year. The article disclosed how players were mentoring and tutoring at nearby University Park Elementary School, as well as helping the Boys and Girls Club, the Children's Hunger Project and participating in camps at the Scott Center for Autism. Tillman disclosed that, during the previous year, the players had contributed 976 hours of community service.

The Fall 2014 issue of *Florida Tech Today* disclosed that the team would play in AT&T Stadium, the home of the Dallas Cowboys, against Tarleton State on Saturday, September 20, 2014. The game would be part of the Lone Star Football Festival. The Panthers beat Tarleton State, then ranked 12th in the country, 37 to 31. Quarterback Mark Cato made big plays at crucial times and hit Tyler Bass for the winning touchdown with 3:56 left in the game. J.J. Sanders and Chris Stapleton each had 12 tackles to lead the defense. Travis Sand was injured but was frequently used in short yardage situations.

The following week, on September 27, the Panthers lost a heartbreaker to Division I FCS Bethune-Cookman by a score of 34 to

33. Bethune-Cookman scored 2 touchdowns in the final 3 minutes to come from behind. Florida Tech had a chance to win at the end of the game when it went for a 2-point conversion which failed. Quarterback Mark Cato completed 20 of 36 passing attempts for 310 yards and 4 touchdowns, while running back Trevor Sand ran for 68 yards.

After a home loss to Delta State on October 2, the Panthers turned it around in the next few games. They won their first ever Gulf South Conference road game when they edged West Alabama by a 33 to 32 score on October 11. That was the first home loss for West Alabama in more than 2 years. Cato hit tight end Gabe Hughes with the winning touchdown with 2 seconds left on the clock.

On October 25, they ran their record to 5 and 3 with a 44 to 9 romp over Mississippi College. Their high-powered offense ran up 599 yards. Cato threw for 304 yards and 5 touchdowns. Xavier Milton was on the receiving end of 123 of those yards with 13 catches while Sand ran for 109 yards on 15 carries.

The Panthers ended their 2014 season with a record of 6 wins and 5 losses and a 3 and 5 record in the conference. The final game of the season was another close loss to traditional powerhouse Valdosta State, 31 to 29. Tight end Gabe Hughes had 4 catches for 143 yards while running back Gary Holmes had 106 rushing yards on only 7 carries.

Xavier Milton led the conference in receiving yards, finishing his career with 1,116 yards and 10 touchdowns, while Trevor Sand led the conference in rushing yardage with 1,105 yards. Linebackers J.J. Sanders and Chris Stapleton were among the defensive leaders of the conference.

Florida Today revealed on November 20, 2014, that several Panthers had been honored by the conference. Xavier Milton was named as Co-Offensive Player of the Year while Mark Cato was named as Offensive Freshman of the Year. Englehart was named Co-Coach of the Year. The Winter 2015 issue of *Florida Tech Today* disclosed that Milton had become the football program's first All-American when he was named to the DAKTRONICS All-American team. *Florida Today* announced on February 12, 2015, that Milton had been named to the second team of the Don Hansen Committee Division II All-America team while linebacker J.J. Sanders was named to the third team. Tight end Gabe Hughes received honorable mention.

The 2014 season was marked by a tragedy that affected the entire team. Alex Brack, a kicker from DeFuniak Springs, was killed in a car crash near his home in November 2014. The relationship that Alex had with the team was demonstrated when his family attended the spring game in 2015. His father Greg put it in perspective when he said to *Florida Today* on March 30, 2015: "We just feel like we're part of this family." Englehart noted of the Brack family: "They are so important to us and to our football family and I am really happy that they are staying connected with all of us so much."

Florida Tech opened its 2015 season against Newberry College on September 5. It was a costly game in terms of injuries as both Quarterback Cato and running back Sand left the game with injuries. Sean Ashley took over at quarterback and completed 18 of 29 for 194 yards and 2 touchdowns but it was not enough to avoid a 31 to 28 loss.

The following week was another challenge when the Panthers travelled to Division I FCS Southeastern Louisiana. Although the defense put up stout resistance by holding the Lions to 1 touchdown, Florida Tech fell by a score of 28 to 17. Disaster struck again when Sean Ashley was injured and the Panthers turned to freshman Landon Galloway at quarterback. Chris Stapleton led the defense with 11 tackles and J.J. Sanders added 9 tackles.

After its first win with a victory over Warner, the Panthers opened their conference season by facing North Alabama which was rated number 8 in the country among Division II teams. Florida Tech showed they could play with anyone in the country when they fell to North Alabama by a score of 55 to 48. Cato returned at quarterback and threw for a career-high 353 yards and 5 touchdowns. Englehart told *Florida Today* on September 28: "The bottom line is everybody on this team knows we are capable, knows we are good enough to beat a team like this in our conference but we have to commit ourselves to being excellent all the time."

The following week, Florida Tech faced Delta State, then rated the number 5 team in the country, on the road. The Panthers responded with perhaps the greatest win in the program's brief history, a 41 to 37 thriller. The Panthers jumped out to a big lead early and then held on down the stretch. Englehart told *Florida Today* on October 4: "We never seem to make it easy."

The Panthers returned home the next week to face West Alabama. They put up 353 yards of total offense in the first half, despite turning the ball over twice in the red zone, to come away with a 24 to 13 victory. Gabe Hughes came up big with more than 100 yards receiving. Hughes told *Florida Today* on October 11: "It was good to get it off my chest and finally score, make a big play out there for my team."

On October 17, Florida Tech improved its record to 4 wins and 3 losses overall with a 34 to 7 road victory over Fort Valley State. Gary Holmes rushed for 103 yards on only 10 rushes. They remained on the road the next week and ran their win streak to 4 straight with a 31 to 14 victory over Mississippi College. Cato had 255 passing yards for 3 touchdowns while also running for 78 yards and a touchdown.

The Panthers returned home on Halloween night to defeat Shorter University by a score of 28 to 24. That made 5 straight wins, running the season record to 6 and 3. *Florida Today* reported on November 1 that true freshman Antwuan Haynes rushed for 242 yards while linebacker Chris Stapleton had 14 tackles, an interception and forced a fumble.

The following week was a huge game for Florida Tech as it faced the number 1 Division II team in the country, the University of West Georgia. The Panthers took advantage of the opportunity with a 28 to 26 upset victory. That made 6 straight wins and moved them into a tie for first in the Gulf South Conference. As reported by *Florida Today* on November 8, Trevor Sand rushed for 104 yards while Mark Cato passed for 183 yards. The defense came up big, even scoring on a fumble return by Tevin Kirkland.

It did not get much easier the next week when the Panthers travelled to Valdosta State which was ranked 18th in the nation. Unfortunately, Valdosta came up with big plays in the fourth quarter to win 39 to 21. That ended the regular season for Florida Tech with a record of 7 and 4. Although they held out hopes that they might receive a playoff bid, the selection committee passed them up.

Florida Today reported on November 19 that post-season honors poured in for the Panthers. Linebacker J.J. Sanders was selected as Gulf South Conference Defensive Player of the Year. Sanders, wide receiver Kenny Johnston, tight end Gabe Hughes, offensive guard Kevin Delgado, and defensive back Manny Abad were all selected to the All-Conference first team as reported on November 19 by *Florida Today*. Wide receiver T.J. Lowder, center Blake Stone, tackle Matt Garcia, defensive lineman Skylar Sheffield, linebacker Chris Stapleton, defensive back Leo Alba, defensive back Trai Cadore and kick returner Antwuan Haynes all were selected for the second team. Englehart was named conference Coach of the Year.

The Winter 2016 issue of *Florida Tech Today* recapped the 2015 football season under the headline "One for the Record Books." The article quoted Steve Englehart as saying: "There were times throughout the year that I think we played as well as anyone in the country. This year was a great momentum builder for the future."

Florida Today reported on March 17, 2016, that Florida Tech would hold its first Pro Day on March 31. As a result of the camp, tight end Gabe Hughes became the first player in program history to sign an NFL contract when he signed with the Miami Dolphins on April 30, 2016.

Two events occurred in early 2016 which were to have negative consequences for football at Florida Tech. On May 13, *Florida Today* reported that the school had suffered a $7.4 million shortfall during the past fiscal year and was looking at a projected $10.1 million shortfall for the current fiscal year. Those shortfalls primarily resulted from lower than projected enrollment of international students. That report quoted incoming president Dwayne McCay as planning to "focus down" on the school's athletic programs. The other event was the retirement on June 30, 2016 of President Anthony J. Catanese. Dr. Catanese had been the initial proponent of football at Florida Tech and one of its most ardent fans.

The 2016 season began on a positive note as they travelled to Newberry College and avenged the previous year's loss with a 42 to 28 victory. The Panthers forced 6 turnovers in order to take control of the game. The following week, Florida Tech shined in its home opener by routing Mississippi College 41 to 0. They followed those games with road victories over Shorter College and Presbyterian College to run their record to 5 and 0. That moved the Panthers up to a national ranking of 16th.

The win streak came to an end when Florida Tech fell to the University of West Florida on October 1 by a 42 to 39 score. *Florida Today* reported on October 3 that the Panthers' plane had arrived in Pensacola 3 hours late and had to play catchup most of the game. The crowd of 6,588 was treated to a 4-hour battle that saw West Florida rush for 458 yards against a defense which ranked third in Division II. The Coastal Classic Trophy was awarded in order to recognize the winner of the game between the only Division II football programs in Florida.

The Panthers had a 2-week hiatus due to cancelling the scheduled game with North Alabama due to Hurricane Matthew. The Panthers then took on Fort Valley State at homecoming in Melbourne. They quickly showed that they were back on the winning track as they routed the visitors by a score of 48 to 14.

The Panthers were back on the road the following week as they travelled to West Alabama. The game became an offensive shootout. Florida Tech outgained West Alabama with 643 yards to 504 yards. However as reported in *Florida Today* on October 23, the Panthers committed too many turnovers at critical points in the game and lost 45 to 35. Their record fell to 5 and 2. However, the following week a win over Valdosta State moved them to 6 and 2 and raised their playoff hopes. Wins over West Georgia and a 42 to 16 rout of Delta State took them to 8 and 2 and a berth in the playoffs.

The team suffered a big setback when starting quarterback Mark Cato, also known as Marquis Gordon Robins II, was arrested for two counts of driving under the influence with property damage and driving under the influence on November 13, 2016. He was arrested after his car hit a fire hydrant and then, crashed into a house at 3:55 AM. *Florida Today* revealed on November 15 that Robins (Cato) had been arrested in March

2015, when University of Central Florida police accused him of driving impaired in a bike lane near UCF. Robins had completed 50 hours of community service for that charge. Florida Tech immediately suspended him indefinitely when he was arrested the second time.

Florida Tech hosted its first playoff game ever on November 19, 2016, when it faced North Greenville. The Panthers, having finished the regular season with 8 wins and 2 losses, were, according to Englehart's statement to *Florida Today* on November 19, "focused and ready." The Panthers fell to North Greenville by a 27 to 13 score. North Greenville was aided by a couple of key interceptions. Despite the loss, it was a great season for a team playing only its fourth season in one of the toughest conferences in the country. Englehart told *Florida Today*: "They had an 8-win season and got a team to the playoffs in 4 years. I just think they have a lot to be proud of."

A highlight of the season was noted in *Florida Today* on December 15 when it was reported that defensive back Manny Abad was named a first team Academic All-American. The Fall 2017 issue of *Florida Tech Today* reported that Abad had become the second player in program history to sign with an NFL team when he signed a 3-year rookie contract with the Tennessee Titans. The Fort Lauderdale native had ended his college career as a 4-time All-Gulf South Conference pick, a 2015 USA College Football All-American and a first team Academic All-American, graduating with a 4.0 cumulative GPA as an accounting major.

Continuing financial challenges at Florida Tech, primarily as a result of declining numbers of international students due to increasing difficulties in obtaining student visas, caused the school to intensify scrutiny of its athletic programs. An analysis conducted by the school's Chief Financial Officer presented to the Athletics Committee of the Board of Trustees on April 4, 2017, indicated that the net loss on football exceeded $700,000 per year, a substantially greater loss than cash flow data would lead one to expect. These losses exceeded the losses of all other sports at the university combined.

The Panthers opened the 2017 season with a 44 to 0 shutout of Virginia University of Lynchburg on September 3. Florida Tech amassed 387 yards of offense while allowing their opponent only 101 total yards. *Florida Today* reported that Brandon Ziarno started at quarterback before being replaced in the second quarter by Trent Chmelik. Chmelik threw for 129 yards and 2 touchdowns.

The Panthers 'next game was a huge challenge as they travelled to Louisiana to face Division I-FCS opponent McNeese State. Mark Cato had completed his suspension on account of off-field misconduct and would be eligible to play in this game. Cato threw for 333 yards and 2 touchdowns, but the Panthers fell to McNeese by a score of 42 to 21.

They then returned home to play Gulf South Conference foe Shorter College on September 14. The Panthers amassed 510 yards of total offense in racking up a 31 to 6 victory. *Florida Today* reported on September 23 that running back Antwuan Haynes won conference Offensive Player of the Week honors as a result of his 188 rushing yards in the game.

Florida Tech hit the road again the following week to face Mississippi College on September 23. They extended their season to 3 and 1 with a 35 to zero shutout. Cato started the game at quarterback but was replaced by Chmelik in the second half. Chmelik responded by completing 9 of 14 passing attempts for 181 yards while Haynes rushed for 139 yards. Patrick Banks led the defense with 8 tackles.

On September 30, the Panthers faced a rugged task when they played conference foe West Florida in Melbourne. The previous year, Florida Tech had fallen to West Florida by a 42 to 39 score on last minute heroics by the Argonauts. This year, Florida Tech lost by last second heroics when West Florida kicked a 44-yard field goal as time expired to win by a 23 to 21 score. Haynes had another terrific game as he racked up 170 rushing yards.

Things did not get easier the following week as the Panthers travelled to North Alabama on October 7 to face an opponent which had been national runner-up the previous year. North Alabama prevailed by a score of 30 to 7. Cato returned at quarterback and completed 13 of 25 for 129 yards. Florida Tech's record sat at 3 and 3 overall and 2 and 2 in the conference.

Florida Tech snapped its 2-game losing streak when it travelled to South Carolina on October 14 to defeat North Greenville by a 42 to 31 score. The Panthers registered 552 yards of total offense with Haynes rushing for 155 yards and Cato throwing for 325 yards.

The Panthers improved their record to 5 and 3 overall and 3 and 2 in the conference with a narrow 41 to 39 victory over 18th-ranked West Alabama on October 21. Mark Cato's 11-yard touchdown run with 51 seconds to play won the game. Antwuan Haynes rushed for 112 yards and 2 touchdowns.

Unfortunately, Florida Tech could not maintain its winning streak the following week when it was routed by Valdosta State by a score of 42 to 14. Haynes, the conference rushing leader, rushed for 59 yards and the Panthers registered 307 total yards.

They returned home for homecoming on November 4 for the last home game of the season against West Georgia. That resulted in a 20 to 14 loss which evened their season record at 5 and 5 and took their conference record to 3 and 4. Cato passed for only 108 yards while

Haynes was held to 32 yards as the Panthers had their lowest offensive output of the year with 172 yards.

The Panthers closed out the 2017 season by travelling to Delta State in Cleveland, Mississippi on November 11. Delta State rolled to a 42 to 20 victory while rolling up 418 total yards and holding Florida Tech to 288 yards. This ended the Florida Tech season with a record of 5 wins and 6 losses (3 wins and 5 losses in the conference). Thus ended a rather disappointing season for Florida Tech. One can only speculate whether Cato's controversial reinstatement after his legal problems affected the team's chemistry but some observers contended that it did have that effect.

Adonis Davis and Antwuan Haynes were selected for All-Conference first team. Romell Guerrier, J.T. Hassel and Kevin Purlett were named to the second team.

Legal woes continued for Florida Tech football continued when backup quarterback Brandon Ziarno was arrested on marijuana charges on June 8, 2018. According to a *Florida Today* report on June 12, Ziarno confessed to Melbourne police that he had sold cannabis to a few of his Florida Tech teammates. On June 14, *Florida Today* reported that Ziarno had been permanently removed from the team due to violating rules of conduct.

In a report in *Florida Today* on August 31, 2018, Englehart acknowledged that it was the team's cohesiveness, his players' chemistry on and off the field that had been the problem with the team the previous year." He disclosed that they had spent a lot of effort in the off-season working on those issues. He continued: "Our guys genuinely care about each other, and the chemistry among our team is much better than it was last year."

They opened the 2018 football season with a 33 to 14 win on the road at Benedict College in Columbia, South Carolina on September 1. Quarterback Trent Chmelik passed for 191 yards and Antwuan Haynes ran for 72 yards. However, it was the defense, led by Evan Thompson, which really shined with 4 turnovers, 3 interceptions, a fumble recovery and 2 defensive scores.

In their home opener on September 8, Florida Tech edged Newberry by a score of 17 to 10. The defense led the way, holding Newberry to 295 yards rushing and a mere 96 yards through the air.

The Panthers pushed their record to 3 and 0 with a home victory over Delta State on September 15. Chmelik threw for 184 yards and Haynes rushed for 88 yards in the 30 to 12 win. Romell Guerrier had 127 receiving yards.

The Panthers' unbeaten skein came to an end on September 22 when they fell at eighth-ranked West Georgia in Carrollton, Georgia by a score of 30 to 21. Chmelik completed 17 of 31 passes for 191 yards. Adonis Davis tied the Florida Tech career record for sacks by racking up his eighteenth career sack.

They returned to the winning track with a road victory over Wingate on September 29. The special teams earned the win with Tyrone Cromwell's block of a point after attempt which was picked up by John McClure and returned for a score to gain the 26 to 23 victory.

The Panthers returned home on October 6 to host Mississippi College. The Panthers trailed 21 to 10 before coming back for a 31 to 24 victory. That took the season record to 5 and 1. Haynes rushed 15 times for 112 yards while Chmelik threw for 184 yards.

The following week was homecoming at Florida Tech and the Panthers faced undefeated Valdosta State. Valdosta proved too much for the Panthers as they took a 24 to 0 halftime lead and spoiled homecoming with a 51 to 32 victory. Chmelik threw for 290 yards, 83 of which were caught by Guerrier.

The following week was a big game for Florida Tech as they travelled to Pensacola to face the University of West Florida in the Coastal Classic on October 20. The Panthers secured one of the biggest victories in program history when they staged a furious comeback to win by a score of 30 to 28 over the nineteenth ranked team in the country. The Panthers were down by 18 points before scoring 27 unanswered points. Chmelik completed 17 of 30 passes for 256 yards and 2 touchdowns. Haynes had 29 carries for 118 yards. J.T. Hassell had 5 tackles, including a tackle for loss. That brought the Panthers' season record to 6 and 2 overall and 3 and 2 in the conference.

The Panthers were on the road again the following week at West Alabama where they fell by a 29 to 22 score. Englehart noted to *Florida Today* on October 29: "We turned the ball over too many times and we didn't score in the red zone. We kept getting field goals and we needed to get touchdowns in the red zone." One highlight for Florida Tech was Richard Leveille's pick-six which gave him 3 defensive touchdowns for the season, a single-season school record.

On Senior Day at Florida Tech on November 3, the Panthers routed North Greenville by a score of 37 to 7, taking the Panthers' record to 7 and 3 overall and 3 and 4 and 3 in the conference. Chmelik was 13 for 18 for 178 yards. Antwuan Haynes became Florida Tech's career rushing leader by rushing for 88 yards on 22 carries.

Florida Tech completed its regular season by routing Shorter College in Rome, Georgia, on November 10 by a score of 55 to 7. The win brought the season record to 8 and 3 overall and clinched a bid to the NCAA Division II playoffs for the Panthers. Florida Tech showed great balance with 241 rushing yards and 246 passing yards.

Florida Tech travelled to Hickory, North Carolina, to face Lenoir-Rhyne of the South Atlantic Conference in the first round of the playoffs on November 17. This would be the Panthers' second playoff appearance in the 6-year history of the program. Lenoir-Rhyne scored 37 unanswered points and took advantage of 6 turnovers to earn a 43 to 21 victory.

J.T. Hassell, Adonis Davis and Romell Guerrier were selected for the first team of the Gulf South Conference All-Conference team. Running back Antwuan Haynes received second-team honors. That was the third consecutive first-team selection for Davis who was the top tackler in the league with a school-record 105 tackles. Guerrier led the conference in 5 different receiving categories.

Florida Tech started its 2019 season on a positive note with a 23 to 22 squeaker over Savannah State on September 8. The Panthers outgained their foe by a 461 to 269 margin.

The following week, Florida Tech travelled to South Carolina to face Newberry College on September 14. The Panthers staved off a last-minute threat by Newberry to hang on for a 30 to 28 road win. Trent Chmelik completed 11 passes of 16 attempts for 210 yards and a touchdown before leaving the game with an injury. Mike Diliello took over for Chmelik and led the Panthers on a 9-play, 75-yard touchdown drive which included 55 rushing yards by Diliello.

The Panthers opened their Gulf South Conference schedule for 2019 when they travelled to Delta State on September 22. They suffered a heartbreaking 30 to 28 defeat when the Statesmen outgained them by 491 yards to 381 yards. A bright spot for the Panthers was redshirt freshman quarterback Mike Diliello who completed 17 passes for 309 yards and 2 touchdowns.

Florida Tech finally experienced the luxury of a home game when it battered West Georgia on September 29 by a score of 44 to 10. The Panthers ran up 510 yards of total offense, 227 through the air and 283 on the ground. Diliello threw for 2 touchdowns while also running for 94 yards.

On October 5, Florida Tech faced Fort Valley State in Melbourne. Turnovers plagued the Panthers, leading to a 33 to 29 defeat. Diliello completed 21 of 35 passes for 288 yards. Marquise Lewis had 7 solo tackles.

On October 12, Florida Tech lost to Mississippi College for the first time in program history. The visiting Panthers fell by the score of 34 to 14. Florida Tech was able to muster only 232 total yards on offense. Malachi Timberlake led the Panther defense with 8 tackles.

On October 19, the Panthers faced the defending national champions of Valdosta State. Although Florida Tech managed to stick with them for the first quarter, Valdosta State soon proved to be too strong and pulled away for a 55 to 28 victory. Trent Chmelik made his first start since being injured in the Newberry game and made a strong showing with 235 yards and 2 touchdowns passing.

West Florida regained the Coastal Classic Trophy when it defeated Florida Tech on October 26 by a score of 38 to 14. The game was the homecoming game at Florida Tech and was interrupted by an extended weather delay. The highlight for Florida Tech was a 91-yard touchdown run by freshman Mike Diliello, his eleventh rushing touchdown of the season.

Florida Tech lost a heartbreaker to West Alabama on November 2 when the Tigers kicked a field goal as time expired to post a 13 to 10 win over the Panthers. The Panthers had led by a 10 to 0 score before West Alabama shut down the offense and Florida Tech was beset with 111 penalty yards.

Florida Tech finally broke its 5-game losing streak on November 9 when Trey Schaneville kicked a 23-yard field goal in the second overtime period to defeat North Greenville by a score of 17 to 14. It was the first overtime game in program history for the Panthers. That brought the Panthers' record to 4 and 6 on the season with a 2 and 5 conference record.

Florida Tech closed out its 2019 season on Senior Day against Shorter College. The Panthers romped by a score of 42 to 3. Quarterback Mike Diliello completed 22 passes of 26 attempts for 209 yards and 3 touchdowns. John McClure had 8 tackles while T.J. Harrell added 6 tackles. The Panthers closed the season with a record of 5 wins and 6 losses and a conference record of 3 wins and 5 losses.

Linebacker Evan Thompson was selectd to the first team of the All-Gulf South Conference team. Defensive back Tyrone Cromwell, tight end Kenny Hiteman, wide receiver Miles Kelly and safety John McClure were selected to the second team. Thomas Roman was selected to the Academic All-District Team selected by the College Sports Information Directors of America. Roman, a junior linebacker, achieved a 3.90 grade point average in aerospace engineering. Seven members of the team were selected to the 2019 Fall All-Academic Team of the Gulf South Conference, including Trent Chmelik, Mike Diliello, Evan Kulyk, Max Linder, Thomas Roman, Evan Thompson and Curtiss Thies.

It was a shock to most when Florida Tech announced on May 11. 2020, that it had eliminated its football team. *Florida Today's* Jon Santucci reported on May 12 that Florida Tech's website stated: "Eliminating the expense of the football program is a necessary step to ensure that Florida Tech can continue meeting its core educational missions." The school assured players that it would honor athletic scholarships for up to 4 years.

The news article was somewhat misleading when it reported that the football program had lost only about $4,500 during the 2018 season with expenses of $3,101,393 and revenues of $3,096,914. Those figures are accurate as to the cash flow but ignore the non-operating costs of facilities and personnel of the university. In reality, costs exceeded revenue by more than $700,000.

The shock to Englehart, his staff and his players was exacerbated by the manner in which the coach learned of the decision to eliminate the program. President Dwayne McCay declined to deliver the news himself but, rather, dispensed an intermediary to deliver the bad news.

It is illuminating to consider the conclusions of the exploratory committee which had delivered the 2010 report and to review the results of the football program with those conclusions. Of course, it is difficult to compare the financial projections of the report to the actual financial results because the report's recommendations as to football scholarships and the amount of funds to be raised prior to playing had been ignored. If those recommendations had been followed, it is quite possible that the committee's conclusion that the program could have a positive cash flow would have been realized. As to the committee's conclusion regarding enrollment, campus spirit and community spirit, there is no data which supports the conclusion that the program would enhance enrollment. There did seem to be some initial increase in enthusiasm for the school at the onset of the program. However, that enthusiasm was never evidenced by student attendance at the games. There were seldom more than a few hundred students in attendance. There was enthusiastic support for the program in the community although it is unclear as to whether that enthusiasm yielded tangible benefits for the university. The report also concluded that the program could be established without damaging the academic culture at the school. Steve Englehart worked hard to recruit the kind of players who would meet that objective and was largely successful in doing so. However, there were instances in which players were indifferent students who did not support that academic culture. Finally, the committee had concluded that football would increase the recognition of the school. In view of the publicity generated by the football team and its play in the Gulf South Conference, there is little doubt that the school gained recognition.

Steve Englehart built an enviable record in his 9 years at Florida Tech. He worked hard to recruit players with high character and with serious academic interests. He built the program from the foundation that John Thomas had created. He produced teams that became formidable competitors more quickly than anyone could have expected. He became a well-known and respected figure in the community and in the region and, thereby, enhanced the respect of Florida Tech. He earned a reputation among his peers for high ethical standards, compassion, hard work and competence.

Englehart's won-loss record at Florida Tech:

Year	Overall	GS Conference
2013	5-7	1-5
2014	6-5	3-4
2015	7-4	5-2
2016	8-3	5-2
2017	5-6	3-5
2018	8-4	5-3
2019	5-6	3-5
Total	44-35	25-26

For Englehart, his won-loss record is not the most significant part of his biography. His positive impact on the many young men he molded is the most important part of his record.

- See also Dodd, Dennis "College Football Attendance Declines for the Seventh Straight Season to Lowest Average Since 1981," at https://www.cbssports/college-football/news/college-football-attendance-declines-for-seventh-straight-season-to-lowest-average-since-1981/, February 24, 2022. See also Bachman, Rachel, "College Football's Growing Problem: Empty Seats," at https://www.wsj.com /articles/college-footballs-growing-problem-empty-seats-1535634001, August 30, 2018.
- For the increase in the number of colleges fielding football teams, see the website of the National Football Foundation at https://footballfoundation.org/news/2019/7/23/775-colleges-and-universities-now-offering-football.aspx.
- Dr. Catanese's efforts to expand the athletic programs at Florida Tech were chronicled in "Think Big: Tony Catanese Doesn't Believe in Small Ideas," *Space Coast Living Magazine*, August 2, 2012.
- Information about membership in the Gulf South Conference was gleaned from https://en.wikipedia.org/wiki/gulf_south_conference.
- The ECAC Futures Bowl is taken from floridatechsports.com>news>2013/11/23.
- Marquis Gordon Robins II was the legal name of Mark Cato. It is unclear how Robins came to be known as Mark Cato at Florida Tech.
- The results of individual games are compiled from reports in *Florida Today*, usually the issues published the day following each game. Other information regarding game results and post-season honors was extracted for news reports on FloridaTechSports.com. (floridatechsports.com>news)

CHAPTER TWELVE:
VOLLEYBALL PERSEVERES

By William C. Potter

Volleyball was inaugurated as an intercollegiate sport at Florida Tech in 1977. The first coach was Sophie Trett, who also coached the fencing team. *Florida Today* disclosed on November 6, 1977, that Trett's Engineers had closed their season with a victory over Saint Leo on the previous day. Earlier that day, they had lost to Eckerd College. *Ad Astra*, the college's annual yearbook, made no mention of volleyball as an intercollegiate sport until 1979 when it noted that the team was coached by Cheryl DeMoss. The 1980 *Ad Astra* noted that the 1979 season had ended with a record of 8 wins and 11 losses, compared to the record of 1 win and 9 losses the previous year. That 1979 team consisted of 11 players and was coached by Dave Clay, a computer science professor, in his first season at the helm. Clay was an eclectic person who was later honored by the Faculty Senate for his outstanding teaching and research.

Sophie Trett coached the volleyball team to success.
Photo from University Archives.

The next mention of volleyball appeared in the 1982 *Ad Astra* which disclosed that the team for the 1981 season had consisted of 11 players and was coached by John Holdsworth. The 1983 *Ad Astra* disclosed that the team now had 19 players and that Holdsworth remained the coach. The 1985 *Ad Astra* recited that the team had a new coach in Alphretta Roberts but disclosed no results for the season.

The 1986 *Ad Astra* disclosed that Florida Tech volleyball for the 1985 season, under a new coach, had experienced its best season ever. The "new" coach was none other than Sophie Trett, returning after a few years hiatus. On October 7, *Florida Today* reported that the Panthers had participated in the Stetson University Women's Volleyball Invitational Tournament, losing to Jacksonville, Stetson and Florida A&M, before recovering to defeat Mercer and Georgia Southern. The team consisted of a pair of sophomores and juniors, with the entire remaining team consisting of freshmen. *Florida Today* reported on October 20, 1985, that The Panthers had, during that single week, defeated Eckerd College, Weber College and Nova University.

Rick Lindon, an Air Force officer at Patrick Air Force Base, took over as coach for the 1986 season. *Florida Today* reported on October 8, 1986, that the team had lost its 3rd game in a row with a loss to Rollins, taking the team's season record to 3 wins and 10 losses. The newspaper reported again on October 10 that the Lady Panthers had played one of its best games of the season on October 9, even though it fell to Saint Leo, taking its record to 3 and 11 overall and 0 and 5 in the conference. Kathie Ludwig and Marissa Poudrier starred defensively for Florida Tech. The Lady Panthers then won 2 in a row, making their record 5 and 11. Marissa Poudrier had 13 kills and 13 blocks in defeating Palm Beach Atlantic.

The 1987 Panther volleyball team was again coached by Rick Lindon. According to *Ad Astra*, the team had 10 members and limped to a record of 3 wins and 26 losses. According to *Florida Today's* reporting on October 20, 1987, Marissa Poudrier, Nicole Barlow, Theresa Hefner and Lynn Grinstead were outstanding servers in a victory over Bethune-Cookman College.

The 1988 team had a new coach, Melanie Clark. *Ad Astra* reported that the team improved to a season record of 9 wins and 14 losses. It also noted that Kathie Ludwig had been named to the all-tournament team at the Jacksonville Gold Tournament. In a game against Webber College on September 24, Laura Hob set a new school record with 10 consecutive serves. An article from *Florida Today* by David Jones on October 3, 1989, highlighted Lynn Grinstead, a junior middle hitter. It noted that Grinstead would not travel with the team for a tournament in North Carolina because she could not afford to lose that much classroom time. Grinstead held a 3.2 GPA and was majoring in marine biology/aquaculture. She not only starred on the volleyball team but was a stalwart as a pitcher on the softball team as well.

In 1991, Barney Andrews took over the program as coach. When the Lady Panthers defeated Saint Leo on October 5, they ran their record to 4 and 5 overall and 2 and 3 in the conference. David Jones observed in *Florida Today* on November 5 that: "After years of struggling, F.I.T. appears on the way to respectability. The squad is full of young, talented athletes and Barney Andrews has turned out to be the steadying influence the program needed after lean times."

Florida Today reported on September 23, 1992, that the Lady Panthers, now coached by Joe Hauser, had lost to Florida Southern, its 4th consecutive loss, to fall to 3 and 5 on the season. Hauser was the team's 4th coach in the last 3 years. Hauser observed, however: "But I think that we are two or three players from being a team to be reckoned with." On November 18, 1992, the Lady Panthers wrapped up the 1992 season with a road win at Saint Leo. *Florida Today* reported that the win brought their season record to 13 and 16 overall and 2 and 8 in the conference. Elisa Bartolo and Edna Escudero led the team with 19 kills apiece. Bartolo, of course, would rise to even greater accomplishments as a softball player.

In 1993, Florida Tech hired a volleyball coach who would lead the Panthers to new levels of success. Mitch Jacobs had been an assistant coach at the University of South Florida and his leadership brought immediate progress to the program. The Lady Panthers completed the season with a record of 17 wins and 16 losses, the 1st season in program history with a winning record and the most season wins in its history. Attendance at home games increased dramatically. As disclosed by *Florida Today* on November 18, junior Cathy Dennis was accorded honorable mention All-Sunshine State Conference honors.

The Florida Tech volleyball season in 1994 was a bit of a step backwards. When the Panthers fell to the University of North Florida on October 31, their record dropped to 12 and 19 overall and 3 and 8 in the conference. However, the 1995 season witnessed a return to a winning record. *Florida Today* reported on November 9, 1995, that the Lady Panthers had defeated Saint Leo the previous night to conclude their season. Their season record of 17 wins and 12 losses tied the record for most wins in a season. Their record of 4 and 10 in the conference was good for a 6th place finish. Kristin Peppel was selected to the 2nd team on the All-Sunshine State Conference team. As reported by *Florida Today* on November 10, 1995, Peppel completed her career as the school's all-time leader in career kills and holder of the record for most kills in a season. As further reported by *Florida Today* on December 7, Peppel topped off her career by becoming the 1st Florida Tech volleyball player ever named to the Division II South's All-Region team. She also joined the basketball team the following season.

The 1996 season brought even greater success. As disclosed by the 1997 edition of *Ad Astra*, the team achieved its best record ever with 20 wins and 11 losses. A victory over Eckerd College on November 20 closed the season with a 6 win, 8 loss conference record, the best in program history. One of the stars of that 1996 team was one of the most notable volleyball players in Florida Tech history, Kari Wanat, class of 1999. Wanat was a first team Academic All-American in 1999 after having received second team honors in 1998. She was the university's Student of the Year in 1999. She graduated as the school's all-time leader in digs with 1,791 and had over 1,000 assists as well. She captained the team for 2 years while making the Dean's List every semester. She graduated with a 4.0 GPA, having majored in molecular biology. She graduated from the Washington University Medical School in 2004 and went on to become the Vice-Chair and Associate Professor of Dermatology and Dermatopathology at the Medical College of Wisconsin. Dr. Wanat was inducted into the Florida Tech Sports Hall of Fame in 2015.

The 1997 Lady Panther volleyball team was another success story. As disclosed by the 1998 edition of *Ad Astra*, the 1997 team made history when it compiled a winning record in the conference by winning 8 while losing 6 games. It also registered a winning overall record of 20 wins and 15 losses. Jacobs told *Florida Today* on November 12, 1997: "Since I've been here, this team has steadily improved a great deal. I am very, very excited." Carrie Green was named to the Academic All-District 1st team while Kari Wanat was named to the 2nd team.

The 1998 season brought another winning record for the Lady Panthers. *Florida Today* reported on November 14 that Florida Tech had fallen to 5th-ranked Barry in 5 games. That took the Panthers' record to 18 and 10 overall and 6 and 7 in the conference. They would finish at 19 and 10 overall and 7 and 7 in the conference.

On July 15, 1999, *Florida Today* disclosed that Mitch Jacobs had resigned as volleyball coach at Florida Tech to become head coach at Division I Fairfield University. In his 6 years at Florida Tech, Jacobs had compiled a record of 107 wins and 87 losses. Jacobs, age 33, by far the most successful volleyball coach in program history, noted: "My strength as a coach is my technical training. I'm solid in tactical ability, in preparation for games." He added: "I'm going to miss the people at Florida Tech. Bill Jurgens has been wonderful to me." The most impressive part of Jacobs' record at Florida Tech was the fact that in 11 of the 12 semesters during his tenure, the volleyball team achieved the highest GPA among all athletic programs at the school.

Jacobs' replacement as head coach of the Lady Panthers was Perri Hankins, who, in a strange turn of events, had been the head coach for whom Jacobs worked at South Florida. Hankins led the team to immediate success during the 1999 season, compiling a record of 17 wins and 10 losses and its best ever conference record of 10 and 4. As reported by *Florida Today* on November 16, the season included wins over Barry and Florida Southern for the 1st time in school history. Disappointingly, that record was not enough to earn a spot in the NCAA Division II South Region tournament.

On February 4, 2000, *Florida Today* reported that Hankins had resigned, having fulfilled the 1-year commitment she made when hired. On March 28, the newspaper disclosed that Cody Hein, a former assistant coach at Barry, had been hired as the new coach of the Lady Panthers. Hein inherited a young team with good potential. Jessica Reid was the sole returning starter. Hein's inaugural team won 5 of their final 8 matches to finish the season at 10 and 15 overall and 6 and 8 in the conference.

The 2001 Lady Panthers volleyball team won 5 of their last 6 games to finish the season with 21 wins and 14 losses, thereby establishing a program record for wins in a season. Sophomore middle hitter Alys Thomas made the all-conference 1st team while Jessica Mirda was named to the conference all-freshman team.

2002 was a rather disappointing season for the Lady Panthers. When they defeated Lynn on November 16, they evened their record at 15 wins and 15 losses. Alys Thomas was named to the 2nd team on the All-Conference Team while outside hitter Jenny Hart was named to the conference all-freshman team.

On April 19, 2003, Florida Today reported that Cody Hein had resigned to accept the coaching position at Chico State University in his home state of California. Hein would remain at Chico State for the next 17 seasons until his untimely death in 2020. On April 26, the newspaper disclosed that Patrick Barrett, who had been an assistant under Hein for the past 3 years, had been named head coach.

An article in *Florida Today* on November 15, 2003, outlined the remarkable careers of 3 senior Lady Panthers who had rewritten the volleyball record book at Florida Tech. Michelle White had set school records for career assists, single game assists and season assists. Natalia Acevedo, a former Palm Bay High star, was the 1st player in school history to have more than 1,000 digs and 1,000 kills in a career. Alys Thomas established records for most career kills, single season kills and attack percentage. The 2003 season concluded with a loss to Florida Southern on November 15, leaving the Panthers with a record of 13 wins and 19 losses.

The 2004 Lady Panther volleyball team was young and struggled as it gained experience. When they lost to Tampa on November 13, their record fell to 4 wins and 23 losses. The 2005 squad made some improvement and completed the season with 9 wins and 24 losses with a 4 and 12 conference record.

Florida Today reported on June 8, 2006, that Coach Barrett was unusually pleased with the recruiting class which signed that spring. He told the paper: "We're pretty excited going into next year. I think the personalities are going to mesh well. It should help push everybody." Unfortunately, the excitement did not translate to victories as the 2006 Lady Panthers won only 2 games while losing 30 and went winless in 16 conference games. Freshman Melissa Reinders was named honorable mention all-conference as well as a member of the conference All-Freshman team.

On January 23, 2007, it was announced that Qi Wang had been hired as head coach of the Lady Panthers' volleyball team. Wang became the 9th coach in the 21-year history of the program. He had previously held head coaching positions at Truman State and Northern Michigan and boasted a .836 winning percentage. Wang had immediate success as the 2007 team posted a 21 and 12 overall record and a 4 win, 12 loss conference record. The 2008 season began with even greater success. When the Lady Panthers defeated Lenoir-Rhyne and Mount Olive on September 11, those victories extended their season record to 10 wins and no losses. Florida Tech completed that 2008 season with a 20 and 14 record, giving them 40 wins in 2 seasons, a new high for the program. Sacha Gumbs was named honorable mention on the all-conference team while Janelle Branch made the conference All-Freshman team. The most notable win was a November 1 victory over Florida Southern, ranked 11th in the nation at the time.

On October 9, 2009, athletic director Bill Jurgens announced that Qi Wang had resigned as coach, effective immediately. He would be replaced by an interim staff to coach the remainder of the season. No reason was given for his resignation but, coming in the middle of the season as it did, a lot of questions remained unanswered. Given these uncomfortable circumstances, it is not surprising that the 2009 squad finished the season with a record of 12 and 15, with a 3 and 13 record in the conference.

On February 10, 2010, A.D. Jurgens announced that Erin Lee had been selected as head coach of the volleyball program. Florida Tech compiled a record of 10 wins and 21 losses during the 2010 season while managing to win only a single game in the conference while dropping 15 conference contests. The 2011 season proved no more satisfying as the Lady Panthers won only 6 games while losing 24 with a 2 and 14 record in conference games. On November 18, 2011, it was announced that Lee had resigned her coaching position. Lee had a positive attitude about her tenure in Melbourne as she said: "I feel that I've helped the girls in volleyball and in life. We've also created a great fan base for volleyball, and I hope that continues."

On January 24, 2012, Florida Tech announced that Nathan Baker had been appointed as head volleyball coach. Baker had previously coached at Tusculum College and the University of West Alabama. Strangely, Baker never coached a game at Florida Tech as it was announced on March 15, 2012, that he had resigned from his position. Amy O'Brien, assistant coach, was elevated to interim head coach pending a search for a permanent coach. On May 4, 2012, Jurgens named O'Brien as permanent head coach. O'Brien had been a standout player at Florida Tech as well as an assistant coach for the past 2 years. She would put an end to the revolving door of volleyball coaches at Florida Tech and bring some direly needed stability to the program. O'Brien told the Fall 2012 edition of *Florida Tech Today* that she had several goals for the team, including to play as a team, compete for NCAA postseason play, achieve a 3.3 team GPA, make a positive impact on the campus and the community, and help promote the team's home games.

Under O'Brien's guidance, the Lady Panthers immediately experienced a dramatic improvement. They completed the 2012 season with a record of 15 wins and 14 defeats with a 5 and 11 record in the conference. Those 15 wins were the most since 2008 while the 5 conference wins were the most since 2003. At one point during the season, they won 7 straight matches. Libero Angie Lassman was selected to the 1st team of the all-conference team and the 2nd team of the All-South Region team. The Lady Panthers followed that season with a solid showing in 2013 with a 15 and 15 overall record and a 5 and 11 conference record. Lassman ended her Florida Tech career with 1,606 digs, good for 2nd all-time at Florida Tech.

Volleyball player Carissa Thiel, a marine biology major, related to the Fall 2014 issue of *Florida Tech Today* that she had spent her summer observing and recording the behavior of great white sharks on a cage diving tourist boat in Mossel Bay, South Africa. She told the publication: "These observations helped us inform the public about conservation and the importance of protecting sharks." Notably, she said nothing about protecting herself.

Florida Tech opened its 2014 volleyball season with a trip to Hawaii where they played 4 matches in 3 days. Although it was undoubtedly a great experience and a memorable start to the season, the season was less satisfying as they finished with a record of 10 and 21 overall and just 2 and 14 in the conference. The 2015 season brought some improvement as the Lady Panthers fought their way to a 13 and 16 overall record with a 4 and 12 conference record. Unfortunately, that improvement did not carry over to the 2016 season as the Lady Panthers compiled an 8 win, 22 loss record, with a 2 win, 14 loss record in the league. Florida Tech improved slightly in the 2017 season as they won 9 while losing 17, including 4 wins and 16 losses in the conference. The 2018 season brought a record of 9 wins and 22 losses and a conference record of 4 wins and 16 losses. The 2019 season was another challenge with a record of only 4 wins against 27 losses and only a single conference win and 19 losses.

On July 18, 2020, the Sunshine State Conference announced that the conference sports, including volleyball, scheduled for the fall of 2020, had been postponed due to the ongoing COVID-19 pandemic. The announcement stated that it was anticipated that some of the games which had been scheduled for fall of 2020 would be played in the spring of 2021. The Lady Panthers returned to the floor for the 2021 spring season and split 4 exhibition matches.

On July 9, 2021, Amy O'Brien resigned as coach of the volleyball program after 9 years heading the program. She compiled 83 wins, the 2nd most in program history. Her overall record was 83 and 154 with a 27 and 113 record in the conference. Although obviously not satisfied with the wins and losses, she had been an exemplary representative of the school and had taught her players invaluable life lessons.

On August 5, 2021, it was announced that Ashlee Crowder had been hired as head volleyball coach at Florida Tech. Crowder took over for the 2021 fall season and led the Lady Panthers to a record of 4 wins and 27 losses, while winning 2 conference games and losing 18. The 2022 season under Crowder saw a dramatic improvement as the Lady Panthers won 13 while losing 16 with a conference record of 5 wins and 13 losses. Katie Erdmann earned 2nd team all-conference honors while Kari Bogen was named to the conference All-Freshman team. They constituted the 1st Lady Panthers named to an all-conference team since the 2015 season. A victory over Palm Beach Atlantic, a perennial NCAA qualifier, highlighted the improving fortunes of Florida Tech in 2022.

In January 2023, Florida Southern College announced that Ashlee Crowder, who had previously been an assistant coach at the school, would return to Florida Southern as head coach. On February 2, 2023, Athletic Director Jamie Joss announced that Jordan Willis had been named as the new head coach of the Panther volleyball program. Willis came from Davis & Elkins College where he had been head coach since 2020.

Notes

- The results of specific seasons, coaching changes and post-season honors are, unless otherwise cited, taken from news articles from https://floridatechsports.com/news.
- The news articles on volleyball which were relied upon were those published on January 23, 2007, November 7, 2007, September 12, 2008, December 15, 2008, October 10, 2009, November 14, 2009, February 10, 2010, November 13, 2010, November 11, 2011, November 18, 2011, January 24, 2012, March 15, 2012, May 4, 2012, November 16, 2012, November 28, 2012, November 23, 2013, September 3, 2014, November 16, 2014, November 18, 2016, November 18, 2017, November 10, 2018, November 23, 2019, November 20, 2021, November 13 2022, November 15, 2022, and February 2, 2023.

CHAPTER THIRTEEN:
TRACK AND CROSS COUNTRY MAKE THEIR MARKS

By William C. Potter

In 1958, the NCAA University Division Men's Cross Country Championship was divided into divisions for smaller colleges and the Division II Championships were begun. Later, in 1973, it was further divided by the creation of a Division III championship. In 1976, the distance for the men's race was set at 10,000 meters (6.2 Miles).

The NCAA began sponsoring women's intercollegiate cross country in 1981. The race distance for women was 5,000 meters from 1981 to 1997, at which time it was lengthened to 6,000 meters.

Cross country has seen some great runners compete for Florida Tech.
Photo from University Archives.

Florida Tech instituted both men's and women's cross country as varsity sports in 1981. Bob Perry, a teacher in the Brevard Public Schools, served as coach for the initial 4 years of the programs, then gave it up after winning a Sunshine State Conference men's title in 1984. Perry returned 4 years later and again won conference men's titles in 1990 and 1991.

On April 15, 1982, the athletic directors of the Sunshine State Conference determined that cross country would be one of the additional women's sports in the conference. The Florida Tech women would eagerly undertake that challenge by winning the conference championship in 1985, 1986 and 1987 under the tutelage of Coach Jeff Small.

The 1983 yearbook, *Ad Astra*, disclosed that the women had finished 5th in the Sunshine State Conference that season. The men, the publication reported, had run to a 3rd place finish. The men would follow up the following season by winning their 1st conference championship in 1984.

Jeff Small took over as coach of both men and women in 1985 and proceeded to put together an impressive record. As reported in *Florida Today* on January 26, 1986, Small had been a Division II track and cross country All-American at Cal Poly-San Luis Obispo. He proceeded to put together an amazing run in which both the Florida Tech men and women won conference championships in 1985, 1986 and 1987.

In 1985, Melanie Thebarge from Charlestown, New Hampshire, began a career that would make her one of the greatest female distance runners in Florida Tech history. She finished 4th in the Sunshine State Conference Cross Country Championship in 1985, improved to 2nd in 1986 and won the conference championship in 1987. Her winning time in 1987 was 19:25. That meet marked the 2nd year in a row that Florida Tech had won both the men and women's conference cross country team titles. Coach Jeff Small noted to *Florida Today* on October 25 that Thebarge won the race with a 47-second margin. She followed up that achievement with a 5th place finish in the South Regional and an 83rd place finish in the 1987 national championship meet. *Florida Today* reported on November 22, 1987, that her time in the national championship run was 19:45 in 19-degree wind chill factor weather in Evansville, Indiana. Thebarge was inducted into the Florida Tech Sports Hall of Fame in 2020. Thebarge continued to run after graduating as reported by the Baltimore Sun on April 18, 1989, when it disclosed that she had come in 2nd place in the Spring Classic 5K at Columbia, Maryland.

Florida Today reported on October 25, 1987, that Florida Tech men and women cross country teams had, for the 3rd consecutive year, each won the Sunshine State Conference Championship. The women were led by Thebarge's 47 second runaway. The men were led by Eric Carlson,

Bill Whalen and Chad Edmonson, who finished 2nd, 3rd and 4th respectively.

The 1987 *Ad Astra* reported that the 1986 men's and women's teams had also run in the Florida State Collegiate Race. That race included several Division I schools, including Florida, Florida State and Miami. The women finished 4th in that race while the men ran to a 5th place finish.

The 1989 *Ad Astra* reported that the 1988 cross country team had some success. Chad Edmondsen and Dan Filippini made the all-conference team on the men's side while Karen Horne was selected all-conference on the women's side.

In 1989, Bob Perry returned to coach the men's and women's teams. He returned in time to coach David Ahmad-Abdallah, a transfer from Nevada-Reno. Ahmad won the 1989 conference championship individually while leading the Panther men to a 2nd place finish and, as reported in *Florida Today* on November 4, sent them to the NCAA Division II South Region meet.

By 1990, the Panther men were back for another conference championship. This time, despite the loss of Ahmad to an injury, it was James Chapman who led the way for Florida Tech. *Florida Today* reported on October 29 that Chapman's 5th place finish, followed by Doug Nehring in 6th and Edwin Ayama in 8th, was sufficient to give the Panthers another championship and qualify all 3 runners as all-conference selectees. The Panther women, led by Kim Wenner's 16th place finish, were 5th among the women. Coach Bob Perry earned his 1st conference Coach of the Year recognition.

On October 27, 1991, *Florida Today* reported that the Panther men had successfully defended their conference crown. Chapman again led the Panthers with a 2nd place finish, supported by Ahmad in 8th, Jim Chambers in 12th, Rick Kaminska in 13th and Jeff Bernabe in 15th. The Lady Panthers took 5th, led by Leslie Simpson's 15th place finish. Perry received his 2nd consecutive Coach of the Year selection.

On September 23, 1992, David Jones noted that Florida Tech's men's cross country returned 3 of their top 4 runners for the year before, including Chapman, their top runner. Perry told Jones: "It has the potential to be a very good year." However, a 3rd straight championship eluded the Panthers. At the conference race, held at Wickham Park in Melbourne, the Panther men finished 3rd, paced by Chapman in 3rd and Kaminska in 4th. The Lady Panthers did not have enough runners compete in the race in order to post a team score but runners Angela Scheer and Kim Wenner finished 21st and 22nd respectively.

Pete Mazzone assumed the reins as cross country coach at Florida Tech in 1993. Mazzone had come to Florida Tech in 1985 and had become a vital part of the management team in the athletic department. He served as director of intramural sports, a strength coach and filled a variety of other roles. As of this writing, Mazzone remains at Florida Tech 38 years after his initial hiring, having even held the position of Interim Athletic Director for a couple of years after many years as Associate Athletic Director. As for cross country, Mazzone would remain as coach until the program was terminated in 2022. On October 17, 2008, Mazzone told *Florida Today*: "You go from brown hair to all of a sudden, a little gray, it's like 'Coach . . . Man, what happened?' So yeah, you look back and you say, 'I've been here a long time.' A lot of things have changed. But it has and it hasn't. People are still the same. There are a lot of good people who have been here as long as I have. And the job is still fun. That's the key to it."

Mazzone's initial year as coach in 1993 was highlighted by Rick Kaminska, who finished 4th in the conference championship race, followed by teammate Fred Hood at 17th overall. Both Kaminska and Hood would go on to race in the NCAA South Region race. Hood was also a pitcher on the baseball team. On the women's side Christine Keenan was the top Lady Panther runner, finishing 9th in the conference meet. Keenan, of course, was notable as one of the greatest basketball players in Panther history and, as noted by *Florida Today* on November 5, 1993 one of only a few athletes in school history to be named all-conference in more than a single sport.

In 1995, The Panther men failed to post a team score when it failed to have 5 runners complete the race due to an injury suffered by one of its top runners. They would bounce back in 1996 and Mazzone would be named Sunshine State Conference Coach of the Year. The Panther men made a 3rd place showing at the conference race and a 17th place finish at the NCAA Southeast Region Championship. The Florida Tech women finished in 5th place in the conference. Mazzone told *Florida Today* on November 21, 1996, that he was optimistic about the future since 10 of his 14 male runners and 5 of his 6 female runners were freshmen. The 1997 *Ad Astra* indicated that the 1996 teams were paced by Karen Horne, an all-conference selectee for the women, and Chad Edmondsen and Dan Filippini, all-conference selectees for the men.

Mazzone again was selected as conference Coach of the Year in 1998 for the 2nd time in 3 years when the Panther men finished 2nd in the conference race. The Lady Panthers improved to 4th place in the conference. *Florida Today* reported on November 8 that Florida Tech had finished 19th in the NCAA Division II South Region Championship, led by Keith Fouts who finished 56th overall. The Florida Tech women finished 21st in the region race, led by a 97th place finish by Nikesha Patterson.

At the 1999 Sunshine State Conference Championship, the Florida Tech men finished 2nd while the women finished 6th. *Florida Today* reported on October 24 that the men were paced by Josh Horst in 5th place and Ryan Moore, Marc Damon and Keith Fouts, who finished 7th, 8th and 9th, respectively. Beth Klice was the top Lady Panther runner in 16th place. *Florida Today* reported on November 7 that the Panther men, paced by Fouts in 59th place, had finished 16th in the NCAA Division II Southeast Region Championship.

The Panther men once again contended for the conference championship in 2000 and once again finished 2nd among the men. *Florida Today* reported on October 22, 2000, that the Panther runners had made dramatic improvements in their times in the conference championship relative to their times on the Saint Leo course earlier in the season. Damon finished 2nd in the men's race while Moore was 9th, Fouts 11th and Chris George finished 18th. Freshman Shannon Chiusano was the top finisher among Panther women in 18th place which led them to a 5th place finish. At the 2000 NCAA South Region meet, the Panthers did well. The men had their best regional performance in several years with a 12th place finish. As reported in *Florida Today* on November 14, Moore paced the Panthers with a 46th place finish while Damon was 61st and Horst was 53rd. The Lady Panthers earned a 19th place behind Chiusano's 79th place finish.

The 2001 Panther men runners placed 3rd in the conference championship race. *Florida Today* reported on October 23 that Ryan Moore was the top Panther runner while Horst 12th place, Gould at 14th place and Damon at 17th also finished in the top-20. The Lady Panthers only had 4 runners so had no team score. Chiusano was the top finisher for the women in 28th place.

The results of the 2002 Sunshine State Conference cross country meet were reported in *Florida Today* on October 20. Florida Tech again placed 3rd behind Moore's 6th place finish. Horst finished 9th followed by Gould at 15th, Chris George at 18th and Caleb Stevens at 19th. The women once again lacked sufficient numbers to post a team score but Jocelyn Boose paced the Florida Tech women with a 19th place finish.

Florida Tech again finished 3rd in the 2003 conference meet. *Florida Today* reported on October 26 that Jon McGonagle had led the Panthers with a 15th place finish, followed closely by Caleb Slavens in 16th place, Steve Gould in 18th, Chris George in 19th, Jared Doescher in 20thand Ryan Brown in 22nd. The Lady Panthers fielded enough runners to finish in 3rd place with Christine Miller in 8th, Charis Parker in 10th, Jocelyn Boose in 11th, Samantha Lanning in 21st and Shannon Chiusano in 23rd.

Florida Tech hosted the 2004 conference championship meet at Wickham Park in October, where both the men and women repeated as

3rd place finishers. As reported by *Florida Today* on October 24, the men were led by Caleb Slavens in 9th place, with Doescher in 12th, Gould in 14th, Joseph Peterson in 20th and Phil Geyer in 22nd. The Lady Panthers also repeated in 3rd place with Boose finishing 16th, Carolyn Salois in 18th, Christine Miller in 24th, Kim Anderson in 28th and Linsey Gasiewicz in 31st.

Florida Tech men finished 14th in the 2004 NCAA Division II South Regional. Caleb Slavens finished in 67th place, followed closely by Steven Gould in 68th. The Lady Panthers finished 11th in the South Regional and, as reported by *Florida Today* on November 7, were paced by Jocelyn Boose's 50th place finish.

The 2005 Sunshine State Conference Championship meet was delayed a week by Hurricane Wilma. When it was finally held on October 29, both the men and women once again finished in 3rd place. As reported by *Florida Today* on October 30, Caleb Slavens paced the men with a 9th place finish while Jocelyn Boose led the women with a 10th place finish, followed closely by Carolyn Salois in 11th place.

At the 2006 conference meet, the men and women each finished in 4th place. Doescher led the way for the men with a 17th place finish, followed by Joe Peterson in 19th place. Megan Pierce led the women in 14th place, Carolyn Salois finished 17th and Jamie Wagner 19th. On November 4, 2006, the men and women each placed 15th in the NCAA Division II South Region Cross Country Championships in Memphis, Tennessee. Salois ran to 29th place to lead the women while Doescher's 40th place showing led the men.

In 2007, the Panther men and women teams each again earned 4th place in the conference meet on October 20, 2007. Freshman Myles Garza led the men with a 9th place run, followed by freshman Morgan Davis at 21st, junior Eric Beckwith at 24th, freshman Ethan Harrell at 26th and senior Joseph Peterson at 27th. Those freshmen gave Mazzone great optimism about the direction of the program. In the women's race, Carolyn Horst finished 7th to lead the Lady Panther runners while Jennifer Lindsay finished 13th and Megan Pierce came in 18th. Myles was named Freshman of the Year for the conference.

At the 2007 NCAA Division II Regional meet, Carolyn Salois-Horst finished in 10th place, good enough to earn her a place in the national championship race in Joplin, Missouri. Myles Garza led the Florida Tech men at the regional meet with a 39th place finish.

At the 2008 conference championship races, the Panthers again each scored 4th place finishes. Myles Garza led the men with a 7th place finish while freshman Nicole Clark finished 9th to lead the women. Mazzone noted: "We've got a good future ahead of us. The conference is definitely tightening up."

The 2008 Panthers followed up the conference meet by competing in the regional championship meet on November 8 in Searcy, Arkansas. The women took 10th place while the men's squad finished 13th. Jennifer Lindsay was the top Lady Panther in placing 29th while Clarke finished 31st. Garza led the men with a 39th place finish while freshman Tyler Subasic was 44th overall.

Sara Trane came to Florida Tech in 2009 from Pixbo, Sweden, as a graduate student in the Psychology School after completing her undergraduate studies at Washington State University, where she had won the Pac-10 steeplechase championship. She had a year of eligibility remaining so that she could run cross-country for the Panthers in 2009. That was enough time for her to set new standards for women's distance running at Florida Tech. She won the Sunshine State Conference championship and followed that up by winning the NCAA South Region championship, both of which were firsts for Panther runners. She then finished 15th at the NCAA Division II cross-country championships to become Florida Tech's first cross-country All-American. Cross-country coach Pete Mazzone spoke about Trane to *Florida Tech Today* for the Winter 2010 issue and said: "All individual accomplishments aside, Sara's biggest asset has been her work ethic and how she approaches her training, her preparation and most importantly the outside factors that come into play with every college student-athlete. She has consistently done the little things that endurance athletes have to do to get the most out of their training – that is getting enough rest, eating right and limiting the outside distractions. She is a very talented student-athlete but to get to the level of success she has accomplished, you have to do everything right." Dr. Trane graduated in 2011 with a perfect 4.0 GPA, earning her Doctorate in Industrial/Organizational Psychology. She was inducted into the Florida Tech Sports Hall of Fame in 2015. Graduation did not mark the end of Dr. Trane's running as The *Orlando Sentinel* reported on December 3, 2017, that Dr. Trane, now age 32, had won the Orlando Utility Commission Half Marathon the previous day.

Trane's presence made 2009 a landmark season for the Lady Panther runners. Behind Trane's 1st place showing, the Lady Panthers improved to 3rd at the Sunshine State Conference Championship meet, coming within 2 points of 2nd place Florida Southern. The women finished 3rd at the regional meet behind Trane's 1st place and Nicole Clarke's 23rd place. Trane, of course, was selected as conference Runner of the Year.

The men also improved dramatically in 2009, finishing 3rd in the conference meet. Myles Garza, Vincent Poczekajlo and Ross Russell all placed in the top 10 in the conference meet. Russell earned conference Freshman of the Year honors. Garza went on to earn All-Region recognition with a 14th place showing in the NCAA Division II Southeast Regional Championships.

Perhaps the most significant accomplishment for the 2009 Florida Tech cross country runners was reported in *Florida Today* on March 9, 2010, with the news that 10 runners had been named to the USTFCCCA All-Academic Team. From the women's team, Nicole Clarke, Stephanie Fonseca, Suzi Gordon, Brittany Reinard, Ali Ronk and Sara Trane were so honored. Reinard, a marine biology major, and Trane were recognized. The men's team runners recognized were Daniel Evans, Myles Garza, Vincent Poczekajio and Ross Russell.

Florida Tech again hosted the conference cross country championships in 2010. The men finished 4th while the women claimed 3rd place. Nicole Clarke took 4th for the women, followed by Suzi Gordon at 18th and Ali Ronk at 20th. William Rolke in 16th place, Ross Russell in 18th and Chris Cacciapaglia in 20th led the men. The men's team finished in 4th place while the women captured 3rd place.

A release on February 18, 2011, described the inauguration of track and field as a varsity sport at Florida Tech. Coach Pete Mazzone was optimistic that he might be able to field a team of 40 to 50 men and women. Mazzone noted wistfully that he was the only coach and that he badly needed help. Later, the winter 2015 issue of *Florida Tech Today* reported that since the Sunshine State Conference did not sponsor track and field, Florida Tech had become a member of the Peach Belt Conference for this sport only and would be eligible to compete in the 2015 conference championship meet.

The 2011 cross country season was notable for the accomplishments of Nicole Clarke on the women's team and Moses Kirui on the men's team. Florida Tech women repeated as 3rd place finishers in the conference in 2011. Once again, Clarke led the way, this time with a 3rd place finish. Stephanie Fonseca ran to a 9th place finish. On the men's side, Florida Tech men finished in a tie for 3rd place behind Kirui's 1st place run. Kirui, a native of Eldoret, Kenya, followed up his SSC Championship by winning the NCAA Division II South Region Championship. He was selected as South Region Athlete of the Year and SSC Runner of the Year. Clarke also reached the national finals by virtue of a 4th place finish at the regional race. The 2011 NCAA Division II Cross Country Championship was held in Spokane, Washington, on November 19 in 25-degree weather with an 11-degree wind chill and light snow. Clarke ended her Panther career by finishing 47th of 186 runners. Kirui struggled with the weather and finished last among the men.

The 2012 Panther men's cross country team was led by graduate student Chris Cacciapaglia who won the conference championship with the 1st win of his career. Teammate David Boiywo finished in 4th place while Ezekiel Zauner claimed 17th place. Despite these efforts, the Florida Tech men were 4th in the team standings. Moses Kirui, who was selected for the all-conference team, did not run in the championship meet. *Florida Today* noted on November 1, 2012, that Cacciapaglia was named Runner of the Year for the conference while David Boiywo also was named to the all-conference team. The Panther men then placed 3rd in the South Region Championship behind a 2nd place finish by Kirui and a 3rd place finish from Cacciapaglia. This led to the men's 1st ever trip to the NCAA Division II National Championship. *Florida Today* reported on November 18 that the Panthers placed 29th in the country in the national championship race in Joplin, Missouri. Moses Kirui came in at 76th out of 245 runners while Chris Cacciapaglia crossed the finish line in 151st place.

The winter 2012 issue of *Florida Tech Today* had a nice piece about Kirui who had begun his collegiate career at New Mexico Highlands where he was twice named to the All-Rocky Mountain Conference Cross Country Team. He came to Florida Tech in order to pursue an Aeronautical Engineering degree. Pete Mazzone, who was described as a father figure to Kirui, noted: "He is the epitome of what a student-athlete really means. He's got an incredible work ethic and determination. He prides himself in his studies and athletic accomplishments. He knows the importance of an education and has seized the opportunity that life has given him. He's going to be a special person."

The 2012 Lady Panther cross country team finished in 6th place in the conference meet. No Florida Tech woman cracked the top 10 finishers.

The Florida Tech men finished 5th out of 6 teams in the 2013 conference championship meet. Justin McMaster had a 6th place finish to pace the Panthers. The men followed up the conference performance with an 8th place finish in the regional meet. McMaster again led the way with a 22nd place finish at the regional meet, followed by Josh Gordon in 35th place and David Boiywo and Jameson Wren in 55th and 56th places, respectively.

The women finished 4th of 7 teams in 2013, although no Lady Panther finished in the top 10 runners. Inka Homeyer, however, became the 1st Lady Panther freshman to run in the NCAA Division II Championship meet where she completed the race 197th out of 245 runners.

The Fall 2014 issue of *Florida Tech Today* noted that Connor Ahlborn of the track and field team had become the 1st Lady Panther to compete at the NCAA Division II Track and Field Championships earlier that spring. Ahlborn would compete in the women's hammer throw. At that same meet, Christian Schiemann had become just the 2nd Florida Tech male to compete. Schiemann competed in the decathlon after qualifying by winning the event at the Lynchburg Multi-Event Meet.

The 2014 Florida Tech cross country teams each finished 5th in the conference championship race. Neither team placed a runner in the top 10 runners. Justin McMaster, a graduate student studying space systems, competed in the NCAA Division II Championship in Louisville. McMaster placed 218th out of 245 runners.

The Winter 2015 issue of *Florida Tech Today* reported that the school's track and field program had joined the Peach Belt Conference as an associate member. That would allow Florida Tech to compete in the conference championships in the spring of 2015. The conference records reflect that Florida Tech placed 7th among the 9 teams competing with 59 points. *Florida Today* reported on April 19, 2015, that sophomore Nathan Knox placed 2nd in the men's javelin and 5th in the shot put. Freshman Rachel Tobin placed 2nd in both the 100- and 200-meter dashes. Sophomore Kevin Jackman placed 4th in the 100-meter final and 5th in the 200-meter event. Freshman Marina DeBiasi finished 4th in the 5,000-meter final. Daniel Schultz received the conference's Elite 15 Award. The Elite 15 Award is given to the student-athlete competing at the championship with the highest cumulative GPA. Schultz, a mechanical engineering and chemistry major, maintained a 4.00 cumulative GPA.

Five members of the Panther track and field team picked up All-Region honors. Tobin, a sprinter from Palm Bay, attained All-Region status in both the 100- and 200-meter events. She had been named Freshman of the Year at the conference meet. Another freshman, DeBiasi, earned a spot on the regional team by finishing 2nd in the 10,000-meter event at the regional event. Alexis Santiago ranked 3rd in the conference in the 100-meter hurdles and joined Tobin in receiving an invitation to compete in the 2015 NCAA Division II Outdoor Track and Field Championships. The 2 men who received All-Region recognition were Knox and Austin Taft. Knox, a Melbourne native, received All-Region recognition in both discus and javelin. Freshman Taft garnered a silver medal in the hammer throw at the Peach Belt Conference Championships and received All-Region recognition in that event. It was notable that Taft had competed in 15 events for the Panthers during the 2015 season.

A Florida Tech release on May 27, 2015, disclosed that 2 Panther track and field team members had been selected for All-America honors by the United States Track and Field and Cross Country Coaches Association. Rachel Tobin had been selected as a result of her 10th overall finish in the 100-meter dash and 5th overall finish in the 200-meter race at the NCAA Division II Outdoor Track and Field Championships.

Alexis Santiago gained the recognition by finishing 10th in the 100-meter hurdles at the championship meet.

Florida Today reported on October 25, 2015, that the Panthers' men's and women's teams had competed at the Sunshine State Conference Cross Country Championships the previous day. The women's team finished in 3rd place while the men finished in 5th place. The women were led by Kerstin Axelsson in 12th, Emily Isley in 18th, Ellyn Willse in 21st and Astrid Bodin in 22nd place. The men were led by Lukas Hassler in 11th place and Tucker Melles in the 17th spot.

A couple of weeks later, the men and women competed in the NCAA Division II South Region Championship for 2015 hosted by Saint Leo. Both teams completed the regional meet in 8th place. The women were again led by Axelsson in 21st place, followed by Isley in 37th and Willse in 59th place. The men were led by 2 freshmen, Melles in the 21st spot and Hassler in the 25th spot.

On October 28, 2015, Bill Jurgens announced that Jason Munsch had been named as head coach of the Panther track and field program. The announcement added that Pete Mazzone would continue to coordinate long-distant runners while Ja'Mar Watson would continue to coach throwers.

2016 marked some major achievements by the Panther track and field teams at the Peach Belt Conference Championship meets. The *Florida Tech Today* issue of the fall of 2016 reported that the teams had taken 7 medals during the meets, including the program's first-ever gold medals won by Nathan Knox and Kevin Delgado. *Florida Today* reported the details of the meet in its edition of April 25, 2016. Knox, a Satellite High graduate, had earned gold by setting a new conference record in winning the discus. Delgado also set a conference record in winning the shot put. Knox took 2nd place in the shot put. Knox followed that up by taking 5th in the hammer throw. Knox's performance was enough to earn him the award as the Male Field Athlete of the Year. Wistenly Alphonse took a silver medal in the high jump by establishing a new school record. For the women, Maia Carter and Alexis Santiago finished in 3rd and 4th, respectively in the 100-meter hurdles. Carter also took silver in the 400-meter hurdles. Terence Brookins took a silver in the 400-meter dash and a bronze in the 200-meter dash. Daniel Schultz was awarded the Elite 15 Award for the 2nd consecutive year.

The 2016 Sunshine State Conference Cross Country Championships were again hosted by Florida Tech at Wickham Park on October 22, 2016. The Lady Panthers took 5th place overall, led by Marina DeBiasi's 11th place finish, followed by Genevieve Lucas in 22nd place and Emily Isley in 23rd place. The men finished in 4th, paced by Tucker Melles' 10th place finish, Christian Lake at 22nd and Malte

Stockhausen at 25th. Both men's and women's teams set new school records for average times.

An article in *Florida Today* on November 6, 2016, noted that former Panther runner Chris Cacciapaglia had won the Space Coast Classic 15K the previous day. What was even more important than the win was the information that he was then defending his doctoral thesis in coral ecology, another example of the kind of scholars that typified Panther runners.

The highlights for the 2017 Panther track and field squads were provided by 3 freshmen, Ryan Harrington, Ondrej Rapp and Joshua Norville. Harrington competed in the 400-meter run and the 800-meter run, as well as the 4 X 400 relay. *Florida Today* reported on March 29 that when he won the 400 and the relay at the Florida DII Collegiate Invitational in March, he was named the Peach Belt Conference Track Athlete of the Week. Norville set a new conference record in the triple jump at the University of North Florida Spring Break Invite. At the Florida DII Collegiate meet, Harrington teamed with Terence Brookins, Erold Farquharson and Brandon Stern on the 4 X 400 relay to set a new school record and post the best time in the conference that year.

Florida Tech Today reported in its Fall 2017 issue that Norville had been named the 2017 South Region Field Athlete of the Year by virtue of having the 5th best mark in the country in the long jump and the 21st best mark in the triple jump. Norville claimed the gold medal in the triple jump at the conference meet and added a bronze medal in the long jump.

On May 31, 2017, *Florida Today* reported that Norville and Rapp had been announced as All-Americans by the U.S. Track and Field and Cross Country Coaches Association. Rapp earned the distinction by finishing 7th overall in the long jump finals at the NCAA Division II Championships with a distance of 7.45 meters. Norville made the All-America 2nd team with his 12th place finish in the long jump in the national championship meet with a jump of 7.03 meters. Earlier, Rapp had won the long jump at the Peach Belt Championship meet with a conference record-breaking leap of 7.50 meters. The Elite 15 Award went to Tyler McCabe, the 3rd consecutive year the award went to a Panther.

Once again, Florida Tech hosted the Sunshine State Conference Cross Country Championships in 2017. The Florida Tech women improved to 3rd place. Freshman Lia Hanus led the Lady Panthers with a 5th place finish while Marina DeBiasi followed in 9th place. For the men, Tucker Melles' 7th place finish and Lucas Hassler's 10th place performance led the Panther men to 5th place in the team standings.

At the 2017 NCAA Division II South Region Championships in Lakeland on November 4, both the men's team and women's team finished among the top 10 teams. Marina DeBiasi led the women by finishing in 18th place followed by Genevieve Lucas at 60th overall. The men took 7th out of 16 teams. Lucas Hassler led the men with an 11th place finish, followed by Tucker Melles at 27th place.

Florida Tech Today reported in its Fall 2018 edition that women's cross country runner Marina DeBiasi had been named as the Sunshine State Conference Scholar Athlete of the Year for 2017-2018. DeBiasi, a chemical engineering major from Plymouth, Michigan, graduated summa cum laude in the spring of 2018 with a 3.92 GPA. Additionally, she won "best in show" at the 2018 Northrop Grumman Engineering and Science Student Design Showcase. DeBiasi was the epitome of a student-athlete or, perhaps more accurately, a scholar-athlete.

Tyler McCabe repeated as the winner of the Elite 15 Award at the 2018 Peach Belt Conference Track and Field Championships, making 4 consecutive years that a Panther had claimed the award. A release from the Peach Belt Conference on June 21, 2018, announced that both McCabe and his teammate Michael Kraska had been named to the 2018 Google Cloud Academic All-America Division II Track and Field/Cross Country Teams as selected by the College Sports Information Directors of America. Kraska, a distance runner, graduated in 2018 with a 3.95 GPA in biomedical engineering. McCabe also graduated Summa Cum Laude with a 3.97 GPA in astronomy and astrophysics.

The Panthers earned 2 bronze medals and 4 top-10 finishes at the Peach Belt Conference Track and Field Championships in Pembroke, North Carolina, in April 2018. As reported in *Florida Today* on April 23, Alexis Santiago won a bronze medal in the women's 100-meter hurdles. Nicardo Cameron earned bronze in the men's 100-meter dash with a time of 10.71 seconds. Lukas Hassler and Tucker Melles finished in the top-15 in the 5,000 meters. Emily Isley, Genevieve Lucas, Lia Hanus and Pauline Cosson all finished in the top-25 in the women's 5,000-meter race.

Upon taking office as CEO of Florida Tech in 2016, President Dwayne McCay had made clear his intentions regarding intercollegiate athletics. As he told *Florida Today* in an interview reported on May 20, 2016, McCay voiced his intent to pare its 22 varsity sports to "choose 10 or so" and "really make the investment so we're competing at a national level." Thus, it was not a surprise when the university eliminated its men's and women's track and field teams in 2018.

The 2018 Sunshine State Conference Cross Country Championships were held in Daytona Beach on November 3. The Lady Panthers finished in 6th place and no Florida Tech women were in the top-10 runners. The Panther men finished 7th and also had no top-10 runners.

The 2019 conference championships were held in Boca Raton on October 26. The Florida Tech men finished in 6th place, led by a 5th place showing by Matte Stockhausen. The women finished in 8th place with no runners in the top-10 runners.

As a result of the pandemic, the conference cross country championships scheduled for the fall of 2020 were postponed until the spring of 2021. Thus, the 2020 championship meet was held at West Palm Beach on February 27, 2021. The Florida Tech men finished 8th of the 8 teams with no Panther runner in the top-10 finishers. The Florida Tech women did not have a team for the conference race.

A Florida Tech release of January 8, 2021, reported that the Sunshine State Conference had announced its Men's Cross Country All-Decade Teams for 2010 to 2019. Moses Kirui was selected for the 1st team while Chris Cacciapaglia was selected for the 2nd team.

Another Florida Tech release of January 25, 2021, reported the conference's announcement of the All-Decade Team for the women. Lady Panther Nicole Clarke was honored as a 2nd team selection.

The 2021 conference race was hosted by Florida Southern at Lakeland on October 23. Once again, the Panther women were unable to field a team to compete for the title. The Florida Tech men again finished 8th of 8 with no runner in the top-10 competitors.

On July 10, 2022, *Florida Today* reported that Florida Tech had announced that its Board of Trustees had approved the elimination of 5 varsity sports and the transition of those sports to club competition. The affected sports were men's and women's crew, men's and women's cross country and men's golf. A later *Florida Today* article on July 10, 2022, explained that the cross country team would convert to club status and join the National Intercollegiate Running Club Association but would be able to compete against varsity teams in numerous other races.

On May 24, 2023, Bob King, the interim President of Florida Tech, announced that men's cross country and men's indoor and outdoor track would be reinstated as varsity sports, effective immediately. In making the announcement, King stated: "This summer, we are carefully evaluating our athletics offerings and adjusting as needed. The addition of these programs will strengthen our athletics offerings while giving our scholar-athletes broader opportunities to showcase their skills."

On July 10, 2023, Athletic Director Joss announced that Marc Small had been appointed as the next Head Coach for cross-country and indoor/outdoor track. Small would fill this role while maintaining his position as Director of Athletic Partnerships and Promotions. Pete Mazzone, who also serves as Associate Athletic Director for Facilities and Equipment, was appointed as Associate Head Coach of cross-country and indoor/outdoor track.

- The information about the history of NCAA cross country and the race distances is derived from the 2010 Division II Men's and Women's Cross Country Championships Handbook found at https://ncaa.com/sports/cross-country-women/d2 and https://ncaa.com/sports/cross-country-men/d2.
- The information about Bob Perry and the beginning of cross-country at Florida Tech is taken from an article in *Florida Today* written by David Jones published on November 5, 1991.
- The releases from the Sports Information Office at Florida Tech are found at https://floridatechsports.com/news. The releases relied upon were dated October 21, 2006, November 4, 2006, October 20, 2007,November 3, 2007, October 25, 2008, November 8, 2008, November 4, 2009, November 7, 2009, December 11, 2009, February 18, 2011, November 17, 2011, November 19, 2011, October 20, 2012, October 30, 2012, November 17, 2012, November 9, 2013, November 23, 2013, May 21, 2014, December 6, 2014, May 13, 2015, May 27, 2015, October 28, 2015, November 8, 2015, October 22, 2016, November 4, 2017, January 8, 2021, and January 25, 2021.
- The releases from the Sunshine State Conference are found at https://sunshinestateconference.com/news. The releases relied upon were dated October 31, 2007, November 5, 2010. The results of the Sunshine State Conference Cross Country Championships are taken from the website of the conference and are found at https://sunshinestateconference.com/archives.aspx.
- The archives of the Peach Belt Conference are found at https://peachbeltconferrence.org/archives.
- As to the appointments of Small and Mazzone, see https://floridatechsports.com/news/2023/7/10/mens-cross-country-small-named-head-coach-mazzone-associated-head-coach-for-mens-cross-country-indoor-outdoor-track.aspx.

CHAPTER FOURTEEN:
LACROSSE COMES TO FLORIDA TECH

By William C. Potter

L acrosse has been, by a wide margin, the fastest growing intercollegiate sport over the past 40 years. The following charts, compiled from the year end Participation Reports compiled by the NCAA for 1981-82 and 2021-22 will illustrate the growth.

Men's lacrosse	Total teams	Total athletes	Division II teams	Division II athletes
1981-82	138	4,193	18	476
2021-22	394	15,954	75	3,393
Women's lacrosse	Total teams	Total athletes	Division II teams	Division II athletes
1981-82	105	2,648	13	358
2021-22	522	13,294	113	2,906

Another interesting evolution has been the change in team size during that period. The average men's team size in Division II men's lacrosse has increased from 26.4 to 45.2 during that time. For women's Division II squads, the average team size has decreased from 27.5 to 25.7.

There are probably several explanations for the explosion of interest in intercollegiate lacrosse. Certainly, one of those reasons must be the increasing awareness of the neurotrauma associated with football. Data indicate that there are few serious injuries in lacrosse relative to other contact sports. The dramatic growth of lacrosse at the college-level has been mirrored by the growth in lacrosse youth teams as well as among secondary schools.

In the midst of this explosive growth in college lacrosse, Florida Tech told *Florida Today* on August 14, 2010, that Ryan McAleavey had been hired as its first coach of men's lacrosse and that the program would begin competition as a club team for a year before beginning intercollegiate competition in 2012. McAleavey came with a wealth of lacrosse coaching experience, most recently as a high school coach in New Jersey.

An article by Mark DeCotis in *Florida Today* on February 13, 2012, related that Florida Tech would play its first-ever intercollegiate game on the following day against St. Leo University. Since the Sunshine State Conference had not yet introduced lacrosse as a conference sport, Florida Tech would play that initial season in the lacrosse-only Deep South Conference, consisting of Tampa, St. Leo, Florida Southern, Rollins and Florida Tech, as well as Wingate University, Catawba College, Mars Hill College and Lenoir-Rhyne University. The Panthers would field a young team with only 2 upperclassmen, goalie Mason Cook and midfielder Matt Durand. They would play their home games at Melbourne Central Catholic's field.

On March 18, 2012, *Florida Today* reported that the Panthers had won for the first time in its inaugural season with a 15 to 13 victory over Shorter College the previous night. Ryan Bailey's 4 goals and 4 assists led the way. They would win only 1 other game in that first season, but the young team demonstrated that it would rapidly improve.

The 2013 men's lacrosse team quickly demonstrated that it was vastly improved. When the Panthers edged Belmont-Abbey on March 6, 2013, they improved their record to 4 wins and 2 losses. The team was led in that game by Andrew Conley's 5 goals.

Florida Tech would finish that 2013 season with a record of 6 wins and 8 losses and a conference record of 2 and 5. This performance by a second-year team was sufficient to cause McAleavey to be named Coach of the Year in the Deep South Conference. As reported by *Florida Today* on April 9, 2013, sophomore midfielder Andrew Conley was named first team all-conference while junior goalie Eric Biller received second team honors.

On June 19, 2013, Florida Tech announced that Corinne Desrosiers had been named the first coach of women's lacrosse at the school. Desrosiers, former head coach at Merrimack College, would have a year to recruit before beginning intercollegiate play in the 2014-2015 season. Desrosiers said: "As a coach at the Division II level, I believe our focus needs to truly be on the well-rounded student-athlete. We have a commitment to family, academics and our sport. However, I would not be in this game if winning on the field were not also important. I will try to bring an environment of energy and focus to this program from day one for all of our young women to thrive in. I get to help write the first chapter in the book of women's lacrosse at Florida Tech, and I can't think of anything more exciting than that."

2014 would mark the inaugural season of lacrosse for the Sunshine State Conference and, as *Florida Today* headlined on February 17, 2014; "Expectations (were) high for Florida Tech squad." A strong freshman class, several transfers and the veteran junior class caused McAleavey to express his excitement about the prospects for the team. The team would have its moments but lost several close games and closed the season with a loss to Florida Southern on April 12. That closed the season with a 3 and 9 overall record and a 1 and 4 record in the Sunshine State Conference.

The Fall 2014 issue of *Florida Tech Today* revealed the quality of student-athletes participating in women's lacrosse at Florida Tech. Katie Reid, a lacrosse player majoring in Aviation Human Factors disclosed that she had spent her summer working in a research group at Jeppeson,

Women's lacrosse has been a strong addition to the sports program at Florida Tech. *Photo from University Archives.*

a global aviation company, where she was involved in projects including apps for aircraft cockpits. The Winter 2014 issue of *Florida Tech Today* disclosed that women's lacrosse coach Corinne Desrosiers had announced the addition of a 7-member class in December 2014, and that the squad would begin its first official season in the spring of 2015.

Florida Today reported on February 16, 2015, that Florida Tech would open its inaugural women's season that evening when it hosted Roberts Wesleyan at Palm Bay High School stadium. Desrosiers predicted: "While we are going to have some tough games this year, I also think that we are going to pull out a few." It took only 2 games for the women to earn its first win as they routed Ava Maria by the score of 18 to 0 on February 21, 2015. Allie Modica either scored or assisted on the first 6 goals of the game.

The Spring 2015 issue of *Florida Tech Today* reported that the women had wrapped up their initial season with a record of 7 wins and 9 losses.

Allie Modica led the team with 51 goals and 17 assists, enough to earn all-region third team honors. Their final game was a loss to Florida Southern in the Sunshine State Conference tournament semifinals. Desrosiers told *Florida Today* on April 25: "I couldn't be more proud of the way we played tonight. To say we are excited for the future is an understatement."

2015 would prove to be a watershed year for Florida Tech's men's lacrosse team. The Spring 2015 issue of *Florida Tech Today* reported that the team had finished with a 12-4 record, which included a 7 game win streak. The team was ranked in the top 15 nationally for the second half of the season.

The April 12, 2015, edition of *Florida Today* revealed that both the men and the women had won games the previous day and both had thereby qualified for the Sunshine State Conference post-season tournament. The men had beaten Florida Southern for the first time in program history with an 11 to 7 victory. Goalkeeper Eric Biller made vital stops to preserve the victory.

Although the men lost to Tampa by a score of 11 to 8 in the championship game of the conference tournament, coach Ryan McAleavey told *Florida Today* on April 27: "We have a sense of pride in this program that I think is going to carry us for a very, very long time. I know the juniors coming up are looking to make it better. It is going to be a lot of hard work, but the guys are up for the challenge."

The women defeated Tampa 20 to 10 for the first conference win in program history. Sara Grenier scored 6 goals, running her season total to 53 for the season. The women went into the post-season with a record of 7 wins and 8 losses (1 and 3 in the conference). They closed the season with a loss to Florida Southern in the conference tournament.

The 2016 women's lacrosse season proved to be a great leap forward for Florida Tech. Perhaps the highlight of the season was reported in the Spring 2016 edition of *Florida Tech Today* which recounted the Lady Panthers' 11 to 10 overtime victory over New Haven, their first-ever win over a ranked opponent and the biggest victory in the short history of the program. The Lady Panthers ended their season on April 29 with a heartbreaking overtime loss to 6th-ranked Rollins in the semifinal round in the conference championship tournament. That completed the season with a record of 10 wins and 7 losses. Allie Modica was named the Player of the Year in the Sunshine State Conference while coach Corrine Desrosiers was named Coach of the Year. Caroline Dunleavy scored her 100th career point in the final game. The Winter 2016 *Florida Tech Today* related that Katie Reid and Arielle Gunderson were the first players in Florida Tech lacrosse history to earn

Intercollegiate Women's Lacrosse Coaches Association Academic Honor Roll status which required a cumulative GPA of 3.5 or higher.

The 2016 men's team was not quite as successful. A 10 to 5 loss to Lynn University on April 23 ended the men's season with a record of 6 wins and 7 losses (1 and 4 in the conference). The season highlight for the Panthers was a 13 to 11 victory on April 2 over Saint Leo, then ranked 19th in the nation. Attacker Brian Bacarella was named to the first team all-conference team as was defenseman Tom Filipow. Freshman attacker Tyler Covey and longsticker Addison Abramson were named to the all-freshman team.

A significant step for Florida Tech occurred prior to the 2017 season when the men moved their home games to campus to be played on the artificial turf field next to the Varsity Training Center. The men began the 2017 season conspicuously with a 20 to 6 victory over Lincoln Memorial on February 11. Nick Wynne led the victory with 8 points. They then proceeded to lose 4 close games in a row before upending Chestnut Hill on March 7. The men followed that win with the biggest win in program history, a 5 to 3 victory over 5th-ranked Seton Hill. Wynne again led the way with 3 goals while goalkeeper Daniel Hock had 19 saves. The Panthers went all the way to the finals of the conference tournament, first beating Lynn in the semifinals by a 13 to 6 score before dropping a 12 to 8 game to Tampa on April 30 in the championship game. That ended their season with a record of 8 wins and 7 losses (4 and 3 in the conference). Five Panthers, Nick Wynne, Logan Sweeny, Addison Abramson, Grant Hughes and Daniel Flock, were named to the first team All-Sunshine State Conference. Abramson was selected to the third team of the USILA/Nike All-America team while Hughes gained honorable mention recognition on the team.

Florida Tech's women's lacrosse team had a remarkable 2017 season. As reported in the Spring 2017 edition of *Florida Tech Today*, the team registered 8 straight victories and was ranked 9th in the country among Division II teams. The team ranked among the top 5 in the country in scoring, scoring margin and caused turnovers per game. The Fall 2017 edition of *Florida Tech Today* disclosed that they finished the season with a record of 14 wins and 4 losses, including 5 wins over top-15 teams. They advanced to the championship game of the conference tournament. They capped the season with their first trip to the NCAA playoffs where they upset East Stroudsburg in the 1st round before falling to Florida Southern in the 2nd round. They ended the season ranked 6th nationally. Desrosiers was again named Coach of the Year in the Sunshine State Conference while Allie Modica was named a 1st team All-American while Sara Grenier was named to the 2nd team.

Modica was the 2017 Female Athlete of the Year for Florida Tech and a 3-time all-conference selection. She concluded her 3-year career at Florida Tech with 191 total points.

The Panther men's team for 2018 finished the season with a record of 9 wins and 6 losses. The season came to an end with a 19 to 12 loss to Tampa in a semifinal game of the Sunshine State Conference tournament on April 26. Leading scorer Logan Sweeney was named to the All-Conference team and received honorable mention All-American honors.

The 2018 women's team had another remarkable season as they again went all the way to the quarterfinals of the NCAA tournament. They won their 1st tournament game with a 13 to 11 win over 7th-ranked Limestone. Once again, their run was thwarted by Florida Southern in a 19 to 10 loss. That ended the Lady Panthers' season with a record of 17 wins and only 3 losses. Lauren Tybor was the Sunshine State Conference Player of the Year while Sara Grenier became the program's all-time leading scorer with 231 goals and 270 points. Caroline Dunleavy concluded her career as the number 2 scorer in program history. *Florida Today* reported on June 11, 2018, that Sam Schiano and Tybor were named to the 2nd team All-America squad while Dunleavy, Grenier and Olivia Going were selected to the 3rd team.

On July 10, 2018, the resignation of Corinne Desrosiers as coach was announced. She left Florida Tech with a record of 48 wins and 23 losses, with a record of 11 and 7 in the conference. Her teams made the conference tournament all 4 years during her tenure and had made the NCAA tournament for the 2 years prior to her resignation. On August 24, 2018, it was announced that McKenzie Rafferty had been hired as the new women's lacrosse coach at Florida Tech. Rafferty had been an assistant coach at Regis University.

Soon after that, men's coach Ryan McAleavey resigned his position on September 19, 2018, after 7 seasons. McAleavey had posted a record of 46 wins and 53 losses during his tenure. Director of Athletics Bill Jurgens wasted no time in filling this position. On September 26, Jurgens announced that assistant coach Mark Penn had been elevated to the position of head coach.

Rafferty's initial season as coach of the women's team in 2019 met with modest success as the Lady Panthers compiled a record of 7 wins and 9 losses for the season. Their record in the conference was 2 wins and 4 losses. The season ended for Florida Tech with a 20 to 7 loss in the semifinal game of the Sunshine State Conference tournament. Sam Schiano earned her 4th consecutive all-conference recognition while also gaining 2nd team All-American honors. Olivia Going also earned 1st team all-conference honors while Brittney Embree and Mollie Kaplan received 2nd team recognition.

Penn's inaugural season as head coach in 2019 yielded a winning record as the Panthers won 7 and lost 5 on the season, with a 3 and 4 record in the conference. Reid Chaconas led the Panthers in scoring while picking up his 3rd all-conference recognition with his selection on the 1st team of the all-conference team. Ryan Land and Logan Sweeney were named to the 2nd team while Addison Abramson, Daniel Flock and Tyler Oblong were given honorable mention recognition.

What began as a promising 2020 women's season was shortened by Covid-19. The women compiled a 6 win and 2 loss-season and were ranked just outside the top-25 before it was cancelled. Mollie Kaplan and Alexis Townsend received honorable mention All-America recognition.

The men's 2020 season was also cancelled after they had compiled a record of 2 wins and 6 losses. Despite the shortened schedule and the disappointing record, senior midfielder Reid Chaconas was named a first team All-American by Inside Lacrosse, thereby becoming the first Panther in program history to receive first team honors.

Covid also resulted in an abbreviated 2021 season for both men's and women's lacrosse. The men compiled a record of 3 wins and 5 losses (1 and 3 in the conference). A 16 to 8 victory over Saint Leo on May 8 and Senior Day was the high point of the season for the men. Reid Chaconas became the program's all-time leading goal scorer as well as ranking 2nd all-time in career points. Chaconas racked up the post-season honors, being named to the first team All-Conference team as well as first team All-American.

The abbreviated 2021 season for the women's lacrosse team was somewhat disappointing as they ended the shortened season with a record of 2 wins and 7 losses, including 1 win and 5 losses in the conference. Olivia Going, however, created some highlights of her own for the program, being named to the 2nd team All-America team, 1st team All-South Region, and for the 4th consecutive year, 1st team All-Conference. Going, from West Islip, New York, topped things off when she was named a 2nd team Academic All-American, having completed her academic career at Florida Tech with undergraduate and master's degrees in accounting and financial forensics with a 4.0 grade point average.

Brad MacArthur took over as head men's lacrosse coach in February 2022. MacArthur came with an extensive record of coaching at the college and professional levels. Most recently, he had been coach and general manager of the Brooklyn Lacrosse Club in Major Series Lacrosse. He guided the Panthers to 10 wins and 6 losses, including a 5 win, 2 loss conference record, in his first year. Their season ended with a 15 to 9 loss to Tampa, ranked number 1 nationally, in the semifinals of the conference tournament. Justin Williams was selected as a first team All-American while Sam Balch was named as an honorable mention All-American. Balch and Williams joined teammate Zach Rozgonyi on the first team All-Conference team. Rozgonyi tallied a team-high 62 points and 43 goals, breaking the school's single-season records in both categories. Midfielder Williams became the school's all-time leader in assists.

Panther women's lacrosse came back strong in 2022. The Lady Panthers compiled a 9 win, 5 loss record with a 2 and 5 conference record. Perhaps the highlight of the season was a 13 to 10 victory over Rollins, then ranked 10th in the country, in the final game of the season. Midfielder Kailee O'Brien was named to the 1st team of the All-Sunshine State Conference team while midfielder Caroline MacLeod and attacker Kayla Minton were named to the 2nd team. O'Brien also received honorable mention All-America honors.

The 2023 men's team finished with a record of 7 and 7 overall and 3 and 4 in the conference. Sam Balch repeated as 1st team all-conference team member and was selected as a member of the 2nd team on the All-American squad. Collin Stewart was selected to the all-conference 2nd team. A promising sign for the future was the selection of Alex Francisco and Nicky Vreeland as members of the conference All-Freshman team. The highlight of the season was a 26 to 8 rout of Emmanuel (Georgia), breaking the program record for goals in a single game. Andrew Walenty paced the Panthers with a hat trick plus one.

The 2023 women's team completed their season with an overall record of 9 and 8 and a conference record of 1 and 6. Kailee O'Brien was a 2nd team all-conference pick and received honorable mention All-American honors.

Men's lacrosse has become a prominent sport in the Sunshine State Conference.
Photo from University Archives.

Notes

- The data regarding the growth of intercollegiate lacrosse is taken from NCAA Sponsorship and Participation Rates Reports for 1981-82 and 2021-22. These reports are available at www.ncaa.org/sports/2013/11/20/sports-sponsorship-and-participation-research.aspx. The data includes only NCAA members and does not include NAIA, MCLA or WCLA.
- For additional information on the growth of lacrosse, see "A Sport on the Rise" published August 5, 2021, at htps://athelogroup.com/blog/a-sport-on-the-rise/
- The results of specific games and post-season honors are, unless otherwise cited, taken from news articles from https://floridatechsports.com/news. The news articles on women's lacrosse which were relied upon were those published on June 19, 2013, February 21, 2015, April 24, 2015, April 29, 2016, May 18, 2016, May 13, 2017, May 18, 2017, May 12, 2018, July 10, 2018, August 24, 2018, September 19, 2018, September 26, 2018, April 26, 2019, May 3, 2019, April 13, 2020, May 5, 2020, May 6, 2020, August 5, 2021, April 23, 2022, May 5, 2022, May 11, 2022, and March 18, 2023. The news articles on men's lacrosse which were relied upon were those published on April 30, 2017, May 24, 2017, April 26, 2018, April 21, 2019, April 24, 2019, April 2, 2020, May 8, 2021, May 12, 2021, February 9, 2022, April 28, 2022, May 26, 2022, April 22, 2023, May 2, 2023 and May 10, 2023.

CHAPTER FIFTEEN:
GOLF WINS SOME CHAMPIONSHIPS

By William C. Potter

M en's golf was one of the early sports at Florida Tech. The 1969 yearbook, *Ad Astra*, related that the team for that year was comprised of 9 members. The 1970 *Ad Astra* reported that the golf team, consisting of 8 players, was coached by Don Rutledge, who was also the basketball coach. By 1971, *Ad Astra* reported that John Cooney had taken over as coach and the team was down to only 5 players. However, that 1971 team, as reported in *Florida Today* on May 9, 1971, compiled a record of 6 wins, 3 losses and a tie, the best record in school history. That article also related that the team had been invited to the NAIA Regional Tournament at Calloway Gardens, Georgia, where it had finished 8th among 11 teams. John Harris and Charlie Sherman led the team at the two-day tournament, each scoring 172 totals. By 1972, the team was back up to 12 golfers. However, *Ad Astra* did not indicate that there was a golf team between 1973 and 1978. *Ad Astra* did describe a 12-member men's golf team coached by Henry Scott in 1979 but there is no record of a golf team.

Tom Nugent worked at Florida Tech in the early 1980's. Nugent had been a college football coach. Nugent worked as a public relations representative for Florida Tech and, not surprisingly, took a strong interest in the athletics program. Among Nugent's duties was his role as Sports Information Director. Athletic Director Bill Jurgens asked Nugent to create a short booklet chronicling both the intercollegiate and intramural athletics programs at the school. Nugent did so in both 1981 and 1982 and the 1982 book related that Lee Thurston was coaching the golf team which would play 12 matches and 4 tournaments, highlighted by a 3-day tournament in Boston against M.I.T., Harvard and others. There is no further record of men's or women's golf teams until they were formally restored as varsity sports in 2003.

It was reported in *Florida Today* on April 27, 2003, that the initial women's team made a strong start on building the program when it enticed Ericka Hildreth, a three-time All-Space Coast high school golfer, to join the team. Al Skellet, who had also been an assistant coach on the men's basketball team, would coach that first women's golf team.

Jay Lally, who is Director of Financial Aid at the university, would serve as the coach of the reinstituted men's golf team.

Both teams began play in the fall of 2003. *Florida Today* revealed on October 14, 2003, that both the men's and women's teams had competed in the UNICCO Fall Invitational held at the Jacaranda Golf Club in Plantation, Florida. The women finished in 4th place, led by Natalia Reimen, while the men, led by Kyle Acchinoe, finished in 14th place.

An article by Carl Kotala in *Florida Today* on April 11, 2004, headlined that "Florida Tech golf teams solid in inaugural season." The article related that the men's team was the only Division II team in the nation to play 5 freshmen. Coach Lally pointed to freshmen Justin Regier and Joowon Ko as leaders of the team. Coach Skellet expressed his hope that the women could finish in the top-half in the conference tournament.

Both the men's and women's teams progressed rapidly. On May 7, 2005, *Florida Today* reported that the men's team had won its first tournament in April 2005, when it won the Bash at the Beach, hosted by Embry Riddle Aeronautical University. That same edition of the newspaper disclosed that Pat Cappola had taken over coaching duties from Lally.

Florida Today reported on March 29, 2006, that, for the first time, both teams had earned first-place honors at an event. The men defeated 6 other teams to win the University of West Georgia Invitational. That was the third title earned by the men, who were led by David D'Agostino. The women's team edged West Georgia to win the title. The women were led by Daniela Iacobelli and Ericka Hildreth.

By April 7, 2006, *Florida Today* could report that the women's team was now ranked in the top 25 in the nation.

Both the men's team and the women's team would soar to new levels of success in 2007. On March 23, 2007, *Florida Today* would report that the men's team, led by Justin Regier, Dan Moline and Jeff Wittup had moved into the number 25 spot in the national rankings.

Both teams experienced success when Iacobelli won the women's medalist honors at the Sunshine State Conference Golf Championships and Anthony Klingensmith captured men's medalist honors as reported by *Florida Today* on April 18, 2007.

Daniela Iacobelli was a graduate of Satellite Beach High School and a member of the Class of 2009 at Florida Tech. As a sophomore at Florida Tech in 2007, Iacobelli won the individual championship at the Sunshine State Conference golf championship. She followed that by winning the NCAA Division II individual championship that same year. The Fall 2007 issue of *Florida Tech Today* reported that she shot rounds of 72, 74, 73 and 74 to finish 5 over par in winning the national championship. Panthers coach Janie Farina told *Florida Tech Today*: "She is a special gal with a special talent." After graduation, Iacobelli would spend 3 years on the LPGA Tour and post wins in the 2012 Symetra Tour Championship, the 2015 Tullymore Classic and the 2019 Island Resort Championship. She was inducted into the Florida Tech Sports Hall of Fame in 2014.

In the fall of 2007, Cappola succeeded Farina as coach of the women's team so that Cappola would now have charge of both teams. He would coach both teams until he retired in 2010. Cappola would pass away in July 2015. Bill Jurgens would tell *Florida Today* on July 17: "His enthusiasm and love of golf was always apparent. He gave a lot to the team and he was very instrumental in advancing the program during the time he coached."

2008 was another strong season for the men's and women's team. As related by *Florida Today* on May8, 2008, both teams made it to the NCAA Division II South Regional. At the regional tournament, Iacobelli came up one shot short in her attempt to return to the Championship Tournament. The men's team finished 7th, led by Kyle Westhorpe, but that was not enough to advance to the Championship Tournament.

In 2009, Iacobelli returned to the NCAA Division II Championship Tournament by winning a 4-hole playoff at the regional tournament. She told *Florida Today* on May 13, 2009, that: "It's not necessarily winning that's important. It's putting your all into it." Although she made a valiant effort, she was unable to win a second national title but was able to finish in 6th place.

In 2010, Florida Tech hired its first full-time golf coach when Chris Saltmarsh came to Melbourne after coaching at Northwood University in Ft. Lauderdale, Florida.

Florida Today disclosed on August 25, 2010, that Saltmarsh would coach both the men's and women's teams. The hiring of Saltmarsh would prove to be a watershed for Florida Tech golf.

A highlight for the 2011 men's team was when Zach Potter took medalist honors at the Titan Invitational while the team finished 2nd. As reported in *Florida Today* on February 9, the Panthers finished 7 strokes behind the winners. The men would go on to play in the NCAA Division II South/Southeast Regional Championships that year, beginning a streak of several years in the tournament.

As reported in *Florida Today* on February 15, 2012, the men's team won the Matlock Collegiate Classic at Lone Palm Golf Club in Lakeland. That was the first tournament win since 2006 for the men. Christian Westhorpe led the Panthers with a 3-under par 213.

By the fall of 2012, the Lady Panthers were once again ranked in the national Division II poll. *Florida Today* reported on September 2012, that the team was now ranked number 7 in the country among Division II teams.

As related in *Florida Today* on May 3, 2014, the 2014 men's team was then ranked 17th in the country and on their way to the NCAA regional tournament at Savannah Quarters Country Club. As Saltmarsh told the newspaper, it had been a great year for the team which had the best scoring season in program history and obtained its highest ranking ever. The team included senior Andrew Wuethrich, juniors Ray Badenhorst, Justin Kalanquin and Ryan Carter, as well as freshman Joe Ellis.

The highlight for the women's team in 2014 occurred when freshman Johanna Larsson from Lidkoping, Sweden, qualified for the NCAA Division II Championship Tournament. As *Florida Today* revealed on May 7, Larsson became the second Panther in program history to qualify, joining Iacobellli as the only Panthers to qualify. Larsson would not prevail but gave Panther fans a lot of optimism for the future.

Florida Tech would have another woman golfer in the NCAA Division II National Championship Tournament in 2015. *Florida Today* reported on May 6, 2015, that Guro Rambjoer had finished 6th in the super-regional tournament to secure a place in the championship. The women's team came within a single shot of advancing to the championship.

The fall portion of the Florida Tech women's team in 2015 was nothing short of sensational. As highlighted in the Winter 2015 issue of *Florida Tech Today*, the Lady Panthers won all 4 tournaments in which they competed that fall, including the Lady Falcon Invitational, the NCAA Division II National Preview, the Myrtle Beach Invitational and the Saint Leo Invitational. Sophomores Guro Ramjoer and Johanna Larsson and junior Felicia Leftinger each won medalist honors in a tournament. The Lady Panthers were ranked 1st in the country among Division II teams.

The following spring, the Lady Panthers continued their success without interruption. As related in the Spring 2016 issue of *Florida Tech Today*, they won 4 of the first 5 tournaments in which they played that spring and again took 1st in the national polls. Felicia Leftinger would become the 4th Florida Tech women's golfer to qualify for the NCAA Division II Women's Golf Championship when she finished 3rd in the 2016 Super Regional Tournament.

The men's team made history in 2017 by qualifying for the NCAA Division II National Championship Tournament for the 1st time. They did so by finishing 4th in the Super Regional Tournament. As reported in the Fall 2017 *issue of Florida Tech Today*, they would end the season ranked 5th in the country.

The year 2017 was also a notable one for the women's team. Brittany LaPadula would make the trip to the NCAA Division II championship after finishing in 2nd place in the Super Regional tournament. As reported in the Winter 2018 issue of *Florida Tech Today*, LaPadula would earn a 7th place finish and would be named an All-American.

The 2017-2018 men's team had a remarkable year, winning the Sunshine State Conference Championship with a 19-under team score. As described in the Fall 2018 issue of *Florida Tech Today*, the final round

268 team score constituted the lowest single round score in conference tournament history.

Florida Today reported that the 2017-18 men's team was ranked in the top 5 nationally throughout the season. Max O'Hagan led that team with a 70.77 scoring average. Han Xue was second on the team with a 72.13 average. Both sophomores were named to the all-conference team while Chris Saltmarsh was recognized as Coach of the Year for the conference. The team followed-up the conference championship by finishing 4th in the NCAA South/Southeast Super Regional, sending them, for the 1st time in program history, to the NCAA National Championship at Reunion Resort. After 3 rounds of medal play, the Panthers sat in 5th place which qualified them for match play for the title. The Panthers fell to Lynn University in the quarterfinals of match play, ending a memorable season. Max O'Hagan and Shanren Brienen were named All-Americans.

The 2017-2018 women's team had another strong season and, as reported in *Florida Today* on May 2, 2018, earned a bid to the NCAA Division II South Region Tournament for the 6th year in a row.

Coach Chris Saltmarsh did a remarkable job when he coached the women's golf team to the NCAA Division II championship in 2019 after the school had announced its intention to discontinue the sport. *Photo from University Archives.*

The 2019 women's golf team triumphed over incredible adversity. In February 2019, it was announced that women's golf would be discontinued as a varsity sport at the end of that season. Despite that announcement, the team accomplished what no other women's sport at Florida Tech had ever done when it won the national championship. As noted in the Fall 2019 issue of *Florida Tech Today*, the Lady Panthers faced

California State University-San Marcos in the final match with the national championship at stake. The Panthers cruised to a 4-1 victory. As reported in *Florida Today* on May 23, 2019, Chris Saltmarsh was named national Coach of the Year while 3 Panther golfers, Noelle Beijer, Lucy Eaton and Paola Ortiz, were named to the All-America team. Ortiz, from Morelia, Mexico, had been named a 2nd team All-American the previous year and won 2 of her 3 match play rounds by large margins. Eaton, from Yorkshire, England, claimed 3rd individually at the NCAA championship tourney. The heroic effort in winning the national championship was, however, not sufficient to forestall elimination of the program.

In July 2022, it was announced by the university that golf would be discontinued as a varsity sport and would become a club sport, joining the National Collegiate Club Golf Association. The association hosts 3 regional tournaments and a national championship each spring and fall. Saltmarsh learned the news while he was attending his father's funeral. Saltmarsh lamented to *Florida Today* on July 10, 2022, that at least when women's golf was terminated, they had an opportunity to finish the season by winning the national championship. Men's golf would have no such reprieve. Saltmarsh, the only full-time golf coach in the history of Florida Tech, would have to be content with the remarkable accomplishments of both the men's and women's teams under his guidance. Chris Saltmarsh is now the coach of men's and women's golf at Catawba College, a private college in Salisbury, North Carolina, that plays in NCAA Division II.

Golf has experienced success at Florida Tech.
Photo from Univesity Archives.

Notes

- Iacobelli's success on the professional tour is described in an article in *Florida Today* on June 25, 2019

CHAPTER SIXTEEN:
TENNIS OVERCOMES OBSTACLES

By William C. Potter

B ill Tiso's article in *The Crimson* on June 4, 1968, stated that tennis was established as an intercollegiate sport at Florida Tech in 1966 with Dr. John Thomas as coach. That is the only record of a tennis coach by the name of John Thomas and it is likely that Tiso was referring to Garland Thomas, who was identified as the tennis coach in several publications in subsequent years. The 1969 yearbook, *Ad Astra*, described the 1969 tennis team as consisting of 6 players coached by Dr. Garland Thomas. It further described Dr. Thomas as a physicist employed by NASA. A later news article published by *Florida Today* on November 18, 1973, described the work that Dr. Thomas was doing with aerial photography.

The 1970, 1971 and 1972 editions of *Ad Astra* disclosed the numbers of team members on the tennis squads for those years but disclosed nothing about the results from their seasons.

The 1973 *Ad Astra* disclosed that the team was coached by B. Eaton and consisted of 12 players, including 1 woman. Again, no results were disclosed. Coach Eaton was probably Captain Bob Eaton, an instructor in the ROTC program at Florida Tech.

The 1974 edition of *Ad Astra* related that the tennis team consisted of 13 players, including a woman. Anthony Kioussis was the coach that year.

The 1975 *Ad Astra* disclosed that the tennis team consisted of 14 players, including a woman. Jack Schwalbe was the first-year coach of the team. The team was led by Steve Bankert, Hans Timke and Carol Shepherd. *Florida Today* reported on February 15, 1975, that the team would open against Embry-Riddle Aeronautical University. *Florida Today* reported on March 5, 1975, that Florida Tech had lost to Stetson 8 to 1. Bankert got the only point for the Panthers with a singles win. That loss brought the season record for Florida Tech to 0 and 6.

Bankert was apparently an enlightened person as well as a good tennis player. *Florida Today* reported on May 15, 1975, that Bankert and the local TKE fraternity chapter had been expelled from TKE for admitting women.

Schwalbe, a Florida Tech administrator who coached in addition to his regular duties, continued as coach for the 1976, 1977, 1978 and 1979 seasons. Bankert became an assistant coach in 1979. The highlight of the 1979 season was provided by Janos Latura, who had an undefeated season as a singles player. As *Florida Today* reported on May 5, 1979, Latura won 17 matches that season while losing none.

On August 12, 1979, *Florida Today* reported that Schwalbe had resigned as tennis coach in order to devote full-time to his administrative duties. Bankert was immediately designated as his successor.

On February 2, 1980, *Florida Today* reported that Florida Tech's tennis team had beaten Saint Leo by a score of 9 to 0. Latura led the team at number 1 singles while Jack Haynie played 2nd singles. On March 8, *Florida Today* reported that Florida Tech had beaten Louis University of Chicago by a score of 8 to 1, taking their season's record to 11 wins and a single loss. On September 15, 1980, *Florida Today* revealed that Florida Tech's 1980 record was 19 wins and only 7 losses. Following the 1980 season, Mike Dickens replaced Steve Bankert as head coach.

The 1982 *Ad Astra* noted that Mike Dickens was the tennis coach of the team consisting of 9 players. No results were given.

The 1983 tennis season marked the debut of one of the most successful players in Florida Tech program history. Khalid Outaleb was a former member of the Moroccan Davis Cup National Team. He immediately assumed the role of playing number 1 singles and doubles for the Panthers. During his initial season with Florida Tech, he compiled a record of 15 wins and 3 losses at number 1 singles. In the course of the season, he defeated Rollins College's Brian Talgo, the 5th-ranked Division II player in the country. Outaleb lost in the semifinals of the conference tournament in a grueling 3-set heartbreaker. However, as reported by *Florida Today* on May 11, 1983, that defeat did not prevent him from receiving an at-large invitation to the NCAA Division II national tournament. Outaleb prevailed in the opening round of the national tournament with a victory over Cal-Hayward's Gary Schalin. However, *Florida Today* disclosed on May 13 that Outaleb had fallen in the 2nd round to Robert Stapper of Southwest Texas.

On March 7, 1984, *Florida Today* reported that Florida Tech tennis was off to a solid start for the 1984 season. After opening with losses to Rollins, University of Central Florida and Florida Southern, the Panthers then reeled-off 11 victories in a row before losing to 15th-ranked Florida International. Outaleb was 9 and 3 at 1st singles and 7 and 1 at 1st doubles when paired with Bob Barbieri.

Florida Today reported on March 29 that the Panthers would host the 1984 Sunshine State Conference tournament at the Pines Tennis Club in Indian Harbour Beach. Outaleb was seeded 3rd at number 1 singles while Outaleb and Barbieri were seeded 2nd at number 1 doubles. Interestingly, Florida Tech had put together a 6-member women's team for the tournament despite the fact that women's tennis was not a varsity sport at the school. At the tournament, *Florida Today* disclosed on March 31, Outaleb won the number 1 singles title over the top-seeded Brian Talgo from Rollins, thereby leading Florida Tech to a 2nd place finish in the tournament and sending Outaleb to the national tournament for a 2nd consecutive year.

Outaleb had a spectacular season in 1985. When he once again defeated Talgo for the conference title on March 29, 1985, that pushed his season's record to 21 wins and no losses. As *Florida Today* reported on March 30, his victory gave the Panthers another 2nd place finish. The win earned him a 3rd trip to the national championship tournament.

1986 would mark Outaleb's final season at Florida Tech. *Florida Today* reported on February 2 that he had led F.I.T. to perhaps its most-notable win in program history when they defeated nationally-ranked Florida International. On March 10, *Florida Today* disclosed that the Panthers had raised their record to 13 wins and 4 losses when they defeated Barry by a 6 to 3 score. Outaleb raised his singles record to 16 and 1 and his doubles record to 16 and 1 as well. For the 3rd consecutive year, the conference tournament was held at the Pines Resort and Tennis Club in 1986. And, for the 3rd consecutive year, Outaleb won the number 1 singles championship. As reported by *Florida Today* on March 29, that victory gave Outaleb a season record of 18 wins and 1 loss in singles matches. In doubles, Outaleb and his doubles partner Peter Johansson dropped a hard-fought match in the finals.

At the 1986 NCAA Division II national championship, Outaleb entered the tournament seeded 4th in singles. Outaleb and Johansson also received a bid as a doubles team. Outlaleb won his 1st 2 matches before falling in the 3rd round to Oliver Amerlinck of Chapman College. The *Florida Today* report of May 18, 1986, also disclosed that Outaleb and Johansson had won their opening doubles match but fell in the 2nd round. Thus ended the Florida Tech career of Outaleb, undoubtedly one of the greatest tennis players in school history. In 2013, Outaleb became the only tennis player inducted into the Florida Tech Sports Hall of Fame. Outaleb played on the Moroccan Davis Cup team from 1984 until 1990. He compiled a 14 win and 3 loss record in Davis Cup competition. Outaleb was the Moroccan national champion in 1984 and 1988.

The 1987 season was a struggle for the Panther tennis team. For the 1st time in 4 years, Florida Tech suffered a losing season with a record of only 5 wins while suffering 18 defeats.

The Panthers turned things around in the 1988 season. *Florida Today* reported on February 27, 1988, that Florida Tech had fallen to powerful Florida International University, but they still possessed a winning record for the season with 7 wins and 3 losses. Juan Soto and Randy Christian posted wins in the singles matches against Florida International. When the Panthers lost 5 to 4 to Florida Atlantic University on March 4, that dropped their record to 9 and 5 on the season. Soto improved his record to 12 and 1 with his singles victory.

Once again, the Pines Resort hosted the Sunshine State Conference championship tournament in 1988. Florida Tech tied for 3rd behind winning Rollins. Juan Soto and Stephan Beskow each reached the men's singles final but Beskow lost the number 3 match while Soto lost at number 5.

Florida Tech pulled off a big victory in January 1989, when it edged Division I Stetson by a 5 to 4 score. *Florida Today* reported on January 29 that the victory was paced by Paul Davis and Juan Soto who each won their singles matches.

Rollins repeated as conference tournament champions in 1989 while Florida Tech again finished 3rd. *Florida Today* reported on March 26 that the Panthers' number 1 doubles team of Beskow and Davis scored a semifinal defeat of the Rollins doubles pair who were top-ranked in the country. Beskow and Davis lost in the finals. The Panthers also finished 3rd in the conference in the regular season with a 6 and 2 record.

Florida Today reported on April 10, 1989, that the Panthers lost to Florida Atlantic 6-3, ending their season at 12-9 overall. Dickens said, "We have a bunch of freshmen and sophomores but they surprised me." Davis, playing at 1st singles, paced the Panthers with a 17 and 4 singles record.

Florida Tech tennis started off strong in the 1990 season. *Florida Today* reported on March 12 that they had won their 8th consecutive victory with a 9 to 0 victory over Barry, bringing their record for the season to 12 and 4 overall and 7 and 1 in the conference. *Florida Today* reported on March 23 that the Panthers had placed 3rd in the conference championships held, once again, at the Pines resort. Paul Davis missed the tournament due to back issues. The Panthers' record stood at 15 and 5 for the year.

Florida Today disclosed on May 10, 1990, that Stefan Beskow had received a bid to play in the NCAA Division II tournament. There, Beskow lost a hard-fought 1st-round battle to Tim Fresenius of Cal State-San Luis Obispo.

In the fall of 1990, Davis and Beskow both played in the NCAA Division II Rolex Invitational tennis tournament. Both made it to the finals where the doubles partners faced each other. *Florida Today* reported on October 5 that Davis had won a close victory over his teammate.

The Panthers' 1991 men's tennis team posted another strong season. *Florida Today* reported on March 23 that the Panthers had posted a 9 to 0 win over Springfield (MA) College, bringing their record to 6 and 8 on the season. Massimo Bosso led the team with a 9 and 5 record at 3rd singles. The Panthers finished 2nd in the 1991 conference tournament. *Florida Today* disclosed on April 7 that the number 2 doubles team of Robertson and Bosso finished runners-up as did Paul Davis in number 2 singles, and Davis and Jeff Lederer in number 1 doubles. Beskow missed the tournament due to an arm injury.

David Jones' story in *Florida Today* on December 17, 1991, related that Mike Dickens had stepped down as tennis coach in mid-November due to his concerns that the program was not receiving adequate funding. Ray Mazzoni, a retired airline pilot and Naval aviator, was named as his replacement. Mazzoni noted that returning players Paul Davis, Massimo Bosso and Paul Robertson gave the Panthers a strong core.

Paul Robertson was a rarity among contemporary collegiate athletes in that he was a star at 2 sports. As a freshman, he made an immediate impact in both soccer and tennis. As his career at Florida Tech progressed, he would gather numerous honors in both sports. *Florida Today* reported on November 12, 1993, that Robertson had been selected to the 1st team of the Sunshine State All-Conference Soccer team.

Mazzoni's inaugural year as coach of Florida Tech tennis would result in modest success. When the Panthers suffered an 8 to 1 loss to Eckerd College on March 27, 1992, their record would fall to 6 wins and 9 losses. As *Florida Today* reported, only a win at number 1 doubles by Davis and Bosso put a point on the board for Florida Tech.

That doubles team of Davis and Bosso also advanced to the finals of the 1993 Sunshine State Conference tennis tournament before falling to a Rollins duo ranked 1st in the country. The Panthers finished 4th in the tournament, far behind powerful Rollins which scored almost double the points of runner-up Barry. *Florida Today* reported on April 3 that Robertson lost in the finals of the number 4 singles while the other Panther singles netters lost in their opening matches.

In 1994, Rollins won its 15th consecutive Sunshine State Conference men's tennis championship. Florida Tech finished in a tie for 4th place. Paul Robertson, Niel Hutchinsion, Hakan Borgstrand and Jamie Hockin paced the Panthers during the 1994 season. Robertson went into the conference tournament with a 13 and 4 singles record for the season.

The 1995 Panther tennis team was hampered by injuries to key players throughout the season. Florida Tech went into the tournament with a 4 win, 9 loss, overall record, including 3 and 5 in the conference. *Florida Today* reported on April 21, 1995, that Number 1 player Hakan Borgstrand suffered from an eye infection and a knee injury. Jamie Hockin, playing at number 2, had back problems while Greg Livingston at number 4 struggled with a sore arm.

1996 was another rough year for Panther tennis. Injuries, visa issues with an international student-athlete and academic issues with another player haunted the team throughout the season. David Jones wrote an article for *Florida Today* on April 19, 1996, which noted that the Panthers record going into the conference tournament was 4 wins and 15 losses. Mazzoni noted: "It's a have and have-not conference. There are five teams really good. Then there's Tampa, Saint Leo and us." Florida Tech's season came to an end with a loss to Saint Leo in the consolation round of the tournament. As *Florida Today* noted on April 21, a bright note for Florida Tech was the play of freshman Sven Bergstrom, from whom much future success was anticipated. Unfortunately, Bergstrom would not have an opportunity to achieve that potential at Florida Tech as the school suspended its tennis program following the 1996 season.

In 2003, under President Anthony Catanese, the decision was made to restore men's tennis as a varsity sport and to inaugurate women's tennis as well. *Florida Today* reported on January 31, 2004, that the women's tennis team would play its first-ever match the following day against Palm Beach Atlantic at the Fee Avenue courts in Melbourne. The men's team, too, would face Palm Beach Atlantic in the same venue on the same day. *Florida Today* would report on February 3 that Clifford Giel, a freshman on the men's team had been named the conference Player of the Week by virtue of his wins at number 1 singles and number 1 doubles in the Palm Beach Atlantic match. Freshman women's player Aya Nakatsuji was also named conference Player of the Week for her performance against Palm Beach Atlantic. Nakatsuji became the 1st-ever Panther woman to win a tennis match when she won at number 4 singles when her opponent retired due to injury. In fairness to Nakatsuji, she was leading when her opponent had to retire.

By the time of the conference championships on April 18, the men were 2 and 3 in the conference and 8 and 11 overall while the women were 0 and 7 in the conference and 4 and 13 overall. The men took 6th place in the conference tourney while the women finished in 8th place. In all, a respectable showing for the newly instituted programs.

In 2005, Marla Reid took over as coach of the Panther tennis program. It was a rugged challenge for both men and women. *Florida Today* reported on April 10 that the men had lost to Webber International and that their overall record thus far was 3 wins and 12 losses. The same article disclosed that the women had defeated Webber and that the women's record was 2 and 12.

On April 21, 2005, Reid told Ken Bradley of *Florida Today*: "You know, we're a young program, only two years old. We have predominantly sophomores on our team. Our team has improved greatly. I think anything is possible." Reid also praised men's players Keith Kessler and Cliff Giel, pointing out that they finished 12 and 3 overall in doubles.

The Panther men finished 8th in the conference tournament. Giel and Kessler continued to lead the Panthers with their doubles play.

The June 27, 2005, edition of *Florida Today* reported that Bill Macom had been named as head coach of men's and women's tennis at Florida Tech. Upon accepting the job, Macom noted: "This is going to be a very enjoyable time in my tennis career." Macom would become a fixture at the school and the longest tenured tennis coach in school history.

A release by the Sunshine State Conference on April 30, 2006, disclosed that the Panther men's team completed the 2006 season with a record of 9 wins and 16 losses but, unfortunately, were winless in conference play while losing 6 matches. The Panther women won 4 while losing 19 and were 1 and 7 in the conference.

The 2007 season demonstrated progress in the tennis program. A release by Florida Tech on April 4, 2007, related that freshman Natalia Ramos of Puerto Rico had been named conference women's tennis player of the week after winning 3 straight set matches at number 2 singles, leading the team to 8 wins which doubled the previous most wins in a season for the women's team. The women completed the season with a record of 9 wins and 12 losses.

The 2007 men's team was highlighted by the doubles team of Clifford Giel and Keith Kessler who won 16 matches while losing only 2. *Florida Today* disclosed on March 21, 2007, that the duo was then ranked 15th in the nation and 4th in the southeast region. At that point in the season, the men's team had won 7 while losing 11 and was 1 and 4 in the conference. They completed the season with a 10 and 16 record.

A release from Florida Tech on March 12, 2008, revealed that Ramos was continuing her tennis dominance and had been named Student Athlete of the Month. At that point in the season, Ramos, playing at number 1 in singles and in doubles, had won 12 straight singles matches without a defeat. Ramos teamed with freshman Abigail Greif to go 15 and 0 in doubles and achieve 20th ranking nationally. The women's team had risen to 23rd in national rankings. During the fall season, Ramos made history by winning the singles title at the Georgia College and State University fall tournament, thereby achieving the 1st fall singles title in program history.

Among the highlights for the men's team in 2008 was the play of freshman James McLane, who finished with a singles record of 17 and 9. McLane was named the Southeast region Rookie Player of the Year by the Intercollegiate Tennis Association.

The 2008 season would be the most successful season in school history for both men's and women's programs. The men would finish with a 15 and 12 record, leaving them ranked 41st in the nation. The women would complete their season with a 15 and 15 record. As a result, *Florida Today* reported on September 23, 2008, that Macom was recognized as Coach of the Year by the U.S. Professional Tennis Association.

The 2009 tennis season witnessed historic accomplishments for Florida Tech tennis in both the men's and women's programs. As disclosed in *Florida Today* on June 24, both teams made their 1st appearances in the NCAA tournament. Both programs completed their season ranked nationally. On the women's side, the doubles team of Ramos and Greif achieved 1st team all-conference honors with a 24 and 3 record. On the men's team, McLane received 2nd team singles all-conference recognition with a 1 and 5 record. *Florida Today* reported on May 7 that the women completed their season with 20 wins and only 9 losses. The men's team finished at 16 and 10. Macom had built a competitive program in a short period of time.

As reported in *Florida Today* on June 9, one of the highlights of the 2010 season was provided by Natalia Ramos when she became the 1st Panther women's All-American in tennis. She finished 8th in the South Region and 14th nationally in singles. She completed the season with an 18 and 9 singles record and led the team to a final ranking of 7th in the region and 20th in Division II nationally. As a team, the Lady Panthers finished 19 and 10 and earned their 1st NCAA tournament victory in history by defeating Albany State in the 1st round. Ramos and Greif also ranked 7th in the region in doubles and 21st in the nation. However, perhaps the most impressive accomplishment for Ramos was that, after graduating as the most-decorated female tennis player in school history, she was set to pursue her graduate degree in Engineering Management at Duke. The Panther men completed the 2010 season with a record of 11 wins and 15 losses.

A notable achievement for the Panther tennis teams in 2010 was described in an article in *Florida Today* on May 30, 2010. The tennis teams hosted a tennis clinic billed as "Aces for Autism" which was a tennis clinic designed to raise awareness and funds for the Scott Center for Autism Treatment. Executive Director of the Center Fran Warkomski related: "Tennis coach Bill Macom had called us and said his team was interested in helping the Scott Center. This was a perfect fit, because the team members are role models for the students."

Although the loss of Ramos had a great impact on the Florida Tech women's tennis program, that void was at least partially filled with by two sisters from Ascona, Switzerland, Kristina and Katarina Huba. A Florida Tech release on April 4, 2011, disclosed that Katarina had been named Panther Student-Athlete of the Week, as she ran her record to 21 wins on the season at the number 1 singles spot. She also had joined with her sister for a 15 and 1 record at number 1 doubles. They would take that doubles record to 19 and 1 by season's end. Katarina would be named all-conference in both singles and doubles while Kristina would make the 1st team in doubles. The 2011 women's team finished the season with a record of 19 and 9 and a 3rd consecutive trip to the NCAA

South Region tournament. The men completed the season with 7 wins and 18 losses.

The 2011-2012 season was marked by a 4th straight trip to the South Regional by the Lady Panthers who racked up a record of 16 wins and 9 losses. The Panther men returned to a winning season with a 14 and 13 record.

A Florida Tech release on October 10, 2012, revealed that Kristina Huba had given Florida Tech its first-ever Intercollegiate Regional Championship a few days earlier by winning 5 straight matches during the tournament. That victory brought Huba to an 8 and 0 record for the fall season.

Florida Today reported on April 28, 2013, that Kristina Huba had made history by being named Sunshine State Conference Player of the Year. Huba, a chemistry major, was ranked as high as 4th nationally and 1st in the South Region. She was also named as an All-American.

Freshman Chloe Chanley, playing at number 3 singles, was recognized by a university release of March 4, 2013, that described her role in pacing the 4th-ranked women's team to a comeback win over Flagler College.

The Lady Panthers earned a record of 16 and 9 for that 2012-13 season. The men managed to break even at 12 wins and 12 losses.

The 2013-2014 men's tennis team was also paced by an international student. Nicolas Clerc, a native of Buenos Aires, Argentina, was recognized as Florida Tech Athlete of the Week on April 1, 2013. According to the release by the school, Clerc, playing at number 1 singles, had won 9 of his last 10 matches and ranked 23rd nationally and 9th in the South Region. The men's team faltered a bit with a 6 and 13 record for the season despite Clerc's record. The women came in at 10 wins and 13 losses for the season. Kristina Huba was recognized as a member of the 2014 All-Sunshine State Conference 2nd team. *Florida Today* reported on May 3, 2014, that Huba finished the year with a 13 and 4 singles record and completed her Florida Tech career with 80 singles wins, the most in school history.

A piece in the Fall 2014 issue of *Florida Tech Today* noted that tennis ace Chloe Chanley had spent her summer studying International Marketing and World Religions at Oxford. Chanley noted: "Since I am an international business major and hope to work abroad, I felt it was necessary to become familiar with the culture in a country other than the U.S."

The 2014-2015 men's team got back on a winning track with a record of 13 and 10. The women also returned to a winning record by winning 14 while losing 10. Both teams were ranked in the top 10 in the South Region and top 50 nationally. The men registered a team GPA of

3.2 while the women registered a 3.6 GPA. Macom was voted the 2015 United States Professional Tennis Association Florida Coach of the Year.

In keeping with Florida Tech's tradition of strong international women's tennis players, Mariana Castaneiras was named Florida Tech's Student Athlete of the Week on November 2, 2015. The release by the university described how the Mexico City native had won the Juan Varon Wildcat Invitational in Daytona Beach the previous week after defeating opponents from Iowa State, Florida A & M and Bethune-Cookman to win the singles competition.

The 2015-2016 women's team, led by Castaneiras, managed a 13 and 10 record. The men achieved a 12 win, 11 loss season.

The 2016-2017 Panther men slipped to a 12 and 15 record. The women continued their winning ways with a 13 and 11 record.

The 2017-18 Lady Panthers maintained a winning tradition with a record of 14 wins and 7 losses. The men achieved an 8 win, 9 loss season. The Spring 2018 issue of *Florida Tech Today* recognized several tennis players who were completing their 4-year careers at that time. Kayla Hergott would finish her career as number 2 in all-time singles wins with 77. Teammate Erin Egoroff would finish with 73 career singles wins. For the men, Aria Canadell had achieved 2nd in all-time singles wins with 69 while Ricardo Carona was 3rd overall with 63 singles victories.

The 2018-19 men's team slipped to a 6 and 13 record. The Panther women managed a record of 11 wins and 8 losses. A highlight of that final season was provided by Lauren Stuckey who won her 77th career singles victory, tying her for 2nd in the record books with her former teammate Kayla Hergott.

Upon taking office as CEO of Florida Tech in 2016, President Dwayne McCay had made clear his intentions regarding intercollegiate athletics. As he told *Florida Today* in an interview reported on May 20, 2016, McCay disclosed his intent to pare its 22 varsity sports to "choose 10 or so" and "really make the investment so we're competing at a national level." McCay made good on the paring part of that statement when the university cut the men's and women's track and field teams in 2018, followed by eliminating men's and women's golf and men's and women's tennis in 2019. In a release dated February 7, 2019, the university announced that men's tennis, women's tennis and women's golf would be terminated as varsity sports at the end of the then current season.

Macom left as the most successful tennis coach in school history. His women's teams achieved a record of 193 wins and 151 losses. Macom's men's teams at Florida Tech won 151 matches while losing 183.

- Results of the Sunshine State Conference Tournament are taken from the news articles cited and also from releases issued by the conference on April 6, 1993, April 12, 1994, April 18, 2004, and April 30, 2006. These releases can be found in the archives on the conference website at sunshinestateconference.com.
- Releases from Florida Tech can be found in the archives at https://floridatechsports.com/news.
- Information regarding Bill Macom's record at Florida Tech was derived from Macom's biography on the website of Saint Mary's (TX) University where Macom currently serves as Director of Tennis. That biography can be found at https://rattlerathletics.com/sports/mens-tennis/roster/coaches/bill-macom/620.

The lack of adequate facilities has hindered the development of tennis at Florida Tech. *Photo from University Archives.*

CHAPTER SEVENTEEN:
FIDGI AND WOMEN'S SOCCER

By William C. Potter

W omen's soccer had achieved widespread popularity on the Space Coast during the 1980's and 1990's. Youth soccer leagues for girls had sprung up throughout the area and had attracted thousands of young girls. Melbourne High School had become a power in girls' soccer and had won multiple state championships. Satellite High School, under the coaching of former Florida Tech star Fidgi Haig, had become a powerhouse in the state and had sent several of its graduates to play at major universities. Thus, when Florida Tech announced in 2003 that it would begin playing women's intercollegiate soccer, the announcement was met with enormous excitement in the community.

Coach Fidgi Haig recognizes Teresa (Brantley) Moon on Senior Day.
Photo from University Archives.

On October 24, 2002, *Florida Today* reported that Tammy Mazza would become the first coach of the Florida Tech women's soccer team. Mazza, a former player at Lynn University, had been an assistant coach for 2 years at Southern Mississippi and 4 years at Florida Atlantic. The Lady Panthers achieved remarkable success during that inaugural 2003 season, winning 7 games while losing 12 with a 2 and 6 record against conference opponents. The 1st victory in program history was a 2 to 1 double overtime win over Carson-Newman. On November 4, Mazza told *Florida Today* that a victory the previous week over Rollins College, then ranked 4th in the South Region, was the biggest victory to date in program history. The news article quoted Mazza as saying: "I couldn't be happier. First-year programs just don't do what we're capable of." Defender Tara Eugenides and midfielder Megan Kramer received honorable mention recognition on the 2003 all-conference team.

Having set high expectations because of the success experienced in their inaugural season, the 2004 season proved to be somewhat of a letdown for the Lady Panthers. *Florida Today* reported on October 25, 2004, that they had lost to Tampa by a 6 to nil score, dropping their record to 0 and 7 in the conference. They had, however, won all 4 of their non-conference matches. Mazza resigned as coach following the season.

On January 20, 2005, *Florida Today* reported that Florida Tech had hired not 1, but 2, of its favorite sons to take over both men's and women's soccer teams. Both teams had gone 0 and 8 in the conference during the previous season. Fidgi Haig would take over as head of women's soccer while Robin Chan would become head coach of the men. Chan and Haig had, of course, been teammates on the powerhouse national championship teams of Rick Stottler. Haig had gone on to compile a record of 246 wins, 19 losses and 9 ties, including 2 state championships, as coach of the Satellite High girls. Chan had compiled a record of 170 wins, 29 losses and 18 ties, including 2 state championships, as coach of the Melbourne Central Catholic boys.

Haig immediately turned the women's program in a positive direction. On October 29, 2005, *Florida Today* reported that the Lady Panthers had closed their 2005 season by defeating Eckerd by a 3 to nil score. That gave them a season record of 7 wins, 7 losses and 2 ties, including a conference record of 3 wins, 4 losses and a tie. *Florida Today* reported on November 11 that senior forward Kelli Huarte was voted to the all-conference 2nd team while junior defenders Rocio Hernandez and Miranda Tessier, sophomore forward Ericka Hildreth and senior midfielder Megan Kramer were all named honorable mention.

The 2006 season witnessed more dramatic improvement. That season ended only after Florida Tech had battled to a double overtime 1-1 tie in the conference tournament semifinal game against top-seeded Tampa which was ranked 8th in the country at the time. Tampa advanced by winning a penalty-kick shootout but the Lady Panthers finished a notable season with a record of 8 wins, 4 losses and 6 ties. Defender Rocio Hernandez was recognized with 1st team all-conference honors while forward Teresa Brantley received honorable mention.

The 2007 team waited until the last game of the season to play their best game when they battled to a 1-1 tie with Tampa on October 27. That completed their season with a record of 9 wins, 5 losses and 2 ties, with a 2 win, 4 loss and 2 tie record in the conference. A remarkable fact was that the entire team that saw the field that last game day were either sophomores or freshmen. Defender Rachel Devlin received honorable mention recognition on the 2007 all-conference team. Haig noted: "This match should give our young team some confidence next season."

The 2008 Lady Panthers made history when they broke into the national rankings for the 1st time in program history, reaching as high as 19th in the nation. They almost saw their season end against Tampa as it had the previous year. The teams met on November 4 in the quarterfinals of the conference tournament and, once again, battled to a tie in regulation. They remained tied after 2 overtime periods and went to a penalty kick shootout, where Tampa prevailed. However, the season continued when the Lady Panthers received a bid to the NCAA Division II South Region Tournament where they won their opening game in a penalty-kick shootout victory over Florida Southern on November 14. Their season came to an end in the 2nd round when they lost to undefeated Rollins on November 16 by a 4 to nil score. This wrapped up the 2008 season with a record of 12 wins and 8 losses. Redshirt freshman midfielder Paula Lillsjo was selected for 2nd team all-conference honors.

As anticipated, the Florida Tech women experienced a very strong season in 2009, reaching as high as 15th in the national polls. When they lost to Florida Southern in the semifinals of the conference championship tournament on November 6, their record fell to 14 wins, 3 losses and a tie. They opened NCAA South Region Tournament play on November 12 with a 1 nil victory over Saint Leo. However, for the 2nd year in a row, their season was ended by Rollins when the Tars handed them a 3-nil 2nd-round loss. The Lady Panthers completed the season with a record of 15 wins, 4 losses and a tie. Teresa Brantley and Melissa Pyles were accorded 2nd team all-region recognition. Brantley was named Sunshine State Conference Player of the Year and Offensive Player of the Year. Brantley, DeeDee Newland and Melissa Pyles all were named to the 1st team of the All-Conference team while Ann-Marie Helgestad, Sara Lewis and Brittany Rainbow gained 2nd team honors. The Lady Panthers shut out 10 of their opponents during that season.

In 2010, the Florida Tech women experienced their most successful season in history. For the first time, they earned a share of the regular season conference championship with a 5 win, 2 loss, 1 tie conference record. They fought their way to the finals of the conference championship tournament before losing to Tampa in overtime. They then took on Florida Southern in the 1st round of the NCAA Division II South Region Tournament. A 4 to 3 penalty kick shootout gave Florida Tech the victory and advanced them to the 2nd round where they blanked Rollins by a 2-nil score. The Lady Panthers then had another nailbiter before defeating Tampa in penalty kicks, giving Florida Tech their 1st ever South Region championship and advancing them to the Elite Eight. Not a team to eschew drama, it took another shootout for the Lady Panthers to dispatch Lenoir-Rhyne in the quarterfinals on November 21, thereby sending them to the Final Four. Florida Tech's magical season came to an end in Louisville in the NCAA semifinal game on December 2 with a 2-nil loss to defending national champion Grand Valley State. That concluded a memorable season with a record of 10 wins, 7 losses and 5 ties. Midfielder Paula Lillsjo was named to the 1st team of the All-South Region team while goalkeeper Mist Eliasdottir, defender Ann-Marie Helgestad and forward Casey Lademann were named to the 2nd team. Lademann and Kelly Whittaker were named to the Final Four All-Tournament Team. Eliasdottir, Helgestad, Lademann and Lillsjo would each secure a place on the 1st team of the all-conference team. The Panthers would be ranked 4th in the final national poll for the season. With 10 starters returning, including 5 All-South Region players, the outlook for 2011 was bright.

Paula Lillsjo, Class of 2011, was without question one of the greatest women soccer players in the history of Florida Tech. A member of the 2010 NCAA Final Four team, she was the first All-American in program history. A midfielder from Sweden, Lillsjo also was selected as a member of the first team on the All-Sunshine State Conference team and the All-South Region team in 2010. Lillsjo was inducted into the Florida Tech Sports Hall of Fame in 2020.

The Panthers would begin the 2011 season ranked 5th in the country in NCAA Division II women's soccer. By mid-September, however, the Lady Panthers possessed a 5 and 0 record and had advanced to be the top-ranked team in the country. When conference play began, the competition became more intense. They ended the regular season with a decisive 5-nil win over Eckerd, bringing their overall record to 10 wins, 3 losses and a tie, with a 4 win, 3 loss and a tie record in the conference. They began the conference tournament with a 1 to nil victory over Nova Southeastern on November 1 but fell in the semifinal round to Rollins by a 2 to nil score. The Lady Panthers received a bid to the NCAA South Regional tournament but lost in the 1st round to Lynn on November 11 by a 1 to nil score. That game marked the last appearance for 7 Panther seniors. Haig noted: "These seniors are very special. The bond that we established is something that will last for years to come." Casey Lademann, Chelsea Pushman, Paula Lillsjo, Kelly Whittaker, Ann-Marie Helgestad and Mist Eliasdottir were each named to the 2nd team all-conference team. Lademann, boasting a 3.93 cumulative GPA, was named to the 3rd team of the Academic All-America team.

The loss of the 7 seniors had its effect as the 2012 Lady Panthers dropped to an overall record of 7 wins, 6 losses and 3 ties. With only 2 conference wins and 5 conference losses, together with 2 ties, Florida Tech failed to make the conference tournament for the 1st time in 5 years. Senior midfielder Kelly Whittaker was named to the 1st team All-Sunshine State Conference team while freshman forward Erika Forsberg made the 2nd team.

It did not take long for the Lady Panthers to rebuild, however, as they completed the 2013 regular season with a record of 10 wins, 5 losses and a tie. Their conference record of 3 wins, 4 losses and a tie was good enough to qualify them for the conference post-season tournament. They opened the tournament with a 2 to nil victory over Saint Leo on November 5. They then faced top-seeded Barry on November 8 where they were eliminated in a fierce defensive battle which was scoreless through regulation time and 2 overtime periods and ended in a penalty kick shootout. The Lady Panthers then advanced to the NCAA Division II South Region tournament where they achieved a 1st round victory over Valdosta State by a 1 to nil score. The 2013 season ended with a 2 to 1 loss to top-seeded West Florida on November 17. Aubri Williamson, a sophomore forward, was named to the All-South Region team while Williamson and fellow sophomore Julia Kantor were named to the 2nd team of the All-Sunshine State Conference team.

The 2014 Lady Panthers fought to a regular season record of 7 wins and 7 losses with 1 tie. They then lost to Saint Leo by a 3 to 1 score in the 1st round of the conference tournament on November 4. Midfielder Courtney Hueston was selected to the 2nd team on the all-conference team. Hueston joined teammate Eva Banton on the 2nd team of the All-South Region team.

On April 16, 2015, the Florida Tech family and the Florida soccer community were shocked when 47-year-old Fidgi Haig died tragically and unexpectedly due to a massive cardiac event. Haig had amassed 97 wins in his 9 years as coach at Florida Tech after having scored 45 goals with 18 assists as a player at the school. The outpouring of grief with his passing was a clear demonstration of the respect which he had earned among his players, fans and colleagues. Viera High School girls' soccer coach Courtney Baines-Lundy, who had played for Fidgi at Satellite High, spoke for many when she told *Florida Today* on April 17, 2015: "Who I am today, and what I have done as a player, coach and person is due to Fidgi's impact in my life." On April 22, 2015, *Florida Today* reported that Bino Campanini eulogized Fidgi by saying: "Fidgi left a mark on our lives that needs no embellishment. His spirit is still with me, and I hope it never leaves." Mike Parsons wrote in *Florida Today* on April 17, 2015: "From the moment that Fitzgerald 'Fidgi' Haig got off the plane from Port-Au-Prince, Haiti, in 1987, he changed the face of soccer in Brevard County."

On May 1, 2015, Dustin Smith, who had served 5 years as an assistant coach under Haig, was named head coach of the women's soccer team at Florida Tech. Smith noted: "You can never replace a man like Fidgi, but I am going to do my best to carry on what we envision for the program."

Smith guided the Lady Panthers to a regular season record of 9-4-2 (5-3-1 in conference) during the 2015 season. They then proceeded to score a 1st round victory over Rollins in the conference tournament when they won 3 to nil on November 3. Freshman Keira McCarthy led the way with her first career hat trick. The Florida Tech run was stopped when they lost to Barry in the conference semifinal on November 7 by a 2 to 1 score. Goalkeeper Julia Kantor and McCarthy were named to the 2nd team of the All-South Region.

The Fall 2015 issue of *Florida Tech Today* featured an article about Ashley Vezina, a chemical engineering major on the soccer team. The article described how Vezina had spent her summer break in Cusco, Peru, studying hydrology and renewable energy at San Ignacio de Loyola.

The 2016 Lady Panthers made a splash on the national scene on October 6 when they travelled to Michigan to face the defending national champions and top-ranked Division II team in the country, Grand Valley State. Keira McCarthy, a Melbourne High School product, scored both goals as Florida Tech prevailed by a 2 to 1 score. Coach Smith observed: "Our conference teams prepare us for anything and everything we could've possibly encountered tonight." The winter 2017 issue of Florida Tech Today noted that the victory ended Grand Valley's 34-game win streak.

The 2016 season ended in the quarterfinal round of the Sunshine State Conference Tournament when the Lady Panthers lost to Barry by a 1 to nil score. This ended the season with a record of 11 wins and 6 losses and a 4 win, 5 loss record in the conference. Eva Banton, Keira McCarthy and Ciera Misner each were named to the 2nd team of the all-conference team while Misner also made the 2nd squad of the All-South Region team.

The 2017 Lady Panther soccer season began modestly but turned out to be a memorable season. Florida Tech completed the regular season with a modest record of 7 wins, 7 losses and 2 ties and a conference record of 4, 5 and 1. However, the Lady Panthers came to life in the post-season. In the opening round of the conference tournament, Florida Tech downed Florida Southern by a 2 to 1 score. They followed that win with a 1 to nil victory over Barry in the semifinals, putting them in the conference tournament final for only the 2nd time in program history. The final game against Tampa on November 5 was a barnburner. The game was a scoreless tie after regulation time and 2 overtime periods. Florida Tech prevailed in the penalty-kick shootout by scoring 4 times while Tampa tallied only twice, thereby giving the Panthers their 1st conference tournament championship in program history.

As noted in the winter 2018 issue of *Florida Tech Today*, the conference championship put Florida Tech in the NCAA Division II playoffs for the 5th time in the past 10 years. However, the post-season run of the Lady Panthers came to an end in the opening round when they suffered a 2 nil loss to Lee University on November 6. Maria Munoz and Keira McCarthy were selected to the 2nd team of the All-South Region team while Elia Stevenson made the 3rd team. Midfielder Munoz was named to the All-Sunshine State Conference 1st team while midfielder Svensson and forward McCarthy were recognized on the all-conference 2nd team.

Teresa (Brantley) Moon heads the ball into the goal.
Photo from University Archives.

Dustin Smith resigned as head coach in September 2018 at the beginning of the 2018 season and was immediately replaced by his assistant Jessica Monarch. Smith had compiled a record at Florida Tech of 30 wins, 19 losses and 5 ties and had led the Lady Panthers to their 1st-ever conference tournament championship in 2017.

The Lady Panthers experienced modest success in their 2018 season. When they completed their regular season on October 23 with a loss to Rollins, their season's record fell to 8-8-1 with a 5-5 conference record. They then faced Rollins again in the 1st round of the conference tournament less than a week later, again losing, this time by a 1 nil score. Keira McCarthy and Maria Munoz were selected to the all-conference 1st team while teammate Maria Sanchez Recureo received 2nd team recognition. Munoz also was selected to the 2nd team of the All-South Region team. Macey Hedelund, a Melbourne native majoring in Biological Sciences, was selected to the Academic All-District 1st team as a result of her perfect 4.0 GPA.

The 2019 season was a frustrating time for Florida Tech women's soccer. They ended the 2019 season on November 5 with a 5 to 1 loss to Lynn. That brought their season record to 3 wins, 11 losses and 2 ties, with a conference record of 1 win, 8 losses and a tie. Maria Munoz, an accounting major, was selected for the Academic All-District 1st team.

Jessica Monarch resigned as head coach on February 25, 2020. Ryan Moon was named as her successor on June 8, 2020. Moon had been a standout player for the Panthers as well as serving as an assistant men's coach since 2011, including Associate Head Coach of the men's team for 2 years. An additional asset that Moon brought to the table was his wife, Teresa Brantley Moon, one of the greatest players in Florida Tech women's soccer history, who would join her husband's staff as an assistant coach. Teresa Brantley Moon had been inducted into the Florida Tech Sports Hall of Fame in 2016.

Ryan and Teresa Moon would have to wait a while to demonstrate whether they could restore Florida Tech women's soccer to its former glory. On July 17, 2020, the Sunshine State Conference President's Council announced that all fall sports, including men's soccer, women's soccer, men's cross country, women's cross country and women's volleyball, would be postponed on account of the COVID-19 then running rampant. The plans announced by the conference contemplated that the postponed sports would be played during the spring of 2021. The announcement further explained that during the postponement of the fall sports, those teams would be allowed to engage in conditioning activities, strength training and practice, so long as those activities could be done without risking the health of the student-athletes.

On December 16, 2020, the Sunshine State Conference announced its Women's Soccer All-Decade Team for the period of 2010 to 2019. Mist Eliasdottir, former net-minder for the Lady Panthers, was recognized as a member of the 2nd team. Eliasdottir, a native of Iceland, had a career that included 3 consecutive NCAA tournament selections, the 1st conference regular season championship in school history and the program's 1st Final Four appearance.

Moon would make his debut as Lady Panther head coach in the spring of 2021 when the team would play 6 games following postponement of the fall 2020 schedule. He quickly demonstrated that

Florida Tech women's soccer was on the rebound as the Lady Panthers were undefeated in their initial 5 games in the spring season before stumbling in the final spring game. Miranda Choplin and goalie Maria Sanchez Recuero led the way for the team.

The success in the spring 2021 season foreshadowed a strong fall season in 2021. The Lady Panthers fought to a regular season record of 8 wins, 2 losses and 5 ties with a conference record of 4 wins, 2 losses and 2 ties. They then opened the conference tournament with their 1st conference tourney win since 2017 by defeating Nova Southeastern by a 1 to nil score. They followed that with a 2 to 1 semifinal win over Palm Beach Atlantic on November 11. Although they fell to Embry-Riddle in the tournament's championship game by a 1 nil score, they were selected to return to the NCAA South-Region Tournament for the 1st time since 2017.

In the opening round of the 2021 NCAA South-Region Tournament, the Lady Panthers won a penalty kick victory over Mississippi College on November 19. Not content with that nail-biting drama, they then won another penalty kick victory over top-seeded Lee University on November 21, thereby advancing to the Sweet Sixteen of the NCAA tourney. Another victory, once again by penalty kicks, over West Florida on December 3 put the Lady Panthers into the quarterfinals of the national tournament. Finally in the quarterfinal round, their run came to an end when they lost to Lenoir-Rhyne in, it almost goes without saying, a penalty kick shootout. Thus ended a storybook season with a record of 10 wins, 3 losses and 9 ties. Post-season honors poured in for the Lady Panthers as JoJo Michaels and Maria Sanchez Recuero were named to the All-Sunshine State Conference 1st team while Marem Ndiongue and Mayara Queiroz Reis were selected to the 2nd team. Michaels and Queiroz Reis were named to the All-South Region 1st team while Sanchez Recuero was named to the 2nd team. The team was ranked 19th in the country in the final poll.

The 2022 season was another strong season for the Lady Panthers as they completed the regular season with a record of 7 wins, 5 losses and a tie, including a 5 win, 4 loss conference record. They then defeated Barry in the opening round of the conference championship by a 1 nil score. The highlight of that victory was achieved when goalkeeper Sanchez Recuero made 5 saves, giving her 280 saves for her career, a new Florida Tech record. That game was followed by a penalty kick victory over Florida Southern on November 3, 2022, which put the Lady Panthers in the championship game. However, the Lady Panthers fell to Embry-Riddle by a 1 nil score in the championship match. Michaels and Queiroz were selected to the all-conference 1st team while Sanchez Recuero, Marem Ndiongue and Kajsa Ekstrom were selected for the 2nd team. Queiroz was named to the All-South Region 1st team while Michaels was named to the regional 2nd team.

Since taking over the reins of the Lady Panthers, Coach Ryan Moon has instilled a desire to win and work ethic that bode well for the future of Florida Tech women's soccer. As Moon said: "If you want to succeed in the college game, there's not really a chance to carry any passengers that aren't going to work hard. We tried to instill that in training, where there's no going through the motions."

Notes

- The success of the 2010 women's soccer team was reported in the winter 2011 edition of Florida Tech Today.
- Teresa Brantley-Moon's accomplishments were also described in the winter 2010 issue of Florida Tech Today.
- The results of specific seasons, coaching changes and post-season honors are, unless otherwise cited, taken from news articles from https://floridatechsports.com/news. The news articles on women's soccer which were relied upon were those published on October 27, 2007, November 4, 2007, November 14, 2008, November 16, 2008, November 5, 2009, November 6, 2009, November 12, 2009, October 31, 2010, November 7, 2010, November 12, 2010, November 19, 2010, November 21, 2010, December 2, 2010, December 8, 2010, December 9, 2010,August 25, 2011, October 26, 2011, November 2, 2013, November 6, 2013, October 26, 2014, November 25, 2014, October 19, 2015, November 3, 2015, November 7, 2015, October 6, 2016, November 1, 2016, November 3, 2016, November 16, 2016, November 3, 2017, November 6,2017, October 23, 2018, November 5, 2018, November 5, 2019, July 18, 2020, December 16, 2020, April 10, 2021, September 1, 2021, November 8, 2021, November 11, 2021, November 14, 2021, November 15, 2021, October 28, 2022, October 31, 2022, November 2, 2022, December 1, 2022, and February 25, 2023.
- Information regarding all-conference selections, the All-Decade Team and postponement of the 2020 season were gleaned from the website of the Sunshine State Conference at sunshinestateconference.com.

CHAPTER EIGHTEEN:
SWIMMING BREAKS RECORDS

By William C. Potter

An article by Mark DeCotis in *Florida Today* on June 8, 2011, described the recently constructed Panther Aquatic Center on the Florida Tech campus. The center, built next to the Clemente Center, consisted of a 25-yard, 9-lane heated competitive pool, with 1 and 3-meter diving stands. An additional part of the center was a heated recreational pool, changing rooms, varsity locker rooms and coaches' offices. The news article even included the interesting but somewhat superfluous information that the competitive pool contained 384,120 gallons of water.

The new facility enabled Florida Tech to add men's and women's swimming as varsity sports. The news article disclosed that Jeni Ritter had been employed as head coach of swimming and diving as well as director of the aquatic complex. Ritter told the newspaper: "I am extremely excited to become a member of the Florida Tech family. Since the announcement of the new Panther Aquatic Center, I have watched the construction progression and can honestly say we have a beautiful state of the art facility. We will not only be able to accommodate both our men's and women's swimming team, but also provide aquatic programming for the campus community."

The Panthers would kick off intercollegiate swimming competition in the fall of 2011. Florida Southern, Nova Southeastern, Rollins, Saint Leo and Tampa fielded swim teams in the Sunshine State Conference at that time. The Panthers men and women faced their first-ever collegiate competition on November 5, 2011, when they travelled to face Saint Leo. Although they lost both men's and women's meets, the 15 Panther competitors scored enough points to find reasons for a hopeful future. Their 2nd meet took place at Rollins on November 12 and, although they again lost both men's and women's meets, Florida Tech inspired confidence when it won its 1st 5 races.

The first collegiate competition at the Panther Aquatic Center featured a meet on December 2, 2011, against Tampa. *Florida Today*, in an article written by Lyn Dowling on December 3, reported that a crowd of 300 fans cheered on the Panthers. Although Tampa prevailed in both meets, there were many bright spots. Steven Moodie became Florida Tech's 1st-ever winner at home when he prevailed in the 50-yard freestyle. Moodie added a victory in the 100-freestyle.

The Sunshine State Conference championships took place from February 15th to 18th, 2012, in Clearwater. Moodie again proved to be a bright spot for Florida Tech as he placed 11th in the 50-yard freestyle, 15th in 100-yard freestyle and helped the 400-yard medley relay team to a 5th place finish. Both the men and the women finished in 6th place in the meet.

The 2013 Sunshine State Conference swimming meet was an historic event for Florida Tech swimming. The Panthers broke 26 school records during the 4-day event while achieving 4 NCAA B cut times.

A highlight of the 2013-2014 season occurred on January 18, 2014, when the Panthers swept Rollins College for the 1st time in program history. That wrapped up the men's dual meet season with a 6 and 4 record while the women completed their dual meet season with a 4 and 8 record for the most season wins in program history.

Jeni Ritter stepped down as coach on April 3, 2014, after 3 years at the helm. She had completed her most successful season in school history that spring when both men and women achieved 4th place in the conference meet, their highest finishes ever in program history. Brian Dumont and Lauren Suarez had become the 1st swimmers in school history to medal at the meet while Dar Raz had become the first Panther ever recognized with all-conference honors. On June 17, 2014, Justin Andrade was elevated from assistant to head men's and women's coach to succeed Ritter.

Florida Tech Today, in its Spring 2016 edition, disclosed that Nir Barnea had become the 1st Panther swimmer in history to win gold at the conference meet when he won the 50-yard freestyle race in a time of 19.98. The publication noted that Barnea, a transfer from LSU, would go on the NCAA meet where he would win All-American recognition as a part of the 200 and 400-freestyle relay teams. The men's 400-freestyle relay team swam to an 8th place finish at the 2016 NCAA championships, thereby earning All-American recognition for team members Nir Barnea, Filip Dujmic, Victor Rocha Furtado and Thomas Steenberg.

The Panther men shocked the competition when the 200-freestyle relay team won the NCAA Division II championship on March 9, 2017, earning the 1st national championship in program history. The relay team, consisting of Nir Barnea, Victor Rocha Furtado, Matthew Gallene and Filip Dujmic, set a school record with a time of 1:19.46. Coach Andrade said: "This is a great group of high character individuals. They trusted the process and worked hard all season long." The 200-medley relay team had previously finished 9th in the meet. The Fall 2016 edition of *Florida Tech Today* would note that 7 Florida Tech swimmers would achieve All-American status during that meet.

Andrade was named Sunshine State Conference Coach of the Year for the 2016-2017 season. No other Panther swim coach has achieved that honor.

The Panther men finished 3rd at the Sunshine State Conference meet in 2018, their highest standing in history. The women completed the meet in 7th place. The Panthers experienced great success at the 2018 Division II NCAA meet. The 400-freestyle relay team of Emanuele

Rossi, Filip Dujmic, Thomas Steenberg and Rocha Furtado placed 4th while that quartet finished 5th in the 200-freestyle relay. Furtado earned runner-up honors in the men's 100 freestyle and 100-freestyle races.

The 200-freestyle relay team won the NCAA Championship in 2017. Coach Justin Andrade celebrated with team members, Victor Rocha Furtado, Matthew Gallene, Filip Dumic and Nir Barnea. *Photo from University Archives.*

Justin Andrade, who had been head coach for 4 seasons and had been Sunshine State Conference Coach of the Year in 2017, resigned on June 20, 2018, to become an assistant coach at the University of Pittsburgh. David Dent, who had served as an assistant coach for the 2017-18 season, was elevated to head coach of the men's and women's swimming team. Dent had been a swimmer at Fairmont State University where he set a number of school records and competed at the 2013 NCAA Division II championships. Dent remains as the head coach as of the writing of this book.

In September 2018, Thomas Steenberg, a recent Florida Tech graduate and a key member of its conference champion 400-freestyle relay team, was named the South Region Division II Scholar-Athlete of the Year, becoming the first Panther athlete to win that recognition. Steenberg had previously been recognized as only the 2nd Panther ever named as Sunshine State Conference Scholar-Athlete of the Year.

The 2018-2019 team made its mark at the 2019 NCAA championship meet when Victor Rocha Furtado finished 2nd in the 100-freestyle race and 4th in the 100 fly. The Panther men's 400-freestyle relay team finished in 4th while the men's 400 medley relay finished in 8th place.

Seven members of the 2018-2019 Panther swimming team were named to the Scholar All-American team, an honor which requires a minimum 3.5 GPA. Savannah Brennan, Valentina Carvajal and Carter Juskevich were named from the women's team. From the men's team, Adi Davidov, Filip Dujmic, Emanuele Rossi and Harry Sale were selected for the honor. Both the men's and women's teams were recognized as a team for their academic accomplishments as Scholar All-American teams.

The 2019-2020 season was highlighted by the selection of Savannah Brennan and Dain Rust as All-Americans. Rust was selected for his 100-breaststroke time while Brennan qualified on account of her time in the grueling 400 individual medley.

On July 19, 2020, it was announced that swimmer Savannah Brennan had been selected as a 1st team Scholar All-American while teammates Nicole Rautemberg and Daniel Aizenberg had been selected for honorable mention recognition. In addition, both the men's and women's teams once again gained Scholar All-American distinction. The women's team boasted a team GPA of 3.8, tops among all sports teams at Florida Tech.

Savannah Brennan and Daniel Aizenberg represented Florida Tech at the 2021 NCAA Division II championships. Both swimmers had previously been named Scholar All-Americans, together with their teammate Nicole Rautemberg. Aizenberg broke his own school record at the NCAA meet to finish 6th overall, good for All-American 1st team honors. Brennan made history by scoring points in the 400-individual medley event.

In October 2021, the Sunshine State Conference announced the conference All-Decade Team. Included on the team was former Panther swimmer Victor Rocha Furtado. Furtado, from Brazil, had won the conference title in the 50-freestyle in 2018 and the 100-freestyle in both 2017 and 2018. He was also a member of the winning 200 and 400-freestyle relay teams in both 2017 and 2018.

At the 2022 NCAA Championships, Daniel Aizenberg garnered a 1st team All-American finish in the 100-backstroke and 2 honorable mention finishes in other events. Savannah Brennan completed her career at that meet, a career that included 3 All-American recognitions and becoming the 1st Panther female swimmer to ever earn points at the national championships when she finished 5th in the 1000-freestyle.

The NCAA Woman of the Year award was established in 1991 and honors senior female student-athletes who have distinguished themselves throughout their college career by their achievements in academics, athletics, service and leadership. In 2022, Florida Tech swimmer Savannah Brennan was nominated and was among the top-30 finalists for the award. There were 577 nominees for the award and the top-30 included 10 from each NCAA division. Brennan, from Oviedo,

Florida, was the first 3-time winner of the Sunshine State Conference's Female Scholar-Athlete of the Year award. She was also a First Team CoSIDA Academic All-America honoree. She completed her undergraduate studies after achieving a 3.97-grade point average with a double major in Genomic and Molecular Genetics and Biomedical Science. After graduation, she then began pursuit of a Master's in Biotechnology. Head swimming coach Dave Dent noted: "During her illustrious career, Savannah was the first female to score any points at NCAA's, the first female All-American, the first female swimmer to win the SSC Scholar-Athlete of the Year award, the first athlete to win the SSC Scholar-Athlete award 3 times in a row, the first Florida Tech scholar-athlete to win the SSC Woman of the Year, and now she is the first Florida Tech scholar-athlete to be named in the Top 30 for the NCAA Woman of the Year. Savannah has garnered an impressive number of accomplishments during her career, no one is more deserving than Sav, she worked harder than anyone day in and day out to accomplish everything she did." Brennan was a 4-year member of the TriBeta biological honors society, where she served as chapter president. During the pandemic, she volunteered in the emergency department of Holmes Regional Medical Center. She also volunteered with Team IMPACT which matches collegiate teams with children dealing with chronic diseases. There could be no more compelling example of the results of Title IX than Savannah Brennan.

In 2023, 9 Florida Tech swimmers qualified for the NCAA Division II championship meet. Daniel Aizenberg, an Israeli, was the conference 100-backstroke champion who would swim in 4 individual races and the 400-medley relay at the national championship meet. Nicole Rautemberg, from Paraguay, would swim in 3 individual races and the 200-freestyle relay. Katherine Helminiak would race in 2 freestyle events. Connor Orth, John Fonnoto and Nathaniel Allen would join Aizenberg on the relay team while Harper Powell, Deborah Xavier and Shaelyn Rutta would join Rautemberg on the freestyle relay team. This would mark the 9th consecutive season that Florida Tech would be represented at the national championships. The highlight of the meet for the Panthers occurred when Aizenberg claimed 1st team All-American honors by finishing 7th in the 100-backstroke. For Aizenberg, that marked his 3rd consecutive All-American showing in that event.

Notes

- The results of specific meets and post-season honors and academic honors are, unless otherwise cited, taken from news articles from https://floridatechsports.com/news. The news articles on men's and women's swimming which were relied upon were those published on February 18, 2012, February 16, 2013, January 15, 2014, April 3, 2014, March 9, 2017, March 17, 2018, September 20, 2018, March 14, 2019, March 16, 2019, July 3, 2019, April 8, 2020, July 10, 2020, October 19, 2021, March 13, 2022, March 10, 2023, and February 22, 2023.
- Information regarding Brennan and Steenberg's selections as Sunshine State Conference Scholar-Athlete of the Year was also gleaned from the website of the Sunshine State Conference at sunshinestateconference.com.

CHAPTER NINETEEN:
NANCY AND VAL CREATE SOFTBALL EXCELLENCE

By William C. Potter

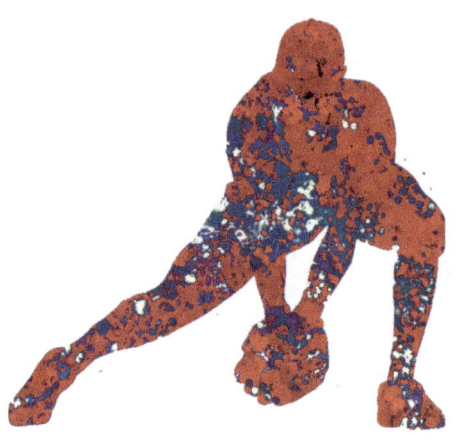

The earliest mention of softball in the Florida Tech yearbook was in the 1982 edition of *Ad Astra* which disclosed a team of 12 players. Dan Hartigan and Jim Green were listed as the coaches.

On April 15, 1982, the athletic directors of the Sunshine State Conference determined that basketball, volleyball, and slow-pitch softball should be the "flagship" sports for women in conference play with cross country and tennis as additional conference sports for women.

The 1983 *Ad Astra* listed John Holdsworth as the coach but gave no information about the results of play. Similarly, the 1884 *Ad Astra* disclosed only that there were 12 players on the team and that John Yana was the coach, assisted by Mike Spragins and Jim Self.

Florida Today reported on March 27, 1984, that the Lady Panthers had started the 1984 season by not only winning their first 6 games but by shutting out each of their opponents. The pitching of Amy Roy and the hitting of Kim Orihuela, Kathy Rogell and Tina Petro led the way for Florida Tech. Orihuela, a graduate of Satellite High School, was notable in that she played both volleyball and softball at Florida Tech.

The Lady Panthers softball team had another successful season in 1985, finishing 2nd in the Sunshine State Tournament. When they lost to Florida Southern in the championship game, their record stood at 14 wins and 11 losses. Orihuela and Sue Ropke were key hitters for the Panther offense that season.

The 1986 season brought a profound change to Florida Tech softball as the Sunshine State Conference changed from slow-pitch to fast-pitch softball. *Florida Today* reported on February 16, 1986, that the Lady Panthers had opened their season the previous day by splitting a doubleheader with Bethune-Cookman College. When they swept a doubleheader from Rollins on March 12, they moved to 4 and 0 in conference play. A doubleheader shutout of Saint Leo on March 26 extended their conference record to 6 and 0. Amy Roy hurled a no hitter in the nightcap against Saint Leo while homers by Kathy Rogell, Kim Orihuela and Sue Ropke powered the Panthers to the sweep.

The 1987 *Ad Astra* disclosed that Bonnie Priester was coaching Panther softball, assisted by Rick Lindon. Lindon was a part-time coach who was also coaching the Lady Panther volleyball team. *Florida Today* reported on February 27, 1987, that Kim Orihuela was up to her old tricks in powering the Lady Panthers to a doubleheader sweep of Bethune-Cookman. Marissa Poudrier added a home run of her own. Florida Tech would go on to post a 19 and 11 overall record with a 15 and 9 conference record, good for 3rd place in the conference. Another notable player on that squad was Barbara Barlow who also played basketball for Florida Tech.

Florida Today's issue of May 8, 1987, disclosed the all-Sunshine State Conference team, dominated by Florida Southern's undefeated squad. First baseman Cindy Casero of Florida Tech made the 1st team while Marissa Poudrier and Kim Orihuela received 2nd team recognition. Poudrier, a Melbourne native, was another dual-sport athlete, competing in volleyball as well as softball. *Florida Today* noted on August 20, 1989, that she was also named a Collegiate All-American Scholar.

The 1988 season brought another significant rule change to women's softball as the pitching rubber was moved from 40 feet to 43 feet. The 1988 Lady Panther softball team, coached by Rick Lindon, had a positive season, finishing 2nd in the Sunshine State Conference. *Florida Today* reported on April 9 that their record stood at 14 and 13 overall and 8 and 6 in the conference. As a result of injuries, the team was down to 9 players at that point. When they split a doubleheader with Eckerd on April 20, their record went to 17 and 17 overall and 11 and 7 in the conference.

Florida Today disclosed on May 17, 1988, that 1st baseman Marissa Poudrier, pitcher Lynn Grinstead, yet another 2-sport athlete, outfielder Jean Yorio and 2nd baseman Cindy VanDoren had all been selected for the all-conference team. Sophomore pitcher Amy Boulay received honorable mention recognition. Grinstead was not only a 2-sport athlete, excelling in both softball and volleyball, but maintained a 3.2 GPA concentrating in genetic engineering.

Greg Meyer would assume the reins as coach of Lady Panther softball at the outset of the 1989 season. Meyer, *Florida Today* would disclose on February 24, 1990, was a former baseball captain at Florida Tech who had become Associate Director of Admissions at the college. The 1989 *Ad Astra* disclosed that, at the time of publication of the yearbook, the Lady Panthers had compiled a record of 11 wins and 2 losses and a conference record of 3 and 1. The Lady Panthers would falter later in the season and finish the 1989 season with an overall record of 17 wins and 19 losses.

When Meyer returned as coach in 1990, he became the 1st softball coach in program history to return for a 2nd season. The stability which he provided enabled a young team to develop. When the Lady Panthers swept a doubleheader from Tampa on April 2, they took their record to 12 and 10 overall and 8 and 4 in the league.

Tom DeFilipow coached the Lady Panthers softball teams for the 1991 and 1992 seasons. The 1991 season began in promising fashion for the Lady Panther softballers when they swept the opening doubleheader from Bethune-Cookman on February 21, 1991. Lynn Grinstead and Sherri Wieda were the starting pitchers for Florida Tech. That promising start, however, did not continue. When Florida Tech swept a doubleheader on March 26, they improved their record to 13 and 14. By the time that they split a twin-bill with Rollins on April 19, Wieda's pitching record had dropped to 3 and 12. Grinstead was the only Panther selected to the all-conference team when she received honorable-mention recognition as reported by *Florida Today* on May 4, 1991.

DeFilipow returned to coach the 1992 softball team in what turned out to be a disappointing season for Florida Tech softball. One highlight of the season was a split of a doubleheader with the U.S. Naval Academy reported in *Florida Today* on March 11. *Florida Today* reported on April 21 that the Lady Panthers had completed their season by losing a doubleheader to Barry University. This closed the season for the Panthers with 12 wins and 28 losses. Their conference record of winning only 4 games while losing 20 was particularly discouraging. A *Florida Today* article by David Jones on April 13 encouraged readers to support an upcoming Florida Tech athletic fundraiser in order to provide scholarships for students like Lisa Hull, a marine biology student who was an infielder on the softball team. Elisa Bartolo was a bright spot for the 1992 team and was a 2nd-team All-Sunshine State Conference choice as she batted .338 and stole 33 bases in 35 attempts.

Paul Ouellette, a former Panther baseball star, was next up to try to turn around the softball program. Ouellette, the 2nd most prolific home run hitter in Panther baseball history, approached the 1993 season with some optimism due to the return of 8 letter winners, including Bartolo and Wieda. That season also saw the implementation of a livelier ball in the game. *Florida Today* reported on February 5, 1993, that one of the initial moves taken by Ouellette was to schedule games on the on-campus field rather than a remote site where they had played for several years. The 1993 season saw some improvement for the Lady Panthers. When they split a doubleheader with Saint Leo on April 2, their record was 10 and 16 for the year. On April 20, the Lady Panthers crushed Rollins College by scores of 12 to 2 and 14 to 1. Bartolo was hovering around the .400 mark in batting most of the season. They did improve their conference record with 5 victories.

The 1994 season proved to be a frustrating one for the Lady Panther softball team. Bartolo was lost to a knee injury in the 6th game of the season, a staggering blow to the team. The team did, however, win eight conference games, their highest win total in the league in 4 years. Their overall record was 9 and 35 while their conference record was 8 and 20.

Certainly one of the greatest players in Florida Tech softball history was Elisa Bartolo, class of 1996, who played both volleyball and softball. Bartolo was NCAA Division II batting champion in both 1995 and 1996. Conference Player of the Year in 1995, she was a 1st team All-American in 1995 and received 2nd team honors in 1996. She graduated holding school records for hits (295), batting average (.466), stolen bases (20!) and runs scored (224). She also held the NCAA Division II record for runs scored. She was inducted into the Florida Tech Sports Hall of Fame in 2001. A *Florida Today* story by David Jones on April 13, 1995, described the "slap" technique that the speedy Bartolo mastered to make her such a dangerous leadoff hitter.

Elisa Bartolo led NCAA Division II in batting average in both 1995 and 1996 with her slap-hitting technique. *Photo from University Archives.*

On June 22, 1994, *Florida Today* reported that Ouellette would step down as head baseball coach and would assume an administrative position with the team. His record after 2 years as head coach was 23 wins and 65 losses. Nancy Bottge, who had served as assistant coach for the 1994 season, would assume the head coaching position. Bottge would bring a new level of success to the program.

Nancy Bottge coached the softball team for 11 seasons from 1995 to 2005. She never had a losing season while guiding the Lady Panthers to a record of 316 wins, 237 losses and 2 ties. This gave her a total of 501 collegiate victories when combined with the record she had compiled at Bloomfield College prior to arriving at Florida Tech. Her final team at Florida Tech compiled a record of 33 and 15, establishing a new record of success in softball at the school.

Bottge's 1995 team experienced immediate success. *Florida Today* reported on April 13 that the team was currently 25 and 20 and had shattered the school record for season victories, which had been set at 19 in 1987. Bottge's initial team finished the season with a 29 and 22 record that would be the 1st with a record over .500 since 1989. On May 3, 1995, the Sunshine State Conference announced that Florida Tech outfielder Elisa Bartolo had been selected as Player of the Year for the conference, having hit .581 for the year with a conference season record of 108 hits.

Bottge had brought Jim Wasicki to Florida Tech as her assistant coach. It was Wasicki who worked with Bartolo in perfecting her slap hitting. Tragically, Wasicki developed cancer and, as reported by *Florida Today* on June 7, 1996, died at the age of 31.

The 1996 Lady Panthers continued on an upward track, setting a new program record for victories with 33 while losing 25. Bartolo was selected to the 2nd team of the NCAA Division II All-America team as well as the All-South Region team. Her teammates Tyme Fruscella, Stacey Tucker and Amy Potter joined her with All-South recognition. Bartolo, Fruscella and Tucker were 1st team all-conference selectees while Potter earned 2nd team recognition. Bartolo hit .549 while stealing 72 bases in 77 attempts. Fruscella led the conference with 52 runs batted in and was named Freshman of the Year for the conference.

The 1997 season brought continued success with a 30 and 25 record. Thus, the Lady Panthers achieved consecutive 30-win seasons.

The 1998 Lady Panthers concluded their season with a 25 and 21 overall record and a 10 and 14 record in the conference. Amy Potter finished her career hitting .342 to lead the team. Bottge told *Florida Today* on April 20: "It was a good year for the old Florida Tech. For the new Florida Tech, we could have done better this year." Potter joined 2nd baseman Shannon Depiesse and pitcher-infielder Lois Elston on the NCAA All-South Region squad.

Florida Today reported on April 17, 1999, that the Lady Panthers were 26 and 13 overall at that point in the season, with a 9 and 8 conference record. On April 24 the Panthers stood at 29 and 19 overall and 12 and 14 in the conference. The 1999 *Ad Astra* reported that they completed the season at 28 and 21. *Florida Today* reported on May 13 that Tyme Fruscella was named to the 1999 All-Sunshine State Conference 1st team while teammates Brianne Pearson and Jana Vander Loop were named to the 2nd team.

Florida Today reported on April 18, 2000, that the Lady Panthers stood at 23 and 19 overall for the 2000 season, with an 11 and 13 conference record. Senior 1st baseman Jana Vander Loop led the team in hitting with a .355 average.

The 2001 season began positively. *Florida Today* reported on March 13, 2001, that the Panthers stood at 13 and 2 for the season. Bottge had passed the 350 career victory mark earlier in the season. By April 17, *Florida Today* could report that the Lady Panthers were 25, 15 and 1 overall with a 6, 12 and 1 record in the conference. Freshman pitcher Christine Custer had gone 16 and 6 while setting a program record for strikeouts with 155 and even pitching a perfect game. A remarkable addition to the team was 43-year old freshman outfielder Kattie Spivey who was reported to have made a number of spectacular defensive plays.

2002 was another winning season for the Lady Panthers. On April 21, *Florida Today* reported that Florida Tech had been swept by Lynn in a doubleheader the previous day. Despite those losses, Florida Tech maintained an overall record of 26 and 24 and a 9 and 15 conference record.

The 2003 team again compiled a winning record with 30 wins, 20 losses and a tie. At the time, those results established the best record in program history. Kristen Lane, a Palm Bay High graduate who was a sophomore majoring in biology, blossomed into a pitching ace for the Panthers. *Florida Today* reported on April 9 that Lane's record stood at 9 wins and 5 losses with a 1.46 earned run average.

A memorable season in Bottge's tenure at Florida Tech took place in 2004 when the Lady Panthers achieved a school-record 21-game unbeaten streak. When Florida Tech split a doubleheader with Barry University on April 21, the Panthers' record stood at 29 wins, 18 losses and a tie, including a 7 and 14 record in the conference. That earned the team its 1st-ever selection in the NCAA Division II South Region ranking at number 8 in the region.

Bottge's final season at Florida Tech in 2005 was perhaps her best season with a 33 win and 15 loss season. In the next to the last game of her career, the Lady Panthers knocked off Nova Southeastern to give Bottge her 500th career win.

Bottge succumbed to cancer on August 8, 2005, at the age of 48. One of her former players, Jesse Lawrence, told *Florida Today* on August 11, 2005: "She was the strongest person I knew and helped make me into the person I am today. Coach Bottge had a presence in life and she never gave up on us and we in turn never gave up on her." David Jones captured her spirit in *Florida Today* on August 13 when he wrote: "Nancy never lost a battle. She just sometimes didn't have enough innings to pull the game out." The Florida Tech softball field was dedicated in her honor on October 14, 2007. She was inducted into the Florida Tech Sports Hall of Fame in 2016.

This collage honors Nancy Bottge, softball coach from 1995 to 2005. Bottge's death devastated her numerous fans and players.
Photo from University Archives.

On September 15, 2005, *Florida Today* reported that Ellie Hanover had been hired to replace Bottge as head coach. Hanover had been coach at D'Youville College, a Division III school in Buffalo.

Hanover's 2006 season started strong. *Florida Today* reported on March 17 that the Lady Panthers had won 16 straight games and stood at 17 and 3 overall and 6 and 0 in the Sunshine State Conference. Catcher and designated hitter Megan Hube was hitting .500 with 7 home runs and 29 RBIs.

When Florida Tech split a doubleheader with Nova Southeastern on April 15, the Lady Panthers' record went to 29 and 13 for the season. A doubleheader sweep of Tampa on April 22 closed the season with an overall record of 31 and 16 and a conference record of 15 and 9. All in all, a very strong start for Hanover's inaugural year as coach.

The Lady Panthers received strong recognition on the all-conference team. Megan Hube, Kristen Fettes, Katie Naumoff and Courtney Harless all received 1st team honors while Karen D'Alberto,

Laura Chisena and Amber West were voted 2nd team honors according to a *Florida Today* article on May 10, 2006. On May 23, *Florida Today* reported that Harless, Naumoff and Hube had each been named to the All-South Region 1st team.

2007 turned out to be an even stronger season for Lady Panther softball. Florida Tech established a school record for wins with 42 while losing only 25. Kristen Fettes led the team by batting .367 while driving in 49 runs and delivering 79 hits. Naumoff was close behind with a .344 average.

Unfortunately, the progress which Hanover had delivered during her initial couple of seasons turned to chaos in her 3rd season. *Florida Today* disclosed on March 13, 2008, that the softball team had not played since February 26 and the university had determined to cancel the remaining games of the 2008 season. A news article by Carl Kotala and Lee Nessel in *Florida Today* on March 14 described a "fractured between the players and Hanover" which Athletic Director Bill Jurgens had tried unsuccessfully to repair despite 2-weeks of attempts at mediation.

Hanover and Jurgens worked diligently to attempt to restore the team during the 2009 season. Florida Tech completed that season with an overall record of 22 wins and 26 losses, with a conference record of 8 wins and 16 losses. The team was almost entirely new, with only Megan Fallon, Brianna Barth and Danielle Healy returning from the previous year's squad. Barth gained 1st team recognition on the all-conference team and 2nd team recognition on the All-South Region team by hitting .340 with 51 hits and also racking up a 10 and 12 pitching record with a 2.14 ERA.

On May 2, 2009, *Florida Today* reported that Hanover had resigned as head coach. Jennifer Seidel, an assistant athletic director, was named to serve as interim coach while a search for a new head coach was conducted. On August 5, 2009, *Florida Today* reported that Valeria Silvestrini had been hired as head coach of the Florida Tech softball team. Silvestrini came to Florida Tech from the University of North Florida where she had been assistant coach, having previously served as an assistant at Charleston Southern and Armstrong State. Silvestrini, a former member of the Argentinean national team, remarked: "Florida Tech is a great school with outstanding leadership. I'm eager to begin this journey."

The hiring of Val Silvestrini has proven to be a propitious decision. As this history is written in 2023, Silvestrini is completing her 14th year at the helm of Florida Tech softball, a reign which has brought unprecedented success on the field and made Val the winningest softball coach in program history.

Val Silvestrini has been Florida Tech's softball coach for 14 years and is the winningest coach in program history.

The 2010 season marked Silvestrini's 1st season as coach of the Lady Panthers. Florida Tech finished with 22 wins and 28 losses. Brianna Barth and Tiffani Bishop were named to the 2nd team on the all-conference team while Barth once again received 2nd team recognition on the All-South Region team. The highlight of the season was a 2 to 1 win over 15th-ranked Nova Southeastern, the program's 1st win over a ranked opponent since 2008.

The 2011 season was marked by a great experience for the team when they travelled in early March to Silvestrini's native Argentina to play 9 games against the country's national team and junior national team. The trip proved to be not only a great bonding experience but an opportunity for an eye-opening cultural exchange. Most of the costs of the trip were covered by funds the team had generated through fund-raising activities.

The Lady Panthers completed the 2011 season with a record of 24 wins and 26 losses. Barth again garnered 2nd team honors on both the All-Sunshine State Conference team and the All-South Region team. Barth was not only a position player but a pitcher as well. She batted a team-high .327 while winning 13 games on the rubber.

The 2012 season brought a 24 and 27 overall record with a 10 and 14 conference record. Lauren Cole achieved 2nd team all-conference honors while Barth received All-South Region honors for the 4th time. Perhaps the highlight of the season occurred when 6 Lady Panthers were named All-America Scholar Athletes. Brianna Barth, Lauren Cole, Emily Densem, Sarah Doring, Sasha Stepaniuk, Kelsey Donahue and Taylor all achieved that honor which required a GPA of at least 3.50.

The 2013 season succeeded in putting Florida Tech over the hump with a winning season as they won 25 while losing 22, while breaking even in the conference at 12 and 12. Freshman Elaine Brown was named the all-conference 1st team after batting .349 and stealing 20 bases in 27 attempts.

The 2014 Lady Panthers jumped off to a strong start. By February 9, Florida Tech had won 8 while remaining undefeated. That start was accentuated by freshman pitcher Rachel Pence who pitched a 5-inning perfect game in the season opener, a 10 to 0 win over Fort Valley State. That fast start soon cooled-off, however, and the Panthers completed the season with 23 wins and 25 losses and 8 wins and 16 losses in the conference. Silvestrini noted:" Our conference was very competitive this year and we lost a lot of very close games." Elaine Brown, Kelsey Donahue and Rachel Pence were all named to the 2nd team of the all-conference team while Brown also made the All-District team.

Silvestrini's diligent and relentless efforts to build success came to fruition in the 2015 season, a season that would prove to be the most successful in program history. The Lady Panthers completed the regular season with a record of 32 wins and 16 losses, including a 25 and 14 record in the South Region. This record earned Florida Tech its 1st ever appearance in the NCAA regional tournament in Florence, Alabama with a 6th seed in the region. The Panthers won their opening game with a 2 to 1 victory over North Alabama, the 1st post-season win in Florida Tech history. They followed that up with a 2 to 1 victory over Rollins, elevating the Panthers to the regional title game. A 4 to 2 victory over North Alabama in the title game gave Florida Tech its 1st-ever NCAA Regional Championship and a trip to the Super Regionals. The Panthers travelled to Rome, Georgia, to face the Shorter Hawks in the Super Regional. The Panthers lost 2 straight to the Hawks, ending the Panther season with a record of 38 wins and 20 losses. Silvestrini reflected on the progress which the program had made which culminated in this special season when she told *Florida Today* on May 17: "I told them they had a chance to change things. They made a great change; three years ago, it began with this group and they are leaving as one of the top 16 teams."

Honors poured in for the 2015 Lady Panthers. Elaine Brown and Nicole Miller represented Florida Tech on the 1st team all-conference team while Brigit Godfrey gained 2nd team recognition and Rachel Pence received honorable mention. Brown made the 1st team All-South Region team while Miller earned 2nd team laurels. Brown hit .416 for the season with a .970 fielding average in center field. Miller had a .343 batting average while Pence had a 22 and 12 record on the mound. Shortstop Godfrey hit .313 while leading the conference with 12 double plays.

The Lady Panthers winning ways continued in the 2016 season as they racked up a record of 39 wins and only 15 losses, including a 17 and 7 mark in the Sunshine State Conference. The 39 wins were the 2nd most in program history. Hailey Leonard was named to the all-conference 1st team while Elaine Brown, Rachel Pence and Nicole Shinsky were named to the 2nd team. Pence set a school record with 31 wins and, as noted in the Fall 2016 issue of *Florida Tech Today*, racked up 229 strikeouts. Leonard led the conference in hits, RBIs, home runs and slugging percentage. Pence was also selected to the Academic All-District team with a 3.8 GPA in Psychology.

The 2017 squad compiled a record of 26 and 25 with an 11 and 13 record in the conference. Senior Rachel Pence once again was the mainstay of the pitching staff. Perhaps the greatest honor for the team that season was its receipt of the National Fastpitch Coaches Association Academic Team Honor which recognized its team GPA of 3.30.

2018 proved to be an outstanding season for Lady Panther softball. The team won 32 games while losing 21. They posted a winning record in the Sunshine State Conference with 16 wins and 14 losses. Narrowly missing the post-season tournament, Florida Tech placed 2 players as 1st team all-conference selections. Melanie Murphy had an outstanding year on the pitching mound with a 17 and 9 record and a new single-season best ERA of 1.00. Murphy and teammate Xiarysse Emerenciana were each 1st team all-conference selections while Murphy also made the 2nd team of the All-South Region team.

The 2019 season was easily the greatest season in the history of Florida Tech softball. Murphy sent a message early in the season when she tossed a perfect game against North Georgia on February 23. Their national ranking reached as high as number 4 while the Panthers won the Sunshine State Conference championship for the 1st time. The 42 wins posted matched the most wins in school history. They made their 2nd trip to the NCAA South Super Regional. The Fall 2019 issue of *Florida Tech Magazine* reported that the team finished the 2019 campaign ranked 10th in the nation.

A victory over Eckerd on April 26 gave the Lady Panthers their 1st ever Sunshine State Conference crown. That resulted in the then 5th ranked Panthers hosting the NCAA South Region. Victories over Alabama Huntsville and Mississippi College sent the Panthers to the Super Regional in Pensacola. The season ended in the NCAA Division II Super Regional with a loss to West Florida on May 17. Murphy told *Florida Today* on May 18, "Florida Tech softball didn't really have a name and then this year we were ranked nationally since the beginning of the season and we kept it there. Everybody saw our name on the list and I think we put Florida Tech on the map this year."

Post-season honors for the Lady Panthers were numerous. Pitcher Melanie Murphy from Melbourne High School became the 2nd All-American selection in program history with her record of 25 wins and 7 losses. Murphy and infielder Jaden Kline were named to the All-South Region team. Murphy, Kline, Shanysse Emerenciana and Mikayla Wessel were each named to the 1st team of the All-Sunshine State Conference team while Xiarysse Emerenciana and freshman Cheyenne Nelson were named to the 2nd team. Murphy completed her 2-year career at Florida Tech with 44 victories and 16 defeats.

The 2020 softball season was truncated due to COVID-19. At the time that the season was terminated, the Lady Panthers had compiled a 16 and 11 record and had won 7 while losing 2 in the conference. A notable accomplishment in 2020 was that of Cheyenne Nelson who was named to the Academic All-District team. Nelson had achieved a 3.94 GPA while majoring in aeronautical engineering. On the field, she had achieved a .324 batting average and a .963 fielding percentage.

2021 was a moderately successful season for Florida Tech softball. When the Lady Panthers swept Nova Southeastern on April 3, that gave Val Silvestrini her 317th win at Florida Tech, making her the winningest coach in program history. In typical Silvestrini fashion, she said: "It's an honor but I never put on cleats at Florida Tech and I never won a game. I think this honor is for all the players that played for me over the last 12 years."

The Panthers completed the 2021 season with an overall record of 13 wins and 15 losses and a 10 and 12 conference record. Cheyenne Nelson was the Sunshine State Conference Player of the Year, landing on the all-conference 1st team as well as 1st team of the All-South Region team. Nelson led the conference in hitting with a .418 average. Tina Velazquez Rolon joined Nelson on the all-conference 1st team and also gained 2nd team honors on the all-region team. Chloe French and Victoria Szrom took 2nd team all-conference honors while Mikayla Lewin received honorable mention.

The Lady Panthers bounced back with a winning record during the 2022 season by posting a 32 win, 20 loss season with a 15 and 15 conference record. Lewin, Nelson, Szrom and Mikayla Wessel each were selected as 1st team all-conference honorees while Jolie Miracle was named to the 2nd team and Ashley Campbell was named to the defensive all-conference squad. Nelson repeated as a 2nd team all-region selection after hitting .372 while stealing 15 bases. Nelson and Lewin each received 1st team berths on the Academic All-District Softball team. Lewin, from Lower Hutt, New Zealand, was a Civil Engineering major who batted .356 with 7 home runs while maintaining a 3.67 GPA. Nelson, from

Snohomish, Washington, had recently graduated with her degree in Aerospace Engineering and a 3.81 GPA.

The 2023 season also saw the Lady Panthers achieve a winning record as they won 28 while losing 22 games. In the conference, they won 16 and lost 14 games. Cheyenne Nelson, now playing as a graduate student, was named to the all-conference 1st team and the all-district 2nd team. Nelson led the Lady Panthers with a .401 batting average and a .988 fielding percentage. Jolie Miracle was selected for 2nd team and defensive team all-conference recognition. Miracle, the Panthers' catcher, set a new program record for runners caught stealing as well as hitting for a .315 average.

Silvestrini has built a solid softball program at Florida Tech. She consistently turns out teams that are competitive in the conference and in the NCAA South Region. Moreover, her players consistently perform extraordinarily well in the classroom, often in some of the most demanding majors in the university.

Notes

- The information regarding Nancy Bottge is taken from the Winter 2007 issue of *Florida Tech Today,* Volume 15, issue 1, and from Bottge's biography for the Hall of Fame on the Florida Tech athletics website. Further information about Bottge's records at Florida Tech is taken from her biography for the Sunshine State Conference Hall of Fame at https://sunshinestateconference.com/hof. Also see the news release from the Florida Tech Department of Athletics mourning her passing at https://news.F.I.T.edu/archive/florida-tech-mourns-passing-of-long-time-softball-coach-dr-nancy-bottge/.
- Information on individual games is taken from reports in *Florida Today*, usually from the edition published the day after the game day, or from Florida Tech news releases described below.
- The results of specific seasons, games and post-season honors are, unless otherwise cited, taken from news releases by Florida Tech's sports information office. The specific releases relied upon for this chapter on softball were dated April 22, 2006, April 24, 2007, May 6, 2009, April 24, 2010, May 7, 2010, June 21, 2010, March 13, 2011,April 27, 2011, May 10, 2011, April 18, 2012, May 2, 2012, May 10, 2012, December 7, 2012, April 21, 2013, May 8, 2013, February 9, 2014, April 19, 2014, May 6, 2014, May 3, 2015, May 6, 2015, May 7, 2015, May 8, 2015, May 16, 2015, May 5, 2016, April 22, 2017, May 3, 2017, October 3, 2017, April 26, 2019, April 30, 2018, May 11, 2019, May 22, 2019, June 14, 2019, May 14, 2020, April 3, 2021, May 2, 2021, May 14, 2021, May 9, 2022, May 11, 2022, April 28, 2023 and April 27, 2023. These releases can be found at https://floridatechsports.com/news.

CHAPTER TWENTY:
WOMEN'S ROWING MAKES A SPLASH

By William K. Jurgens

The 1972-1973 academic year was the inaugural year for the women's rowing program at Florida Tech. Women's rowing was just beginning at several universities in Florida: Jacksonville University (JU), University of Tampa, and the University of Central Florida (known in 1972 as the Florida Technological University, FTU). The coaching staff for the women during their first year were Gene Jeffords, Doug Linden, and Chuck Hildebrand, all of whom had been or were active rowers on the Florida Tech's men's rowing program. During this year, the crew focused on rowing technique and rowing together as a team. To highlight the year, the women's rowing program arranged a race against JU in Jacksonville. Using equipment loaned by JU, the women's eight were victorious by open water. Chuck Hildebrand remembers being thrown in the Saint Johns River off JU's launching dock. Throwing winning coxswains and coaches into the water after races is a tradition in rowing that dates back over a century. Members of this victorious eight were Gene Jeffords (coxswain), Anne Gauzens, Kathy Pazera, Marian Dionne, Caty Levay, Donna van de Sande, Bobbie Ohler, Sue Sandilands, and Susie Goff.

1970s

In the 1975-1976 academic year the Dad Vail Regatta added events for women's teams. The Florida Tech women's rowing program continued to grow in numbers through its first four years of existence. Norton Schlachter coached the Florida Tech women for two years, beginning in the fall of 1974 and ending in the spring of 1976. In 1975, before there were women's events in the Dad Vail Regatta, the Florida Tech women finished second in the Southern Intercollegiate Rowing Association Championship (SIRA) to a strong women's varsity eight from the University of Tampa. Going into the 1976 Dad Vail Regatta the Florida Tech women's eight had dominated its competition in both the Florida Intercollegiate Rowing Association Championship (FIRA) and the SIRA championship, avenging its 1975 loss to Tampa. Funding from the university was not available for the women's crew to attend the Dad Vail Regatta, so the crew members participated in fundraising activities to achieve their goal of participating in this season-ending regatta.

To assist the women's crew in their efforts to raise the necessary funds, Florence (Flossy) Evans said she wanted to help. Mrs. Evans was the first woman to be named to the university's board of trustees, which occurred in January 1974 (*Topics*, Fall 1974). Mrs. Evans provided the women's crew with 500 dollars, which she said was to be used to raise money for their program; one of their fundraisers was selling shirts for the Governor's Cup Regatta hosted by Florida Tech. Mrs. Evans provided the team with an additional 500 dollars to cover expenses for the 1976 Dad Vail Regatta. Billie Brown said she and Marian Dionne went to Mrs. Evans' home to pick up the checks. The women's varsity eight finished an impressive second to Ithaca College, ahead of third place Purdue University, fourth place Rollins College, fifth place Wesleyan University, and sixth place Washington College. Participants in Florida Tech's varsity eight were coxswain Marian Dionne, stroke Joan (Blondie) Nordstrum (captain), 7-Valerie Barber, 6-Lynette Clark, 5-Jeanne Flanagan, 4-Libby Fick, 3-Vicki Dean, 2-Eve Gsteiger, and bow Cathy Meyer. It is amazing that a university the size of Florida Tech with its small percentage of enrolled women could be among the top women's rowing programs in the country.

The Florida Tech women's program remained strong for the 1977 Dad Vail Regatta. Casey Baker replaced Norton Schlachter as the head women's rowing coach, and the program continued to dominate the rowing competition in the state and southeast. The women's varsity eight finished first in the 1977 SIRA over second place University of Central Florida (UCF), third place Duke University, and fourth place University of Alabama Huntsville. The women's varsity eight again had an impressive second place finish in the Dad Vail Regatta. It should be noted that there were several different teams in the 1977 women's varsity eight final from the previous year's (1976) final. The winner in 1977 was the University of Western Ontario from Canada, followed by second place Florida Tech, third place Purdue University, fourth place Ithaca College, fifth place George Washington University, and sixth place Wichita State University. Members of the 1977 women's varsity eight were coxswain Billie Brown, stroke Eve Gsteiger, 7-Valerie Barber, 6-Libby Fick, 5-Jeanne Flanagan, 4-Cathy Meyers, 3-Kit Beran, 2-Andrea Bagdigian, bow Lynette Clark, and coach Casey Baker.

The 1977-1978 women's program continued with top-finishing results. In the fall (1977) Head of the Charles Regatta the women finished 5th in the women's four-with event. Members of the crew were coxswain Billie Brown, stroke Eve Gsteiger, 3-Valerie Barber, 2-Kit Beran, 1-Jeanne Flanagan, and coach Casey Baker. At the 1978 Dad Vail Regatta the women finished 3rd in the varsity eight event behind first place Wesleyan University and second place University of Western Ontario. Finishing behind Florida Tech were fourth place Ithaca College, fifth place Purdue University, and sixth place New Hampshire University. Members of this varsity eight crew were coxswain Mary Bayers, stroke Kit Beran, 7-Valerie Barber, 6-Barb Reed, 5-Jeanne Flanagan, 4-Andrea Bagdigian, 3-Susie McDonough, 2-Beth Brindisi, bow Char Fuller, and coach Casey Baker.

Also, in 1978 four members of Florida Tech's women's varsity eight crew combined with rowers from the University of Tampa (UT) and UCF to form the Florida Women's Composite Eight for the purpose of competing against Vesper Boat Club's top women's eight in a scheduled race in Miami. Vesper Boat Club, located on Boathouse Row in Philadelphia, was the training site in 1978 for national team rowers under national team eight coach John Hooten. During their trip to Miami the composite eight did well in a scrimmage against Yale University and defeated Vesper Boat Club in a 2,000-meter race. The Florida Women's Composite Eight was coached by Dennis Kamrad of UCF and Casey Baker of Florida Tech (FT). Members of this select group of Florida women rowers and the schools they represented were coxswain Billie Brown (FT), stroke Maryann Welsh (UCF), 7-Terry Smythe (UCF), 6-Judy Kapler (UCF), 5-Valerie Barber (FT), 4-Kit Beran (FT), 3-Jeanne Flanagan (FT), 2-Margaret McNiff (UT), and bow Debbie Berg (UT).

Being a part of this 1978 Florida Composite women's eight helped further the rowing ambitions of Valerie Barber and Jeanne Flanagan. Valerie Barber was a member of the 1978 U.S. National Team's eight that rowed in the World Rowing Championships in New Zealand. Barber was also a member of the 1980 Olympic Rowing Team. Jeanne Flanagan credited the composite crew races with helping her gain recognition by national team coaches, which led to her being a member of the 1984 Olympic Rowing Team's eight that won a gold medal. Flanagan was also a member of the 1980 U.S. Olympic Rowing Team. Additionally, Flanagan was a member of the U.S. National Rowing Team in 1979, 1981, 1982, and 1985. Flanagan's vast experience led the national team coaches to place her in the stroke position of the 1985 U.S. National Rowing Team's eight.

1980s

An important part of Florida Tech's combined overall championship (men and women) in the 1982 Dad Vail Regatta was the gold medal performance by the women's heavyweight four-with. This crew won their event by an impressive 10 seconds over second place St. John's University, third place Simmons College, fourth place Michigan State, fifth place UCF, and sixth place West Virginia. Members of the 1982 women's heavyweight four-with were coxswain Jo Ann Alden, stroke Christy Bredenkamp, 3-Sue Brown, 2-Laurie Kuestner, bow Sharon Gallagher, and coach Mike Davenport. In addition to coaching the Dad Vail Regatta's winning women's varsity four-with in 1982, Coach Mike Davenport coached the 1981 women's varsity eight to a fifth-place finish, the 1983 women's varsity eight to a win in the petite final, and the 1983 JV eight to a third-place finish. After Florida Tech, Coach Davenport became the head women's rowing coach at Washington College (Chestertown, Maryland); a position that he held for 26 years. In recognition of his many successes at Washington College, Coach Davenport was inducted into the 2022 Washington College Athletic Hall of Fame.

Women's crew has experienced success over the years.
Photo from University Archives.

1990s

In 1992 the Florida Tech women's varsity lightweight eight embarked on a special record-breaking season. This crew had been victorious among the rowing teams it faced in the FIRA and SIRA rowing championships. Mary Fox, coach of the women's lightweight eight, was confident that this crew had what it takes to become a Dad Vail Regatta champion. Coach Fox had this to say about this special group of nine women, "this boat had a fierce competitiveness within themselves but not arrogant, never boasting. Quite the opposite, they were happy, delightful, and inclusive." Denise Fleming, a senior member of the lightweight eight, said, "when you row you strive to reach a perfect state where there is no check" (Check is when the flow of the boat slows down at the catch). She further said, "this Nirvana state resulted from members clicking together and it felt like we glided above the water." In the finals of the women's varsity lightweight eight, Florida Tech won by an amazing 25.7 seconds, which is one of the largest margins ever recorded between a first-place team and second-place team in a varsity event. The distance for this large margin equates to approximately six boat lengths. There was a heated battle going on between the next three crews for second place. At the finish line just four-tenths of a second separated the next three crews: Boston College placed second, University of Rhode Island placed third, and Holy Cross University placed fourth. The fifth and sixth finishers were Delaware University and Villanova University. Members of the 1992 women's varsity lightweight 8 were coxswain Rachael Hannah, stroke Michelle Berard, 7-Heather Counter, 6-Joan Mills, 5-Olifia Gudmundsdottir, 4-Jen Kreps, 3-Monica Bedmar-Perez, 2-Jen Bernan, bow Denise Fleming, and coach Mary Fox.

In the 1998 Dad Vail Regatta the women's pair won a bronze medal. The women's pair was made up of Sarah Peters at stroke and Tracy Stofferahn at bow with Matt Kaminski as coach.

NCAA and SSC Participation for Florida Tech Women's Rowing Program

In 1997 the National Collegiate Athletic Association (NCAA) and the Sunshine State Conference (SSC) increased opportunities for women's rowing programs by providing championships. Before discussing Florida Tech's participation in the NCAA Women's Rowing Championship, it is helpful to understand what transpired in women's rowing for it to become an emerging sport with the NCAA. Emerging sports are given some leeway in meeting the NCAA sport sponsorship requirements. One consideration for emerging sports is they do not have to meet sport sponsorship requirements for championship status as long as they are making steady progress towards meeting those requirements. A big reason NCAA emerging sports came into existence was to address the imbalance in the percentage of female student-athlete participation levels compared to the percentage of male student-athlete participation levels, particularly in institutions with varsity football programs. The student-athlete ratio of male to female is compared to the percentage of men to women in an institution to determine if there are equitable varsity sport participation rates for men and women. Title IX is a civil rights law that prohibits schools or educational programs that receive federal assistance from discriminating against anyone based on sex. The Title IX law regulates fairness in sport sponsorship numbers as well as in other areas, such as athletic scholarships, facilities, operating budgets, coaching salaries, and number of coaches. The success of rowing as an emerging sport has to do with traditionally large numbers of participants in this sport. The large number of participants can be attributed to multiple events in dual races and regattas, which promotes larger squad sizes. Additionally, since everyone on the team competes in every race, there are higher team satisfaction levels and opportunities for student-athletes to develop through competition.

2000s

NCAA rowing began in 1997 with all three divisions combined. Though NCAA DII and DIII institutions were invited in limited numbers, they had to participate in events against DI programs. Fortunately, in 2002 Division II and Division III institutions began their own NCAA competitions with separate governing committees to regulate how their respective competitions would be conducted. Florida Tech women's rowing program has taken advantage of this opportunity by qualifying and competing in 10 NCAA DII women's rowing championships since 2002. With the emergence of NCAA rowing championships, the Sunshine State Conference (SSC) began a conference championship in rowing. The first SSC Women's Rowing Championship was held in 1997 with the winner being Florida Tech. Since its inception in 1997, Florida Tech has led the conference with nine SSC championships, Barry University is second with seven, Nova Southeastern is third with six, Rollins is fourth with two, and Embry Riddle is fifth with one.

Florida Tech participated in five consecutive NCAA DII women's rowing championships. In 2003, 2004, and 2005, Coach Casey Baker's women's rowing team won the team rowing championship at the SSC and went on to qualify and compete in the NCAA women's rowing championship. In 2006 Florida Tech women's rowing team received an at-large bid for its varsity eight to participate in the NCAA championship. This team also won the SSC rowing championships and finished third in the varsity eight event at the NCAA championship. Members of this crew were coxswain Desiree Tetrault, stroke Whitney Given, 7-Jessie House, 6-Andrea Cross, 5-Rachel Purvis, 4-Maddie Smerin, 3-Nicky Weiler, 2-Audrey Farson, bow Anna Beamon and coach Casey Baker. Coach Adam Thorstad took over as the head coach of the women's program in 2007, and his varsity eight continued the winning tradition by finishing first in the SSC championship and received an at-large bid for the varsity eight to compete in the NCAA rowing championship in which they finished sixth.

In 2005 the women's program entered the collegiate four-with event at the Head of the Charles Regatta. The Charles River separates Boston from Cambridge and over 200,000 fans line both shores to watch this fall rowing classic. The women's four not only won this race but set a course record. Members of this crew were coxswain Desiree Tetrault, stroke Maddie Smerin, 3-Nicky Weiler, 2-Whitney Given, bow Jessie House, and coach Casey Baker.

2010s (2010 – 2019)

Prior to 2019, Coach Adam Thorstad's teams competed in three NCAA Division II rowing championships. In 2010 the team finished fourth with the varsity four-with capturing a silver medal. Members of the women's varsity four-with were coxswain Stephanie Spangler, stroke Ashley Sicard, 3-Megan Taylor, 2-Marie McBride, bow Amanda Deveaux, and coach Adam Thorstad. In 2017 the at-large varsity eight finished third. Members of this 2017 at-large varsity eight were coxswain Taylor Stoni, stroke Natalia Arasa Bonavila, 7-Morgan Billig, 6-Theresa Gadilhe, 5-Graysen Pensch, 4-Samantha Martinez, 3-Irina Durovic, 2-Aurelia Gervasi, bow Federica Pala, and coach Adam Thorstad.

In the 2018 NCAA DII National Championship, the team finished third with the varsity eight capturing third and the varsity four-with finishing fourth. Members of the 2018 women's varsity eight were coxswain Taylor Stoni, stroke Natalia Arasa Bonavila, 7-Federica Pala, 6-Theresa Gadilhe, 5-Anna Kayser Gallego, 4-Julie McCarthy, 3-Irina Djurovic, 2-Svetlana Ristin, bow Graysen Pensch, and coach Adam Thorstad. Also, in 2018 the women's team entered the varsity heavyweight four-with event at the Dad Vail Regatta and won a gold medal. Members of this 2018 Dad Vail Regatta champion crew were coxswain Taylor Stoni, stroke Natalia Arasa-Bonavila, 3-Federica Pala, 2-Theresa Gadilhe, bow Irina Djurovic, and coach Adam Thorstad.

The historic 2018-2019 academic year for the women's rowing program began with a first-place finish in the collegiate four-with event at the Head of the Charles Regatta. Members of this crew were coxswain Taylor Stoni, stroke Natalia Arasa Bonavila, 3-Federica Pala, 2-Svetlana Ristin, bow Theresa Gadilhe, and coach Adam Thorstad. In the spring the Panther crew finished first at the 2019 Sunshine State Conference Championship. In this two-event championship the women's crew finished first in the women's eight and first in the four-with. The next goal was to participate in the Dad Vail Regatta in which there were

NCAA Division II events in the eight and four-with. What makes this rowing event important is DII programs travel from as far away as California to compete in this late season regatta. A late season result is 24 days prior to when the NCAA selection committee meets to determine who qualifies for the NCAA DII championship, and these results carry more weight than regular season results. Another reason teams want to participate in the Dad Vail Regatta's DII events is to compare their head-to-head boat speed with other regional teams and avoid leaving who qualifies up to subjective evaluation. The Florida Tech women's eight won gold in the 2019 Dad Vail DII eight event. Members of this crew were coxswain Taylor Stoni, stroke Natalia Arasa Bonavila, 7-Federica Pala, 6-Svetlana Ristin, 5-Theresa Gadilhe, 4-Anna Kayser Gallego, 3-Irina Djurovic, 2-Liza Lutter, bow Graysen Pensch, and coach Adam Thorstad. Like their teammates in the eight, the Florida Tech DII four-with captured gold in the 2019 Dad Vail Regatta. Members of this were coxswain Nataisha Patrawalla, stroke Shaula Rey, 3-Julia Seibold, 2-Rebecca Miller, bow Emily Hall, and coach Patrick Burns.

In the 2019 NCAA Division II Women's Rowing Championship Florida Tech finished second behind Central Oklahoma, which was the highest finish for the Panthers since the event began in 2002. The women's varsity eight finished a strong second to Central Oklahoma. Members of the second-place women's varsity eight were coxswain Taylor Stoni, stroke Natalia Arasa Bonavila, 7-Federica Pala, 6-Svetlana Ristin, 5-Theresa Gadilhe, 4-Anna Kayser Gallego, 3-Irina Djurovic, 2-Liza Lutter, bow Graysen Pensch, and coach Adam Thorstad. The women's varsity four-with finished third in the 2019 NCAA Division II Women's Rowing Championships. Members of the third-place women's varsity four-with were coxswain Nashaita Patrawalla, stroke Shaula Rey, 3-Julia Seibold, 2-Rebecca Miller, bow Emily Hall, and coach Patrick Burns.

In the fall of 2019, the women's four-with finished first in the collegiate four event at the Head of the Charles Regatta. This crew, like the 2005 women's four-with, set the current course record for this event. Members of this crew were coxswain Nataisha Patrawalla, stroke Natalia Arasa Bonavila, 3-Liza Lutter, 2-Svetlana Ristin, bow Theresa Gadilhe, and coach Adam Thorstad.

2020s (2020 – present)

The 2020 spring rowing season was cancelled due to the Covid Pandemic.

The 2020-2021 women's varsity rowing program qualified for the NCAA Division II Rowing Championships and finished third in the varsity eight and third in the varsity four-with, which resulted in the Panthers finishing third overall in the NCAA DII Women's Rowing Championship. Members of the third-place women's varsity eight were coxswain Abby Smith, stroke Anna Kayser Gallego, 7-Ismini Noni, 6-Liza Lutter, 5-Maclain Zajcek, 4-Hannah Schulcher, 3-Sydney Spicer, 2-Simona Vilenskyte, bow Graysen Pensch, and coach Adam Thorstad. Members of the third-place women's varsity four-with were coxswain Nashaita Patrawalla, stroke Julia Seibold, 3-Becca Miller, 2-Sophia Ferrizzi, bow Gabby Rodenzo, and coach Adam Thorstad. The 2021 first place finish in the Sunshine State Conference Women's Rowing Championship was the fourth out of the past five conference rowing championships won by Florida Tech; this is a remarkable feat given that Nova Southeastern University and Barry University are previous NCAA Division II women's rowing national champions. Coach Adam Thorstad for all his accomplishments was recognized by his peers six times as Sunshine State Conference Coach of the Year.

After the 2021-2022 season, the university dropped the women's rowing program as a varsity sport and designated women's rowing as a club sport. For the 2022-2023 season, Coach Adam Thorstad and his assistant coach, Catherine Davie, coached the women's and men's rowing programs as club sports. In the fall of 2022 Coach Thorstad put together a women's four-with and a men's four-with for the Head of the Charles Regatta in which the women finished first and the men finished 11th. This fall rowing classic includes college and post college rowers. The strong performance in the 2022 Head of the Charles Regatta is a tribute to the commitment and hard work of the coaches and rowers. Funding for participation and travel to this regatta was provided by members of the Friends of Florida Tech Rowing (Florida Tech rowing alumni). Coach Adam Thorstad's commitment to the Florida Tech rowing program during the 2022-2023 season was invaluable for continuity in the men's and women's rowing programs.

2023 Season

The 2023 season was a record-breaking season for the women's rowing team. The women's four-with had an undefeated spring season. Coaches for this team were head coach Adam Thorstad and assistant coach Catherine Davie. On March 18th, the women's rowing team won the four-with for their first victory of the spring season at Rollins College. In the Hatter Invitational on March 25th, the women's four-with won its second race of the season against two crews from UCF. In the state rowing championship (FIRA), the Panthers defeated second place Embry Riddle Aeronautical University (ERAU), and third place Barry University. The women's four-with continued their winning ways at the SIRA Rowing Championship by winning their event and defeating second place Kansas State University.

Going into the 2023 Dad Vail Regatta, the women's four-with was seeded second behind Lafayette University; a team that had won the collegiate varsity four-with in the 2022 Head of the Charles Regatta; a race in which the Panthers finished third. The Dad Vail Regatta's four-with race final proved to be a strong test for the Panthers as they progressed through the 2,000-meter course on the Cooper River in Pennsauken, New Jersey. After 500 meters, Florida Tech had a deck length lead over Lafayette College with Boston University (BU) in third and the University of Western Ontario in fourth. As the teams moved through the 1,000-meter mark in the race, both Lafayette and BU tried to cut into Florida Tech's lead, but to no avail as the Panthers rowed an outstandingly consistent race in which they led from start to finish. The final order of the race was Florida Tech first, Lafayette University second, University of Western Ontario third, and BU fourth. Members of the 2023 women's open four-with Dad Vail Regatta national champion crew were coxswain Mckenna Barr, stroke Brynn Romberger, 3-Ashton Clark, 2-Sydney Whisler, bow Sydney Freiberger, and coach Adam Thorstad.

The final race of the season was at the American Collegiate Rowing Association (ACRA) National Championship, which is the national championship for club rowing programs. The women's varsity four-with had two frosh/novice rowers in the boat, so it is not surprising that this boat continued to improve throughout the season. In the finals of the women's varsity four-with, the Panthers won by an amazing 20.1 seconds, which is over five boat lengths. Having an undefeated season in the Florida Tech women's varsity four-with is a deserving reward for their hard work, consistent rowing performances, and unflinching determination to be the best they could be. Members of the 2023 ACRA national champion open four-with crew were coxswain Mckenna Barr, stroke Brynn Romberger, 3-Ashton Clark, 2-Sydney Whisler, bow Sydney Freiberger, and coach Adam Thorstad.

References

- Adam Thorstad (women's head rowing coach from 2007 through 2023).
- Andrea Bagdigian interview (team member during the '70s).
- Billie Brown assisted with early years of women's crew (team member during the '70's).
- Casey Baker interviews (women's head rowing throughout the history of rowing).
- Chuck Hildebrand shared coaching experiences (team member and women's coach during this time).
- Denise Fleming-Linnenbaugh interview (member of 1992 women's varsity lightweight eight).
- Doug Linden interview (men's team member and women's coach during the '70s).
- Eve Gsteiger-Duddy provided team results (team member during this time).
- Gene Jeffords (men's team member and women's coach during the early '70s).
- Jeanne Flanagan (video by Jeanne Flanagan produced for Florida Tech Legacy Banquet on July 23, 2022).
- Kathy McDevitt-Wojtas interview(Women's team member during the '80s).
- Lindamood, R. (1994). *Marietta crew: A history of rowing at Marietta College*
- Marietta College of College Advancement. Marietta, Ohio.
- Marian Dionne assisted with team information (team participant during the '70s).
- Mary Fox interview (women's head rowing coach in 1992).
- *Topics* (Fall 1973). Five New Trustees Named to F.I.T. Board. Published Quarterly by the Department of Public Relations. Florida Institute of Technology, Vol. 1, Number 1.
- Valerie Barber helped gather information on teams (team member during the '70s).

CHAPTER TWENTY-ONE:
OTHER SPORTS AND SPIRIT GROUPS

By William K. Jurgens

P hysical education classes had a favorable impact on getting students involved in sports at Florida Tech. Students first voiced their desire to have a Physical Education (P.E.) program as early as 1968 (*Crimson*, April 18, 1968). In an article titled *Weight Room in Operation*, the editors expressed the following: "the lack of Physical Education classes on campus leaves a large gap in the requirements of a well-rounded person." According to Pete Mazzone, who in 1985 became the director of Physical Education, Jim Stoms, Dean of Management Science (which later became the College of Business) promoted his desire to add physical education classes to Dr. Andrew Revay, head of engineering at the time. Stoms and Revay felt that P.E. classes would benefit students at Florida Tech by providing students with instruction in life-long recreational activities that involved skill development, physical activity, and mental discipline. Stoms also felt that receiving credit for taking courses encouraged students to take these one-credit elective classes to relieve the stress resulting from academic rigor. The P.E. classes from the outset were well received by students. Boris Altatears (September 26, 1976) reported in a *Crimson* (student newspaper) interview with new athletic director Bill Jurgens, who said the following about physical education classes: "the objective of physical education is twofold: develop interests in a wide range of physical activities and generally improve the health of the participant." Also present in this article was a schedule of P.E. classes to be offered beginning in the 1977-1978 academic year. These classes included three officiating classes (flag football, softball, and basketball), introduction to sailing, introduction to archery, introduction to volleyball, introduction to wrestling, fencing, and rowing for beginning (introduction), intermediate, and advanced classes (Altatears, September 26, 1976). In many instances the P.E. classes promoted participation in sports such as fencing, sailing, rowing, volleyball, and wrestling. As an example, wrestling was an active club sport in 1978-1979 (*Ad Astra*, 1979), and fencing became a club sport for 35 years after first being a P.E. class.

In the mid- '70s the emerging sports as club and varsity were supported together by the athletics department. An example of this supportive effort was indicated in the *Crimson* (September 26, 1976) when the schedule for the upcoming team meetings was listed. The sports, date, and location (all meetings were in the Gymnasium) of the meetings were for the following Florida Tech sports: baseball, basketball, crew (men and women), golf, rifle club, sailing club, soccer, swim club, and tennis. Another example of the club sports and varsity sports being together under Florida Tech Athletics were the early athletic awards banquets in which club sports and varsity sports received varsity awards, e.g., sailing, judo, and riflery. With the advancement of varsity sports and club sports, they eventually became two separate entities by the early 80s.

The importance of physical education classes to the students was evidenced in 1998 when the administration wanted to drop the physical education program. At this time, the students submitted a petition with over 600 student signatures to retain the P.E. program to President Lynn Weaver (Stiles, April 14, 2000). The justification the administration gave for discontinuing the P.E. classes was that the Clemente Center for Sport and Recreation would be coming online in 2001 and similar classes would be offered in this new facility (Stiles, April 14, 2000). After receiving the petition, Dr. Weaver asked that a meeting with students be held to discuss their concerns in the All-Purpose Room (later named the Hartley Room) of the Denius Student Center. After hearing several of the more than 50 students in attendance and several administrators, Dr. Weaver thanked the students for their passion for the P.E. program and said the P.E. program would continue in its present format.

Fencing

Fencing became a sport at Florida Tech because of adding physical education courses as part of the academic curriculum. The first instructor for the fencing class was Maestro Sylvio Vitale. Maestro Vitale relocated to Melbourne, Florida after serving as the varsity fencing coach at MIT for 27 years (Museum of American Fencing, May 19, 2023). In his first year of instructing students, he was joined mid-year by Sophie Trett as an unpaid assistant. Trett was an experienced fencer, and it was clear that she wanted to learn from a highly qualified coach of Maestro Vitale's caliber. Unfortunately, he passed away after his first year at Florida Tech. This left a motivated Sophie Trett to take over the fencing P.E. class and later forming a fencing club made up of students who had started out in the class.

Trett also had experience in coaching volleyball and became Florida Tech's volleyball head coach in 1977 in addition to her fencing responsibilities. Neal Julien, as a coach apprentice, who worked with Trett for 12 years after taking her P.E. class in the late 1990s. Julien said "Trett's coaching style and leadership skills were exceptional." As an example, Julien said, "Trett had high expectations for team members, but her expectations were different for each fencer." He also said, "Trett had a great deal of patience but did not waiver in letting someone know when their work ethic fell short of the expectations she had for them." Most important to Trett was that students gave the necessary effort. Julien said Trett liked to see everyone happy after their class.

Sophie Trett had many roles within the athletic program at Florida Tech, including her outstanding performance as coach of the fencing team.
Photo from University Archives.

Beginning in the fall of 1977 Sophie began her illustrious 35-year career of coaching and instructing fencing at Florida Tech. In 1979 Tom Nugent, in the booklet *F.I.T. Intercollegiate Athle*tics, said that with Sophie Trett, the fencing activities will be growing. Nugent also said that Trett was instrumental in the newly formed (1977) women's volleyball program as its first coach.

By 1981 the fencing club was competing in four or five matches a year plus tournaments (Nugent, 1981). Florida Tech hosted its own tournament, called the "Sophie Trett Fencing Tournament." The fencing teams in Florida were in several regions. Florida Tech was in the Central Florida Region, which included the University of Central Florida, University of South Florida, Florida Southern College, and University of Tampa (Julien, May 19, 2023). Typically, the P.E. fencing class had 15 to 20 students register, though in later years this number decreased to around eight to ten students. Never was a class cancelled because it had less than eight students register. The competitive season for the fencing club lasted the entire school year.

To host a fencing tournament, sophisticated equipment is required, which Florida Tech was able to acquire over the years. The piste is a metallic threaded matt on which fencers compete. The vest is also made of a metallic thread that when the sword touches the vest the points on a foil and epee close. The sabre is the third sword in which fencers compete and scoring with this instrument is from a slicing motion to the vest. Florida Tech under Trett taught foil. To win a preliminary round five touches or whoever is ahead after three minutes is needed. Whereas, later in the tournament direct elimination bouts which require 15 touches or three, three-minute periods are needed to win.

Neal Julien began assisting Trett after he completed the P.E. fencing class in 1999. He said he enjoyed assisting Trett and learning from her leadership skills, as well as her teaching methods on how to become a better fencer. Julien said that modern fencing is constantly changing and Trett's style of fencing was called the classical style. Julien had this to say about the fencing program at Florida Tech: "I never fenced before but when I finally began competing four years after I began, fencing people would say they enjoyed watching the classical style that Trett had taught me."

Sophie Trett was the strength behind the fencing program, both the club and the P.E. classes. After 35 years, Trett felt it was time to retire, and her protege, Neal Julien took over for her in the 2012 – 2013 academic year. However, after a year his new job required him to travel which resulted in him having to give up teaching the sport he loved. Pete Mazzone, who is director of the Physical Education program, tried to find a replacement, but there was no one available to instruct the fencing class, which resulted in the discontinuance of fencing. Fortunately, there are two independent fencing clubs in the Melbourne area at this time which have spearheaded an increase of skilled fencers if there is ever an interest by the students to return fencing to Florida Tech as a club (Julien, May 19, 2023).

References

- Altatears, B. (September 26, 1976). *New athletic director institutes more offerings. Crimson.* Retrieved from Florida Tech's Evans Library by archivist Anna Norris.
- Stiles, D. (April 14, 2000). *PED back and kicking. Crimson.* Volume XXXIV, No. 25. Retrieved from Florida Tech's Evans Library by archivist Anna Norris.
- Editorial Staff (April 18, 1968). *Weight room in operation. Crimson.* Retrieved from Florida Tech's Evans Library by archivist Anna Norris.
- Interview of Pete Mazzone, Director of Physical Education, circa 2023. Pete Mazzone served as the director of the Physical Education program from 1985 to present.
- Museum of American Fencing. (May 19, 2023). *Vitale, Sylvio.* Retrieved from: https://museumofamericanfencing.com/wp/vitale-sylvio/.
- Neal Julien was interviewed on May 19, 2023. Neal Julien was a student and later an instructor of P.E. fencing classes.
- Nugent, T. (1979). *Fencing. Intercollegiate Athletics at F.I.T.* Florida Tech Press.

Rifle Team

The varsity and club rifle teams existed at Florida Tech because of having an Army ROTC program. ROTC became a program at Florida Tech in the fall of 1969 (The Crimson, April 18, 1968). At that time, the ROTC program required Florida Tech to provide a shooting range on campus for its members. To satisfy this requirement, Florida Tech, according to dean of students Ray Work, built a rifle range that became functional in 1970 (Woolverton, April 29, 1970). This 10-point rifle range was expanded in 1975 to include an office, meeting room, and a walk-in vault to secure the smallbore rifles and ammunition. The Rifle Range at Florida Tech was one of the best in Florida. Consequently, state championship matches were held on the Florida Tech campus. Colonel George S. Jones served as the Professor of Military Science from 1969 to 1973. When Colonel Jones retired, he became the registrar at Florida Tech, and served for one year as the interim department head for Oceanography.

The rifle team had great success but died out when ROTC no longer required shooting as part of its curriculum. *Photo from University Archives.*

Stan Prokop was one of the first members of the ROTC Rifle team. He began in 1969 and was on the team through the spring of 1973. Prokop was the captain of the team in 1973. In 1972 Dale Pierce became a member of the Rifle Team. An incentive for Pierce to join the Rifle

Team was when he heard the team got steak dinners when they traveled to away matches. As a freshman, this was a strong incentive for him. After this introduction to the Rifle Team, Pierce ended up making the varsity his first year. In 1972 Sgt. Kelley served as the Rifle Team coach. Though a strong marksman himself, Sgt. Kelley brought in Lones Wigger, who was the reigning world champion, to work individually with team members on their shooting skills. Wigger was a member of the Army Marksmanship Unit (AMU). Sgt. Kelley coached the Rifle Team through the spring of 1975.

In the fall of 1975 Master Sergeant Jack Wesson took over as coach of the rifle team. Wesson continued in this capacity through the spring of 1979. In the 1979-1980 season Captain Wilson and Master Sergeant Giles served as the rifle team coaches. Pierce competed on the varsity team for five years. In 1973 Pierce finished second in the NRA state competition. To improve the competitiveness of the rifle team, the university administration purchased two Anschutz rifles in 1975, which were considered the best competition rifles in the world. Other rifles used by the rifle team included ten Remington 40X and ten Winchester 52 rifles; these rifles had Redfield match sights. The rifle team was comprised of students who were classified as ROTC cadets and civilians. While the ROTC cadets got their ammunition free, the civilians, at this time, had to pay for theirs. In 1975 the southeast regional collegiate championship was held in Loyola, Louisiana in conjunction with Mardi Gras. Pierce finished second in this competition. This location made it attractive for teams to attend. Riflery is the only sport where men and women compete equally. According to Pierce, the women on the F.I.T. Rifle Team were as good or better shooters than the men. During this time Debbie McDonough was a top shooter who made the varsity rifle team at Florida Tech. All shooting teams were part of the NRA Intercollegiate Rifle Club Championships. Riflery as an NCAA sport did not begin until 1980. For some matches there was a civilian team and a military team. In 1976 the F.I.T. varsity Rifle Team won the NRA state championship in small bore, and Dale Pierce won the individual NRA state champion title in small bore. The state championship match was held in Florida Tech's Rifle Range. In 1976 Dale L. Pierce was awarded the Veterans of Foreign Wars Trophy as the top collegiate shooter in the country. This trophy was first awarded in 1926 to teams made up of four civilian members. Beginning in 1971 the trophy was awarded to the top collegiate individual in the country with the highest aggregate score in the National High Power Rifle Championship.

The growth of riflery on the Florida Tech campus was the result of large numbers of students in the rifle club, such as 35 in 1975 and 27 in 1977. The club team members served as a feeder system for the varsity teams, which typically numbered 12 members with four on the first team and four on the second team. A big incentive for being one of the top shooters on the team was the possibility of receiving an athletics scholarship. Typically, ROTC cadets were already receiving scholarship assistance for their commitment to military service after graduation. However, the top civilian shooters on the team were awarded athletic scholarships for their exceptional performance. Another benefit, for being on the rifle team was attending the department of athletics' awards banquet and receiving awards for their years of participation. In 1976 an engraved pewter mug was awarded to senior members of the rifle team.

According to Art Tank, the Mardi Gras competition determined the southeastern champion for the United States. In the 1979 and 1980 spring seasons, Florida Tech finished first by defeating a strong Texas A & M team. In 1980 there were 39 teams from 33 universities that participated in this championship. The rifle team was ranked 12th in the country and first in the southeast during these two years. In 1980 the Florida Tech rifle team took first team honors at the Mardi Gras event, 67 points ahead of the second-place team, and Art Tank finished second individually behind the winner by just two points. The international small-bore guidelines that were used for this event included: prone, offhand (standing), and kneeling. A common practice was for the top shooters to have a key to the Rifle Range and after the initial years of the program the rifles used by top team members were purchased by them and not the school.

According to Bill Tolson, captain of the rifle team during the 1979-1983 time period, Florida Tech did a lot of postal matches in which teams were on the honor system to send in their targets for scoring and the top individuals and teams were awarded trophies. There were also a lot of in-state competitions that included going to the University of Tampa and the University of Florida every year. Out-of-state competitions were at the University of Kentucky and to the Mardi Gras match in Thibodaux, Louisiana. The coach would determine who was on the "A" and "B" teams. A school would not always send both teams because of costs. There was a minimum of five people on a travel team in case one got sick. Kris Cobham and Katy Bell were female members on the rifle team in the 1981-1982 season and Cobham served as the second team captain. In the 1982-1983 season Kris Cobham and Jerry Cleaver were female members of the first team. Kris Cobham was captain of the team in 1983-1984 and 1984-1985. Second team captain in 1983-1984 was Mike O'Dell. Coach of the team in 1980-1981 was Captain William Coleman. Master Sergeant Chuck Chaney took over as coach in 1981-1982 and remained as coach through the 1983-1984 season. George Tolson became a civilian coach beginning in 1979 and remained with the team for eight years until the spring of 1987. George Tolson was instrumental in assisting the rifle team through the transition of ROTC no longer requiring rifle as part of their training program and therefore no longer providing coaching personnel.

In 1985, the varsity rifle team was discontinued as a varsity team sport. Dropping the Rifle Team was the result of ROTC no longer requiring shooting for its on-campus cadets. Further, ROTC no longer provided military personnel to coach the team, and athletic scholarships were no longer provided (*Ad Astra*, 1987). Beginning in 1986 the office and meeting room of the Rifle Range were assigned to coaches and athletic staff personnel (*Ad Astra*, 1987). The Clemente Center for Sports and Recreation now stands where the Rifle Range was located.

References

- The Crimson (April 18, 1968). *ROTC for F.I.T.*. Volume 1, No. 5. Evans Library Archives.
- Woolverton, D. (April 29, 1970). *Emphasis is on growth, quality education at F.I.T. Florida Today.* Retrieved from Anna Norris.
- The Veterans of Foreign Wars Trophy. Retrieved from the web site on June 27, 2023: https://competitions.nra.org/media/9052/tro-102-veterans-of-foreign-wars.pdf.
- *Ad Astra* (1973). *Rifle Team.* Retrieved from the Evans Library Archives.
- *Ad Astra* (1975). *Rifle Team.* Retrieved from the Evans Library Archives.
- *Ad Astra* (1977). *Rifle Team.* Retrieved from the Evans Library Archives.
- *Ad Astra* (1979). *Rifle Team.* Retrieved from the Evans Library Archives.
- *Ad Astra* (1980). *Rifle Team.* Retrieved from the Evans Library Archives.
- *Ad Astra* (1982). *Rifle Team.* Retrieved from the Evans Library Archives.
- *Ad Astra* (1983). *Rifle Team.* Retrieved from the Evans Library Archives.
- *Ad Astra* (1984). *Rifle Team.* Retrieved from the Evans Library Archives.
- *Ad Astra* (1985). *Rifle Team.* Retrieved from the Evans Library Archives.
- *Ad Astra* (1987). *Rifle Team.* Retrieved from the Evans Library Archives.
- Interview with Dale Pierce on April 19, 2023.
- Interview with Art Tank on May 12, 2023.
- Interview with Bill Tolson on June 16, 2023.

Sailing

The Florida Tech sailing program is comprised of a sailing club and a racing team. In the '70s there were as many as 70 students participating in the club, the racing team, and in physical education classes. The racing team competes with teams throughout the state of Florida and hosts regattas on the Indian River Lagoon. Social events are also associated with the home regattas. Sailing club members pay dues for membership but can check out boats free of charge (Nugent, 1979).

Melbourne was an ideal location for a sailing team.
Photo from University Archives.

The Florida Tech sailing club has had a rich tradition for over 50 years. As early as 1969 there has been a sailing club. From the spring of 1974 to the spring of 1979, the sailing club race team received varsity letters for their participation on the race team. As a club sport there has not always been a coach for the team. This was the case in 1974-1975 season when in the program for the athletics awards banquet the team members are listed but not a coach. The management of the sailing club is done by student officers elected by team members. The 1974-1975 officers of the sailing club were Daniel Machowski, commodore, Bob Millen, vice-commodore, Mike Ray, Secretary, and Russ North, rear commodore. What has remained consistent for over 50 years is the dedication of the sailing club members. This consistent level of participation has proven that sailing is an important part of the extracurricular activities at Florida Tech.

Though the maintenance of the boats has been a time-consuming responsibility for the students, the university has always assisted the team with funds provided through the student government association, which has a committee whose purpose is to allocate funds to club organizations based on a club having existed for more than a year and the club having successfully achieved its stated goals. David Noble, a student on the sailing race team, taught physical education (P.E.) classes during the fall of 1978 and spring of 1979, which produced additional revenue for the sailing club. The sailboat used for teaching the P.E. class was a 23-foot Raven class sailboat that would accommodate up to six sailors.

What enhances participation in the sailing program is its proximity to the Indian River Lagoon to the school (less than two miles), the width of the river (a mile and three-eighths outside of the Melbourne harbor), and the prevailing offshore breeze, which is ideal for small-boat sailing. The greatest asset for the sailing team is the Florida Tech Anchorage, located on the south side of the Melbourne Harbor. At the Anchorage there is ample room to store their boats, a shed to store their equipment, and a water-level launch dock for easy access.

David Noble was captain of the sailing team in 1978-1979 and 1979-1980, and in 1980-1981 Craig O'Bara was captain of the team. In 1978 the team bought six 420s from the St. Petersburg Yacht Club for a total of $1,000. With the addition of these sailboats, the team members no longer had to wait their turn to go out. Also, the race team grew in student participation once the boats became water worthy. It took only a brief time before they got four boats on the water. The governing body for collegiate sailing in the southeast was the South Atlantic Intercollegiate Sailing Association (SAISA). During this time period, there were typically six students on the racing team. They also practiced in three Sunfish class sailboats. The race team competed against the

College of Charleston, Florida State University, University of Florida, University of Miami, and Eckerd College. The top four finishers in this district would advance to the national championship. With their four 420s, in 1979 Florida Tech sailing team hosted Florida State University, University of Florida, and Eckerd College. Though the Panthers did not win, they competed well in this event.

Members of the Florida Tech sailing team in 1977-1978 began taking part in the Southern Racing Circuit. This was considered big boat sailing and teams would come from all parts of the world to compete in this class of sailing. Noble recalls his teammates sailing on different big boats, one of which was named TNT. The Southern Racing Circuit had competitions that included sailing from St. Pete to Fort Lauderdale, a triangle race off Fort Lauderdale, and a Fort Lauderdale to Key West race. Noble recalls that there were no big boats sailing team that displayed better teamwork than F.I.T.

Chris Duer participated on the sailing team from 1996-2000. Duer recalls the team sailing on the Lindenberg 28 Fast Lane, which could handle a crew of five to seven sailors. It was the sale of the Lindenberg 28 that made it possible for the sailing team to purchase four Flying Juniors. This purchase took place in 1998 when the team traveled to St. Petersburg to pick up Flying Juniors from Eckerd College. With these four new sailboats the sailing team grew from 12 to 20 members.

The competition in the 1990s for the right to represent the Southern Atlantic Intercollegiate Sailing Association (SAISA) had become more difficult with strong sailing programs in both the north and south districts. The top programs in the north district were the College of Charleston, University of North Carolina, and North Carolina State, and the top programs in the south district were Eckerd College, F.I.T., University of Florida, and the University of South Florida. With just four spots available in SAISA, it was difficult to advance to the nationals. However, the frosh four from F.I.T. were selected to compete in the nationals that were being held in New Hampshire. The frosh four from F.I.T. finished in the top five in the country.

Chris Duer has only fond memories of his time as captain of the sailing team, for example, when he crammed three of the four frosh sailors along with his future wife into his small car and traveled to New Hampshire for the national sailing championship. Duer said that all the challenges he faced as a member of the sailing club and race team helped make him self-sufficient. He also said that the thing that keeps him connected to the university is the sailing club. He emphasized that when he travels to sailing regattas, he often finds children of his former teammates competing with his children, and this contagious love for sailing has resulted in some of this younger generation aspiring to become Olympic sailors.

The present-day sailing club continues to fare well as an intercollegiate racing team. Assisting the Panthers in team racing is the sailing coach of the Melbourne Yacht Club, Coach Gonzalo Crivello. Another part of the sailing tradition at Florida Tech has been the close relationship of the sailing club to the Melbourne Yacht Club. This close bond between the two organizations is a testament to the selfless supportive nature sailors have for one another.

References

- 1974 *Ad Astra* was located as an archive in the Florida Tech Evans Library
- Nugent, T (1979). *Sailing. F.I.T. Intercollegiate Athletics.* Florida Tech Press
- Interview with Dave Noble on July 5, 2023
- Interview with Chris Duer on July 5, 2021975 Florida Tech Athletic Awards Banquet Program. Retrieved from the Evans Library Archives.

Judo

The Judo team emerged in conjunction with the available space in the new gymnasium, which was opened for sporting events in the fall of 1968. Heading up the formation of the judo team was student-coach Bill Harkins. Under his leadership, the judo team grew to sixteen members in the 1969-'70 season. The team trained on the second floor of the Hedgecock Gymnasium. On the back wall of this location, Harkins had placed a large performance board with the judo team's insignia on it. Under the insignia were the names of team members and the judo belt each had earned.

With the growth of the judo team, a competitive schedule was developed in 1969-1970. The judo team competed favorably in the Florida Judo Association, the Southern Collegiate Judo Association, and in the East Coast Judo Association. It was stated in the 1970 *Ad Astra*, "the successes of the judo team prove that it is a well-established team." The challenging competitions in which the team participated were the Florida State Championship, Southeastern Invitational Tournament, S.E.C.J.A. Weight Class Tournament, Florida State College Weight Class Tournament, S.E.C.J.A. Five Man Team Tournament, a second late-season Southeastern Invitational Tournament, and the Florida State Promotional Tournament.

The judo team continued its winning ways in the 1970-1971 season. Members of this team were Michael Behl, Curtland Betchley, Chester, William Jarett, Louis Locklear, Dean Smelhil, H. Soto, Edward Uzialko, and student-coach Alfred Yee Litt. Members of the 1971-1972 season were Russell Ballage, Roger Barrios, Curtland Betchley, William Jarett, Dean Smelhil, Edward Uzialko, and Alfred Yee Litt.

The Florida Tech judo team had been invited to the first four annual athletic awards banquets because of their success as an intercollegiate sport. Those members of the 1972-1973 judo team who earned varsity letters were Curtland Betchley, Edward Uzialko, William Jarett, Alfred Yee Litt, Michael Behl, Louis Locklear, and student-coach was Edward Vzialko.

The leadership of the judo team in 1973-1974 was again in the hands of Alfred Yee Litt who had been a prominent member of the team for the three previous seasons. Members of the 1973-1974 team included his brother Daryl Yee Litt, along with Russell Ballagh, Steve Forma, Dave Hamel, Steve St. John, and Dean Smelhil.

Participation in the judo team declined after the 1973-1974 season. However, in the 1980s martial arts clubs were increasingly being formed which attracted large numbers of students, such as the Tang Soo Do Moo Duk Kwan club, that had as many as 40 students. The interest in judo remained strong throughout the years. In the 2000s judo physical education courses became popular with the students, especially given the quality of instructors who taught the classes.

References

- *Ad Astra* (1970). *Judo*: Retrieved from the Evans Library Archives.
- *Ad Astra* (1971). *Judo*. Retrieved from the Evans Library Archives.
- *Ad Astra* (1972). *Judo*. Retrieved from the Evans Library Archives.
- *Ad Astra* (1973). *Judo*. Retrieved from the Evans Library Archives.
- *Ad Astra* (1974). *Judo*. Retrieved from the Evans Library Archives.
- Correspondence with Pete Mazzone who is the Director of P.E. since 1985.

Cheerleading

Cheerleaders have been an important part of Florida Tech athletics.
Photo from University Archives.

The participation in cheerleading by the Florida Tech students began in 1967-1968 at the same time as the men's basketball began to expand its competition to four-year colleges. According to *Ad Astra* (1968) there were four women on the team who cheered for the basketball team at its off-campus site (Melbourne High School). The 1968-1969 cheerleading squad was formed just in time to cheer on the team in the new Florida Tech gymnasium, which opened in the early part of 1969. Members of this cheerleading squad were Cheryl Shephard, Kathy Sapia, and Gale Rohde. Though the participation of women on the cheerleading squad were small in numbers due to the limited academic course offerings in the 60s, their enthusiasm was unmatched. This enthusiasm and encouraging chants by the cheerleaders never wavered through the next 50-plus years. However, the cheerleading squads did take on different forms of cheerleading such as cheering, tumbling, dancing, jumps, and stunts. Men also joined the predominately women squads to assist with the cheering and stunts. As the enrollment of women expanded so did the size of the cheerleading squads. In the 1973-1974 season there were six members of the squad that included Kathy Lane as captain, along with Sue Freiss, Karla Hailfinger, Koko Knoot, Jan Ruzicka, and Lisa Sharpes. The 1978-1979 cheerleading squad saw the addition of two men; this team was comprised of Marla Carlson (Sayles), Sandy Foy, Vicki Garrett, Patrick Langley, Vickie Kenyon, Fran Paulock, Joella Pyle, and J.C. Thesken. The growth of the cheerleading squad continued into the 80s with the 1980-1981 squad comprised of three men and seven women. Members of this squad included Kim Metzger, co-captain, Rick Henry, co-captain, Catherina Dubbleday, Linda White, Carolyn Kinebrew, Elizabeth Dimailig, Amy Roy, Mike Payne, Ron Raedeke, and Brian Burton.

The 1986-1987 cheerleading squad continued in the steps of the previous squads by providing spirited support for the men's and women's basketball teams. The 1987 *Ad Astra* yearbook had this to say about the cheerleaders that year: "If there is one organization on campus which helps to induce school spirit, the Cheerleading Team is it." Members of this squad were Michael Angeli, Jeff King, Kathy Kiamedas, Robin Loomis, Judy Mainzer, Colleen McAller, Bruno Romer, Joy Shearer, and Hope Taylor. Joan Rasaci did a great job coaching the 1986-1987 squad. Following Coach Rasaci were many talented coaches who dedicated themselves to the cheerleaders on the team.

In the 1994 *Ad Astra* yearbook there is an article about being a cheerleader, and the anonymous author expresses well the importance of these dedicated Florida Tech student-athletes: "Many people do not realize that the cheerleaders have a difficult job to perform. These students must create energy and motivation within themselves in order to pass it along to the crowd. Their job becomes vital when a shift in momentum goes against Florida Tech. They must find that spark in the crowd to shift the edge back to the Panthers. Firing up the spectators is probably the second hardest task next to keeping themselves on the positive side. Their dedication and fervor helped the Panther Men defeat Barry in the homecoming game. The cheerleaders injected some liveliness into the crowd during half-time with an impressive routine. Even when Barry made a last second tying shot, the influx of high spirits helped the Panther Men win the game in overtime." The members of the 1993-1994 cheerleading squad were Roxanne Dorman, Jennifer Ball, Mylene Martin, Ramona Francs, Tanja Sluzenski, Andre Takacs, Rebecca Tagg, Lashonda White, Lablonda Cary, and Lynda Bottos. Coaches were Debra Williams, head coach, and Jane Shouppe, assistant coach.

The cheerleading teams continued their success through the turn of the century and in 2017 became a varsity sport with all the benefits associated with this status. Leading the team through this new phase of the program was coach Alexa Sumner. Adam Lowenstein (January 21, 2020) reported in the *Florida Tech News* that the Florida Tech cheerleaders reached the pinnacle of success when they won three events at the 2020 International Cheer Union University World Cup Cheerleading

Championships, giving them the title of World Champions in the Elite Small Coed Team Cheer, Dance Team, and the Dance Team Pom Doubles competitions. To be a competitor in this world competition, Florida Tech was selected by USA Cheer to represent the United States from among hundreds of teams. The second-place finisher to Florida Tech was Mexico's Tecnologico de Monterrey Borregos. As recognition for this accomplishment, there is a large banner hanging from the rafters in the Clemente Center that proclaims the 2020 Florida Tech Cheerleaders as the University World Cup Cheerleading World Champions in the three events mentioned above. This accomplishment took a lot of hard work and dedication by the 20 members of the cheerleading squad and their head coach, Alexa Sumner.

The transition of the varsity cheerleading team to the Spirit Squad is described by Josie Keenan in a *Crimson* article (Keenan,. February 19, 2023, updated March 2, 2023). Keenan states that the varsity cheerleading squad was discontinued after the 2021-2022 season, which left the present members of the squad to come up with a plan on how the cheerleading squad could move forward as a club. In keeping with the tradition of over 50 years of support for teams by the cheerleading squads, the squad members led by Allison Poling, president and captain of the dance team, Julia Martinus, public relations coordinator, Elise Medhus, treasurer and cheer captain, Gabby Cadolino, Emma Saurman, Ashauntie Reid, and Faith Westby, restructured their cheer and dance teams to be called the Spirit Squad. These Spirit Squad leaders achieved remarkable results in what they accomplished in their first year. There is no other group on campus that shows more pride in being a part of the university than cheerleaders, and the Spirit Squad did just that for the 2022-2023 academic year. They performed at the men's and women's basketball games, the hockey games, Homecoming, Orientation, and many other university events. According to Allison Poling, "This past year we had a team of 14 dancers and 13 cheerleaders. Plus two competition teams with 12 dancers and 11 cheerleaders." The leaders of the Spirit Squad have shown what can be done when a dedicated group of Florida Tech students get together to make something happen.

References

- Andy Lowenstein (January 21, 2020). *Florida Tech News*. Retrieved from https://news.F.I.T..edu /campus/florida-tech-cheerleading-crowned-world-champs-at-icu-university-world- cup/.
- *Ad Astra* (1968). *Cheerleading*. Retrieved from the Evans Library Archives.
- *Ad Astra* (1969). *Cheerleading*. Retrieved from the Evans Library Archives.
- *Ad Astra* (1979). *Cheerleading*. Retrieved from the Evans Library Archives.
- *Ad Astra* (1981). *Cheerleading*. Retrieved from the Evans Library Archives.
- *Ad Astra* (1987). *Cheerleading*. Retrieved from the Evans Library Archives.
- *Ad Astra* (1994). *Cheerleading*. Retrieved from the Evans Library Archives.
- Allison Poling provided an email on July 25, 2023, describing the 2022-2023 Spirit Squad.
- Keenan, J. (February 19, 2023, updated March 2, 2023). *Florida Tech Cheer and Dance team debut as the Spirit Squad. Crimson*. Retrieved from: https://www.crimson.fit.edu/campuslife/florida-tech-cheer-and-dance-team-debut-as-the-spirit-squad/article_2aec26f6-b068-11ed-86bd-9fddb420a350.html.

Pep Band

A pep band existed from time to time throughout the history of Florida Tech. In the April 10, 1977, edition of the *Crimson* student newspaper, there was a request by a student, Don Rosetti, for anyone seriously interested in being a part of a drum and bugle corps to contact him, and he said "No experience necessary! Come and learn!" A relatively large percentage of students at Florida Tech have a background in musical instruments. What is amazing about Florida Tech students who play musical instruments is that they are very good at it. In the 1998 *Ad Astra* yearbook it talked about the expanded Band Program at Florida Tech and that students, faculty, and staff could continue their musical interest through practicing, rehearsing, and performing in one of the musical groups now offered at Florida Tech. Florida Tech in the early 2000s began, through its humanities department, offering classes in orchestra. It was not unusual for a student to be in the orchestra, pep band, and perform as a band in one of the school plays.

Having a pep band was important to the Florida Tech athletics program. The need for a pep band hit home in 1999 when the men's basketball team was displaced from its campus court while construction of the new Clemente Sports and Recreation Center was taking place. At this time, Florida Tech was playing Embry Riddle Aeronautical Institute at the Melbourne Campus of Brevard Community College. Not only did the Panthers lose, but Embry Riddle brought their pep band and the spirit they created made the fans think it was Embry Riddle's home court. This experience served as a catalyst for the athletics department to support a pep band that would play during the men's and women's basketball games. The Florida Tech athletics director took on the role as advisor to the pep band. Through the early 2000s the band grew to as many as forty members. The athletics department helped arrange a reciprocating deal with the University of Tampa in which the Florida Tech Pep Band would host Tampa's pep band when they traveled to Melbourne, and Tampa would likewise host the Panther Pep Band when it traveled to their place. The athletics department provided a bus for the Florida Tech Pep Band. A highlight of this trip was the two bands would get together to form one big band. The athletics director at the University of Tampa said he spent more time watching the bands than the game.

It was uncommon for a pep band to play at both games (men and women) of a double header, but the Florida Tech Pep Band managed to play for both the men's and women's basketball teams. Because of class conflicts, the pep band members would come and go during double headers. However, during the break between games, the athletic department would provide them with pizzas and drinks.

Another practice by the athletics department to show the Pep Band they were appreciated was during basketball's senior recognition day, the Pep Band seniors were also called to the court to be recognized. Pep Band seniors were awarded an engraved wooden plaque with a picture of the recipient playing their instrument.

The Pep Band was instrumental in developing and promoting a fight song for the university. They would shorten the original version to fit into the timeframe they had to play. The fight song was written by a local composer with assistance from the music director at Florida Tech. Several times throughout a game the pep band would play the fight song and chant some of the lyrics. They worked closely with the cheerleaders to coordinate their music with the routines. The Pep Band along with the cheerleaders provided entertainment and a school spirit that was contagious to everyone in attendance.

The Pep Band's skill as musicians was recognized and appreciated by the Florida Tech fans. Some fans even requested CDs of their performances. What is remarkable about their high level of play was they had no professional band instructor. They did it all by themselves, which included the selection of music, planned rehearsals to maximize performance, and election of student officers whom they trusted and believed in. The members of the Pep Band not only enjoyed playing their instruments, they also learned valuable lessons in leadership and what it takes to be a part of an effective organization. The latest edition of the Pep Band has provided the university with over 20 years of continuous service.

References

- *Crimson* (April 10, 1977) *F.I.T. drum and bugle corps now forming.* Volume 10, No. 12. Retrieved from Evans Library.
- *Ad Astra* (1998). *Pep Band.* Retrieved from Evans Library Archives.

CHAPTER TWENTY-TWO:
INTERCOLLEGIATE ATHLETICS:
THE ADDED VALUE FOR STUDENT
ATHLETES AND THEIR STUDENT PEERS

By Frank M. Webbe, Ph.D.

Visit any primary school in the United States and you will observe children engaging in physical education, recreation, and intramural athletic competitions. Visit secondary schools and you will find the same activities with the addition of after-school interscholastic competitions. If you visit college campuses you will observe many recreational activities, students involved in self-initiated games and sports, intramural and club sports, and inter-collegiate athletic events. Clearly, physical activity occupies a consistent and important niche not only in American educational institutions, but in educational venues around the globe. Why would this be?

For the intrascholastic-intramural activities the rationale is quite simple. Educators have concluded over more than two millennia that physical exercise not only complements mental exercise, but also contributes to a more profound learning environment. For most of those two plus millennia these conclusions were born out of anecdotal, observational evidence and theory and rarely were questioned – except by some students who found no appeal in physical exercise or felt bullied by physically larger and stronger students in their gym or physical education classes. Kajal Sharna, an educator and blogger with the Asian Schools in India, proposes the following ten purposes for sport and exercise in their curriculum.

1. Stay Healthy
2. Good Fitness Level
3. Develop Leadership skills
4. Positive Mentoring
5. Boost Emotional Fitness
6. Develop Social Life
7. Develop Discipline
8. Better Performance in Academics
9. Develop Self-esteem
10. Develop Cooperation and Teamwork

These objectives (and expectations) are mirrored in schools the world over where athletic programs are described, with some systems espousing narrower and more targeted purposes compared to the list Sharna developed. For example, in 19th and 20th century British public schools, athletics were imposed by some headmasters to control and channel aggressive and hyperactive young boys. Other masters and headmasters valued athletics as one means for identifying leaders and emotionally robust young men (Mangan, 2000), hence the quotation attributed to the Duke of Wellington following the ultimate battle against Napoleon Bonaparte's legions: "The battle of Waterloo was won on the playing fields of Eton" (Oxford Dictionary of Quotations, 2014).

As noted, the early rationale for school-sponsored physical activities and athletic competitions was based upon non-empirical conclusions about the benefits that prompted inclusion of sport and exercise in school curricula. Beginning in the latter half of the 20th century empirical studies and well-designed qualitative research provided some support for the presumption of benefits. For example, Taras (2005) reported that of 14 studies that considered the association between or effect of athletics participation upon academic performance, five used prospective, experimental designs. The outcomes of those studies provided weak support for a beneficial role of exercise on classroom performance. In a

backhanded conclusion, Taras notes that these studies also showed no detriment to academics related to time spent in the athletic pursuits. Recent studies have supported the role of sport and exercise in the organizational structure of children's developing brains (Tomporowski, Moore, & Davis, 2011).

More recently, The Institute of Medicine in 2013 published a compendium of evidence-based facts regarding the role of exercise and sport in contributing to optimum physical, emotional, and mental development in children. Among their key takeaway points were the following:

- Evidence suggests that increasing physical activity and physical Fitness may improve academic performance and that time in the school day dedicated to recess, physical education class, and physical activity in the classroom may also facilitate academic performance.
- Available evidence suggests that mathematics and reading are the academic topics that are most influenced by physical activity. These topics depend on efficient and effective executive function, which has been linked to physical activity and physical fitness.
- Executive function and brain health underlie academic performance. Basic cognitive functions related to attention and memory facilitate learning, and these functions are enhanced by physical activity and higher aerobic fitness.

- Single sessions of and long-term participation in physical activity improve cognitive performance and brain health. Children who participate in vigorous or moderate intensity physical activity benefit the most.
- Given the importance of time on task to learning, students should be provided with frequent physical activity breaks that are developmentally appropriate.
- Although presently understudied, physically active lessons offered in the classroom may increase time on task and attention to task in the classroom setting.

Currently as summarized in the following infographic, the Centers for Disease Control include comprehensive exercise and physical education as a key element in promoting children's physical, mental, and emotional health (CDC, 2023). Thus, the question as to whether exercise and sport play a positive – some would say necessary – role in children's development has been answered in unequivocable fashion.

Most children enter post-secondary educational venues with physical growth nearly complete. However, brain development continues through the teen years into the mid-20s. The National Institute of Mental health presents evidence that transition from childhood into teen years and then to adulthood reflects significant changes in the structure and function of the brain. Many of these changes are portrayed in the NIMH infographic below. A key take-away regards the continued flexibility of development of the adolescent brain. Normal growth can be facilitated (as by exercise) or impaired (as by emotional stress). These are the reasons that environmental events may leave indelible scars on a developing brain.

Of critical importance to determining the role of sport and exercise on college campuses as teens mature into young adults is the inclusion of emotional, social, and cultural health in addition to cognitive health and development. Thus, regardless of a student's membership on a team versus playing pick-up games, actual sport activity contributes to a healthier and more balanced lifestyle. This brings us now to the critical question:

The Teen Brain: 7 Things to Know

From the **NATIONAL INSTITUTE** *of* **MENTAL HEALTH**

Did you know that **big** and **important changes** happen in the brain during adolescence? Here are **seven things to know about the teen brain**:

1 Adolescence is an important time for brain development.

Although the brain stops growing in size by early adolescence, the teen years are all about fine-tuning how the brain works. The brain finishes developing and maturing in the mid-to-late 20s. The part of the brain behind the forehead, called the prefrontal cortex, is one of the last parts to mature. This area is responsible for skills like planning, prioritizing, and making good decisions.

2 Brain development is related to social experiences during adolescence.

Changes to the areas of the brain responsible for social processes can lead teens to focus more on peer relationships and social experiences. The emphasis on peer relationships, along with ongoing prefrontal cortex development, might lead teens to take more risks because the social benefits outweigh the possible consequences of a decision. These risks could be negative or dangerous, or they could be positive, such as talking to a new classmate or joining a new club or sport.

3 The teen brain is ready to learn and adapt.

The teen brain has an amazing ability to adapt and respond to new experiences and situations. Taking challenging classes, exercising, and engaging in creative activities like art or music can strengthen brain circuits and help the brain mature.

4 Teen brains may respond differently to stress.

Because the teen brain is still developing, teens may respond to stress differently than adults. This could increase teens' chances of developing stress-related mental illnesses such as anxiety and depression. Recognizing possible triggers and practicing effective coping techniques can help teens deal with stress. More information on managing stress is available at **www.nimh.nih.gov/stress**.

5 Most teens do not get enough sleep.

Research shows that the sleep hormone melatonin works differently in teens than in children and adults. In adolescence, melatonin levels stay high later at night and drop later in the morning, which may explain why teens may stay up late and struggle with waking up early. Many teens do not get enough sleep, making it harder to pay attention, control impulses, and do well at school. Getting good sleep at night can help support mental health.

6 Mental illnesses may begin to appear during adolescence.

Ongoing changes in the brain, along with physical, emotional, and social changes, can make teens more likely to experience mental health problems. The fact that all these changes happen at one time may explain why many mental illnesses—such as schizophrenia, anxiety, depression, bipolar disorder, and eating disorders—emerge during adolescence.

7 The teen brain is resilient.

Despite the stresses and challenges that come with adolescence, most teens go on to become healthy adults. Some changes in the brain during this critical phase of development actually help support resilience and mental health over the long term.

Finding help

If you or someone you know has a mental illness, is struggling emotionally, or has concerns about their mental health, there are ways to get help. Find more information at **www.nimh.nih.gov/findhelp**.

Talking openly with your doctor or other health care provider can improve your care and help you both make good choices about your health. Find tips to help prepare for and get the most out of your visit at **www.nimh.nih.gov/talkingtips**.

> If you or someone you know is struggling or having thoughts of suicide, call or text the 988 Suicide & Crisis Lifeline at **988** or chat at **988lifeline.org**. In life-threatening situations, call **911**.

National Institute of Mental Health

www.nimh.nih.gov

NIH Publication No. 23-MH-8078
Revised 2023

Why do American colleges and universities sponsor intercollegiate athletics?

This seemingly simple question has many answers and a full discussion extends well beyond the scope of this chapter. I direct the reader to Guy Lewis's 1970 paper in the *American Quarterly* for a more expansive development of the background to this question, though that still only represents a start.

A first line of inquiry identifies the brief history of sport in American college campuses. Historians credit the rowing contest between Harvard and Yale in 1852 as the first true intercollegiate athletic event held on American soil. Reports of this event abound so whether it was indeed the first, it was at least the most publicized. Subsequently to this event other colleges in the northeast, notably Brown, Dartmouth, and Pennsylvania joined and participated in the intercollegiate rowing competitions. I mention this grouping to establish that sport competitions originated at the demonstrably best academic institutions in America. It was no accident that rowing was the seminal intercollegiate sport, and Harvard and Yale were the initiators. The "Boat Race," the annual competition between the Oxford and Cambridge boat clubs in England began in 1829. The adoption of the boat race represents just one of many traditions and structures borrowed by American colleges in efforts to be viewed as equivalent to (or better than) the venerable British flagship universities.

Intercollegiate sport teams in US colleges did not develop from a vacuum. Most intercollegiate sport competitions extended from clubs that already existed at colleges and universities. In addition to rowing, beginning in the 1850s baseball, football, track and field, rugby, cricket, and soccer clubs existed on many campuses, and soon the clubs spawned intercollegiate teams. Although school administrators and professors may have encouraged the development of these sport clubs, historians of sport agree that development and management of these clubs originated with student organizations and existed primarily as outlets for physical effort. At some of the more established schools that patterned instruction and courses on classical learning philosophies, athletic involvement and competition was viewed as consistent with academic structures that originated in the Greek academies, propelled by the philosophy of human development espoused particularly by Plato. In those classical academies, rhetoric, sciences, art, and physical activity represented a complete path to education (Lewis, 1970; Rodriguez, 2020). As the years rolled by, more colleges began operation and sport clubs plus intercollegiate sport teams proliferated. According to the U.S. Department of Education's National Center for Education Statistics (NCES), 4,294 four-year colleges and universities currently exist in the United States. Of those, 1,118 affiliate with the NCAA, 250 with the National Association of Intercollegiate Athletics (NAIA), and smaller numbers with the National Christian College Athletic Association (NCCAA) and other organizations. Thus, no more than half of all participate in organized leagues for inter-collegiate sport competition.

When Jerome Keuper conceived and then implemented Florida Institute of Technology in the late 1950s, he was consumed with very practical issues such as finding buildings that could be used as classrooms, identifying scientists with sufficient academic credentials to instruct, and obtaining supplies with no budget. Finding students among the various workers in the space industry may have been the easiest task. Long before the movie *Field of Dreams* appeared on the big screen, President Keuper exuded confidence that if he built it, the students would come. He did; they did (Patterson, 2000).

To some, the development early on of athletics and sport teams at Florida Institute of Technology may have seemed out of place or at least premature when basic academic buildings, qualified instructors, and an academic infrastructure still were in a fledgling state. Keuper had attended highly rated academic institutions, earning his bachelor's at MIT, his master's at Stanford, and his physics doctorate at University of Virginia. One constant at these schools was the presence of many successful intercollegiate athletics teams, and many more sport clubs and intramural athletic opportunities. Indeed, today MIT hosts 33 intercollegiate teams, the most of any NCAA Division III program in the country. Similarly, Stanford hosts 36 intercollegiate teams. But king of NCAA Division I with 40 teams is Harvard.

American institutions of higher learning have been unique globally in sponsoring athletic competitions. One hundred years ago the global ramifications appear to have been unknown. Sponsorship of inter-institutional athletic contests as well as providing financial and material support to student-athletes is rare elsewhere in the world, and often involves sports that are less common at US colleges – think the rowing competition between Oxford and Cambridge.

One could ask the question: would Harvard, Yale, Brown, Oxford, Cambridge, etc. have developed into lesser academic institutions in the absence of intercollegiate rowing and other sports? As is the case with historical what if questions, the answer is moot but the speculation about the answer can illuminate factors to consider, both pro and con. Such questions also provide a guide for where we might look to understand the value – or lack thereof – of formal intercollegiate sports on college campuses.

The original rationale for forming athletic clubs was to provide a physical companion to relieve stress from mental study. In most of the cases that have documentation these clubs were organized and operated by students (Lewis, 1970). The role of physical activity in enhancing mental and emotional well-being now has been established empirically in many studies. Reduction in anxiety, relief of depression, reduction in troubling cognitions all are proven effects of consistently performed physical exercise over a period of several months. [The usual rule is that exercise must raise cardio-respiratory fitness and be performed at least for 30 minutes at a time over 3-4 days per week for a minimum of 10 weeks to demonstrate effects equivalent to prescription medications.] The point here is that according to modern scientific findings, regular physical activity balances the individual's mental and emotional life. In the mid 19th century, such research findings were not available so the rationale for forming sport clubs at colleges and universities was more grounded in allowing a break from study routines so that muscle and cardio-respiratory exertion supplanted mental exertion for a time. Nothing wrong with that rationale as it turns out.

As noted previously, the mid-19th century adoption of rowing by Ivy League Schools clearly copied the tradition from Oxford and Cambridge. In general, athletics in universities and colleges outside the United States is mostly club level. However, the tradition of athletics in schools likely descended from the popularity in the English public schools. There, athletics were used to teach leadership, encourage "gentlemanly" sportsmanship within a competitive environment, and physical development. Not to be forgotten was the use of athletics to drain energy from active adolescents. All these objectives appear to have influenced the creation of club sports on college campuses in the United States (Hart, 1890). Obviously, the competitive approach spurred development of intercollegiate contests. At some point in the early 20th century a point was reached where the expectation of club and intercollegiate sport on college campuses was integral to student recruiting, and later to alumni development.

Initially F.I.T. offered graduate classes and associate's classes, typically held in the evenings. The advent of BS programs in Electrical Engineering and Mathematics in 1961 coincided with the creation of the first sport team, baseball. As chronicled in Chapter 2 of this volume, additional sports developed quickly. President Keuper's objective in founding F.I.T. was to provide education for working professionals in the nascent space industry. Original instructors were senior scientists and engineers employed by the major engineering and space-systems firms supporting the Atlantic Missile Test Range. By 1961 as heralded by the offering of bachelor's degrees and beginning of sports teams, Keuper's concept of the school expanded rapidly, approaching the structure of a modern STEM university. The offering of additional undergraduate majors such as biological sciences and business administration attracted more students. This paved the way for more athletic teams. The athletics program provided entertainment and diversion for the student body, undergraduates, and graduates alike. Such offerings were not trivial. Melbourne, Florida in the early 1960s certainly was not a hot bed of culture or entertainment. Particularly sports played on-campus such as basketball and volleyball attracted many student attendees. Support of the sports teams also tugged at recollections of school spirit from high school. Intercollegiate sport also extends opportunities to the community to engage with the students and faculty.

For the student athlete, team membership and intercollegiate competitions offer avenues for development of leadership skills, social bonding, time management, delay of gratification, physical expression, and emotional learning. Relationships formed with teammates often last a lifetime. Regrettably, adverse events with poor outcome also may have repercussions that last a lifetime. It is an irony that the physical exercise aspect of sport that can provide a barrier against anxiety and depression does not always protect the varsity student athlete. Indeed, the pressures that build up as a function of the sport and team may conspire to derail the individual into stress-induced physical and emotional pits. One of the most rewarding changes in college sport support has been recognition that the mental health of student athletes cannot be assumed. The athlete who practices and plays through pain and discomfort often shuns expressions of that pain to any outside the team, and frequently not to teammates. The creation of the Mental Health Task Force by the NCAA in 2013 began the critical exploration and documentation of mental-health needs by student athletes and set the stage for implementing mental-health support on all member campuses. Florida Institute of Technology was one of the first in Division II to implement recommendations. Indeed, the foresight of Athletic Director Bill Jurgens had prompted development of such resources to direct student-athletes to centers on campus where mental-health problems could be discussed and treated by professionals several years earlier.

References

- Centers for Disease Control. *About CDC Healthy Schools.* https://www.cdc.gov/healthyschools/about.htm. Accessed June 6, 2023.
- Centers for Disease Control. *Health Benefits of Physical Activity for Children.*https://www.cdc.gov/physicalactivity/basics/adults/health-beneF.I.T.s-of-physical-activity-for-children.html Accessed June 6, 2023.
- Hart, A. B. (1890). *The Status of Athletics in American Colleges. The Atlantic*, July Issue.
- Institute of Medicine. (2013). *Educating the Student Body: Taking Physical Activity and Physical Education to School.* Washington, DC: The National Academies Press. https://doi.org/10.17226/18314
- Lewis, G. (1970). *The Beginning of Organized Collegiate Sport. American Quarterly, 22*(2), 222-229.
- Mangan, J. A. (2000). *Athleticism in the Victorian and Edwardian Public School: The Emergence and Consolidation of an Educational Ideology.* New York: Routledge.
- Rodríguez, J. (2020). *Was Aristotle indifferent to sport? Analysis of The Nicomachean Ethics, Rhetoric, Politics, Metaphysics and On the Soul. Ágora para la Educación Física y el Deporte, 22*, 167-186. https://doi.org/10.24197/aefd.0.2020.167-186
- Sharna, K. *Importance of sports in school.* https://www.theasianschool.net/blog/importance-of-sports-in-school/ Accessed May 2, 2023.
- Taras, H. (2005). *Physical activity and student performance at school. Journal of School Health, 75*(6), 214-218. doi: 10.1111/j.1740-1561.2005.00026.x. PMID: 16014127.
- The National Center for Education Statistics (NCES). *https://nces.ed.gov/* Accessed July 1, 2023
- Tomporowski, P., Moore, R. D., & Davis, C. L. (2011). *Neurocognitive Development in*
- *Children and the Role of Sport Participation. In F. M.* Webbe (Ed.), *Handbook of Sport Neuropsychology* (pp. 383-393). New York: Springer Publishing Company. ISBN: 9780826115713

CHAPTER TWENTY-THREE:
THE IMPACT OF VOLUNTEERS

By William K. Jurgens

Those who have served Florida Tech athletics as volunteers have made a significant impact on the success of the program. The volunteers have made contributions in the areas of fundraising, leadership, service projects, and filling important roles that enhance the quality of Florida Tech athletics. These volunteers received no monetary compensation for their many hours of service; however, their altruistic nature is not taken for granted. Having a chapter on volunteers exemplifies the importance Florida Tech Athletics places on their contributions. Many of the volunteers discussed in this chapter have been inducted into the Florida Tech Sports Hall of Fame for their contributions, while others have had athletic facilities named for them in honor of their contributions, or by receiving special recognition awards. This chapter will shed some light on their contributions and the importance of these volunteers to the university and its athletics program.

2018 Hall of Fame Inductees (from left) Bill Potter (volunteer), Lynisha Nelson (basketball), Justin Sedlak (basketball) and Kieran Breslin (soccer).
Photo from University Archives.

Andy Seminick

During the early years of Florida Tech athletics, the university named Andy Seminick as its athletics director. It is not surprising that Andy Seminick was given this title during the formative years of the university. Seminick, a legend in major league baseball, was an all-star catcher for the Philadelphia Phillies, and the primary catcher for the Phillies from 1943 through 1951. He was also a prominent member of the Phillies' Whiz Kids when they captured the 1950 National League Pennant from the Brooklyn Dodgers. Tim McCarver, who was a television announcer for 23 World Series said on national television that Andy Seminick was the best catcher he ever saw block home plate. In Dodgertown, the former spring training facility for the Los Angeles Dodgers, there is a picture on the wall showing Seminick blocking the plate as Jackie Robinson slides into home. Seminick also served as manager of Phillies' minor league teams, and in this capacity, he coached Mike Schmidt, future inductee into MLB Hall of Fame, and four-time All-Star catcher Bob Boone. Pat Williams, who played for Seminck when he managed a minor league team in Miami, spoke at a Panther Athletic Association (PAA) luncheon about Andy Seminick as a leader. In his speech, Williams shared that when their team lost, Seminick would go around the locker room making contact with each player and saying to each, "We will get them next time." Andy Seminick taught me a lot about leadership. I remember saying to Andy, "when I criticize someone, you never respond by saying a negative thing about anyone." I thought this is a person I want to emulate.

Seminick had a great impact on the Florida Tech baseball program as a coach in its early years before leaving for spring training to manage within the Phillies' organization. For the team's first uniforms, Seminick got a set of uniforms from the Philadelphia Phillies and Martha Work, wife of Vice President for Student Affairs Ray Work, personally altered the uniforms with help from her mother. Seminick also served as a scout for the Phillies, and his love for Florida Tech baseball was evidenced when he met a young high school player named Randy Muns from Texas. Randy took Seminick's advice and enrolled in Florida Tech beginning in the fall of 1975. Seminick's advice to Muns was that he would get the exposure needed at Florida Tech to play professional baseball, which proved a reality for Muns who after graduation played minor league baseball for the Chicago Cubs organization.

Seminick was also a stalwart in raising funds for the athletics program. An important part of Florida Tech's fundraising was A Sporting Affair in which sports memorabilia was auctioned off.

Seminick was always sending letters and calling friends to donate sport items. On one occasion Seminick was in the Florida Marlins' clubhouse at its spring training facility in Melbourne, Florida when just prior to a game he came upon Jim Leyland, the manager of the Marlins. As he often did with others, Seminick asked Leyland if he had anything he would like to donate to Florida Tech athletics, which Seminick said was important to him. Leyland without hesitation took the baseball jersey off his back and signed it for Seminick. At another time, Seminick got two of his Whiz Kids teammates, Hall of Famers Robin Roberts and Curt Simmons, to be guests at Florida Tech Athletics' A Sporting Affair. At this event, the three of them autographed the book titled *The Whiz Kids: and the 1950 Pennant* for the attendees. In this book Seminick is mentioned and photographed 81 times. Richie Ashburn, a teammate of Seminick's, said, "If there was a leader, I would have to say it was Andy Seminick. Although I don't think anybody ever said Andy was our leader, he commanded respect because of his toughness and his great work habits" (Roberts & Rogers, 1996). Further, Ashburn said, "Andy was quite, really a nice guy. The fans loved him, and his teammates loved him" (Roberts & Rogers, 1996).

For all Seminick's support, The Florida Tech baseball field was named the Andy Seminick Baseball Field in 1987. When the baseball field was relocated to a new site on the campus of Florida Tech, the field was renamed in 1999 the Andy Seminick – Les Hall Baseball Field, which added the name Les Hall in honor of Florida Tech's legendary baseball coach. Additionally, a large, framed oil painting of Andy Seminick in his Phillies uniform hangs on the wall near the doors to the main court in the Clemente Center. This painting serves as a tribute to Seminick's many contributions to Florida Tech Athletics. Andy Seminick was inducted into the Florida Tech Sports Hall of Fame on February 14, 1987. Seminick passed away on February 22, 2004, at the age of 83. The funeral home was filled to standing room only, and there were many Florida Tech representatives in attendance, along with many former baseball players, including MLB Hall of Fame inductee Mike Schmidt, whose lives had been influenced by Seminick.

Dr. Joe Doller

Another important volunteer was Dr. Joe Doller who practiced podiatry locally. Doller's background was well suited for being a part of an athletics program having served as head athletic trainer for the NFL Cardinals (Nugent, 1981). He was also the head athletic trainer for the MLB Chicago Cubs and the NFL Chicago Bears (Nugent, 1981). Doller joined Seminick as an athletics administrator when he was given the title of Assistant Athletic Director. He was also a founding member of the Florida Tech Athletic Advisory Council. Doller was a strong supporter of basketball, and as such arranged for the Harlem Globetrotters to play on two occasions in Florida Tech's gymnasium as a fundraiser. Dr. Doller was the de facto athletic trainer for Florida Tech athletics. Student-athletes were told to go to his podiatry office whenever they needed an athletics trainer. Everyone knew Doller for his vociferous support of the basketball team. The Doller family made generous donations to improve the equipment in the athletic training room. For their generosity, the athletic training room in the Clemente Center was named the Doller Athletic Training Room. For his numerous contributions to Florida Tech, Joe Doller was inducted into the Florida Tech Sports Hall of Fame on February 11, 1988.

William (Bill) Potter

Bill Potter's service to the Florida Institute of Technology spans over 40 years. Potter was a member of the university's board of trustees from 1981 to January 2022. As a member of the Board of Trustees, he also served as its chair from 1990 to 1997. As busy as he was running a law practice and serving on the Board of Trustees, he also served as chair of the Florida Tech Athletic Advisory Council, a committee that advises the university president on athletic related matters. Being associated with Florida Tech Athletics was natural for Potter. He played college sports as an undergraduate at Brown University, and when he went to law school at the University of Michigan, he was an avid fan of all Michigan's athletic programs. His love for "Go Blue" has stayed strong with him through the years with his attendance at many Michigan bowl games, as well as basketball games, and other Michigan sporting events.

The Athletic Advisory Council, with Potter as its chair, undertook another fundraising event called A Sporting Affair in 1991. The Athletic Advisory Council brought in an expert on fundraising events, Darcia Jones-Francey, to help the Council move forward with this event. The goal of A Sporting Affair was to raise money from the cost of admission and the auction of items that included sports memorabilia, items from local businesses, and trips to various locations. All these items and travel arrangements were donated. This event brought in an average of $95,000 a year, which also went towards athletic scholarships.

At Florida Tech, Potter was a mainstay at the men's and women's basketball and soccer games. And, on many occasions he traveled to away games because he loved sports and watching Florida Tech compete well against formidable competition. His over 40 years of association with Florida Tech Athletics has given him great insight and an appreciation for the numerous contributions and achievements of the coaches, administration, and student-athletes. Potter's appreciation for the history of Florida Tech Athletics motivated him to begin writing a book on this subject. He asked Bill Jurgens, athletic director emeritus at Florida Tech, to co-author this book with him, and he wasted little time in pursuing this undertaking in his typical drive, thoroughness, research, and persistence. When the Sunshine State Conference wanted to revise its bylaws, Bill Potter's name surfaced as someone whose expertise in legal matters qualified him for this undertaking. Without hesitation Potter volunteered his service to update the present bylaws of the Sunshine State Conference. In 2016 when the trustees formed the Athletics Committee, Bill Potter was the clear choice to serve as its chair. He admirably chaired this position until he retired in January 2022. For his many years of service to the Board of Trustees, he was given the respected title of Board of Trustee Emeritus. A statement that best characterizes Bill Potter is that "William C. Potter has a strong commitment to his family, outstanding service to his community, and patriotic duty to his country." Florida Tech Athletics is a better program for the service and support provided by Bill Potter. In recognition of his many contributions to Florida Tech Athletics and the leadership he provided, Bill Potter was inducted into the Florida Tech Sports Hall of Fame in 2018.

Phil Gaarder

Prior to volunteering at Florida Tech, Phil Gaarder was a down range operations director for NASA space launches, and during this time he could be seen in the launch control room monitoring the progress of each launch. Gaarder put his operations experience to good use in the setup and operations of many fundraising events at Florida Tech. Gaarder's skills came along at the right time (mid 1980s) when Florida Tech athletics was looking for ways, outside the university's budget, to increase its funding of athletic scholarships. Gaarder was also a member of the Athletic Advisory Council and later a member of the board of the Panther Athletic Association. He is responsible for implementing the Spring Wine Festival on the corner of Babcock St. and University Blvd. This event provided non-stop entertainment, carnival rides, and the selling of beer, wine, and hotdogs. Gaarder was also the main operations person for A Sporting Affair's dinner-auction. There was no task too difficult for Phil Gaarder to handle. Another undertaking by Gaarder was the concession stand that was implemented for the basketball, baseball, softball, and soccer games. This undertaking by Gaarder proved to be highly profitable, given the large attendances at Florida Tech athletic events during this time. Gaarder was also a leader in the Panther Athletic Association (PAA), serving as its president for three years. During his tenure, the Panther Athletic Association had regular lunchtime meetings with guest speakers, such as Tommy Lasorda, Pat Williams, Lee Corso, and Richard DeVos (owner of the Orlando Magic and co-founder of the Amway Corporation). Gaarder was like having a full-time employee. We began giving an award for outstanding service at the PAA luncheons and after Gaarder won the first two annual awards for service, it was decided to name the award "The Phil Gaarder Outstanding Service Award," so others could be recognized for their service. Gaarder's fundraising efforts represented a large portion of the funds raised to support athletic scholarships. This increase in fundraising led to an increase in athletic scholarships for soccer and baseball, which had a lot to do with their successes in the late 80s and early 90s. For his contributions to Florida Tech Athletics, Phil Gaarder was inducted into the Florida Tech Sports Hall of Fame on November 22, 1996.

Percy Hedgecock

Before joining Florida Tech, Percy Hedgecock was the founder and first Mayor of the town of Satellite Beach, Florida. He served as Mayor from 1957 to 1973. Hedgecock was also an accomplished slow-pitch softball coach with the Satellite Beach Comets. His teams won five national championships and four world softball championship titles. For his successes in softball, he was inducted into the Hall of Honor of the Amateur Softball Association in 1982. His reputation for being a successful coach and helping others was widely known by everyone in South Brevard. When asked to serve on the Athletic Advisory Council, Hedgecock readily accepted. In 1981 he was voted as the chair of the Athletic Advisory Council. Percy was aware of the importance of athletic scholarships, especially having coached players who needed financial assistance to attend college. The Athletic Scholarship Fund was established in 1982. To get this new fund underway, Hedgecock said that he would donate $15,000 and personally raise an additional $15,000 for this fund. The Athletic Advisory Council (AAC), under Hedgecock's leadership, realized that athletic scholarships were costly, therefore, the AAC expanded its efforts by establishing the Panther Athletic Association (PAA) in 1986. The AAC helped with the establishment of a board of directors for this new organization. The founding members of the PAA voted Phil Gaarder as its president. The dues from PAA memberships raised over $20,000 a year. The PAA continued to grow, and to assist in this growth, Richard DeVos (owner of the Orlando Magic and co-founder of the Amway Corporation) was asked to speak at this Panther Athletic Association Luncheon to promote memberships. DeVos' motivational speech resulted in 17 new members signing up at the luncheon.

For Percy Hedgecock's generosity and devotion towards raising funds for athletic scholarships and his service on the Florida Tech Board of Directors from 1981 to 1987, the Florida Tech gymnasium was dedicated the Percy L. Hedgecock Gymnasium on January 7, 1986. When the Percy L. Hedgecock Gymnasium was replaced by the Charles and Ruth Clemente Center for Sports and Recreation in 2001, it was decided that a bust of Percy Hedgecock should be commissioned to honor his legacy. Dale Dettmer and other board of trustees donated to this sculpture of Hedgecock. The sculpture was placed near the doors to the main court in the Clemente Center. At the dedication of the bust, Hedgecock's brother, Hub Hedgecock, was present and when the bust was unveiled, its likeness of Percy Hedgecock brought tears to his eyes. Percy Hedgecock was also inducted in the Florida Tech Sports Hall of Fame on February 15, 1986.

Jim Mitchell

John Reynolds reviews game statistics with Jim Mitchell. Jim has broadcast both men's and women's basketball for many years. *Photo from University Archives.*

Jim Mitchell has been the television, radio, and live stream voice of Florida Tech Basketball for 43 years. During this time, he broadcast over 600 games. That is an amazing accomplishment given that he volunteered his services without ever missing a game. He was an experienced radio broadcaster prior to his arrival at Florida Tech. Mitchell also traveled to away games to announce over the radio whenever radio broadcasts were available. He traveled as far as Fairbanks, Alaska to announce two Florida Tech games in a tournament. Mitchell announced games over WFIT. 89.5 FM, WYAK Channel 56, ESPN Melbourne, Sunshine State Conference, and Florida Tech Sports.com. When Florida Tech began its live television broadcast over WYAK Channel 56, Mitchell was the lead play-by-play announcer for all games. Most noteworthy were the two games in the 1989 Florida Tech Holiday Classic in which Florida Tech played the University of Massachusetts on Friday night and Boston College in the final on Saturday. The success of the Florida Tech men's basketball team in these two games were fully captured by the enthusiastic and experienced Mitchell. It was not uncommon for students who watched home basketball games from their dorm rooms to leave their rooms and head over to Hedgecock Gymnasium to watch the games in person. Jim Mitchell's professionalism as a play-by-play announcer was also evidenced when in a 2020 home game with Rollins College the basketball rim broke. It took the game operations staff over an hour to replace the rim. During this time Mitchell described the action taking place as if it were a game. When people left the arena, thinking that the game would be postponed, they watched from their live stream devices as Jim Mitchell described the action taking place on the court. Additionally, the commissioner of the Sunshine State Conference and the Supervisor of Officials, knowing that some people involved were asking that the game be postponed, watched Mitchell as he continued his steady account of what was happening. However, the rim was replaced and Mitchell, without missing a beat, continued announcing the game to its conclusion. Days after the game many people came forward and said they were captivated by the job Mitchell did in keeping their interest in what was happening. For his 43 years of volunteer service (37 years at the time of his induction) as a broadcaster for Florida Tech Athletics, Jim Mitchell was inducted into the Florida Tech Sports Hall of Fame on March 19, 2016.

The Athletic Advisory Committee in 1982. Left to right, front row, Kevin Yelverton, Adger Smith, Carolyn Findlay, Percy Hedgecock and Joe Dollar. Left to right, back row, Tom Adams, Bill Sullivan, Barry Fullerton, Bill Jurgens, Phil Gaarder, Joe Glover, Joel Boyd and Andy Seminick. *Photo from University Archives.*

Ted Dockstader

Ted Dockstader is affectionately known as "Doc." Dockstader serves as the volunteer manager of the Florida Tech men's lacrosse team, and throughout his eight-year tenure with the team he has displayed a humble and unassuming presence. After you watch him, you can see that he acceptingly takes on menial tasks like bringing a 150-foot hose to the water break area, doing the laundry in the Anthony Catanese Varsity Training Center, and assisting coaches with needed tasks. To do all these tasks requires his presence at least a half-hour before practice and often over an hour after the team departs. Throughout this entire time, Dockstader displays an attitude of enjoyment and pride. These actions by Dockstader gained him the respect and appreciation from the entire team.

Dockstader's background includes being a 1975 graduate of Florida Tech. After graduation, he enlisted in the U.S. Army where he served for 25 years and achieved the rank of Lieutenant Colonel. His work ethic and desire to serve others resulted in him volunteering his time and energy to the Florida Tech men's lacrosse team in 2016. Eight years later he still approaches this job with the dedication and commitment to make a difference for the team.

At the 2023 Athletic Awards Banquet he was recognized with a plaque for his service to the men's lacrosse team. In presenting him this award, the Florida Tech Athletics Department had this to say about Dockstader, "Leadership can be defined as the ability of an individual to influence and guide members of a team, and Ted Dockstader meets this definition, and in doing so he is selfless in his time and action."

Martha Work

Martha Work was the wife of former Vice President of Student Affairs, Dr. Ray Work. Martha Work was considered by many during the early days of Florida Tech athletics as its #1 fan. She attended almost every basketball and softball game in the programs' early histories along with cheering for volleyball, soccer, and baseball. She was known for ringing a cow bell throughout basketball games before the NCAA implemented noise abatement rules.

Martha was a graduate of The Ohio State University, where she met fellow student and future husband Ray Work. When Florida Tech was still Brevard Engineering College (BEC) she, along with Ray, worked with the emerging basketball team players at Florida Tech. Her background as a basketball player was the impetus for the love and enthusiasm she showed at every basketball game. In addition to her love of sports, she served as a leader with the Girl Scouts for over 50 years, even hiking with them on the Appalachian Trail.

In the mid-80s Martha was a member of the Women's Locker Room. With Florida Tech women's basketball starting in 1986, there was a need to raise funds to support the expansion of women's sports at Florida Tech. To achieve this goal, the Women's Locker Room was formed with the members being prominent women from the Melbourne area and the university. Special events were established by the leaders of this group, which included cheese and wine receptions hosted by members of the Women's Locker Room, and interaction gatherings between the members of the Women's Locker Room and women student-athletes, which took place inside the Percy Hedgecock Gymnasium. Members of the Women's Locker Room paid a membership fee and as a special benefit for their contributions, each member's name was placed on the lockers of women student-athletes.

Tim Wakefield

Tim Wakefield has never forgotten his teammates, his coach, or his university from his playing days at Florida Tech. His affinity for Florida Tech is evidenced by the many times he responded to requests from Florida Tech to support the baseball facility's development efforts and his acceptance to become a member of the Florida Tech Board of Trustees in 2014. Besides always answering the call, he returned to his alma mater for Homecoming gatherings to be with former teammates. There were times when he won the homerun derby contest against Florida Tech baseball alums. You could see he still had the power to hit line drive homeruns, which was indicative of the records he still holds for Florida Tech baseball's number of homeruns in a season at 22 and all-time homeruns at 40. Much like what Andy Seminick did for Florida Tech in its early days of baseball, Wakefield would take the time to gather equipment from the Red Sox organization that they no longer needed and bring it to Coach Hall for his players.

Wakefield's humble disposition, strong work ethic, and unrelenting will to succeed, were personal attributes he displayed as a professional baseball player and in the communities for which he served. In 2010 Tim Wakefield received the Roberto Clemente Award, which goes to the MLB baseball player who, "best represents the game of Baseball through extraordinary character, community involvement, philanthropy and positive contributions, both on and off the field (Major League Baseball, May 23, 2023)."

Tim Wakefield had many memorable accomplishments as a major league baseball player. Wakefield was a starting pitcher for the Pittsburgh Pirates in 1992, and in that year, he went on to win two games in the National Leagues Championship Series against the Atlanta Braves. In 1995 he received the National League's Comeback player of the Year Award in his first year with the Boston Red Sox. A highlight for Wakefield was being a part of the Boston Red Sox's 2004 and 2007 World Series Championship teams. And, in 2009 he was a member of the National League All-Star team. He retired from the Boston Red Sox after the 2011-2012 season with 200 career wins and 186 of those wins were with the Red Sox, which placed him third on the Red Sox's all-time winningest pitchers behind only Cy Young, (192) and Roger Clemens (192) (Edes & McDonald, February 17, 2012).

When there was an urgency to reach the financial goal for beginning construction of the Florida Tech baseball field in time for the 1999 spring season, it was Tim Wakefield who stepped forward with a contribution that made it possible. Also, when donations were needed for lighting the baseball field, Wakefield's donations helped make it a reality. For his continuous support of Florida Tech Baseball, the new covered batting cage for baseball and softball was named the Tim Wakefield Batting Cage. Also, for his accomplishments as a player on the Florida Tech baseball team and his accomplishments as a major league baseball player, Tim was inducted into the Florida Tech Sports Hall of Fame on January 9, 1993.

Hundreds of Other Volunteers

These nine volunteers played an important part in the history of Florida Tech athletics. However, there were hundreds of other volunteers who assisted coaches, served on committees, assisted with fundraising efforts, and served as managers. These individuals contributed to the teams' successes or provided valuable resources that also helped the program achieve greater success than otherwise would have been possible. Florida Tech was built on volunteerism and for the past 60 years this tradition has been an important part of the university's growth.

References

- Bruce Gaarder provided a biography of his father, Phil Gaarder, which was received on May 14, 2023.
- Buckley, S. (September 18, 2014). *Buckley: Tedy Bruschi, Tim Wakefield full of pride. Boston Herald*. Retrieved from: https://www.bostonherald.com/2014/09/18/buckley-tedy-bruschi-tim-wakefield-full-of-pride/
- Edes, G. & McDonald, J. (February 17, 2012). *Knuckleballer Tim Wakefield retires. ESPNBoston.com.* Retrieved from: https://www.espn.com/boston/mlb/story/_/id/7585718/tim-wakefield-retires-17-seasons-boston-red-sox.
- Major League Baseball. (May 23, 2023). *Roberto Clemente Award.* Retrieved from: https://www.mlb.com/community/roberto-clemente-award.
- Nugent, T. (1981). *F.I.T. Intercollegiate Athletics.* Florida Institute of Technology, Melbourne, Fl.
- Pat Williams speaking about Andy Seminick at Panther Athletic Association Luncheon.
- Randy Muns ('78) interview on May 14, 2023.
- Roberts, R. & Rogers III, P. (1996). *The Whiz Kids: and the 1950 Pennant.* Temple University Press, Philadelphia, Pa.

CHAPTER TWENTY-FOUR:
C0VID-19 AND INTERCOLLEGIATE SPORTS

By William C. Potter

As COVID-19 spread throughout American society in 2019, 2020 and 2021, college campuses faced unique challenges in slowing the spread of the pandemic. Intercollegiate athletics were inevitably impacted as the virus propagated itself. The nature of intercollegiate athletics which often included student-athletes in close contact in intimate venues, created unique problems for athletic administrators.

A story in *Florida Today* by Eric Rogers on March 20, 2020, reported that Florida Tech has suspended in-person classes, athletics and most campus events. The announcement by the school stated that the suspension would begin immediately and would continue for the remainder of the spring semester. Effective March 23, all classes would become on-line classes. Dormitories and student housing would remain open. Immediately following the announcement, Florida Tech athletic officials confirmed that all sports events were suspended indefinitely, effective immediately. The athletic announcement continued: "The suspension applies to all athletic competitions and practices for the health and safety of all who are essential to these activities."

The NCAA issued its first publication addressing the subject on May 1, 2020, when it issued its "Core Principles of Resocialization of Collegiate Sports." It followed up that publication with a release on July 16, 2020 titled "Resocialization of Collegiate Sport: Developing Standards for Practice and Competition." Those publications largely deferred to individual members and athletic conferences to determine how and when they would practice and play intercollegiate sports. These publications contained some paternalistic advice that was of limited usefulness or hackneyed that it was not helpful. For example, the publications advised that testing strategies should be developed and that masking and physical distancing should be practice "when feasible." Perhaps the most salient information coming from the NCAA was the edict that any student-athlete could decline to participate in athletics during the pandemic without fear of losing his/her athletic scholarship.

On July 17, 2020, the Sunshine State Conference President's Council announced that all fall sports, including men's soccer, women's soccer, men's cross country, women's cross country and women's volleyball, would be postponed on account of the COVID-19 then running rampant. The plans announced by the conference contemplated that the postponed sports would be played during the spring of 2021. The announcement further explained that during the postponement of the fall sports, those teams would be allowed to engage in conditioning activities, strength training and practice, so long as those activities could be done without risking the health of the student-athletes.

On July 22, 2020, *Florida Today* confirmed that the Sunshine State Conference Presidents Council had postponed all fall sports competition until spring. It also announced that the spring sports of men's and women's lacrosse, men's golf, baseball, softball, and women's rowing, which normally had a short fall season, would not compete in fall of 2020. A decision as to whether to conduct winter sports would be made no later than October 1. The article quoted interim Athletic Director Pete Mazzone as saying: "We will, as a collective group, continue to remain positive and work hard knowing that one day soon we will be competing again." The conference plan was that competition for fall and spring sports would be held in the spring 2021 semester. The Sunshine State Conference later announced that the winter sports would be suspended at least through the end of the 2020 calendar year. Practice and conditioning for all sports would be permitted during the fall 2020 semester "provided health and safety conditions allow these activities."

The fall 2020 issue of *Florida Tech Magazine* (Volume 29, Issue 2) described the "Return to Learn" recommendations which had been developed by Florida Tech's Pandemic Response Committee. The committee, chaired by Senior Vice-President of Student Life Bino Campanini, made recommendations which included daily wellness screenings, mandatory face-coverings in high-traffic areas, communicating social distancing guidelines, restricting public access to campus, increasing safety cleanings, plexiglass barriers, limiting attendance in buildings, limited dining and changing fall break. The plan included isolation and quarantine policies for those who contracted COVID-19.

In the fall of 2020, teams were able to resume practicing pursuant to a Phased Resocialization Plan developed by the athletic administration in coordination with the university's Pandemic Response Team. That plan was a 4-phase plan which phased in teams for small groups of practice at the outset of the semester to full-team practices for the last 4 weeks of the semester. An article by Daniel Supraner in the winter 2021 issue of *Florida Tech Magazine* (Volume 29, Issue 3) described the phases as beginning with Phase 0 which took place from August 17 through September 6, 2020. During Phase 0, there were no practices and only remote meetings were held by the use of Zoom videoconferencing. Phase 1 took place from September 8 to September 21. During Phase 1, teams were permitted to hold practices in groups of 10 or less to focus on individual training and conditioning, physical distancing was required. Phase 2 took place from September 22 to October 5 and teams were able to practice in larger groups but were encouraged to continue with small groups. After October 6, Phase 3 took effect and teams were able to return to normal practices, although masks continued to be required and social distancing was encouraged when practicable. Supraner's reporting described how athletic department administrators, coaches and student-athletes had worked together to establish a plan that would permit on-campus practices beginning with the fall 2020 semester. Interim Athletic Director Pete Mazzone and head athletic trainer Luis Velez worked closely with the university's Pandemic Response Team to create a resocialization plan, including university and CDC guidelines for mask usage and social distancing, that would reacclimate student-athletes to college-level training. Mazzone explained to

Supraner: "Our resocialization plan consisted of phasing in our teams during the semester, from small groups of practice to actual full-team practices for the last four weeks of the semester." Velez told Supraner: "This resocialization plan not only helps reduce risk of injury, but it also creates a culture of healthy habits to sustain participation in sports during this pandemic."

In December 2020, Mazzone and Velez met with the university's Pandemic Response Team and were charged with responsibility to devise a plan to safely conduct intercollegiate athletics after the winter break in January 2021. Charged with that responsibility, Velez authored a document somewhat verbosely but descriptively titled "Proposed Athletics Spring COVID-19 Surveillance Testing and Resocialization Strategy Spring 2021." The comprehensive plan required that all student-athletes would be tested within three days of returning to campus. All test results would be transmitted to the trainer for their team. During the first week after their return, student-athletes would be limited to small group, non-contact practices. The plan included frequent meetings discussing the testing protocols and reiterating the importance of hygiene, mask use and social distancing. At the end of the first week, pool testing was to be conducted with regularity. It was determined that no teams would travel overnight that spring. An interesting issue was the requirement that an opponent be notified in the event that any student-athlete tested positive within 48 hours after competing against that opponent. The plan contained a testing flowchart which illustrated the actions which would be taken in response to testing results. Positive tests would result in contact tracing and isolation. The plan also contemplated the maintenance of a spreadsheet that documented all positive tests and contacts with detailed information about each student-athlete on the spreadsheet.

Mazzone and Velez followed-up that document with a document titled "Strategic Planning for Spring 2021 Intercollegiate Competition Regarding COVID-19 Session One." That document set forth several issues that needed to be addressed as intercollegiate competition resumed in the spring semester of 2021. Among those issues were concerns regarding the accommodation of visiting teams, travel by Florida Tech teams, COVID-16 surveillance testing and in-season contact tracing.

Prior to the 2021 Spring semester and the restart of intercollegiate athletics, Head Trainer Velez penned a letter to all student-athletes. Velez made it clear that the university's goal was "to not only prioritize your health, but also that of your team, campus, the surrounding community, and your opponents." The letter set forth the testing requirements for student-athletes prior to return to campus as well as the surveillance testing that would be conducted throughout the Spring Semester.

During that same time, a document was also provided by Mazzone and Velez to all coaches describing the surveillance testing and resocialization process to be followed by teams during Spring Semester 2021. The coaches were informed of the testing that would be required prior to the return to campus by a student-athlete and the pool testing that would take place thereafter. This direction to coaches also describe the isolation and tracing that would take place in the event of positive tests.

On August 18, 2021, the NCAA published a "Fall Resocialization Update." Based on that update, Florida Tech published a "COVID-19 Positive Return to Play Policy." That direction suspended surveillance testing and mandated testing only for student-athletes who reported symptoms consistent with COVID-19 or suspected to have COVID-19. In the event of positive tests, contact tracing could be instituted if ordered by the Campus COVID-19 Case Manager Krishna Patel. All student-athletes testing positive were required to isolate for at least 10 days. Since the vaccine was available by the time of release of this policy, a distinction was made between vaccinated and unvaccinated people who had experienced contact with someone who had tested positive. Vaccinated students were monitored whereas unvaccinated students underwent mandatory testing. The policy also included detailed direction regarding team activities that would be permitted following a positive test result from a team member. Under some circumstances, the policy envisioned that a team could be required to pause its activities.

Prior to commencement of the 2021-1922 academic year, Velez and newly arrived Athletic Director Jamie Joss published a document titled "Information Regarding COVID-19 Risk Mitigation Strategy for Athletics During the 2021-1922 Academic Year." The notable provision in that document was that vaccinated student-athletes would be contact traced and tested only if exposed to someone who had tested positive. Unvaccinated student-athletes, on the other hand, would be subjected to surveillance testing every 1 to 2 weeks. Similarly, masks would be required for unvaccinated student-athletes but not for vaccinated student-athletes.

The Athletic Department also published "Athletic Team 2021-1922 Travel Guidelines." Those guidelines also made distinctions between vaccinated and unvaccinated personnel. Travel parties were limited to players, coaches, trainers and drivers. Masks were required for all travelers. In the event that a traveler developed symptoms while traveling, it was mandated that they seek care at an urgent care facility and, if positive, be isolated prior to return to campus.

That document was followed by a document titled "Florida Tech Athletics COVID-19 Information for Spring Semester 2022," which urged all student-athletes be vaccinated for COVID-19. It further requested that all scholar-athletes, regardless of vaccination status, be tested prior to return to campus for Spring Semester. A second round of testing was to be administered by the athletic training staff at the time each team returned of on the first day of the new semester. Unvaccinated athletes would be subjected to weekly surveillance testing while vaccinated athletes would be subject to testing "as warranted." Masking while indoors continued to be required for all scholar-athletes.

Perhaps the greatest challenge for athletics administrators occurred in December 2021 when several basketball players on both the men's and women's teams tested positive for the virus. Under conference rules in effect at the time, if it was determined that a team was unable to field a team for a scheduled game, that team would forfeit the game and it would be recorded as a loss. It fell upon head trainer Velez to recommend that the team was unable to play the games due to the lack of adequate substitutes. This recommendation did not make Velez overly popular with some of the players and coaches but clearly demonstrated that Velez had his priorities in proper order.

All scholar-athletes in spring and fall sports, regardless of vaccination status, were required to undergo testing on January 10. 2022. For those playing winter sports, only those athletes who were not fully vaccinated were required to undergo testing that day.

Notes

- The NCAA publications cited in this chapter are taken from the website of the NCAA at https://www.ncaa.org/sports/2020/2/28/covid-19-coronavirus.aspk.
- The Sunshine State Conference publications cited in this chapter are taken from the conference website at https://www.sunshinestateconference.com/news/2020/7/17general-ssc-announces-decision-regarding-fall-2020-competitions.aspk and at https://www.sunshinestateconference.com/news/2020/12/8/general-sunshine-state-conference-update-regarding-fall-and-winter-sports.aspk.
- The documents published by the Athletic Department of Florida Tech cited in this chapter were provided to the author by Head Athletic Trainer Luis Velez. Velez was not only the primary author of these documents but was the person primarily responsible for carrying out the policies and procedures mandated by these documents.

APPENDICES

Appendix One: NCAA Champions

1988 Men's Soccer
Team Members: Baldur Bragason, Bino Campanini, Robin Chan, Gary Eyles, Steve Freeman, Martin Gordon, Edward Grosso, Fidgi Haig, Tylan Hannan, William Hill, Todd Hubmer, David Jackson, Dylan Lewis, Kip Ortiz, Ian McNally, Christopher Payne, Chris Smilas, Andy Smith, and Bill Twait.
Coaches: Head Coach Rick Stottler, Asst. Coach Homer Bozorg; & Asst. Coach Giles Malone

1991 Men's Soccer
Team Members: David Beneway, Mark Cartwright, Thad Terry, Andrew Fox, Dylan Lewis, Paul Robertson, Keiran Breslin, Keith Ames, Greg Kemp, Jeremy Wall, Colin Semwayo, Richard Sharpe, Edward Enders, Colin Prest, Joe Daly, Alvaro Fuster, David Jackson, Justin Viezbicke, Daniel Meeroff, and Chris Rogan.
Coaches: Rick Stottler, Head Coach; Homer Bozorg, Asst. Coach; Giles Malone, Asst., & Graduate Asst. Bino Campanini

2007 Women's Golf – Individual Champion
Player: Daniela Iacobelli
Coach: Janie Farina

2017 Men's Swimming – 200 Freestyle Relay
Team Members: Nir Barnea, Victor Rocha Furtado, Matthew Gallene and Filip Dujmic
Coach: Justin Andrade

2019 Women's Golf
Team Members: Noelle Beijer, Megan Dennis, Alexis Dizinno, Lucy Eaton, Hailey Ko, Marybeth McGuire, Paola Oritz, and Lauren Watson
Coaches: Head Coach Chris Saltmarsh and Assistant Coach Mitch Greenberg

Appendix Two: Sunshine State Conference Team Champions

Event/Year	Coach
Women's Cross Country	
1985	Jeff Small
1986	Jeff Small
1987	Jeff Small
Men's Cross Country	
1984	Bob Perry
1985	Jeff Small
1986	Jeff Small
1987	Jeff Small
1990	Bob Perry
1991	Bob Perry
Women's Soccer (regular season)	
2010(tie)	Fitzgerald Haig
Women's Soccer (tournament)	
2017	Dustin Smith
Men's Soccer (regular season)	
1988	Rick Stottler
1989 (tie)	Rick Stottler
1991	Rick Stottler
1993	Rick Stottler
Men's Soccer (tournament)	
2022	Robin Chan
Women's Basketball (regular season)	
1991-92	John Reynolds
1992-93	John Reynolds
1996-97	John Reynolds
2001-02	John Reynolds
Women's Basketball (tournament)	
1991-92	John Reynolds
1992-93	John Reynolds
2001-02	John Reynolds
Men's Basketball (regular season)	
1989-90 (tie)	Tom Folliard

2011-12	Billy Mims
Softball (regular season)	
2019	Val Silvestrini
Men's Golf	
2018	Chris Saltmarsh
Women's Rowing	
1997	Matt Kaminski
2001	Matt Kaminski
2003	Casey Baker
2004	Casey Baker
2005	Casey Baker
2017	Adam Thorstad
2018	Adam Thorstad
2019	Adam Thorstad
2021	Adam Thorstad

Appendix Three: Dad Vail Regatta Men's Champions

1975 Men's Varsity Lt/Wt 8+	1975 Men's JV Lightweight 8+	1975 Men's Fr/Nov Hv/Wt 8+
Coach Bill Jurgens	Coach Bill Jurgens	Coach Norton Schlachter
Coxswain Gene Jeffords	Coxswain Jeff Benes	Coxswain Walt Faulconer
Stroke Tom Deluna	Stroke Matt Stoudt	Stroke Pat Langley
7 – Skip Schied	7 – Bill Fries	7 – Eric Smith
6 – Steve Wright	6 – Dave Chaffee	6 – Pete Allor
5 – Andy Doan	5 – Gene Angus	5 – Mike Davenport
4 – Bob Stickler	4 – Steve Johnson	4 – Mike Leblanc
3 – Bill Alonso	3 – Al Deluna	3 – Jerry Sheppard
2 – Doug Engler	2 – Bill Aspen	2 – Bill Ihle
Bow Gene Ferraro	Bow Bill Reynolds	Bow Don Heckenstaller
1975 Men's Fr/Nov Hv/Wt 4+	**1979** Men's Fr/Nov Hv/Wt 4+	**1979** Men's Fr/Nov Hv/Wt 8+
(Jensen Beach Campus)	Coach Steve Wagner	Coach Steve Wagner
Coach John Hennon	Coxswain Willard White	Coxswain Dave Kniskern
Coxswain Eric Botnick	Stroke Chris Wasik	Stroke Stevie Bator
Stroke Bill Bater	3 – Mark Howell	7 – Mark Pohlhammer
3 – Glenn Bunting	2 – Alan Mayo	6 – Marc Delmonico
2 – Jay Niec	Bow Jim Kenny	5 – Mike Dean
Bow Tim Tress		4 – Geoffrey Healy
		3 – Chris Wasik
		2 – Alan Meeker
		Bow Bruce Stelzner
1980 Men's Frosh/Nov Hv/Wt 8+	**1981** Men's JV Hv/Wt 8+	**1982** Men's Heavyweight 8+
Coach Glenn Bunting	Coach Bill Jurgens	Coach Bill Jurgens
Coxswain Juan Hinestrosa	Coxswain Steve Stevens	Coxswain Steve Stevens
Stroke Mike McDevitt	Stroke Greg Hogan	Stroke Mike McDevitt
7 – Steve Fluhr	7 – Don Enderlin	7 – Jim Kenny
6 – Tom Terry	6 – Al Meeker	6 – Chris Wasik
5 – Don Enderlein	5 – Gary Jacob	5 – Steve Fluhr
4 – Greg Hogan	4 – Tom Terry	4 – Greg Hogan
3 – Gary Jacob	3 – Mike Miller	3 – Gary Jacob

2 – Steve Somosky	2 – Al Shawcross	2 – Mark Pohlhammer
Bow Mike Lenihan	Bow Lyle White	Bow Scott Barberides
1982	**1982**	**1983**
Men's JV Heavyweight 8+	**Men's Lightweight 4+**	**Men's Varsity Lt/Wt 8+**
Coach Bill Jurgens	Coach Bill Jurgens	Coach Bill Jurgens
Coxswain Ken MacLeod	Coxswain Howie Klein	Coxswain Howie Klein
Stroke Al Shawcross	Stroke Dave Forcucci	8 – Steve Somosky
7 – Steve Murphy	3 – John Sodano	7 – Bruce Schwab
6 – Mike Dean	2 – TR Hernacki	6 – Dave Forcucci
5 – Don Gross	Bow Kent Eff	5 – John Mattson
4 – Steve Somosky		4 – Paul Kempin
3 – Steve Hall		3 – Wayne Ice
2 – Dave Hill		2 – Dave Hill
Bow Bruce Schwab		Bow TR Hernacki
1983	**1983**	**1984**
Men's JV Heavyweight 8+	**Men's Varsity Lt/Wt 4+**	**Men's Frosh/Nov Hv/Wt 8+**
Coach Bill Jurgens	Coach Bill Jurgens	Coach Eric Smith
Coxswain Phil Namour	Coxswain Tim Edsell	Coxswain Pat Mangonon
Stroke Dennis McCormick	Stroke Larry Green	Stroke Dennis Davitt
7 – Bob Nield	3 – John Sodano	7 – Brett Patterson
6 – Scott Siebert	2 – Ron Finelli	6 – Vince Ferris
5 – Don Gross	Bow Kent Eff	5 – Sam Stevens
4 – Alan Meeker		4 – Tom Bohrer
3 – Mark Rice		3 – Jack Zimak
2 – Mark Kirsch		2 – David Vecella
Bow Steve Hall		Bow Shannon Ridgeway
1985	**1986**	**1987**
Men's JV Heavyweight 8+	**Men's JV 8+**	**Men's Varsity Lt/Wt 8+**
Coach Bill Jurgens	Coach Bill Jurgens	Coach Bill Jurgens
Coxswain Rick Marks	Coxswain Ken McCleod	Coxswain Dave Wagner
Stroke Alan Taggart	Stroke Barry Sokol	Stroke Pete McLoughlin
7 – Jack Zimak	7 – Dan Bertossa	7 – Dan Twadell
6 – Rob Mildish	6 – Alan Taggart	6 – Steve Hult
5 – Barry Sokol	5 – Chip Stetson	5 – John Totman
4 – John Hubbard	4 – Don Misener	4 – Jon Tate
3 – Eric Hess	3 – Bob Shaffer	3 – Frank Fandetti

2 – Mike Kelly	2 – John Hubbard	2 – Don Carrier
Bow Dan Bertossa	Bow Sam Stevens	Bow Bob Blair

1987	1988	1994
Men's Fr/Nov Hv/Wt 8+	Men's Varsity Hv/Wt 8+	Men's Hv/Wt 4+
Coach Steve Fluhr	Coach Bill Jurgens	Coach Casey Baker
Coxswain Dave Bolinski	Coxswain Jim Barrett	Coxswain Jim Kerr
Stroke Art Schofield	Stroke Wayne McFarlane	Stroke Aleksandar Stojanovic
7 – Jim Petrowski	7 – Andy Loeffler	3 – Paul Clark
6 – Dave Streever	6 – Rob Mildish	2 – Craig Mischler
5 – Andy Loeffler	5 – Jim McDevitt	Bow Kevin Harris
4 – Ken Zugel	4 – Scot Killen	
3 – Darrin Plaisance	3 – Chris Cornell	
2 – Josh Bardwell	2 – Art Schofield	
Bow Keith Bagot	Bow Jim Petrowski	
1995	1995	1996
Men's Varsity Lt/Wt 4+	Men's Varsity Hv/Wt 4+	Men's Varsity Lt/Wt 8+
Coach Casey Baker	Coach Casey Baker	Coach Casey Baker
Coxswain Dan Morales	Coxswain Jenny Weitzel	Coxswain Julie Davis
Stroke Boris Stojanovic	Stroke Andreja Vasiljevic	Stroke Vukan Petrovic
3 – David Livingston	3 – Nikola Sjerobabin	7 – Boris Stojanovic
2 – John Yurich	2 – Craig Mischler	6 – Dave Livingston
Bow Sean Parks	Bow Greg Harding	5 – John Yurick
		4 – Andy Holtery
		3 – Jason Werking
		2 – Peter Velkin
		Bow Drew McKay
1998	2004	2007
Men's Varsity Lt/ Wt 8+	Men's Frosh/Nov Hv/ Wt 4+	Men's Frosh/Nov Lt/ Wt 8+
Coach Casey Baker	Coach Marc Mandel	Coach Tim Watson
Coxswain Anna Wimer	Coxswain Nathan Schultz	Coxswain Christa Blaisdell
Stroke Vukan Petrovic	Stroke Gabe Candelaria	Stroke Logan Sailer
7 – Jose Arellano	3 – Lars Johnson	7 – Mateo Arimany
6 – Andy Holtery	2 – Justin Eickmeier	6 – Mark Moyou

5 – Jonathan Hand	Bow Jeff Tessier	5 – Stanley Van Etten
4 – Chris Marrot		4 – Charley Pearson
3 – Jason Werking		3 – Mike Mathews II
2 – Kevin McCalis		2 – Matt Strand
Bow Drew McKay		Bow Travis Schramek

2013	2015	2016
Men's Hv/Wt 4+	Men's Hv/Wt 8+	Men's Hv/Wt 8+
Coach Jim Granger	Coach Jim Granger	Coach Jim Granger
Coxswain Jacqueline Horbert	Coxswain Aaron Evans	Coxswain Aaron Evans
Stroke Frank Campione	Stroke Jose Gomez-Feria	Stroke Nikola Selakovic
3 – Jose Gomez-Feria	7 – Ernestas Zarskis	7 – Matas Lukosevicius
2 – Alec Bertossa	6 – Nikola Selakovic	6 – Josep Babinac
Bow Troy Toggweiler	5 – Joe Horn	5 – Kevin Coyle
	4 – Martynas Mickus	4 – Andrew Konecny
	3 – Andrew Konecny	3 – Ljubomir Gavric
	2 – Philip Machen	2 – Philip Machen
	Bow Kevin Coyle	Bow Krisjian Markovc

2022
Men's Varsity Hv/Wt 4+
Coach Jim Granger
Coxswain Mark Roberts
Stroke Arnedas Kelmelis
3-Justas Kuskevicius
2-Domantas Morocka
Bow Jackson Moore

Appendix Four: Florida Tech All-Americans

All-American Honoree	Year	Sport	All-American Team
Steve Freeman	1988	Men's Soccer	First Team
Dwight Walton	1989	Men's Basketball	Third Team
Steve Freeman	1989	Men's Soccer	First Team
Dwight Walton	1990	Men's Basketball	Third Team
Chris Payne	1990	Men's Soccer	First Team
Robin Chan	1990	Men's Soccer	Second Team
Dwight Walton	1991	Men's Basketball	Second Team
Tom Finney	1991	Baseball	Third Team
Dylan Lewis	1991	Men's Soccer	First Team
Paulette King	1992	Women's Basketball	First Team
Richard Sharpe	1992	Men's Soccer	First Team
Eddie Enders	1992	Men's Soccer	First Team
Paulette King	1993	Women's Basketball	First Team
Richard Sharpe	1993	Men's Soccer	First Team
Richard Sharpe	1994	Men's Soccer	First Team
Martin Peat	1994	Men's Soccer	Second Team
Elisa Bartolo	1995	Softball	Second Team
Elisa Bartolo	1996	Softball	Second Team
Ryan Jackson	1997	Baseball	Third Team
Sanja Radenkovic	1997	Women's Basketball	Honorable Mention
Felicia Bell	2002	Women's Basketball	Honorable Mention
Jonathan Baksh	2005	Baseball	First Team
Jonathan Baksh	2006	Baseball	Third Team
Steve Condotta	2007	Baseball	Second Team
Gary Ogilvie	2010	Men's Soccer	Honorable Mention

Paula Lillsjo	2010	Women's Soccer	Third Team
Justin Sedlak	2011	Men's Basketball	Second Team
K.C. Clabough	2011	Baseball	Second Team
Ryan Mcchesney	2011	Baseball	Third Team
Briauna Hagins	2012	Women's Basketball	Honorable Mention
Julius Reid	2013	Men's Basketball	Honorable Mention
Kayk Wilson	2013	Women's Basketball	Honorable Mention
Kayk Wilson	2015	Women's Basketball	Honorable Mention
Jordan Majors	2015	Men's Basketball	All-Freshman
Austin Allen	2015	Baseball	Second Team
Scotty Ward	2015	Baseball	Third Team
400 Freestyle Relay (1)	2016	Men's Swimming	First Team
Allie Modica	2016	Women's Lacrosse	Second Team
Corbin Jackson	2016	Men's Basketball	Honorable Mention
200 Freestyle Relay (2)	2017	Men's Swimming	First Team
400 Freestyle Relay (3)	2017	Men's Swimming	First Team
200 Medley Relay (4)	2017	Men' Swimming	Honorable Mention
Victor Rocha Futrado	2017	Men's Swimming	Honorable Mention
Nir Barnea	2017	Men's Swimming	First Team
Adi Davidov	2017	Men's Swimming	Honorable Mention
Grant Hughes	2017	Men's Lacrosse	Honorable Mention
Allie Modica	2017	Women's Lacrosse	First Team
Sara Grenier	2017	Women's Lacrosse	Second Team
Sam Schiano	2018	Women's Lacrosse	Second Team
Lauren Tybor	2018	Women's Lacrosse	Second Team
Caroline Dunleavy	2018	Women's Lacrosse	Third Team
Olivia Going	2018	Women's Lacrosse	Third Team
Sara Grenier	2018	Women's Lacrosse	Third Team
Logan Sweeney	2018	Men's Lacrosse	Honorable Mention
Victor Rocha Furtado	2018	Men's Swimming	First Team
200 Freestyle Relay (5)	2019	Men's Swimming	First Team
400 Medley Relay (6)	2019	Men's Swimming	First Team
200 Freestyle Relay (7)	2019	Men's Swimming	First Team
400 Freestyle Relay (8)	2019	Men's Swimming	First Team
Victor Rocha Furtado	2019	Men's Swimming	First Team
Sam Schiano	2019	Women's Lacrosse	Second Team

Melanie Murphy	2019	Softball	Third Team
Reid Chaconas	2020	Men's Lacrosse	First Team
Mollie Kaplan	2020	Women's Lacrosse	Honorable Mention
Alexis Townsend	2020	Women's Lacrosse	Honorable Mention
Dain Rust	2020	Men's Swimming	Honorable Mention
Daniel Aizenberg	2021	Men's Swimming	First Team
Olivia Going	2021	Women's Lacrosse	Second Team
Reid Chaconas	2021	Men's Lacrosse	Second Team
Justin Williams	2022	Men's Lacrosse	First Team
Sam Balch	2022	Men's Lacrosse	Third Team
Kailee O'brien	2022	Women's Lacrosse	Honorable Mention
Daniel Aizenberg	2022	Men's Swimming	First Team
Savannah Brennan	2022	Women's Swimming	First Team
Luis Tovar Romero	2022	Men's Soccer	First Team
Sjur Drechsler	2022	Men's Soccer	First Team
Daniel Aizenberg	2023	Men's Swimming	First Team
Sam Balch	2023	Men's Lacrosse	Third Team
Kailee O'brien	2023	Women's Lacrosse	Honorable Mention
(1) Team Members: Nir Barnea, Filip Dujmic, Victor Rocha Furtado And Thomas Steenberg.			
(2) Team Members: Nir Barnea, Victor Rocha Furtado, Matthew Gallen And Filip Dujmic.			
(3) Team Members: Nir Barnea, Victor Rocha Furtado, Thomas Steenberg And Filip Dujmic.			
(4) Team Members: Nir Barnea, Victor Rocha Furtado, Thomas Steenberg And Matthew Gallene.			
(5) Team Members: Emanuele Rossi, Dain			

Rust, Filip Dujmic And Victor Rocha Furtado.	
(6) Team Members: Emanuele Rossi, Dain Rust, Filip Dujmic And Victor Rocha Furtado.	
(7) Team Members: Emanuele Rossi, Harry Sale, Filip Dujmic And Victor Rocha Furtado.	
(8) Team Members: Emanuele Rossi, Harry Sale, Filip Dujmic And Victor Rocha Furtado.	

Note

- This appendix was compiled from the list of all-Americans set forth on the Florida Tech Athletic Website at floridatechsports.com/sports/2022/11/30/all-americans-2.aspx.
- In a few cases, there were inconsistencies in the spelling of names. In those cases, I relied on the spelling used in *Florida Today* news reports.

Appendix Five: Florida Tech Sports Hall of Fame

Year Of Induction	Inductee	Category
1986	Casey Baker	Men's Rowing/Men's And Women's Rowing Coach
1986	Jeanne Ann Flanagan	Women's Rowing
1986	Percy Hedgecock	Volunteer Booster
1986	Ray Work, Jr.	Athletic Director/University Dean
1987	Fran Reininger	Men's Rowing
1987	Andy Seminick	Baseball Coach
1988	Dr. Joseph Doller	Volunteer Booster
1988	Nino Lyons	Men's Basketball
1989	Robert Dunlap	Administrator Who Instituted Crew Program
1990	Joseph Eckelman	Men's Rowing
1991	John Narciso	Baseball
1992	Thomas Bohrer	Men's Rowing
1993	Calvin Griffith	Volunteer Booster
1993	Tim Wakefield	Baseball
1995	Steve Freeman	Men's Soccer
1995	Chip Greek	Baseball
1995	Davon Kelly	Men's Basketball
1996	Tom Folliard, Jr.	Men's Basketball
1996	Phil Gaarder	Volunteer Booster
1996	Les Hall	Baseball Coach
1996	Chris Payne	Men's Soccer
1999	Bill Jurgens	Rowing Coach/Athletic Director
1999	Christine Keenan	Women's Basketball
1999	Paulette King	Women's Basketball
2001	Elisa Bartolo	Softball/Volleyball
2001	Richard Sharpe	Men's Soccer
2001	Rick Stottler	Men's Soccer Coach
2001	Dwight Walton	Men's Basketball
2003	Martha Work	Volunteer Booster
2003	Robin Chan	Men's Soccer
2003	Tom Folliard, Sr.	Men's Basketball Coach
2003	Wayne Mcfarland	Men's Rowing
2003	Rob Terry	Men's Basketball
2005	Bino Campanini	Men's Soccer
2005	Tom Finney	Baseball
2005	Dylan Lewis	Men's Soccer

2005	Sanja Radenkovic	Women's Basketball
2008	1988 Men's Soccer Team	
2008	1991 Men's Soccer Team	
2008	1982 Men's Varsity 8 Crew	
2008	1988 Men's Varsity 8 Crew	
2013	Dr. Valerie Barber	Women's Rowing
2013	1992 Baseball Team	
2013	Eddie Enders	Men's Soccer
2013	Fitzgerald (Fidgi) Haig	Men's Soccer
2014	Dr. Anthony Catanese	University President
2014	Daniela Iacobelli	Women's Golf
2014	2001-02 Women's Basketball Team	
2014	1982 Women's Varsity 4 Crew	
2015	Jonathan Baksh	Baseball
2015	1989-90 Men's Basketball Team	
2015	1975 Men's Lightweight 8 Crew	
2015	Dr. Sara Trane	Women's Cross Country
2015	Dr. Kari Wanat	Volleyball
2016	Dr. Nancy Bottge	Softball Coach
2016	Teresa Brantley Moon	Women's Soccer
2016	Mark Cartwright	Men's Soccer
2016	Steve Condotta	Baseball
2016	Jim Mitchell	Basketball Announcer
2016	Brandon Palmer	Men's Basketball
2017	Kieran Breslin	Men's Soccer
2017	Lynisha Nelson	Women's Basketball
2017	Bill Potter	Volunteer Booster
2017	Justin Sedlak	Men's Basketball
2020	Paula Lillsjo	Women's Soccer
2020	Paul Ouellette	Baseball
2020	Martin Peat	Men's Soccer
2020	Melanie Thebarge	Women's Cross Country
2020	Peter Walcott	Men's Basketball
2020	Dr. Frank Webbe	NCAA Faculty Representative

Appendix Six: Florida Tech Members of Sunshine State Conference Sports Hall of Fame

Year Of Induction	Inductee	Category
1994	Andy Seminick	Baseball Coach
1998	Tim Wakefield	Baseball
1998	Steve Freeman	Men's Soccer
1999	Richard Sharpe	Men's Soccer
2001	Paulette King	Women's Basketball
2002	Rick Stottler	Men's Soccer Coach
2003	Elisa Bartolo	Softball/Volleyball
2005	Dylan Lewis	Men's Soccer
2006	Dr. Nancy Bottge	Softball Coach
2007	Sonja Radenkovic	Women's Basketball
2007	Casey Baker	Women's Rowing Coach
2008	Robin Chan	Men's Soccer
2008	Christine Keenan	Women's Basketball
2009	Bino Campanini	Men's Soccer
2011	Dwight Walton	Men's Basketball
2011	Chris Payne	Men's Soccer
2015	Fidgi Haig	Men's Soccer/ Women's Soccer Coach
2016	Daniela Iacobelli	Women's Golf
2022	Dr. Frank Webbe	NCAA Faculty Representative

Appendix Seven: Florida Tech Academic All-Americans

Honoree	Year	Sport	All-American
Kari Wanat	1997	Volleyball	Second Team
Kari Wanat	1998	Volleyball	First Team
Casey Lademann	2011	Women's Soccer	Third Team
Trey Collins	2015	Men's Soccer	First Team
Evan Enders	2017	Men's Soccer	Second Team
Ian Hlavica	2017	Men's Soccer	Second Team
Thomas Steenberg	2018	Men's Swimming	First Team
Harry Sale	2019	Men's Swimming	Second Team
Logan Sweeney	2019	Men's Lacrosse	Third Team
Guillermo Segovia	2019	Men's Soccer	First Team
Olivia Going	2021	Women's Lacrosse	First Team
Savannah Brennan	2021	Women's Swimming	Third Team
Savannah Brennan	2022	Women's Swimming	First Team
Alexander Carpenter	2022	Baseball	Second Team
Daniel Aizenberg	2023	Men's Swimming	First Team
Sean Catron	2023	Men's Swimming	Second Team

Note

- This appendix was compiled from the list of academic all-Americans set forth on the Florida Tech Athletic Website at floridatechsports.com/sports/2022/11/30/academic-all-americans-2.aspx.

Appendix Eight: Membership of Sunshine State Conference

Current Members

Institution	Location	Founded	#Enrolled	Joined	Mascot
Barry University	Miami Shores	1940	7,400	1988	Buccaneers
Eckerd College	St. Petersburg	1958	1,850	1975	Tritons
Embry-Riddle Aero. University	Daytona Beach	1926	7,520	2015	Eagles
Florida Southern College	Lakeland	1883	3,074	1975	Moccasins
Florida Institute of Technology	Melbourne	1958	9,590	1981	Panthers
Lynn University	Boca Raton	1962	3,520	1997	Fighting Knights
Nova Southeastern University	Davie	1964	20,576	2002	Sharks
Rollins College	Winter Park	1885	3,127	1975	Tars
Saint Leo University	Saint Leo	1889	9,523	1975	Lions
University of Tampa	Tampa	1931	9,628	1981	Spartans

Past Members

Institution	Location	Year Joined	Year Left	Current Conference
University of Central Florida	Orlando	1975	1984	Big 12
University of North Florida	Jacksonville	1992	1997	ASUN Conference
Saint Thomas University	Miami Gardens	1975	1987	The Sun (NAIA)

Note

- Enrollment numbers are taken from the websites of each institution.

BIBLIOGRAPHY

Books

- Cleveland, Weona. "Crossroad Towns Remembered: A Look Back at Brevard and Indian River Pioneer Communities." Florida Today, 1994.
- Cleveland, Weona. "Mosquito Soup." The Florida Historical Society Press, 2014.
- Melbourne Area Chamber of Commerce Centennial Committee. "Melbourne: A Century of Memories." 1980.
- Patterson, Gordon. "Florida Institute of Technology." Arcadia Publishing, 2000.
- Raley, Karen, and Ann Raley Flotte. "Melbourne and Eau Gallie (Images of America)." Arcadia Publishing, 2002.
- Roberts, R. & Rogers III, P. (1996). *The Whiz Kids: and the 1950 Pennant.* Temple University Press, Philadelphia, Pa.
- Stone, Elaine Murray. "Brevard County: From Cape of the Canes to Space Coast." Windsor Publications, 1988.
- Wakefield, Tim. "Knuckler: My Life with Baseball's Most Confounding Pitch." Mariner Books. Reprint Edition March 6, 2012.

Periodicals

- Blakemore, Erin. "Title IX at 50: How the U.S. Law Transformed Education for Women." National Geographic Magazine. June 22, 2022.

- Carey, Kevin, "Men Fall Behind in College Enrollment: Women Still Play Catch-Up at Work" New York Times, September 10, 2021.
- Hildes-Heim, N. (1982, May 9). *Florida Tech excels in Dad Vail Regatta. The New York Times.*
- Hildes-Heim, N. (1988, May 15). *Temple is upset in regatta final. The New York Times.*
- Mertens, Maggie. "50 Years of Title IX: How One Law Changed Women's Sports Forever," Sports Illustrated, May 19, 2022.
- Patterson, Gordon. "Countdown to College: Launching Florida Institute of Technology." Florida Historical Quarterly, Volume 77, Number 2, Fall 1998.
- Patterson, Gordon. "Space University, Lift-Off of Florida Institute of Technology." Florida Historical Quarterly, Volume 79, Number1, Summer 2000.
- Pielke, Roger "The Decline of Football is Real and It's Accelerating," Forbes Magazine, January 28, 2020.

Websites

- Bachman, Rachel, "College Football's Growing Problem: Empty Seats," at https://www.wsj.com/articles/college-footballs-groing-problem-empty-seats-1535634001, August 30, 2018.
- Dodd, Dennis "College Football Attendance Declines for the Seventh Straight Season to Lowest Average Since 1981," at https://www.cbssports/college-football/news/college-football-attendance-declines-for-seventh-straight-season-to-lowest-average-since-1981/, February 24, 2022
- For the increase in the number of colleges fielding football teams, see the website of the National Football Foundation at https://footballfoundation.org/news/2019/ 7/23/775-colleges-and-universities-now-offering-football.aspx.
- "How Title IX Transformed Women's Sports" at https://www.hutirt.com/news/title-nine-women-sports retrieved on December 7, 2022.
- Major League Baseball. (May 23, 2023). *Roberto Clemente Award.* Retrieved from: https://www.mlb.com/community/roberto-clemente-award.
- Buckley, S. (September 18, 2014). *Buckley: Tedy Bruschi, Tim Wakefield full of pride. Boston Herald.* Retrieved from: https://www.bostonherald.com/2014/09/18/buckley-tedy-bruschi-tim-wakefield-full-of-pride/

- Edes, G. & McDonald, J. (February 17, 2012). *Knuckleballer Tim Wakefield retires. ESPNBoston.com.* Retrieved from: https://www.espn.com/boston/mlb/story/_/id/7585718/tim-wakefield-retires-17-seasons-boston-red-sox

Note

- For additional information on the growth of lacrosse, see "A Sport on the Rise" published August 5, 2021, at https://athelogroup.com/blog/a-sport-on-the-rise

ABOUT THE AUTHORS

Authors

William C. Potter is a graduate of Brown University and the University of Michigan Law School. He practiced law in Florida from 1965 until 2002, when he moved to Europe to serve as Head of the Rule of Law Department of the Office of the High Representative in Bosnia and Herzegovina. He served on the board of directors of several banks and businesses, including a publicly-traded defense contractor. He served as a Trustee of

Florida Institute of Technology from 1980 to 2022, including serving as Chair from 1990 to 1997. He currently serves as a Trustee Emeritus. He was inducted into the Florida Tech Sports Hall of Fame in 2017. He was inducted into the Space Coast Business Hall of Fame in 2016. He is the author of the book *A Bosnian Diary: A Floridian's Experience in Nation-Building*, published by the Florida Historical Society in 2005 and the book *Melbourne Orlando International Airport: A History from 1928 to 2022*, self-published in 2022. Potter is a retired officer of the Florida Air National Guard, where he served as Judge Advocate General for Florida.

William K. Jurgens served as the Director of Athletics at Florida Institute of Technology from 1976 until January 2020. He then served the school as Vice-President for University Relations before retiring in 2021. Jurgens began his career at Florida Tech in 1969 when he became head crew coach. The Panthers' crews won 17 Dad Vail national championships under Jurgens' leadership. As an athlete, Jurgens has rowed on the U.S. national

team in international competition. He earned his undergraduate degree from Jacksonville University and a Master's of Science Education from Florida Tech. He has been a member of the Board of Directors of the U.S. Rowing Association and a member of the U.S. Olympic Rowing Committee. He has been a member of the board of the Dad Vail Regatta since 1990 and continues to hold that position. In 2016, Jurgens received the Jack Kelly Award from USRowing, which recognizes superior achievements in rowing or an individual who serves as an inspiration to American rowers. Jurgens is a member of the Florida Tech Sports Hall of Fame, the Jacksonville University Athletic Hall of Fame and the Space Coast Sports Hall of Fame.

Contributors

Father Douglas Bailey was the Florida Tech Catholic Campus Minister and University Chaplain from 1983 until his retirement in 2020. Father Doug was not only a spiritual advisor to thousands of students but he also taught classes in World Religion and in Bioethics. He held daily masses and conducted Bible study classes, Rosary and untold other activities for the benefit of  students. The students who benefited from his wisdom and compassion included not only Catholics but numerous other religious denominations. Father Bailey received his undergraduate degree in philosophy, followed by a Master's degree in Religious Studies. He was ordained in 1976. In recognition of his service, an endowment was established titled "Father Douglas F. Bailey SDS, Endowment to Support Catholic Campus Ministry" to underwrite expenses related to the Campus Catholic Ministry.

Dr. Anthony J. Catanese is President Emeritus of Florida Institute of Technology. Dr. Catanese earned his bachelor's degree in city and regional planning from Rutgers University, a masters in urban planning from New York University and his Ph.D. in urban and regional planning from University of Wisconsin-Madison. Among the  many academic positions held by Dr. Catanese were his service as Dean of the College of Architecture at the University of Florida. Dr. Catanese served as President of Florida Atlantic University from 1990 to 2002. As President, he led an initiative to establish a Division I football team at FAU. He became President of Florida Tech in 2002. Among his many accomplishments at Florida Tech was the expansion of the intercollegiate sports program to 21 sports. He served as President of the Sunshine State Conference from 2007 to 2009. He was inducted into the Florida Tech Sports Hall of Fame in 2014. Dr. Catanese retired as President of Florida Tech in 2016 and currently serves as President Emeritus. He has authored 14 books and 18 chapters in books, as well as more than 65 articles in academic journals.

Dr. Frank M. Webbe serves as an Emeritus Faculty member of Florida Institute of Technology, having taught and conducted research in the School of Psychology for more than 25 years, including time as Dean of the school. Dr. Webbe earned his undergraduate degree, Master's degree and Ph.D. from the University of Florida, where he was a member of  Phi Beta Kappa. His research focused on two areas of neuropsychology: Alzheimer's disease and sports-related concussion. He is a charter member of the Technology Professional Interest Area of the International Society to Advance Alzheimer Research, as well as a charter member of the Sports Neuropsychology Society. Dr. Webbe served as Florida Tech's Faculty Athletics Representative to the NCAA for many years and participated in the Task Force on Student-Athlete Mental Health which focused attention on mental and emotional challenges to student-athletes. He was the Florida Tech Teacher of the Year for psychology during nine school years. He is the author of more than 50 academic publications and edited The Handbook of Sports Neuropsychology. Dr, Webbe was inducted into the Florida Tech Sports Hall of Fame in 2020 and the Sunshine State Conference Hall of Fame in 2022.

ACKNOWLEDGEMENTS

This book was truly a pleasure to write given the inestimable contributions of so many people who in many cases span over 50 years of association with Florida Tech Athletics. Through athletics you learn the importance of teamwork and writing this book felt like there was a team of players who constantly provided support and encouragement regardless of how many times they were asked to clarify and expand on what they had previously provided. To begin with, John Courtney who was a member of the first basketball team at Florida Tech talked about how he and a friend went to Dr. Ray Work, Vice President for Student Affairs, with the idea of having a basketball team and Work subsequently gave them two basketballs and numbered jerseys which later had "Engineer" printed on them. Dick Bowman was always a pleasure to talk to about his insights on being the men's basketball coach during the late '60s and the school's association with the NAIA. Don Rutledge, who in 1969-1970 was the coach of basketball, baseball, and golf teams, was kind enough to travel to Florida Tech from Orlando to talk to the authors and leave them his scrapbook on basketball. Two other contributors were Anna Kephart Norris, University Archivist, and Christina Hardman, Associate AD for Communications, who always had the time in their busy schedules to provide photographs and research information that were invaluable in writing the history of Florida Tech athletics. Also, Christena Callahan, Director of Creative Services, assisted with the design of the cover for the book. Susy Jurgens took on the task of proofing the book for which she spent many 10-hour days proofing both an electronic version and a hard copy of the book. Barry Eager also spent hours scanning photos and posters from various sources including his video productions of the Florida Tech Sports Hall of Fame.

The Development and Alumni Affairs Office, which includes Gary Grant, Senior Vice President for Development and Alumni Affairs, who also proofed the book and made suggestions; Gina Yates, Assistant Vice President of Alumni Affairs, who provided contact information for contributing alumni; and Alyssa Carney, Administrative Assistant for Office of Advancement, who assisted with research on cheerleading.

Alumni who assisted with historical accounts of their participation in the sports programs were Randy Muns, Bino Campanini, Marian Dionne, Valerie Barber, Eve Gsteiger-Duddy, Gene Jeffords, Chuck Hildebrand, Doug Linden, Ken Watts, Ray Walker, Steve Fluhr, Glenn Bunting, Andrea Krikorian, Billie Brown, Dale Pierce, William Tolson, Art Tank, Neal Julien, David Noble, Chris Duer, Jimmy Woodard, Kathy Wojtas, Tom Folliard and Denise Flemming-Linnenbaugh.

Rob Dunlap and Bruce Gaarder, who are the sons of Bob Dunlap and Phil Gaarder, provided historical information and reflected on their fathers' contributions to the athletics' program.

Coaches who provided information on their teams and names of members were Casey Baker, Giles Malone, Jim Granger, Adam Thorstad, Tim Watson, Marc Mandel, and Mary Fox.

Milo Zonka of Sheltaire, Zachary Gower of Melbourne Flight School, and Derek Fallon, of Melbourne Flight School, assisted in facilitating aerial photographing of the athletic facilities.

This is the second book on which Lois M. Deveneau has worked with William Potter in designing, formatting and providing publishing assistance. Once again, her work and guidance have been essential in creating a credible publication.

The authors owe a debt of gratitude to all those who unselfishly gave of their time to help make this book what we hope will be a valuable and useful historical account of Florida Tech Athletics.

Finally, both authors must acknowledge the contribution their families have made to the authors' affection for Florida Tech athletics and, consequently, their incentive to write this book. For Bill Jurgens, that sacrifice by Susy Jurgens and their children, Mandy and Scott, included countless nights of missed meals and late nights when Bill was carrying out his responsibilities at athletic events and travelling to distant venues. For Bill Potter, his wife Wendy and his children, Alison, Andy and Carrie, endured many nights sitting in the stands at Florida Tech athletic events and dutifully supporting Panther teams as soon as they were old enough to cheer.